"Well resea_____ must-
read not on_____ student
of the swing____

   —Missis:____

"This is a g_____ an col-
lectors will _____ one of
jazz's greate____

   —Caden____

"This long-_____y."

   —Los An____

Bunny Berigan

Elusive Legend of Jazz

Robert Dupuis

LOUISIANA STATE UNIVERSITY PRESS
Baton Rouge

Designer: Patricia Douglas Crowder Typeface: Linotron 202 Caledonia
Typesetter: G&S Typesetters, Inc. Printer and binder: Thomson-Shore, Inc.

LIBRARY OF CONGRESS CATALOGING-IN-PUBLICATION DATA
Dupuis, Robert, 1926–
      Bunny Berigan : elusive legend of jazz / Robert Dupuis.
      p. cm.
      Discography: p.
      Includes bibliographical references and index.
      ISBN 0-8071-1648-3 (cloth)
      1. Berigan, Bunny, 1908–1942. 2. Trumpet players—United States—Biography. I. Title.
ML419.B297D8 1991
784.4'165'092—dc20   90-21408
[B]   CIP MN

ISBN 0-8071-3068-0 (pbk.)

Published with support from the Louisiana Sea Grant College Program, part of the National Sea Grant College
Program maintained by the National Oceanic and Atmospheric Administration of the U.S. Department of Commerce.

The author offers grateful acknowledgment to the editors and publishers who granted permission to reprint
selections and excerpts contained herein:
      "First Fig" by Edna St. Vincent Millay. From Collected Poems, Harper & Row. Copyright 1922, 1950 by
Edna St. Vincent Millay. Reprinted by permission of Elizabeth Barnett, Literary Executor. Excerpt from
Remembering Bix reprinted by permission of Ralph Berton. Excerpts of articles first appearing in Billboard
© 1930, 1938, 1940 BPI Communications, Inc. Used with permission from Billboard. Excerpts from
"Plunkett's" by Josh Billings reprinted from Esquire Jazz Book, 1947 (New York, 1946), courtesy of Da Capo
Press. Excerpts from articles in Down Beat reprinted with permission. Except from The New Edition of the
Encyclopedia of Jazz (Rev. ed.) reprinted by permission of Leonard Feather. Excerpts from Lyrics on Several
Occasions reprinted by permission of the Estate of Ira Gershwin and Mrs. Ira Gershwin. Excerpts from "That
Old Gang of Mine" by Benny Goodman with Richard Gehman, which appeared in Collier's, January 20,
1956, reprinted by permission of the Estate of Benny Goodman. Excerpts from Conversations with Jazz
Musicians reprinted by permission of Gale Research, Inc. Excerpts from I'll Quit Tomorrow by Vernon E.
Johnson. Copyright © 1980 by Vernon E. Johnson. Reprinted by permission of Harper & Row, Publishers,
Inc. Excerpts from Ian Crosbie's "Bunny Berigan" reprinted from Jazz Journal by permission of the publisher. We Called It Music, by Eddie Condon, copyright © 1947, 1962 by Eddie A. Condon. Reprinted by
permission of McIntosh and Otis, Inc. Excerpts from The Big Bands (4th edition) by George T. Simon
reprinted with permission of Schirmer Books, a division of Macmillan Publishing Company. Copyright ©
1967, 1971, 1974, 1981 by George T. Simon. Excerpts from Melody Maker used with permission of the
publisher. "Squareface," words by Winston Tharp, music by Eugene Gifford. © 1935 Edwin H. Morris &
Company, a division of MPL Communications, Inc. © renewed 1963 Edwin H. Morris & Company, a division of MPL Communications, Inc. International copyright secured. All rights reserved. Excerpts from articles by Whitney Balliett reprinted by permission; © 1982 and 1987 Whitney Balliett. Originally in the New
Yorker. Excerpt from the obituary of Bunny Berigan copyright © 1942 by The New York Times Company.
Reprinted by permission. Excerpt from The Illustrated Encyclopedia of Jazz by Brian Case and Stan Britt
reprinted by permisison of Salamander Books, Ltd. Excerpts from Giants of Jazz: Bunny Berigan by John
Chilton, notes on the music by Richard M. Sudhalter, © 1982 Time-Life Books, Inc. Excerpts from Variety
reprinted by permission of the publisher. Excerpts from liner notes by Bozy White to Shoestring SS-100,
Bunny Berigan—Vol. 1 (1938–39) and from liner notes by John McDonough to Shoestring SS-115, Bunny
Berigan, 1931, reprinted by permission of Bozy White. Excerpts from liner notes to Soundcraft LP-1013, The
Saturday Night Swing Club—On the Air, reprinted by permission of Ed Burke, producer.

Frontispiece: Bunny Berigan at the height of his career, ca. 1937. From the Frank Driggs Collection.

The paper in this book meets the guidelines for permanence and durability of the Committee on Production
Guidelines for Book Longevity of the Council on Library Resources. ∞

My candle burns at both ends;
It will not last the night;
But, ah, my foes, and, oh, my friends—
It gives a lovely light!

—Edna St. Vincent Millay

Contents

Illustrations

At rehearsal with band
With the Tommy Dorsey Orchestra
"Holly" Caffey and Berigan
At the Roosevelt Hotel, Jacksonville, Florida
Berigan band promotional photo
Suffering from the bus blues
On Hollywood sound stage
Bunny's last band
Cover of Victor's memorial album
Cover for "Wacky Dust" sheet music
New marker for Berigan's grave site
Fox Lake, Wisconsin, welcome sign
Loretta Berigan at cemetery
Joyce Berigan in her home
Patricia Berigan Slavin in her studio

Acknowledgments

No book comes into being through the efforts of one person. Particularly in writing of the life of a subject who has been dead more than forty years, much help is needed. I am most grateful to those who have helped me in assembling the needed information, in getting it into reasonable form, and in bringing it to final form. Along the way were those who helped simply by giving enthusiastic encouragement to my efforts. I would like to single out those who have been most responsible for helping me bring this project to completion.

First, the members of the Bunny Berigan family: Bunny's widow, Donna, spent long parts of three days with me in Houston when the state of her health demanded confinement to bed with regular respiration therapy. This did not appear to affect her memory. Daughters Patricia Berigan Slavin and Joyce Berigan were gracious and encouraging in interviews by telephone and in person, as well as in subsequent letters. Bunny's sister-in-law Loretta Berigan, who lived with Bunny's parents for a time, was most helpful in providing family background information as well as encouragement through a continuing correspondence. Robert Berigan, Bunny's cousin, and his wife, Lorraine, were helpful with some genealogical information and general advice. Madeline McArthur Troisi, Donna's sister, has also provided valuable insights. I thank them all.

Many who knew Bunny during his brief life—childhood friends, fellow musicians, listeners—were good enough to grant interviews for this book. Without exception, they did so happily, eagerly, glad to contribute to a biography of a man they loved. Their names appear in the footnotes or in the text, and I again thank them sincerely. Some have maintained contact through written and telephoned correspondence, providing ever more insight about Berigan. Of this group I must single out Johnny Blowers, Joe Dixon, Al Gage, Clif Gomon, Buddy Koss, Gene Kutch, Tom Morganelli, Neal Payne, Bobby Smith, and Paul Weston. Their interest and encouragement were vital to this project. Perhaps Bunny's most loyal friend and conservator was Artie Beecher, whose efforts in Bunny's behalf are told herein. Artie was a professional musician from Beaver Dam, Wisconsin, who died at age eighty on May 18, 1990, on the eve of the seventeenth Bunny Berigan Day. He helped me greatly by arranging interviews with several childhood friends of Berigan and by sharing his own knowledge of his friend.

Several people contributed by providing recordings, tapes, photographs, specialized aid and information, and help with copying manuscript or other needed material, or simply by giving much-needed encouragement. Among those, I wish to thank Johnny Blowers, Bess Bonnier, John Corrado, Vince Danca, Larry Doyle, Frank Driggs, Bill Dupuis, Allen Freiwald, Jim Gallert, Charlie Gilbert, Burrell Gluskin, John Grams, John Hauck, Stan Hench, Bill Hunkins, Buddy Koss, Gene Kutch, Creighton Lederer, Leonard Minkwic, Tom Morganelli, Larry Peplin, Ron Pikielek, Duncan Schiedt, Marian Schultz, Mary Sullivan, and Brian Welch. The good people of Fox Lake, Wisconsin, and environs have made known their pleasure at seeing a book about their local hero come to completion. To those not named herein I offer thanks for much-appreciated moral support. Literary agent Marie Brown was the first person in the publishing business to see merit in my project when she read some of my early efforts during a writing seminar. She continued to express faith in the manuscript as it developed, and I am grateful to her for this faith and for practical assistance.

Persons from three institutions provided much-appreciated assistance. The librarians at the main branch of the Detroit Public Library and the Grosse Pointe Public Library were invariably helpful and conscientious. Bernadette Moore at the RCA Archives in New York was kind in giving me access to these records. Dan Morgenstern, director of the Institute of Jazz Studies at Rutgers University, has helped at several stages. His tip-of-the-fingers knowledge has amazed me.

Tom Cullen was generous in sharing his considerable insight about Berigan gleaned from his years of research, conducted alone and in collaboration with Bozy White. Cullen's research includes invaluable information on Berigan's Wisconsin years, tapping the rich memories of musicians, relatives, and friends. Deborah Mickolas has given tapes of many of her Berigan recordings, personal interviews, and other information, and has shared her youthful enthusiasm for Berigan. I thank both Tom and Deborah.

Bozy White has been researching the Berigan story for more than forty years. Bozy began his work alone but eventually joined Cullen in an effort to produce a biography-discography of Berigan. When this partnership ended, he teamed up with Martin L. Kite, a music researcher from Washington, D.C., until Kite's untimely death. At this writing, he is collaborating with Dr. Ian Crosbie of England, a physician and jazz writer, in a renewed effort to complete the definitive bio-discography of Berigan. Their book is eagerly awaited by jazz lovers and discographers everywhere.

I readily acknowledge that much of the information about Bunny Berigan's life as a working musician, particularly between the fall of 1925 and July, 1941, that I provide in this book was derived from an outline organized and typed by Bozy White and reflecting his and Tom Cullen's joint research efforts. I first used this outline not knowing it was Bozy's work and without his knowing that I had been given a copy of many parts of it. This source provided me with such information as names, dates, locations, events, and quotations from the music trade press and other periodicals, as well as radio remote broadcast listings and information about recording sessions not found in the standard reference books. I also used quotations from and paraphrases of interviews with musicians conducted by Mr. White and Mr. Cullen.

Without this early research headed by Mr. White much vital Berigan information would have been lost. Recognizing that I might not otherwise have been able to uncover certain facts because of the deaths of so many musicians and others associated with Berigan, Mr. White has graciously given his permission for my extensive use of information from his outline so that readers of my version of the Bunny Berigan story would not be deprived of the details of Berigan's life as a working musician. The Martin L. Kite materials are used with Mr. White's permission. The Tom Cullen materials cited herein are used with Mr. White's and Mr. Cullen's permission.

Norm Krusinski, "Bunny Berigan's No. 1 Fan," has been of inestimable help to me. Simply stated, he has freely lent or given me access to all of the considerable Berigan information he has in his possession, including countless tapes and records of Berigan music, as well as interviews with pertinent subjects. He has been my prod to complete the biography. His enthusiasm for Berigan is boundless, and I would not be surprised if some of it had rubbed off. Thank you, Norm.

Two professionals who helped shape this book must be cited. Thomas Jackrell brought not only his professional indexing skills but an abiding love of, and knowledge about, jazz to his creation of this Index. Editor Julie Schorfheide also contributed more than just technical skills, as she added ideas, enthusiasm, understanding, and empathy to this project. I thank them both.

The rest of this is a family affair, but it must be shared anyway. I thank my sister, Norma Dupuis, and my daughter Denise Morey for lending their sharp-eyed proofreading skills at various stages of the manuscript's life. There is one person without whose efforts this book could not have come into being: my daughter Diane Dupuis. She brought her professional skills to bear as she line-edited nearly the entire manuscript at its most crucial stages, offering ideas, suggestions, and sometimes virtual orders. Throughout this whole process we had but two major content confrontations—one of which I won! Truly, she helped give birth to this book, giving me yet one more reason to love her.

Finally, to my wife, Jean, I can only say that I hope holding this book in her hands will in some way repay her for the months-into-years of my preoccupation with this project. Throughout, she not only has been supportive but has contributed excellent ideas, asked valid questions, offered positive criticism, brought meals to me at the computer, served as cheerleader, and been a wonderful companion as we have traveled about the country gathering information. I hope she thinks it all was worth it.

Bunny Berigan

Introduction: Getting Started

I survey the Community Building in Fox Lake, Wisconsin, on a third Sunday in May when the weather is not only cooperating but contributing to the success of the event. The Community Building resembles a barn—not a surprising fact, since it is located in the heart of the dairy-farming area that I have always associated with Wisconsin. Today the old structure is not being used as a barn might. Long, knockdown tables surrounded by folding chairs cover the floor. White, rolled paper "cloths" valiantly try to shield the tables' surfaces from sweating pitchers and glasses and the grease of potato chips and the crumbs of pretzels that adorn them.

Bill Sargent's Big Band is playing vintage arrangements: Tommy Dorsey, Benny Goodman, Glenn Miller, a little Count Basie, a few old stocks of 1940s music, with some contemporary numbers thrown in. Automatically, I begin to compare this band with the one I played in back in 1943 to 1944. Maybe forty years of selective memory has improved our sound, but we were good. Several of my high school crowd are still professional musicians. Some played for a while with Stan Kenton, Bobby Sherwood, or in other name bands. I decide to delay my final assessment of Sargent's group. Meanwhile, the draft beer is welcome on this precocious May day; we empty and refill the pitchers quickly. The crowd's mood is festive. We've come to have a good time and so far are succeeding. Infants and ninety-year-olds are here. Local businessmen and their wives are here. The Legionnaires are here; a smattering of teens. We've come from across the street and across the state and from California and South Carolina and Michigan.

Some are dancing. The hardwood floor of the old building serves well for this activity. The sound system is a mixed blessing: without it, the room swallows the sound; with it (for, of course, the amplifiers are turned up much too high), the sound bounces and echoes.

I have been told that the young first trumpeter, The Soloist, will attempt something very brave soon after the first intermission. As that time approaches I watch him very closely, imagining how I would feel—how he must feel—to be trying this number. I decide that he's probably hoping that everyone drinks *lots* of beer and talks through the music. He's wondering how he ever let himself get into this position. Doubts are racing through his mind: Will his lip hold out? Can he reach that damn high E-flat? Can he hold it if he reaches it? What about the low stuff in the coda? Why does the solo have to wander all over the horn?

The Soloist lays out of the tune the band is playing now. He removes the valves from his trumpet one by one, carefully applies a fresh coat of valve oil, then spins them back into the casing to spread the oil evenly before screwing the tops on. He's looking hard at the third valve. Is it sticking? This would be a *terrible* time for that. Should he have gotten a new set of springs last week? Too late now! The band begins the last chorus of its number, and for the third time, The Soloist opens the spit valve and blows, but any excess saliva has already been expelled. Then, just to be sure, he pulls out the other two valve slides and shakes them with a snapping motion to rid them of any phantom moisture. He's probably banking now on the crowd to keep talking right through the music, the way most crowds do.

Only this isn't most crowds. This is Bunny Berigan's crowd. In Bunny Berigan's home town. Bill Sargent has brought his band to Fox Lake to play for the Eleventh Annual Bunny Berigan Day festival. And he has asked The Soloist to play Bunny's famous solo and theme, "I Can't Get Started." Other groups in previous years had played that song too, with other trumpet players taking a chorus or two. This is the first time, though, that anyone is attempting to do the celebrated full-band version, virtually a concerto for trumpet. Fully half of the audience knows this masterpiece note for note. Most of us have heard Bunny's record dozens or perhaps hundreds of times. We know each accent, each shading, each nuance, how much vibrato Bunny assigned to each note. Many of us could discuss with clarity the differences between the April 13, 1936, Vocalion version with Bunny and His Boys and the August 7, 1937, twelve-inch Victor of Bunny Berigan and His Orchestra.

Certainly, this is not most crowds. Merrill Owen is here, the one who "discovered" Bunny and hired him away from Fox Lake so many years ago. Tom Cullen is here, who devoted parts of more than twenty-five years to researching Bunny and his music. Art Beecher, drummer, area resident, onetime Berigan friend and jammer with Bunny, is here. Bill Hunkins is here, lured by the prospect of acquiring new records or tapes, or of sharing his. Many of Bunny's relatives are here. Die-hard fans and childhood Berigan acquaintances are here. This is definitely not a random crowd.

The Soloist winds his way to the front-center of the stage. The band sounds the sustained chord that begins the introduction. Here we go! The Soloist plays the first cadenza a little uncertainly, but no major flaws intrude. Sustained chord again. Shorter phrase. Not bad! Third chord. Whew! My palms are wet with empathetic sweat. He gets through the tough one very well, and I'm hoping he won't miss the cadenza after the fourth band chord. OK. He hits the G at the end cleanly. Now he's telling himself that he's got some straight melody for a while. I wonder when he'll notice that nobody's talking; everybody's listening!

As the saxes take over the melody line, The Soloist and I relax momentarily and breathe. I take a look around to see the reaction of the crowd. The guy with the dour face beneath the baseball cap looks as though he's thinking that The Soloist has some nerve to be playing Bunny's song. Most are smiling, though, apparently enjoying the chance to hear even a facsimile of the gem they know. I'm wishing he had played it his own way instead of trying Bunny's stuff, even though he's doing a decent job. I hear myself admiring him for trying it, especially here. Bill Sargent sings the vocal chorus with the Ira Gershwin lyric that always seemed to have been made for Bunny's high-pitched voice. Then The Soloist takes over for the exquisite, dramatic build to the final phrases. When, with a sense of visible relief, he hits the final high E-flat, The Soloist gets a warm round of applause. Most of us are on our feet. The gray-haired tenor man in the front row turns around and gives The Soloist a big smile, and they slap fives: way to go, kid, you did just fine!

During the next intermission, Commander "Skip" Schweitzer conducts the pleasant business of the day. The Fox Lake American Legion Post 521 sponsors Bunny Berigan Day as a fund-raiser for the local scholarship fund. Annually, the scholarship prize goes to the most deserving music student from local high schools who plans to attend college. The Legion takes considerable pride in the fact that the fund has grown each year since 1974. This year the winner happens to be a trumpeter, a handsome, husky blond whose apparent wholesomeness and demeanor could serve as a great advertisement for the Wisconsin dairy industry or for the American Legion. He offers an unremarkable acceptance speech. The music resumes.

During this final set I tune out the music to reflect on my reasons for coming to Bunny Berigan's hometown. As a high school trumpeter who listened better than he played, I felt a sense of loss when Bunny died before I had a chance to hear him in person. In all these years no one has completed a biography of Bunny. When a career change opportunity presented itself, I decided to go for it. So, for nearly a year I had been gathering information about my boyhood hero. I had read everything I could find about Bunny, much of it repetitive, some of it wrong. Letters and phone calls and conversations with others interested in preserving Bunny's place in jazz history had led me here to interview as many people as I could, to gather information, and to absorb the atmosphere of his birthplace. My friend Norm Krusinski (whose business card reads "Bunny Berigan's #1 Fan") has come with me to introduce me to some of the people who might be willing to help. Before the set ends, I am able to interview Merrill Owen, still proud of his discovery of so many years ago. And I meet Tom Cullen and Artie Beecher. They make it plain that they have talked with many who have begun biographies of Bunny, but none who has finished. Would they be willing to help this newcomer? Would I be considered the interloper? Their silent assessment of me drowns out the music; their decision on whether to help is not immediately apparent.

The concert and scholarship presentation constitute only half of the day's activities. Still to come is the traditional jam session at the Legion Hall in the middle of town. Many of us in this first audience will simply walk or drive the few blocks, stake out some sitting room at the hall, and continue with the day's drinking and listening. The session proves to be one of those truly democratic entities: anyone who has the nerve is welcome to bring an instrument and join in. The preferred style and repertoire are Dixieland and early swing. Gray hair, or none, is the predominant look. The piano is a nondescript upright that *may* have been tuned for the original Bunny Berigan Day. The ceiling is low. The temperature is high. The spirits are soaring. The acoustics remain poor. The beer continues to flow. The session is on.

Initially, a somewhat-organized group plays the standard Dixie repertoire. No doubt: they've played together before. Their interplay with one another and the way they feed upon the ideas in the previous solo are the giveaways. My ear catches the sound of a trombone whose operator knows what he's doing. I love his chorus on "Louisiana." As afternoon becomes evening, the performing group constantly changes. Sometimes two or three trumpets or cornets are on stage simultaneously, sometimes just one. Always a full rhythm section plays, but on almost every tune the personnel changes. I wonder who the older lady on the piano is. She's sitting on a 7-Up case on top of the piano bench. Man, can she swing! I'm told it's Fran Campbell from the Dells, wife of Herb Campbell. The names don't mean anything to me now, but they will.

The red-shirted Old Cat with the pot belly comes on stage with his cornet. Oh, yes! He can play. He invests that nice, full tone into a chorus of "Rockin' Chair" and everything lays just right. He's got good range and decent technique. He's so at ease. I wonder how many times he has played this tune. After he's played several numbers—all with authority, all well worth careful listening—the Old Cat steps down to quaff a few more beers.

Now the winner of the scholarship takes his place on stage, holding his Bach Stradivarius. This is a trumpet used by many professional players, one coveted and owned by many high school and college trumpeters whose talents do not test the capabilities of the instrument. I'm interested to hear what The Winner can do. The young woman on drums was the scholarship winner a few years ago. She displays a good sense of time; knows what to do. Some of the older guys on stage smile quiet approval as she kicks off "Muskrat Ramble" with a four-bar intro. With a journeyman trumpeter leading the way, they romp through two or three choruses, and then it's The Winner's turn. Wow! He doesn't seem to know the chord changes and is floundering more than a little. This must not be his milieu, I'm thinking, and besides, he's probably nervous.

I am dividing my time between listening to the music and talking with some of the local people. I meet several of Bunny's cousins who are related by way of his father's brother, Bob Berigan. The wife of the town undertaker enjoys jazz, I learn. I'm hoping that some of the contacts I am making will turn out to be helpful. A neighbor of the Berigan family introduces herself. She gives me her address and indicates that she would be willing to share some information and clippings with me.

After a while the Old Cat comes back up. The Winner is about to receive his first course, noncredit, no tuition due, under the newly won scholarship. They swing into "Indiana." By now Bill Sargent has taken over on drums, providing some spark and apparently having a ball. The "regular" piano man has returned and the group finds a fine, cohesive groove. The Old Cat plays two choruses and really shows good form. The melody is always there, but he is improvising some lovely lines to complement and enhance the original. The phrasing is sure; the tone is pure. He builds a rhythmically interesting, compelling solo, then gives way to the tenor man. Nothing much happens there, but now The Winner takes another turn. Maybe the tempo and changes will be more to his liking. Unfortunately, within two measures I can tell he is again overmatched by the tune; he just doesn't seem able to follow the changes or do anything with them. After one painful chorus he bows out to the trombone. Then the Old Cat leads them in an out-chorus to which almost everyone contributes.

The Old Cat asks the players what to do next. The Winner names "Saints," the Old Cat nods, and Bill kicks it off from the drums. They solo in about the same order; this time The Winner seems determined to do better. He chooses to go upstairs and show off his range by playing almost the entire solo *a la* Maynard Ferguson, the trumpeter whose stratospheric style holds special appeal for the younger crowd. Instantly, everyone except the coterie of The Winner's local friends realizes that it still is not working. Too often the wrong high note escapes; too often he reaches, then loses it; too often the great effort simply doesn't add up to a musical statement. The out-chorus ends the lesson. The Old Cat takes the last half-chorus up an octave, and when The Winner reaches a high, clear final note, he hears the

Old Cat pick off the third above it just like it was a middle C. The Old Cat wasn't gloating; The Winner wasn't defeated. They had reached a mutual, unspoken understanding about some dues to be paid, some listening to be done, and probably lots of wrong notes to be played before The Winner can expect to hold his own with the likes of the Old Cat.

Soon after, the Eleventh Annual Bunny Berigan Day festival draws to a foamy close. As I make my way back to the motel, I reflect that Fox Lake, Wisconsin, is an unlikely site for a jazz festival of any kind. It just happens to be the place where Bunny Berigan grew up, some sixty miles southwest of Hilbert, where he was born on November 2, 1908. His parents resided in that tiny town for a brief time.

Approximately two hours' drive northwest of Milwaukee, Fox Lake sits in the heart of the beautiful, bountiful, rolling hills of Wisconsin's dairyland. It is the image of Middle America, small-town version. Fox Lake includes three churches, the library, the consolidated school, the canning factory, the American Legion Hall, the printing shop, the farm-implement dealer, the tackle and bait shop, and—oh, yes— fourteen places of various description where the locals may purchase liquor, beer, or wine. The town itself does not wear the same prosperous, forward-looking aura of the surrounding farmland, which, though mortgaged to the tops of its silos, looks fertile and flourishing this May.

Three miles outside of the town is Saint Mary's Cemetery. I find the grave marker, a modest, red marble stone: "BERNARD BUNNY BERIGAN 1908–1942 Internationally Famous Musician." An engraving of a trumpet separates the two dates. Twenty-five feet away, I gaze at the seemingly endless, gently rolling, green fields. I easily imagine that they must have looked much the same seventy years ago when Bunny was growing up among them. In Bunny's playing the same timeless quality prevails. This is the quality that draws several hundred faithful to the eleventh formal remembrance of this small town's native son.

Fox Lake, Wisconsin, is far removed from 52nd Street, New York, New York. There Roland Bernard Berigan earned the respect and awe of colleagues; there he fully developed his unmistakable sound and style; there he performed as sideman and leader in more than six hundred recordings; there he became number one call for radio and recording-studio gigs; there he spent countless nights giving away at jam sessions what he was so well paid to do during working hours; there he downed unmetered quantities of Scotch whisky; there he met, married, left, and reunited with the beautiful Donna; there he was surrounded by appreciative, sometimes adoring fans; there he immersed himself in music, this swing he helped to create, and altered the voice of jazz for all time. In New York, too, Bunny Berigan died at age thirty-three, broken in spirit, physically spent, deep in financial debt.

More than forty years later, the artistry of a trumpet player with a throaty, quivery voice compels half a thousand people to come to tiny Fox Lake to demonstrate their abiding allegiance. What is it in the music and the legend of Bunny Berigan that commands this lasting respect and devotion? I think I know.

1

April Played the Fiddle

Song recorded April 10, 1940
with Tommy Dorsey and His Orchestra

Perhaps someone will do a study some day to determine how many of the great instrumentalists, classical and jazz, began to play on an instrument other than the one on which they achieved fame. Even discounting the obligatory, struggle-filled piano lessons, part of so many American childhoods, the percentage surely must be substantial. Bunny Berigan is one of those. He began playing the violin at an early age, urged on by a family that was more than casually musical.

"Ah, yes," one can imagine Bunny's proud mother, Mayme, recounting, "my grandfather, Fred, brought his violin with him from Germany when he came to America. My father, John, played cornet and violin. We all played something. It just seemed the natural thing to do." In fact, Mayme—really Mary—was an organist and pianist and taught piano to youngsters in and around Fox Lake for many years. She could also double on alto and baritone horns, as could her sisters, Cora and Theresa. An uncle of Bunny's played the clarinet and another aunt played drums, as did Bunny's brother, Don, three years Bunny's senior. "My father," Mayme might have continued, "brought a violin home when Bunny was only six. He gathered Don and Bunny around him and told them that the first one who learned to play the violin could have it. Well, you know, Bunny won that violin. And for such a little one, he surely could play it."

With early instructions from his grandfather and his mother, Bunny did make good progress. Music was an important part of the family's daily life. Bunny's father, William "Cap" Berigan, did not join in the music making, but he encouraged the participation of all of his family in the pursuit of music. Bunny's first public musical performance was as an eight-year-old vocalist.

Mayme's smile broadened as she recalled the arduous practicing they did at home in anticipation of the event. The proud mother with musical talent and a penchant for detail had prepared the boy well. He displayed a high, clear voice with a good sense of pitch. She had been sure that the audience at the Farmers Institute in Fox Lake would be impressed. She remembered the panicked feeling when she discovered just before their number that the piano was tuned much too high. She attempted to catch Bunny's eye and delay the start until she could figure out the difference and modulate to an approximation of the proper key. But Bunny heard the opening chord and was ready to begin. He carried it off like a trouper. Afterward, Mayme reported that Bunny said "Gee, Ma, that was tough! But I got it, didn't I?" Mayme never tired of repeating this story, whether apocryphal or factual, at family gatherings and interviews.

At the time of this debut, rural Wisconsin was somewhat removed from the events of the world, even though 1916 was the year before the United States would be drawn into World War I. These events did provide fuel for some of the discussions at the firehouse, the local stores, and Schlitzberg Hall, which served as a general meeting place, but they did little to disturb the tranquillity that prevailed. Before Bunny was a year old, Cap had given up his job in Hilbert as a railway express agent and returned to Fox Lake, where he became a territorial salesman for the Badger Tobacco & Candy Company, selling candy and cigarettes. Members of both sides of the family lived in or around Fox Lake. John Schlitzberg, Mayme's father, lived part of the time with Cap and Mayme and their growing family. He owned a furniture store in town, served the town as undertaker, led the community band, and ran the dance hall. In Bunny's milieu the work ethic prevailed; idle moments were few. The days were full of a variety of activities; music almost always filled the house. The long Wisconsin winters enforced some limitation on outside activities.

John Schlitzberg was of the old school when it came to music. He stressed great attention to detail: repetition of a measure or note until it was "right"; the "correct" technique—the finger bent just so, the bow held with exactly the prescribed pressure, the posture erect. The scene is easily imagined: "No, no! That note is there to be *accented*. *Accent* it! Why do you not give that note its full value? Are you going to hold that note all day? Are you listening to what you are playing? Yes, better!" Every measure, it seemed, prompted such a comment from Schlitzberg, all in a still-thick German accent sometimes difficult for the young Bunny to understand. But if his grandfather's language sometimes confused him, and if the precision required and the repetition demanded sometimes weighed heavily on him, Bunny rarely complained. Early on, he sensed that he could communicate with and through music, that somehow—in ways he did not fully understand or appreciate—somehow he was able to make music that pleased himself. At times it surely pleased others, too. Those notes on the page, that crude fiddle, his grandfather's stern methods, the hours of practice: in some way these elements combined to produce a feeling of comfort and confidence, fed by the approval of those close to him.

On those occasions when the growing boy felt oppressed, confined, misunderstood, or unappreciated, solace was near at hand. His mother had only to invite Bunny to play with her piano accompaniment. The doting mother, a noted hugger, was at once the world's greatest audience and its firmest, gentlest critic. Perhaps Mayme was a rural version of the typical stage mother, but playing songs with her at the piano was satisfying to Bunny. Her smiles of approval, at once maternal and musicianly, predominated. The reasons for her disapproving frowns rarely had to be verbalized; the young violinist's innate musical ear usually told him what error his hands had committed. More and more, Mayme's corrections became encouraging questions rather than directions. Long before Bunny ever picked up his first trumpet, he had demonstrated that he could differentiate between music that was right and that which was not. "Gee, Ma, that was tough! But I got it, didn't I?" was the prophetic utterance of an eight-year-old whose taste, ear, and musicianship far exceeded his tender years and experience.

The violin lessons that Bunny received at home from his mother and grandfather served him well when he graduated to the teaching of "professor" Clarence H. Wagner. The professor was a highly respected teacher in the Fox Lake–Beaver Dam area. His title had apparently been bestowed upon him by his pupils and admirers. Many years after Bunny's rise to fame, Wagner would say, "With the violin

Bunny was very good. He made progress on it very quickly. But with the trumpet he was not so good."[1] The trumpet had been introduced by John Schlitzberg when Bunny was about eleven, for while the official lessons were to be given by Wagner, Schlitzberg was hardly one to be passed over or shunted aside.

The story has been retold in the same way in countless places. Schlitzberg came home one day with the horn—Don says it was a cornet—and surprised Bunny. "Here! This is you; play you!" An abrupt beginning to a career, perhaps, but this presentation was followed by regular instruction on the trumpet and other brass instruments. After all, the Fox Lake Juvenile Band, led by John Schlitzberg, needed brass players, and he would see to it that the band got what it needed. A well-circulated photograph shows Bunny, age ten or eleven, posed with fourteen other stalwart members, holding an alto horn. The group contains several Schlitzbergs and Berigans and is presided over by the formidable leader. Several alto, baritone, euphonium, and bass horns, as well as trombones, are visible. Perhaps that area of rural Wisconsin suffered a shortage of trumpets or cornets in 1919. Probably it was after this picture was taken that Schlitzberg presented Bunny with his trumpet, recognizing the need for greater balance. As with most small community bands until recent years, the instrumentation depended upon the availability of instruments from closets, attics, and parlors of family, neighbor, and friend. Whatever its source, grandfather's gift was being played by Bunny before he was twelve years old.

Progress on the new instrument must have been swift and sure. The Juvenile Band, with Bunny now on trumpet, played for community concerts and enjoyed an excellent reputation in the area. They were called upon to welcome soldiers returning from overseas duty. At one point, probably during 1920, Bunny began playing his first dance jobs. Berigan's Orchestra was led by Mayme at the piano and featured Bunny on trumpet, Don on drums, and Uncle Walt on sax and clarinet. An aunt might be added, playing horn, to increase the

---

1. Bob Wilson, "Beauty, Drive, and Freedom" (Typescript in possession of author), 6. This typescript was given to Donald Berigan, who in turn gave a copy to Norm Krusinski, who gave a copy to the author. It contains information and direct quotations of Berigan family members that do not appear elsewhere. My research has led me to believe that Wilson's material has come from his interviews of the subjects quoted and that it is accurate. A copy of this typescript may also be found at the Institute of Jazz Studies, Rutgers University, Newark, N.J.

group to five. Sometimes, when only three instrumentalists were called for, the uncle was eliminated. The practice—in large and regular doses—the concerts, the dances, and the continuing lessons combined to effect noticeable improvement in Bunny's trumpet playing. During this period, Bunny underwent an appendectomy and was hospitalized. To be certain that his prize band member lost no ground while incapacitated, John Schlitzberg brought several mouthpieces to the hospital so that Bunny could keep his lip in shape.

Howard Streich runs the Buick garage and dealership on the site formerly occupied by Schlitzberg Hall. He recalls the day some of the neighborhood playmates were climbing and sliding down the mill hill. "I was just a small kid—maybe seven or eight. Bun was five, six years older. He became real sick. In fact, he had appendicitis, but, of course, we didn't know it then. He was in agony while we rolled him home in a coaster wagon. We all helped to pull. From there he went to the nearest hospital, in Portage. I guess it nearly killed him!"[2]

Other friends from Bunny's childhood in the Fox Lake–Beaver Dam area seem eager to share their memories of this region's most famous son. I found none of the resentment that I expected might be accorded the local boy who went "big time" and whose show-business wife spent several extended periods here. Most of the townspeople are eager to share some association, some knowledge, or to claim some proprietary piece of Bunny's early years. Jack Smith's description of Bunny's early years at home is typical of that made by several of his friends of that time: "Bun wasn't too active because he was a little sickly when he was young. He couldn't be in any football and not much baseball. His mother protected him; she didn't want him to get hurt. She really favored Bun over his brother. She'd see to it that Bun practiced. He would ride horses over at our place. He was such an easygoing guy. He had all this talent and people recognized it, and I guess he did, too, but he never exploited it or bragged about it. He was a regular guy."[3]

Erlyne Keefer Eisenbarth, whose brother Hubert was Bunny's bandmate, adds, "Bunny practically lived here. They'd all come in and practice by the hour. He left his horn here, slept here. In fact, he

2. Howard Streich, interview with author, May 19, 1986, tape in author's possession.

3. Jack Smith, interview with author, May 19, 1985, tape in author's possession. Subsequent quotations from Smith are taken from this interview.

ate a lot of bakin' powder donuts and chocolate cookies in our house. He was *absorbed* with the music; he practiced all the time. Was he good-looking as a teenager? He was"—she rolls her eyes and smiles wistfully—"*beautiful!*"[4]

In her basement, Eisenbarth is proud to display photographs of musicians and musical instruments. Most relate to her brother "Hubie" and her uncle, "Windy" Jacobs, whose Five Aces once played one hundred nights in a row, all within forty miles of Beaver Dam. Bunny is in many of the photographs. One in particular, dated December 21, 1924, shows the Merrill Owen band playing at Sam Wah's Chop Suey Restaurant in Milwaukee. The sixteen-year-old Bunny is no longer sickly: his broad shoulders fill the tuxedo jacket; his neck and chest are well developed; his head is large, the face wide and handsome; he stares at the photographer with what Erlyne might describe as bedroom eyes—soft, vulnerable, inviting.

"Diver" Litscher, who lived near the Berigans, relates,

Bun was born on November 2, 1908, and I was born on November 2, 1909. We palled around together a lot, and even though I'm younger, I ran with Tony mostly. You know, Tony is what we all called Bun's brother, Don. Tony and I would go to the dances together and drink and raise hell. But Bunny got along well with his parents and the other kids. He was calm and easygoing. He was his mother's boy, though. She babied him and sometimes it made Tony mad. It seemed like she talked baby talk to Bun when he was twenty years old. When he was young, Bunny couldn't play all the games like baseball and football. I guess his mother was afraid he'd hurt his fingers or something. Later on, Tony and I would try to borrow Bun's coupe. At first he'd say no, but then he would [lend us the car].[5]

Bunny's musical education was boosted along by the addition of a phonograph to the household. The Berigan family considered such an extravagance to be a necessity, a natural extension of the total musical experience they wanted for the family. Don and Bunny delighted in it, not necessarily with the full knowledge of Cap and Mayme. The young brothers were attracted by some strange new sounds, stirring sounds quite different from the "dance" music they were playing for the locals. Naturally, Bunny was especially attracted to listening to

4. Erlyne Keefer Eisenbarth, interview with author, May 19, 1985, tape in author's possession.

5. Emerson "Diver" Litscher, interview with author, May 19, 1985, tape in author's possession. Subsequent quotations from Litscher are taken from this interview.

some of the trumpet stylists of the day. A surprising number of these "hot" records made their way to peaceful, unsuspecting Fox Lake, and Bunny became hooked. His ear was eager, discerning. At first he could not believe that the notes that he read on countless scores were the same ones used to create this new excitement. He was convinced that some other system, some special scheme must designate these notes that sounded so different. Bit by bit, Bunny started playing along with the records, extending the sections he copied by a bar or a partial phrase at a time, until he had approximated the notes of the soloist. Bunny's ear and memory were such that even with records he borrowed from friends and returned, he could remember whole solos once he worked his way through them and could repeat them without benefit of the record. Before long, the young soloist was adding a note of his own here and there, changing ever so slightly what some of his early recording heroes had committed to history via the miracle of the acoustic record.

Bunny's environment provided him with ample opportunity to enhance this skill. At this period Fox Lake was a resort town. Summers would usher in flocks of fun- and sun-seekers from Chicago and Milwaukee. Fox Lake, the lake around which the town is built, provided excellent fishing and swimming. Three trains a day made transportation easy. Many of the records that found their way to Fox Lake arrived on one of these trains, brought by a friend who had access to the latest recordings carried by the shops in the big cities. Bunny's liberty-taking with the recorded solos began to range further and further. He was playing regularly for concerts and street dances with his grandfather and for dances with his mother. More and more, small improvisations began to appear in his playing at the dances. He delighted in embellishing a melody with a hot lick, whether his own or one he had learned from the records. These deviations from the melody were less likely to show up on the violin than they were on the trumpet. Word began to spread as people were attracted to this immature trumpeter-violinist who seemed to possess musical talent and savvy beyond his years. Bunny began playing professionally, outside the family sphere, when he was thirteen.

2

Ten Easy Lessons

Recorded June 8, 1938
by Bunny Berigan and His Orchestra

"That's what attracted me to him in the first place—that
great big tone. It was amazing, especially for such a young fellow."
The speaker is Merrill Owen, Bunny's first employer. At eighty-
three, Owen still played solo piano gigs in the Madison area. He exhibits understandable pride in his longevity and in his recollection of
the first time he met thirteen-year-old Bunny.

John Schlitzberg would have us come up about every three weeks from
Beaver Dam to play in his dance hall—Schlitzberg Hall. I was up there this
one night, and after we had set up for the dance I went out to hear the band
Mr. Schlitzberg led. All of a sudden I heard a big trumpet sound coming
from—it was actually a hayrack, is what it was. I didn't know who he was. I
was surprised at how good he played for being so young. So I went up to him
and told him to come up to the dance hall after you're through here and I'll
tell them to let you in. And he says, "Oh, you don't have to tell them. That's
my grandfather that you're playing for." So that's how I happened to meet
Bunny. He didn't want to play that night. But that tone of his was quite remarkable for someone so young.[1]

Bunny's reluctance did not last long.

Merrill Owen and his so-called Pennsylvanians were a popular
dance band throughout the Fox Lake–Beaver Dam–central Wisconsin area. A quintet that played in a Dixieland style, all of the members
were local boys. The important-sounding title was actually the idea of

1. Merrill Owen, interview with author, May 20, 1984, tape in author's possession. Subsequent quotations from Owen are taken from this interview.

an itinerant circus advance man and sign painter whose imagination got the better of him.

The Charleston dance craze had hit even rural Wisconsin in the early 1920s, and dances were a major recreation. Dixieland and other "jazz" sounds were the thing. Good trumpet players were hard to come by, though a surprising number of good jazz musicians—trumpeters included—sprang out of the upper Midwest.

I asked Bunny if he would like to come down to Beaver Dam and rehearse with my band and see if we could work something out [Owen recalled]. Bunny agreed. He'd come to Beaver Dam after school, or after his lesson with Doc Wagner. He only rehearsed with us for a week or two, and I offered him a job. He could play violin and trumpet, and sometimes even valve trombone.

All of our lead parts were written for the violin or piano. So at first Bunny had trouble reading the parts. Had trouble with the keys, you know, transposing from the violin part to the trumpet. So I went down to Madison and bought him a C-slide for the trumpet. That did it! He only used that C-slide for a few weeks, then he was able to get along just fine without it.

Six dollars a night! That was Bunny's first wage rate, and it was consistent with the going pay for that type of job. It was good money for a fourteen-year-old, especially so since the Pennsylvanians of Merrill Owen were engaged for seventy-one consecutive one-nighters shortly after Bunny joined the band. Owen's 1919 Buick touring car with side curtains provided transportation to and from the jobs. Typically, the instrument cases were carried on the running boards, the bass drum tied to the spare tire at the rear. Thus did Bunny begin learning his life's work, about two years after acquiring his first trumpet.

Bunny's success led almost immediately to some conflicts within the family. The early ones were sartorial. Mayme recalled that shortly after Bunny began playing with Owen, he confronted his mother with all of the strength and courage he could muster: "Ma, I feel so foolish on the bandstand in these short pants and long stockings!"[2] After consultation, his mother and father conceded that the budding professional musician should be allowed to wear long trousers.

Other problems with Bunny had mainly to do with his schooling. After that first summer job with Owen's band, Bunny returned to

2. Wilson, "Beauty, Drive, and Freedom," 8.

school. He continued to play with the band on weekends and occasionally on weeknight jobs that were near Fox Lake. School could not compete, however, with the lure of the band business.

Bunny was a sensation on the road a month after he joined our band [Owen remembered]. The Fox Lake and Beaver Dam crowd used to follow us for miles. We drew well. At some of those lake resorts we'd play to two thousand couples during a weekend. Sometimes Bunny'd take off and do passages he had heard on Armstrong or Red Nichols recordings. Then he'd bring his fiddle along and occasionally he'd play a waltz. He also played a valve trombone at this time, and he'd sing: rhythm novelty tunes like "Jada," "Red Hot Mama," and "I Wish I Could Shimmy Like My Sister Kate."

That was in 1922 when we started, and we played the biggest place in the state of Wisconsin with five pieces and no amplification—just a megaphone. That was Rosenheimer's Pavilion [in Cedar Lake]. It stood for a long time. Bunny could fill that hall with sound. For a kid it was amazing the way he played that trumpet. All the bands around Fox Lake would have liked to sign him.

Owen's last statement is confirmed by Bunny's rapid moves. After playing with Owen and others in 1923 and most of 1924, Bunny joined Cy Mahlberg's band in Fond du Lac in 1925. In September of 1925, Bunny went to live with his uncle "Big Bob" Berigan in Madison. The move was related to Bunny's continuing school struggles; musically, it proved to be just what Bunny needed. The young trumpeter was eager to play with the more advanced groups in Madison. His parents felt that if they allowed him to live with his uncle there, he would be able to play at the desired musical level and, with much of the travel time eliminated, would be able to complete high school.

Bob Berigan was a drummer with the Benson-Emanuel band, one of the many area bands managed by the Al Thompson agency. The coleaders were both University of Wisconsin students; both became doctors. Many years later, Dr. Clifford Benson recalled, "Bunny was just sixteen when he sat in with our band one Friday night. He played great, but he wasn't a very good reader. The very next morning we took him to Thompson, the booking agent, and he put Bunny with Ned Ivey. Ivey's the one who taught Bunny how to read so well."[3] Later, Bob Berigan played drums with the Berigan-Smith Band, an outfit his nephew co-led with Erle Smith, a prominent reed player in

3. Clifford Benson, telephone interview with author, October 5, 1989, transcript in author's possession.

the area. Although he also played for part of 1926 with Jesse Cohen, for most of the three years after his move to Madison, Bunny was featured with the Berigan-Smith Band. Included in this band was Russ Morhoff, a tuba player who would later share membership in other bands with Bunny. Smith-Berigan was a popular band, but by no means did it provide Bunny with his only jobs in the Madison area. He was playing in dance bands and pit orchestras and in some of the places frequented by the University of Wisconsin students, with whom he appeared to blend. The once-frail and overprotected little boy had developed into a husky, handsome young man, looking very much the part of the university student.

But in reality Bunny had never been a good or enthusiastic student, with the notable exception of his music. As early as the eighth grade, still in Fox Lake, Bunny was talking about quitting school. Jack Smith related that Bunny "got in an argument with the manual training teacher. I was a little late, just coming in the door and Bun was on his way out. There was a scene—a little hot air. So Bun told him to go to hell. As he passed me Bun told me, 'I quit school,' and I thought he was just teasing. I joked with him, but he went down the path and that was it."

Actually, his parents were able to keep him attending for yet a while, but Bunny never showed any inclination toward traditional school studies, and the move to Madison followed soon after. Once Bunny found his acceptance as a trumpet player in Madison, the termination of his formal education was only a question of time. Despite frequent references in print to his being a University of Wisconsin student—some sources claim athlete, scholar, graduate!—Bunny left Wisconsin High, a laboratory school of the University of Wisconsin, with credits for approximately the eleventh grade.

When Bunny was between fourteen and twenty years old, his musical education—as well as his musicianship and reputation—burgeoned. In addition to playing with Merrill Owen until early 1925, he played (the stints obviously overlapping) with Cy Mahlberg in the summer of 1925; with "Windy" Jacobs in the Madison–Beaver Dam area in 1925; with the Berigan-Smith Band from 1925 to 1927; at fraternity dances, restaurants, and the Campus Soda Grill from 1926 to 1928; in the pit orchestra of the Orpheum Theater beginning in November, 1927; and in the pit orchestra of the Capitol Theatre beginning in January, 1928. He was playing at every opportunity, as well as practicing. Owen stated that Bunny was doing a lot of formal practice when he was with Owen. Bob Berigan claimed that this was not the case in Madison. Certainly while in Madison under his uncle's guardianship, Bunny was playing a great deal, leaving less time for formal practice. Erlyne Eisenbarth remembered clearly that all the boys in her brother's band—and especially Bunny—practiced almost endlessly.

Another point of disagreement concerns the influence of Chicago teacher Forrest Nicola, who taught a nonpressure method of playing brass instruments. Owen seems certain that Bunny did receive instruction from Nicola in this technique. As the name implies, this method advocates using the musculature of the brass player's embouchure (the manner of applying the lips to the mouthpiece) to make the lips vibrate faster and thus produce higher notes. An alternate, and very common, practice involves pressing the mouthpiece more and more firmly against the lips, thus tautening them to produce higher and higher tones. The latter method is easier initially but places more stress on the lips. Bob Berigan did not believe that Nicola had much influence on Bunny's playing. Regardless of this, Bunny's method of tone production must have relied heavily upon solid, basic technique, attainable only through hours of dedicated practice. Further, Bunny's later stamina, his survival in the gruelling studio sessions and the long strings of one-nighters that found him playing lead and solo horn on almost every tune, must be related to his knowledge of how to avoid abusing his lip through excessive pressure. Many years later, renowned trumpeter Don Jacoby, longtime president of the Dallas Federation of Musicians, would observe, "The bell of his horn pointed up, and it seemed like his lower lip flattened out. He would set the mouthpiece on that flat lower lip and also had a beautiful 'setting' on his upper lip. It was a real strong-looking embouchure; it must have been to get the results he did."[4] Clearly, Bunny's early training, including that received in his own home and up to the time he left the Madison area, was solid and was undergirded by hours of purposeful practice.

When he was not playing or practicing, Bunny spent as many hours

---

4. Don Jacoby, to author, March 21, 1988, in author's possession.

as possible studying other players. He was an avid listener to the phonograph, and early on he was attracted especially to Louis Armstrong's playing. Bunny once recalled hearing Armstrong in Chicago and acknowledged studying "Satch's" playing on records. "I got one of those crank-up jobs," he said, "and would play Armstrong records by the hour."[5]

Don, too, recalled that he and Bunny would play records by the hour, sometimes late and loud, to the distress of the neighbors. At some of these sessions Bunny would try to teach Don to play the cornet. "I would sit on a chair—I was about sixteen or seventeen—and Bun would climb on back of the chair behind me," Don wrote. "He would tell me to hold the horn and blow through it and he would press keys on it—and I would be playing 'Tiger Rag' or some other song."[6] More often, Don would play his drum set while Bunny played along with the records. Erlyne Eisenbarth also remembered that at some of the practice sessions in her home the boys would play records and try to imitate them. Armstrong and Bix Beiderbecke are some of the players she remembered hearing over and over.

The Paul Whiteman Orchestra was extremely popular and was a special favorite of Mayme's and Bunny's. Whiteman's version of "Wang Wang Blues" with Henry Busse was recorded on August 9, 1920, before Bunny was twelve. Armstrong first recorded with King Oliver's Creole Jazz Band on April 6, 1923, when Bunny was fourteen. Beiderbecke made his recording debut with the Wolverines on February 18, 1924, when Bunny was fifteen. Red Nichols appeared "on wax" with the Cotton Pickers the next year, on August 21, 1925, and with the Red Heads, November 13, 1925, around the time of Bunny's seventeenth birthday. Recordings of other fine trumpet players were also available.

Bunny began listening to a variety of records at about age thirteen, but during the latter stages of his apprenticeship in Madison he was concentrating most avidly on Armstrong, as were the other emerging jazz musicians. Clif Gomon was one of the many excellent Madison trumpeters in the late 1920s. He met Bunny at the Ward-Brodt music

5. *Down Beat*, VIII (September 1, 1941), 7. This interview of Berigan was in response to Louis Armstrong's picking Bunny as his favorite trumpeter.
6. Donald Berigan, May 21, 1978, from notes written for the program for the Fifth Bunny Berigan Day, copy in author's possession.

store in Madison in 1928. Clif and Bunny later played together in the talent-laden band at the Club Chanticleer for about eight or nine months in 1929. As Gomon related,

At that time Louis was our favorite, and we used to arrange our intermissions at the Chanticleer so that we could listen to Louis' broadcasts. At 10:30 or 11:00 we'd take our break and go in the back room and turn on the radio and listen to Louis every night. Almost any morning at 8:00 you could go to the Ward-Brodt music store and find Bunny there. He was checking to see if there were any new records out by Louis or Red Nichols—especially Louis, though. If they did have any, Bunny'd take them home and memorize Louis' chorus and then play it that night on the job. He was that studious about it. And of course, I did the same—copying Louis' records. By doing that, we got ideas from Louis and from different ones; we'd play some of their ideas and put them into our own ideas on a chorus, and after a while those ideas kind of become your own. You don't think of them as Louis'; they just kind of work right in with your style and you develop a style in that way. I'm sure it worked that way for Bunny, too.[7]

Art Beecher was a drummer from Beaver Dam, Wisconsin, who played successfully with several of the territory bands. As the name implies, these bands remained in a rather loosely defined area, building a local reputation and returning over a period of months or years for engagements at dance halls and special functions. A friend of Bunny's, Beecher remembered a generous sprinkling of Fletcher Henderson records among the others Bunny and his friends listened to.[8] Probably Rex Stewart, later a driving force on cornet with Duke Ellington, was on some of these 1928 Henderson sides, as Armstrong had been on earlier ones.

Trombonist Keith "Curly" Roberts, a Lancaster, Wisconsin, native, was playing with the Hal Kemp band in November, 1927, when it was on tour in the Madison area. Noting that Kemp was seeking a replacement for trumpeter Earl Geiger, Roberts recommended that Bunny be considered. Berigan sat in with the band at Fort Atkinson's Shorecrest Ballroom, probably on his nineteenth birthday. Kemp and John Scott Trotter, his pianist and arranger, made the assessment. Trotter is quoted in many places as saying that Berigan had "the tinniest, most awful, ear-splitting tone you ever heard." According to

7. Clif Gomon, interview with author, August 30, 1985, tape in author's possession. Subsequent quotations from Gomon are taken from this interview unless otherwise indicated.

8. Art Beecher, interview with author, May 19, 1986, tape in author's possession. Subsequent quotations from Beecher are taken from this interview.

one writer, Trotter ascribed to Bunny a "pea shooter tone." Roberts, on the other hand, recalled that Kemp offered Bunny the job because his big tone matched that of the other trumpeter with the band, Wade Schlegel. Further, Roberts stated that Bunny's father refused to let him tour with the band, clinging to the hope that Bunny would complete high school.[9] Whatever the case, Bunny remained in Madison with his multiplicity of jobs, school no longer of any concern to him. Within weeks of the audition he had arranged for Bunny, Roberts left the Kemp band and returned to Madison. There he joined Bunny in the pit orchestra of the Orpheum Theater, where Bunny had begun playing in mid-November, 1927; they both moved to the new Capitol Theatre when it opened in late January, 1928.

Trotter's assessment notwithstanding, Bunny's contemporaries, many of them excellent musicians who would also later achieve some measure of acclaim, developed admiration for Berigan's tone quality and general sound. Owen, who "discovered" Bunny, was attracted by his sound, and fellow trumpeter Gomon remembered Bunny's playing in this way: "He had power, and plenty of that; and plenty of range, too. His tone was a good round, solid, live tone, and believe me, he made good use of it. We both used Holton horns at that time and both used the Number 2 mouthpiece that came with it. I always did." Perhaps the duplication of equipment, combined with their similar listening habits, partly explains the assessment by Herb Campbell, their bandmate, who formed his opinion through many months of playing with both trumpeters: "If you closed your eyes and listened, you couldn't tell the difference between Clif's and Bunny's playing."[10]

"Curly" Roberts and Bunny played together at the Orpheum and Capitol theaters until April, 1928, when Roberts went to New York to study with Charles Randall. Roberts remembered that Bunny

9. Vince Danca, *Bunny: A Bio-discography of Jazz Trumpeter Bunny Berigan* (Rockford, Ill., 1978), 3; Mort Goode, liner notes for RCA AXM2-5584, *The Complete Bunny Berigan, Vol. I;* Keith "Curly" Roberts, interview with Tom Cullen, June, 1959, tape in author's possession. Many of the questions on the interview were formulated by Bozy White. This taped interview was given to the author with Cullen's permission by John Grams, who used it as part of a tribute to Berigan on his radio program on station WTMJ, Milwaukee, and preserved it. Subsequent quotations from Roberts are taken from this interview, used with permission of Bozy White. Information on Berigan's work in Madison theaters researched by Tom Cullen, in Bozy White Outline.

10. Fran Campbell to author, June 23, 1985, in author's possession. Campbell, of Wisconsin Dells, Wis., is a pianist and the widow of Herb Campbell, a prominent trombone player in the Madison area.

"played a good, solid horn and had a big tone. At that time Bunny played a Holton trumpet, but later he switched to a Conn—22B, I think it was called—which was the biggest horn they made. It took a good man to fill—which he did."

Bob Berigan and Erle Smith have both called Bunny's tone in the mid- to late-twenties "excellent," and the elder Berigan remarked that his nephew was developing great style during that period. Bob Berigan added, "He could play some clinkers at times, but he was never afraid to try the difficult. It was exciting to listen to him."[11]

The large number of outstanding jazz musicians who emerged from the Madison area and from other parts of the upper Midwest may seem surprising at first. Some explanation may be found in the fact that many German, Scandinavian, and Dutch families migrated to the area, bringing with them a rich musical tradition, which they perpetuated. Bunny's family-fed supply of instruments and musical instruction was not unusual. Further, entertainment initially was found largely in the home and the church and relied heavily on the ingenuity and talents of the residents. Dancing—especially the Charleston—and singing were popular; both required musicians. The traditions of the residents' homelands were naturally assimilated into the new settlements.

Madison's proximity to Chicago and, to a lesser extent, to Milwaukee, contributed to the popularity of the new forms of music, first ragtime, then a freer style of jazz. The presence of the University of Wisconsin brought an influx of those wanting to be associated with the newer, more exciting forms of art, especially music. Chicago took the lead in fostering jazz and introducing it to the rest of the country. Relatively easy access from Madison to the jazz parlors of Chicago and Milwaukee encouraged the development of a large number of Wisconsin-based instrumentalists, urged on by the college community's insatiable appetite for jazz. Riverboat and lake cruisers in the area still feature jazz bands for summer listening pleasure, as they did decades ago.

Beginning in approximately the mid-1920s, hundreds of excellent musicians developed their skills in this general area. Some of the names have enjoyed national renown: "Doc" DeHaven, Heine Beau,

11. Wilson, "Beauty, Drive, and Freedom," 11.

Chuck Hedges, Lucy Reed, Gene Puerling, Les Paul, Gene Schroeder, Vaughn Monroe, Dick Ruedebusch, Rollo Laylan, Herb Campbell, Keith Roberts, Shorty Sherock, Buddy Clark, Freddie Slack, Jackie Cain, Woody Herman, Joe Dodge, and Billy Maxted. Others, because of personal choice, or lack of proper opportunity, or because of less lofty talents, remained in the area, providing listeners even now with a rich, indigenous musical heritage.

Beecher called Bunny's playing at that time "better than all the rest—even then." Roberts, in spite of his Kemp recommendation, maintained, "At that time, Bunny wasn't the top trumpet player in Madison by any means. There was Cec Brodt, Clif Gomon, Cliff Benson, Frank Powers, "Fuzzy" Fosgate. They were all good jazz men, good improvisers." Benson confirmed this assessment, adding that Brodt had won a trumpet competition at about this time. Clearly, Bunny, the young trumpeter, had positioned himself at the forefront of an elite group of emerging jazz musicians in an area that had an almost unlimited enthusiasm for the new American phenomenon—jazz—and that was producing some of its better performers.

3

Back in Your Own Back Yard

Song preserved on an air check, March 27, 1938
Bunny Berigan and His Orchestra
from the Paradise Restaurant

"I called Bunny late at night from New York," recalled "Curly" Roberts. "I think they finally reached him at the Green Circle in Madison. I told him what the setup was: Frank Cornwell was asked to form a band for Janssen's restaurant in Philadelphia while he was still playing in the New York Janssen's. His brother, Ardon Cornwell, was a very fine arranger and pianist, and everything seemed to jell that way. Bunny got to New York on the train the second day after I called him," Roberts continued. "Ardon and I went to Grand Central Station to meet him, and what with the big crowd or going to the wrong train, we missed him. When we got back to the apartment, there was Bunny."

The men were living in what Roberts called a typical 1928 New York brownstone on 53rd Street between 5th and 6th Avenues—just a block from what later came to be called Swing Street. They lived in a furnished efficiency apartment, one of those that catered to musicians. It came complete with kitchen and grand piano. The band formed within two weeks after Bunny arrived, rehearsing at the Helen Morgan Club on 52nd Street before moving to Philadelphia. The band included, besides Berigan and Roberts, Julie Towers on alto sax and clarinet; Joe Usifer (who later changed his name to Paul Lavalle, and still later directed the Band of America), also on sax; Ardon Cornwell as arranger and pianist; Lacey "Speed" Young on guitar; Russ Morhoff on bass; and drummer Billy Southard. They were known as the Lacey Young Orchestra, since the guitarist fronted the group. Roberts decided to join up "because Bunny was on the band."

When they moved to Philadelphia to begin playing at the plush new restaurant, Roberts and Bunny initially roomed together at the Central Apartments. Later they moved to the Chatfield Apartments and were joined by saxophonist Walt Dorfus and Towers in sharing quarters. Since none of the young musicians owned cars, they cabbed to work daily. Roberts recalled that they played for the shows every night but Sunday, when they played for an afternoon dinner session. "Our book had about 250 to 300 numbers—good arrangements by Ardon. He gave the 'hot' men a chance to take off, and the men could really improvise fine. Jimmy Dorsey had taken lessons from Towers, who was a *fine* clarinet man."

A newspaper advertisement heralded the opening of the new restaurant: "And now Janssen wants to see you in Philadelphia. . . . The Famous Hofbrau in New York has been duplicated at 1309 Walnut Street. . . . The same food—the same service—Everything the same—Opens TOMORROW evening, April 11th at 7 PM. . . . August Janssen, Jr. will be there to greet you—For reservations call Pen. 4204." And, indeed, Frank Cornwell did come to the Philadelphia Janssen's, but only for the opening and perhaps another night or two, after which he was not associated with the band.[1] It was Ardon's band and it was a good one, as more than one member attested.

Apparently Philadelphians agreed, for the beautiful new restaurant attracted sell-out crowds. Another newspaper advertisement depicted the restaurant offering "Special Hofbrau Platter including Bread, Butter and Coffee served at 55 cents to 85 cents—quick service. Serviced 11:30 AM until 4:30 PM. . . . Hofbrau table d'hote dinner $1.50 . . . the best in town serviced from 5:30 PM until 9 PM. . . . Continuous a la fonte service—music and dancing from 6 PM until 1 AM . . . No cover charge at any time."[2]

Newspaper listings reveal regular broadcasts of the "Janssen's Hofbrau Orchestra" during the initial months of the job. The band was building a well-deserved reputation. In spite of this and every apparent advantage, however, the restaurant was losing money. No one could understand this loss because "standing room only" was a

1. Philadelphia *Bulletin-Enquirer*, April 10, 1928, in Bozy White Outline; Julie Towers, interview with Bozy White, February, 1953, transcript in White and Cullen Research Materials, copy in author's possession. All Philadelphia newspaper citations on these pages from research by Martin L. Kite, in White Outline.
2. Philadelphia *Evening Bulletin*, May 2, 1928, in Kite Papers.

nightly occurrence. Roberts speculated that the restaurant's troubles were caused by a purchaser for the restaurant who was using his position to acquire inventory for his own business. Whatever the case, in about mid-August the Young band left the Philadelphia Hofbrau. They had been scheduled to take over at the Gateway Casino in Atlantic City in early August, but the job never materialized, perhaps because the summer season was so far advanced. *Billboard* erroneously reported that on August 4 the "Lacey Young Orchestra which recently concluded a four month run at Janssen's Hofbrau, Phillie, has moved to the Gateway Casino here, where the combination will knock out the dance timers for the balance of the fall. . . . Gateway Casino is under the management of August Janssen, Jr." Possibly the Philadelphia job extended into September, when the band arrived in New York and soon began a run at the China Royal Restaurant in Brooklyn. This lasted through approximately November, 1928. Again, the band was involved in regular, almost daily, broadcasts. Roberts recalled that the run was short and that the band could not find further work. When he received a call from a friend in Florida, he left to play in Tampa, arriving, he believes, on Halloween night. Clearly, the "Speed" Young band was breaking up in the fall of 1928. Either because of lack of work or tooth problems affecting his lip, Berigan returned home on December 22, 1928, ready to resume his musical activities there. The local Fox Lake newspaper reported his return in its December 27 issue.[3] Thus ended Bunny's first joust with the music scene in the New York tilting grounds.

His New York experience was actually a double exposure for Bunny. On the one hand, he made many valuable contacts musically, was heard by many, and was judged by listeners and colleagues alike to be a coming major talent. Perhaps one of the most valuable contacts Bunny made was in meeting and earning the friendship of Rex Stewart, later a mainstay with the great Duke Ellington band. The stylish cornetist was then beginning a two-and-one-half-year stint with the Fletcher Henderson band, which was to be the model and inspiration for the bands of Benny Goodman and other leaders of the swing era. The depth of the Berigan-Stewart friendship is not known, but Stewart was present near the beginning of Bunny's professional

3. *Billboard,* August 11, 1928; Fox Lake *Representative,* December 27, 1928. Most *Billboard* citations in this book from research by Bozy White, and most Fox Lake *Representative* citations from research by Tom Cullen, all from Bozy White Outline.

career. Stewart introduced Bunny to Tommy and Jimmy Dorsey, who were, in 1928, just beginning to make records as the Dorsey Brothers Orchestra. And it was the Dorseys who chose the personnel for a significant number of the record sessions in the late 1920s and early 1930s, so this exposure opened many doors for Berigan.

Bunny was also introduced to alcohol during this relatively brief period in Philadelphia and New York. The initiation started during the Philadelphia run where, according to Roberts, Bunny was playing in "fast company." He began drinking with some of his bandmates, notably Towers and Southard, thus seeding a habit that has received much attention through succeeding years. This exposure—perhaps inevitable—was one that likewise played a major role in Berigan's life.

Once back in Madison, Bunny wasted little time getting his career rolling again. Frequently playing in two places during the same evening, by about March, 1929, he was leading one of the Al Thompson units that played throughout the upper Midwest. Madison's Club Chanticleer opened on March 1, 1929, and Bunny was soon featured there with a familiar group of musicians. On April 2, "Mr. B. and His Orchestra" played a one-nighter at the Green Circle, a popular spot for dancing. On April 5, the University of Wisconsin Military Ball—"The Greatest Social Event in the Spring Season," according to the announcement in the school's *Daily Cardinal*—featured "Bunny Berrigan's [*sic*] 12 Piece Band."[4] This job represented quite a plum for Bunny, since the area boasted several more-established bands that might have expected to land this job. The chief justice of the Wisconsin Supreme Court was present to welcome guests on behalf of the state. On April 19, Bunny led a band that opened the summer season at Esther Beach, one of the dance halls especially popular with the college crowd.

After playing the weekend of May 10 through 12 at Esther Beach, Bunny left Madison for Champaign-Urbana, Illinois, to play with Pete Drum and Paul Beam and their Apostles of Music. They opened at the Lakeside Ballroom on May 17, but the stay was a short one for Bunny. He left to join another territory band. This, too, was a brief stay, and on about June 10, Bunny began playing with Joe Shoer and His Orchestra at the Castle Farms Dream Garden in Cincinnati, a

4. University of Wisconsin *Daily Cardinal*, April 4, 1929, in Cullen Research Materials (hereinafter cited as Cullen Materials).

large, beautiful facility. From there the Shoer band drove to Lexington, Kentucky, to open at the Joyland Casino in early July. The Joyland's one hundred–degree heat drove the band to unusual measures. A photograph shows the players immersed in the swimming pool, their instruments held aloft. This two-week gig actually ended after four weeks. The Shoer band apparently dispersed at this time, Bunny darting back to Madison, where he soon fronted a group at Club Chanticleer.

This stand at the Chanticleer lasted from approximately the first or second week of August until about September 16. Within a few days, Bunny was contacted from New York. On September 21, 1929, he again left for New York, a young man in a hurry.[5]

5. Fox Lake *Representative, ca.* September, 1929, in Cullen Materials. All information about Berigan's Madison and Champagne-Urbana performances and his performances with Shoer is from research by Martin L. Kite, Tom Cullen, and Bozy White, in Bozy White Outline.

4

Forty-second Street

Song recorded April 11, 1933
with the Boswell Sisters

Bunny Berigan arrived in New York on September 23, 1929, eager to test his skills in the toughest, most exciting arena of all. His timing could have been better. Within a month the stock market crashed, launching the Great Depression. With the excitement of the new job, Bunny probably took little note of the economic scene. He was more concerned about his tooth problems, which in turn could affect his lip. Here he was in New York, ready to become a member of the band that played at August Janssen's New York Hofbrau restaurant, one of the liveliest in the city.

Bunny's concern about his teeth was not new. Photographs of Bunny from this period betray a discolored, crooked front tooth. Bunny's old roommate Keith Roberts insisted that this was a persistent problem with Bunny until Nat Natoli, a fellow trumpeter, helped Bunny make some corrections. Natoli was considerably older and more experienced than Bunny, having played in the studios for many record and radio sessions. While Bunny and Natoli recorded together for the first time in 1932 with Paul Whiteman, the two trumpeters certainly would have met long before that, perhaps as early as 1930 when Natoli played with Whiteman. Bunny may even have received some help with this problem before leaving Madison in the fall of 1929.

The return to the New York Hofbrau of the Frank Cornwell band—this time featuring Bunny Berigan—was announced with this advertisement: "TONIGHT—America's Finest Restaurant—Janssen Wants to See You—Fall Opening Celebration—Return of Frank Cornwall and Crusaders—A REVUE of beautiful girls and many other attractions."[1] The band was headed by the violin-playing leader, and Bunny occasionally doubled on his violin. Musicians and the regulars thought that this was a better band than the one Frank Cornwell originally fronted at the Hofbrau.

Once again, regular radio broadcasts originated from Janssen's, beginning on November 18 and running through June, 1930. WOR broadcast these performances daily except Sunday and Tuesday. The hours were irregular, with no discernible pattern. Such broadcasts, in keeping with then-prevalent trade practices, often served as filler for the regular programming. Some of the players felt that the band did not show to best advantage on these broadcasts. Song-pluggers and publishers would apply pressure on the band by feeding it stock arrangements of new tunes to read during live shows, thus preventing polished performances. This advertisement in the November 20, 1929, *Variety* illustrates the point: "We doff our hats to Frank Cornwell who, with his famous Crusaders at Janssen's Hofbrau and during his regular broadcasts via station WOR, shows rare discrimination and fine judgment in consistently featuring: 'How Am I to Know?,' 'Singin' in the Rain,' 'Just You, Just Me.' [Signed]—Robbins Music Company."[2]

The band worked a full schedule at Janssen's. Beginning at 6:30 P.M., they would play for two shows and dancing, with only a brief intermission before the second show. The shows were varied but always included a line of tall, provocatively dressed show girls, as well as dancers, singers, and variety acts. Following the second show, they played for another hour of dancing, packing up at about 1:00 A.M.

Frequently, that is when the fun began. A trip to Harlem's Clam House, run by Gladys Bentley, or to nearby Plunkett's, both of which featured good after-hours jazz and jazz talk, became a regular part of the evening's routine. Josh Billings' description of Plunkett's helps to recall the flavor:

1. New York *Times*, October 10, 1929, p. 35. This and most other citations from the New York *Times* from research by Tom Cullen and/or Bozy White, in Bozy White Outline.

2. Opinions about the broadcasts can be found in the Roberts interview and interviews with other band members, in White and Cullen Research Materials; *Variety*, November 20, 1929, p. 66, in White Materials. This is an example of how publishers (in this case Robbins) could influence what tunes the bands played. Through such advertisements Janssen's received free publicity, and the band was expected to play the music that was given to them. Most citations from *Variety* from research by Bozy White, in White Outline.

The Sixth Avenue "El" turned over to Ninth Avenue along narrow 53rd Street and the premises of 205½ W. 53rd were always in the shadow. There was the usual metal-sheathed door and the round peephole. There were a number of passwords, but the most reliable was, "Tommy Dorsey sent me."

Once inside, you would see Hairless Jimmy Plunkett and . . . Gene O'Byrne. Jimmy had lost his locks, even his eyebrows and the hair on his chest, through a typhoid attack. Because of this, it was his everlasting habit to wear a cap and numerous sweaters. The bar at Plunkett's was about ten feet long and on the shelves above it were a half-dozen nondescript beer steins.

In those free and easy days tabs represented more of the business than cash.

There were two booths in the small back room, but they were seldom used except for a siesta or the occasional visit of an angry wife. Every day the barreled beer arrived at Plunkett's in a different truck. Sometimes it was a florist delivery car, sometimes a milk wagon and on one occasion it was even a hearse.

Eddie Condon's dressing room, the icebox Tommy Dorsey talks about, was loaded to the ceiling with thousands of dollars worth of instruments—everybody's—from Jimmy Dorsey's famous collection of gold saxophones to Pee Wee Russell's crud-caked clarinet or Bix Beiderbecke's cornet in a corduroy sack. Also in the icebox was a miscellany of laundry, hats, odd raccoon coats, baggage belonging to some members between hotels or on the road—and even Arthur Schutt's gold-headed cane.

You could get a haircut or shave at Plunkett's any time from Tommy O'Connor, one time car pusher in the coal mines in Scranton. The space from the top of the icebox to the ceiling was jammed with more instruments of more unknowns—Eddie Condon's guitar, Joe Venuti's fiddle, Jack Teagarden's and Glenn Miller's trombones, Max Kaminsky's and Wingy Manone's trumpets, Davie Tough's and Gene Krupa's drums. The camaraderie at Plunkett's was something special. Why, when the Dorsey Brothers started their orchestra, Jimmy Plunkett was their manager.[3]

Camaraderie was an accepted and expected part of life in the New York jazz community. Berigan quickly became known for being good company and for fitting in with the music crowd. Beginning at about this time, and extending throughout his career, Bunny became known as a generous spender, always ready to help a musician who had the "shorts." Rex Stewart and Bunny became reacquainted during this time—perhaps at the Clam House—and Bunny probably met the

---

3. Josh Billings, "Plunkett's," in *Esquire Jazz Book, 1947* (New York, 1947), 31–32.

Dorsey brothers in the same fashion. Jimmy Dorsey told researcher Tom Cullen that he and Bunny first met at Plunkett's when Bunny complimented Jimmy on his recording of "Beebe" (a virtuoso saxophone piece recorded June 13, 1929). This would indicate that Bunny did not meet the Dorseys—at least Jimmy—until his second trip to New York, in approximately October, 1929.[4] Word of his musical exploits at Plunkett's and similar hangouts spread among the fraternity.

Late in April of 1930, conditions combined to create another change for Berigan. As the early hardships of the Depression set in and money grew tight, business at the Hofbrau declined. The bandsmen read the signs and foresaw that they would soon be replaced by a cheaper band. Worse, Cornwell had not lined up other bookings. The band began to disperse as individuals found new gigs. Bunny notified "Curly" Roberts of the impending breakup, and Roberts again advised him to seek a chair with the Hal Kemp band. Kemp, and perhaps John Scott Trotter, who had maligned Bunny's tone in the earlier Kemp audition, reversed their evaluation. While it is true that Berigan had matured and improved rapidly in the interim, the fact that he had now achieved status among fellow musicians seems to have come strongly into play. In any event, Bunny was offered, and he accepted, a job with the Kemp band.[5]

Now Bunny's timing was excellent. By about May 28, Janssen's Hofbrau had replaced Cornwell's band with the Joe Frasetto band. *Variety* reported that Janssen's Hofbrau had been designated as "restricted territory" for bands by the American Federation of Musicians, who alleged that the Frasetto band, from out of town, had worked there below union scale pay.[6]

Meanwhile, the Kemp band began an engagement at the Nixon Cafe in Pittsburgh on April 21. Shortly thereafter, Bunny came on the band. On May 14, the Kemp band recorded four titles at Brunswick studios. The next day the band departed for England from the West 18th Street Pier at 9 P.M. on the British liner *Majestic*. They arrived at Southampton on Wednesday, May 21, at 10:30 P.M. Excited though he was by the rapidly unfolding events and the promise of the trip, Bunny had left something important behind.

4. Tom Cullen, interview with author, May 21, 1985, tape in author's possession.
5. All information about Frank Cornwell from research by Bozy White.
6. *Variety*, July 2, 1930, in White Materials.

5

The First Time I Saw You

Song recorded May 13, 1937
by Bunny Berigan and His Orchestra

"It was when Darrell and I would do the adagio. He would have me fully extended up on his shoulders, and I would come out of that into a split and bend backward, facing the orchestra. There were these beautiful blue eyes, almost at my level, staring into my eyes. He was playing the violin for our adagio, although he usually played the trumpet. . . . Well, we just had to meet. Yes, it was a romantic way to meet your future husband. Awkward, too! We were booked into the Hofbrau . . . , and Bunny was in the orchestra when we came in."[1] That is how Donna Berigan Burmeister recalled meeting Bunny at Janssen's Hofbrau in the fall of 1929. The passing of more than fifty years robbed Donna's memory of some details—she could not call forth Janssen's name—but her recollection of the major events and important feelings has survived, largely intact.

"Bunny was kind of shy. He had Frank Cornwell arrange a double date for him, and we went to one of the clubs with Frank and his wife. We had to sneak out on that first date, and the others, too, because the girls in the show weren't allowed to associate with the musicians. Somebody wrote that we went to the Cotton Club that first date, but that's not true."

Donna and Darrell performed as a brother-and-sister dance team; Darrell McArthur was Donna's elder by five years. Born in Berlin, New Hampshire, on April 19, 1912, Donna moved with her family to Syracuse, New York, at an early age. She started dancing by observ-

1. This quotation from Donna Berigan Burmeister and all those from her throughout the book are taken from a series of interviews with the author, September 6–8, 1984.

ing Darrell's lessons, and it quickly became apparent that Donna had an aptitude for dancing: she would remind Darrell and demonstrate some of the segments of his most recent lesson after they returned home. Soon a team emerged; Donna, aged thirteen or fourteen, and Darrell began performing in the Syracuse area. By the time she was about sixteen, Donna became one of the first women to sign on with Fitch's Minstrels, with whom the team performed for a while. The dancers' career was blossoming nicely when they were booked into Janssen's.

"It was a big place; a nice place, right on Broadway and 52nd Street." A smile softens Donna's face as memory casts aside the haziness.

Always had a fast-moving show, with the line of tall girls and the shorter ones who did the tap routines. All the usual variety acts. When the orchestra did "Piccolo Pete," that's when Bunny took out his little piccolo. We had several dates while we were both still at the Hofbrau. That was a fun time, and things were getting serious between Bunny and me.

We wanted to get married before he went to Europe with Kemp, but I was really too young to get my mother's permission. And, of course, Darrell was against it because it would break up the act. We had worked very hard to get where we were: five hours of rehearsal nearly every day; lots of traveling. We were doing pretty well.

Donna remembers Bunny's four-and-a-half-month stay abroad as ten months.

After he came back, Darrell and I were playing in this hotel in Detroit [the Addison]. It was run by the Purple Gang. They treated us real nice, gave us anything we needed. Only thing was, they didn't let us leave the hotel. Sent everything we wanted up to our rooms. Anyway, Bunny was playing somewhere nearby, I think, and he came to see me in Detroit. That's when we decided to get married.

Of course, Darrell was having a fit. I asked him who he was going to get to take my place. Finally he decided to get this girl from Pittsburgh. She was a tap dancer and it took us three months to break her in. She came to Detroit and we broke her into the act there. She never did learn to do the adagio. She did the ballroom and the others, but in the act I'd do the adagio and she'd do the rest. Do you know, Darrell didn't talk to me hardly for seven years? He held a grudge. He was just getting started to be well known.

Photographs from this period, preserved with some difficulty, reveal the appeal, grace, and beauty of the young dancer Donna

McArthur. Her oval face, framed by long, blonde hair, features a generous, sensual mouth whose smile contrasts with her eyes' sadness. Although intended to be glittery publicity shots, the photos seem, oddly, to project a comfortable wholesomeness.

On May 25, 1931, Donna and Bunny were married at Saint Patrick's Church in Syracuse. The photograph run in that evening's edition of the Syracuse *Herald* shows nineteen-year-old Donna and twenty-two-year-old Bunny posed outside the church with their wedding party. A strapping Bunny towers a full six inches over his bride. He looks nervous. Donna's floppy picture hat turns back to reveal the same lovely face with the full, smiling mouth. The photo's caption identifies the new Mrs. Berigan as "a dancer, a protege of Sonya Marens. She has appeared with her brother, Darrell McArthur, and has also been presented on the RKO Keith circuit several times." Berigan is portrayed as "a trumpeter with Freddy Rich's orchestra." The caption continues: "The bride and groom left immediately for New York City." Donna recalled that they took no time for a honeymoon. The Depression loomed out there. Bunny had some shows to do; he had a reputation to enhance; he had ι career to further; he had some music to play.

6

At Your Command

Song recorded June 15, 1931
with Fred Rich and His Orchestra

Almost exactly a year before marrying Donna, Bunny had sailed for Europe with the Kemp band. John Chilton provides an excellent overview of the trip:

In the middle of May [May 15, 1930] the band left for England, the first stop on a European tour. For Berigan, his first (and last) trip abroad was an unqualified success. Despite the band's heavy schedule of daytime theater appearances and nightclub dates that lasted until 3 a.m., Berigan found time to make friends and have fun. He impressed pianist Eddie Carroll with his high-speed memorizing of trumpet parts and caught the ear of the editor of *Rhythm* magazine with his interpretation of a brand-new song, "On the Sunny Side of the Street." The editor asked him to write out a chorus, and published the result in the magazine's August 1930 issue, a rare tribute to a musician as little known as Berigan was then. Author-bandleader Patrick Cairns (Spike) Hughes, after meeting Berigan, called him "one of the nicest kids in the profession."

He was certainly one of the most lighthearted. When a Salvation Army band marched past the Kemp band's dressing room at the Dominion Theatre one day, Berigan snatched up his horn, fell in with their ranks and marched along playing a perfect harmony part, to the immense amusement of his colleagues.

He also surprised and delighted some of the British jazz fans who heard him both in the band's regular routines and at the Saturday afternoon tea dances at the Cafe de Paris. The Kemp band's regular act was that of a collegiate show unit. They sang glee-club songs, played arranged novelty numbers on bottles filled with water to various levels and provided mellow background sounds for their leader's beautifully played subtone clarinet. But on Saturdays they had jam sessions with musicians such as Jimmy Dorsey and Muggsy Spanier, then on tour with the Ted Lewis band, and Berigan could cut loose, astonishing jazz buffs with the heat and intensity of his improvisations.

After London, the band went on to engagements in Belgium and France before sailing from Le Havre on the *Ile De France*. They arrived in New York six days later, on September 30.[1]

Certain details made this a memorable trip for many. On the third day out on the way to England, most of the band members became seasick. This was the night they were asked to play for the benefit of the influential passengers, whose reactions might help determine their reception in London, and for the critical ears of the incumbent English orchestra on board. They pulled it off—just barely. An examination of the "heavy schedule" cited by Chilton provides insight into why road travel with a band is basically a young person's job. Arriving on May 21 at Southampton, the band almost immediately began a three-shows-a-day run at London's Coliseum Theatre.

On Monday, May 26, the band added to the Coliseum schedule an engagement at the Cafe de Paris on Coventry Street. The shows there began at about 11 P.M. and ran as late as 3 A.M. This doubling lasted for approximately a week, until the Kemp band closed at the Coliseum on Saturday, May 31. The run at the Cafe de Paris lasted until Thursday, August 14, during which time the band doubled with engagements at the Plaza Theatre in July and August for a total of about three weeks. From August 11 to 14 the band "tripled," adding shows at the Dominion Theatre at 6:00 and 8:30 P.M. These shows featured, in addition to Kemp's band, a large ballet corps and the Lon Chaney film *Phantom of the Opera*. All of these runs came to an end on Thursday, August 14. As if this were not enough, the band squeezed in charity shows and other concerts. Regular radio broadcasts emanated from the Cafe de Paris.

Billboard reported on the tour:

Hal Kemp . . . is scoring a sensational hit this summer at the Cafe de Paris in London with his Carolina Club Orchestra, according to reports received in local music circles.

The Kemp orchestra, one of the foremost dance bands in the National Broadcasting Company's list, which firm arranged the London date, has made rapid strides in the music industry in the last two years and before

1. John Chilton and Richard M. Sudhalter, *Giants of Jazz: Bunny Berigan* (Alexandria, Va., 1982), 11–12. These notes by Chilton are from the booklet accompanying the Time-Life record album.

starting out on the present job was regarded as one of the foremost "name" orchestras in the East. The band has been in London since May.

The Prince of Wales and other members of the British Royal Family have heard him play and have danced to his music at the Cafe Paris.

Prince George recently had six of his musicians out to play for him at his country home. . . . All the Kemp boys sing as well as play.

The combination will conclude its London stay in a few weeks and is scheduled to make appearances in Belgium, Germany, Italy and Spain before returning to the States late in the fall.[2]

The Kemp band was riding high and having fun, too. Ted Lewis and his orchestra were in London during much of the Kemp period and featured Jimmy Dorsey and the uninhibited trumpeter Muggsy Spanier. The Lewis band was also enjoying great success in England, more because of the antics and melodramatics of the clarinet-playing leader than his musicianship. Whenever possible, exchange sitting-in took place, but jam sessions, because of both bands' heavy schedules, were rare. Gus Mayhew, a stellar trombonist with Kemp, recalled one afternoon session at the Cafe de Paris during the period when the band had only one assignment. Jimmy Dorsey came to sit in, replete with a rhinestone-covered clarinet that had been given to him. Mayhew delighted in recounting that Dorsey was in midflight on his decorated instrument doing a lampooning imitation of his leader, when in walked Ted Lewis himself![3]

Because of Britain's tightening economic situation, authorities imposed sanctions upon the use of foreign musicians for recording and for entertainment purposes in general. In spite of this, Van Phillips, an American working in Britain's record industry, arranged to record six visitors with an unidentified local rhythm section. Berigan and four other Kemp band members joined Jimmy Dorsey, who came from the Lewis band. The group, augmented by strings and led by Phillips, recorded two medley selections from English musical shows. Issued on Shoestring SS-110, these recordings are musically disappointing but are of some interest historically. In reaction to the session, authorities pressured the Lewis and Kemp bands to leave the country immediately. The intervention of influential local musicians probably prevented their deportation from England.

When jam sessions could be arranged, local jazz musicians eagerly

2. *Billboard*, August 16, 1930.
3. Gus Mayhew, interview with Bozy White, May, 1959, in White Materials, copy of transcript in author's possession. Subsequent information from Mayhew is taken from this source.

joined in with the likes of Berigan, Dorsey, and Manone. Free to blow what he felt, instead of what was demanded by the constraining and contrived Kemp charts, Bunny astounded the British jazz enthusiasts with the intensity of his playing and with his inventiveness. Even though Bunny can be heard to break through in some of the recordings he made with Kemp, the overwhelming "show" nature of the group, accounting as it did for much of the band's commercial success, served as a strait-jacket to Bunny's drive and capabilities. His jazz-trumpet voice was still developing rapidly and required the nurturing environment of appreciative listeners and, especially, fellow musicians.

While the National Broadcasting Company had arranged the English part of the trip, Kemp's brother booked the Continental portion. As the first part ended, singer "Whispering" Jack Smith and Cookie Fairchild, part of the popular piano team of Fairchild and Linholm, hosted an all-night party to celebrate the Kemp band's successful stand. They rented the entire La Potimier Restaurant in Leicester Square in London for the bash. After packing, playing, and partying throughout the night, the band found the English Channel crossing the next day a queasy experience. Thus ended a stay in England that found the Kemp band lauded by the British media, idolized by adoring patrons, and commanded by royalty.

The Ostend and Paris engagements were somewhat less successful, partly through circumstances the band could not control. Arriving in Ostend, Belgium, on Saturday, August 16, the Kemp band almost immediately began an engagement at the Royal Palace Hotel, closing out there at approximately the end of August. After a train ride to Paris, they began an extended appearance at the prestigious Les Ambassadeurs club. *Billboard* fleshed out the story:

> Cold and rainy weather which has prevailed thruout most of France during the so-called summer season has, strange to relate, afforded the various dance bands an unusually good break.
>
> Unseasonable weather at all the Northern Coast resorts has driven many of the visitors to the Riviera this summer, and the casinos and restaurants along the Mediterranean have been forced to book bands and attractions ahead of the usual "season."
>
> Noble Sissle and his band, who have been featured at the new Ambassadeurs in Paris for the season, have been forced to lay off for three weeks, due to Hal Kemp's jazz blowers being booked into the Ambassadeurs for a late summer date.

However, Sissle and his boys lost no time during the layoff. The management of the Casino at Monte Carlo, which seldom books "name" bands before December, wired Sissle to bring his band to that spot as soon as it was free at the Ambassadeurs, to remain for the full three weeks. They will return to the Ambassadeurs at the conclusion of the Monte Carlo run.[4]

Cold weather scared off normal tourist trade. The stand was not uneventful, however, as another *Billboard* article related:

Hal Kemp and his orchestra, who opened at the Ambassadeurs here recently for an indefinite run, following the Noble Sissle tooters, have been forced by police order to quit their run at the fashionable Champs Elyssees resort.

The order to oust the Kemp combo followed the introduction of talking pictures last week into a number of Parisian theaters, thus throwing many French musicians out of work.

Officials of the Parisian musicians' union announce that 75% of the motion picture theater musicians are threatened with unemployment. They state that, while the unemployment is caused by the sound films, the invasion of foreign bands is also an important factor.

The Kemp music makers, despite the police edict to quit the Ambassadeurs, continued to play under the management's orders, but packed up their music when the Paris police threatened to fine them $100,000 francs, approximately $4,000, unless they ceased their playing. A French orchestra took their place.[5]

A later *Billboard* story indicated that Kemp's troubles in Paris stemmed from the band's failure to secure work permits. Some speculated that the lack of an appropriate bribe of the proper officials lay behind this pressure.[6] In any case, the band set sail on September 24 from Le Havre aboard the *Ile de France*, arriving in New York on September 30.

Later that same day, Berigan took part in an audition with Jimmy Dorsey that, while unsuccessful, proved prophetic, for despite the steady employment and the great acceptance of the Kemp band, Bunny was growing restive. The Kemp band, highly commercial, was providing too tight a musical straitjacket. In Late September or early October, however, the band, still enjoying Bunny's services, began an extended engagement at the Daffydill Club in Greenwich Village.

4. *Billboard*, September 20, 1930, p. 22.
5. *Ibid.*, October 4, 1930, p. 24.
6. *Ibid.*, October 11, 1930, p. 25; see interviews in White and Cullen Research Materials for these speculations.

Since the Kemp band had been abroad for the several previous months, their book did not yet include all the newer numbers. Many were played for the first time at the Daffydill. Mayhew recalled that frequently the band would read a number through just once. If they did well, Kemp would assign Bunny or someone else an extended solo, and the tune became part of the book.

While the Kemp band played at the Daffydill, WEAF broadcast their performances for one-half hour on three days weekly. In addition, the band completed four recording sessions at the Brunswick studios in late October and in early to mid-November, cutting a total of eight titles. The Daffydill closed its doors on November 8, a victim of the growing economic depression. NBC continued the three weekly Kemp broadcasts through Monday, November 17, from its studios.

On November 22, Kemp's group opened at the Golden Pheasant Restaurant in Cleveland, replacing the Paul Specht Orchestra. Again, they broadcast on a regular schedule over WTAM, an NBC affiliate. During this stand, pianist Claude Thornhill, on a strong recommendation by Mayhew, joined the Kemp band. In the past, Kemp had used two pianos on some occasions for special effect; Thornhill and Trotter were paired for a short while before the latter took a temporary job in Florida. The Golden Pheasant engagement ended on January 23, 1931.

The Berigan era in the Kemp band was winding down. Following a series of one-nighters, the Kemp aggregation landed in New York City to begin a series of recording sessions. The travel, often featuring bad weather and coupled with Bunny's intention to marry Donna, led Bunny to seek a more stable, more lucrative situation. Featured on some of the numbers, Bunny recorded with Kemp on February 13, 14, 16, and 18, and again on April 23, playing on a total of twelve titles. Fellow trumpeter Harry Prebal recalled that Jack Purvis was playing on some of the one-nighters for Bunny, and Bunny was phasing into what became his main source of income for the next several years: playing for the CBS radio network's New York house band.[7]

7. Information from Harry Prebal in White Materials; information about Hal Kemp from research by Tom Cullen and Bozy White, in Bozy White Outline.

7

Blue Skies

Song recorded June 25, 1935
with Benny Goodman and His Orchestra

Bunny wanted to end the musically limiting, but valuable, stay with the Kemp organization, as his audition with Jimmy Dorsey on returning from Europe indicates. With that late-1930 audition, Bunny and Dorsey had hoped to land a booking at a familiar place, Janssen's Hofbrau Restaurant in New York. Jimmy was to front the band in what could have been a long-term stay. At the time, Dorsey looked upon the failed audition as one of the disappointments in his life. The band included Bunny, Tommy Dorsey, Bud Freeman, Joe Sullivan, Dick McDonough, and Gene Krupa, as well as Jimmy Dorsey. As he reflected on the decision years later, Jimmy laughed at the reason the manager gave for not hiring the band: when not playing as an ensemble, these men were "not capable of good solo work!"[1] As it turned out, this assessment probably served to forward Bunny's career. The extra several months of exposure via radio and records with Kemp helped to solidify the young trumpeter's growing reputation both inside and outside the jazz community and certainly helped foster his hiring by CBS.

The demands on the musicians tended to blur the distinction between jazz and other, perhaps more classically trained, players in the early 1930s. Increasingly, employment came from the radio studios, and though record sales were suffering greatly from the general economic situation, the musicians who played in the recording studios maintained extremely busy schedules. Frequently, these prime re-

1. Jimmy Dorsey, interview with Tom Cullen, *ca*. June, 1952, transcript in author's possession. Subsequent quotations from Dorsey are taken from this interview.

cording jobs were held by the same close-knit group of radio studio elite, many of whom had more work than they could handle. The general arrangement for staff men was to have a contract, or simply an understood expectation, for a minimum amount of radio work, which usually developed into more than the minimum. Even so, the schedules frequently allowed some time for free-lance playing, most often in the recording studios. These situations were demanding; they required versatility. One radio show might require a symphonic performance, the very next a freewheeling, almost improvisational ability. The music frequently required solos. Always the players were required to be excellent readers; second and third run-throughs were luxuries to be avoided.

If the demands were great, the rewards were commensurate, as illustrated in this *Variety* piece: "While musicians and musical organizations in general are fighting the mechanical age in the music biz, a select few are praying for it to stick. These are the radio musicians, employed by the networks, but mainly by NBC studios in NYC. Some of the steadily employed NBC instrumentalists are grossing as high as $700–800 weekly. Some are doing so many shows a day that they can be seen RUNNING from studio to studio."[2]

One week later, *Variety* reported: "Phono disc makers are laying off the big recording names as their contracts run out . . . . Disc sales are off 50%." John McDonough gives a compelling description of the music industry in general, and the recording industry in particular:

It was a mortally wounded industry which saw its sales sink like an iron ingot—an astounding 94 percent plunge in the five years preceding 1932. Certainly no time for any businessman to consider risk or innovation. Besides formulas had been devised by cigar-chomping Jesse White/Roscoe Karnes types that governed the men who wrote the music and the ones who played it, formulas that shunned any hint of innovation, imagination or individuality. Hacks shuffled and reshuffled the standard deck of chord changes, segues and lyrics imagery. Publishers, who collected a two cent mechanical royalty on every record of a title, deluged recording supervisors and sales people with their output. And the record companies recorded it because in 1931 they were clinging to the formulas like everyone else.

By then the American Record Company (ARC) had bought up most of the little independent companies that had been born to prosperity in the '20s only to face certain bankruptcy and consolidation during the depression. By

2. *Variety*, March 11, 1931, p. 68, in White Materials.

the end of '31 ARC was manufacturing under something like 17 of these different labels and logos, plus a few "private labels" sold through retail chains like Sears (Conqueror) or S.H. Kress (Romeo). Soon even such venerable aristocrats as Brunswick and Columbia would become part of this rag-tag army of corporate hobos.

Turning out a product for all these labels became a simple matter of routine, although even such an authority as Brian Rust admits that the precise circumstances of how they were made remains something of a mystery today. One thing is sure, however: any given performance could be and often was issued on different labels under different artist names. These names were a strange mixture of real people and fabricated pseudonyms. It's not at all certain that the name of an actual person on a record meant he had any creative control, or that he was even present during the session.

All that was about to change as the performances on this album were being made. Radio would reorient the American ear and records would follow in the path it cleared. Bing Crosby and Morton Downey would become great "recording stars." Then the second great big band era would break open and sweep the nation—one engineered not by baton wielding showmen but a generation of brilliant virtuosos who thought of themselves as musicians, not entertainers. It's no coincidence that studio band sessions were virtually abandoned by ARC by the end of 1935. With Benny Goodman, Duke Ellington, Glenn Miller, and so many more, the star system came to the home turntable. It broke the power of the publishers. It picked the record industry up and sent it soaring through the '40s, '50s, '60s and beyond.

Bunny Berigan—buried in the ensembles of these 1931 relics—would be part of that very considerable process. He would become an enduring star. He would rise because he lived in an environment or popular culture that rewarded style, creativity, innovation. Berigan had it all.[3]

Into this milieu Bunny Berigan eagerly plunged full-time, signing on with the CBS band under Fred Rich's leadership in late February, 1931. He apparently landed this choice assignment without the requirement of a formal audition. Tommy Dorsey and several of the other staff people recommended Bunny wholeheartedly, not only because he had all the qualifications, but because he was becoming good company and a bit of a character. And when Bunny soloed in a jazz vein, everybody listened to catch what the new marvel would try next. Rich was no doubt well aware of who he was getting, probably through direct contact at Plunkett's. And Bunny surely knew what he was getting. In most cases the music he would play was no less con-

3. John McDonough, record jacket notes for Shoestring SS-115, *Bunny Berigan, 1931.*

stricting than that in the Kemp band, probably more so. But the money was great; the work was steady; his colleagues were the tops in their field, and they appreciated every new sound that came from his horn and let him know it. Plus—this was New York!

After finishing a series of mid-February recording sessions with the Kemp band, Bunny began spreading his talents to the sessions of other leaders, notably Fred Rich, whose records were released under a variety of pseudonyms. During this time, Bunny made his first known recordings with Tommy Dorsey. On February 26, Bunny reached two milestones when he recorded four titles with the Dorsey Brothers under their own name for Brunswick, representing the first known time (discounting the session in England) Bunny and Jimmy Dorsey recorded together. The Dorseys were among the most influential forces in the New York music scene. Jimmy later observed that they would use Bunny on every session they could. At about this same time, the Dorseys were booking numerous dances and concerts at colleges and clubs in the area. Three such dates produced musical landmarks: the appearance of Bix Beiderbecke and Bunny on the same bandstand. For Bunny, many record dates followed with such leaders as Victor Young, Sam Lanin, and Bert Hirsch, the last on the Hit of the Week label. The Hit of the Week records were paper-based, with recording on one side only. They enjoyed a short period of popularity, partly due to their lower price. Bunny recorded an early five-minute Hit of the Week session, a short-lived idea for producing longer-playing records.

When Bunny was hired, CBS was moving aggressively to expand and upgrade its network offerings. Bunny was not a replacement but rather an addition to the staff. Over the following several months, in an attempt to equal or surpass NBC, CBS further augmented its ranks with several of radio's eventual stars, including Bing Crosby, Kate Smith, the Boswell Sisters, Morton Downey, and Arthur Tracy the Street Singer. In March, 1931, CBS had seventy-seven affiliated stations throughout the country; NBC had seventy-six. By January, 1932, CBS boasted ninety stations. Often the network contracted stars and broadcast their programs without a sponsor, on a sustaining basis, until one could be found. Of course, virtually all music on radio at that time was broadcast live. In contrast to today's formula-driven, market-oriented, preprogrammed radio sounds, the freshness of 1930s broadcasts is stunning. The radio world also thrived without the benefit of disc jockeys. The studio orchestras played for the regularly scheduled programs, which featured the greater and lesser stars in the networks' galaxies. In addition, the orchestras played filler programs, usually of fifteen-minute or half-hour duration. Sometimes, because of listener response, a musical group would be given a permanent program and would be featured in its own right.

Other jazz-oriented musicians on staff or on part-time call with CBS at the time Bunny began with Rich included Joe Venuti, Eddie Lang, Glenn Miller, both Dorseys, Carl Kress, Artie Shaw, and Adrian Rollini. Jerry Colonna, who later became Bob Hope's comedy sidekick, was an excellent staff trombonist. Many equally talented musicians who did not express themselves with the jazz voice also formed this elite musical circle. This family extended beyond the walls of CBS. Theater pit orchestras, recording studios, and clubs often served as meeting places for musicians from the rival networks. Together, such musicians as Jack Teagarden, Benny Goodman, Jack Jenney, Charlie Margulis, Harry Bluestone, Miff Mole, Arnold Brilhart, and Nat Brusiloff at once created and eagerly appreciated a new form of music—swing. This new musical form had been "invented" and was being developed in the clubs, theaters, and dance halls of Harlem by black musicians excluded as a race from the lucrative studio jobs. Their white colleagues sought out—live in Harlem and on record—the influential disseminators of swing: Fletcher Henderson, Don Redman, Benny Carter, Roy Eldridge, Duke Ellington, Jimmy Lunceford, Chick Webb, Willie Smith, and Coleman Hawkins, among others. The community of swing thrived despite society's racial intolerance, reflected in the studios.

Tolerance was, at least, a feature of CBS's policy regarding substitutes. If a regular staff player scheduled himself into a conflict with a record date, or perhaps just suffered a hangover from too much Plunkett's the night before, he would simply arrange for a substitute on his own. He chose his replacement carefully to ensure high musical standards. What the studios did not tolerate was an unfilled chair at showtime. Camaraderie there was, and competition, too. First-call players rarely attended a rehearsal. Instead, subs would play and mark the parts. Then, the first-call would arrive for the show—sometimes breathless, sometimes whiskey-breathed—and read his part for the first time. During the show, musicians, with wagers placed, listened carefully for mistakes and tallied them. After the show, bets would be settled; at two dollars or more per mistake, a player could lose a bundle on an off night.

Bonnie Lake sang with Artie Shaw, Jack Jenney, and Nat Cole, and composed such songs as "Man with a Horn" and the Dorsey Brothers Orchestra theme song, "Sandman." Her husband, Jack Jenney, was for some time first-call trombonist at NBC. Lake recalled that some of the top men were playing "anywhere from twenty to twenty-eight shows per week. They hired substitutes to play the rehearsals and mark their parts. And they had cabs waiting outside to take them to the next job. I saw it! They'd *run* from NBC and change their jackets on the way. They had guys who'd carry their horns and everything and get them to the next show. This went on and on. They were making money like—millionaires. And they lived terribly well." She remembered the clique meeting "every night" at such clubs as the Onyx or Hurley's or the Famous Door. Lake recalled Hurley's as "anything but attractive: it had a tiled floor with a partly exposed kitchen that made pretty bad hamburgers. But it was the meeting ground of *everybody* in show business. On the corner of 49th Street and 6th Avenue, it was the crossroads of the entertainment world."[4]

This madcap atmosphere, with all the rushing about, gave rise to events that produced many humorous anecdotes. Lake recalled one that involved trombonist Miff Mole. "Between shows they would all run down to Hurley's for a few drinks. The NBC studios all opened out onto the same hallway, lined up one after the other. Well, one night after his Hurley's break, Miff ran upstairs to play the show. He dashed for his chair and someone had moved it. So he grabbed another chair, sat down, and played the show, played the whole show. They didn't know until afterwards that he'd played the *wrong* show. He was supposed to be across the hall."

In the midst of this whirl of excitement, Bunny and Donna were

4. Bonnie Lake, interview with author, June 28, 1985, tape in author's possession. Subsequent quotations from Lake are taken from this interview. Lake was part of the Radio Row scene in the 1930s.

married on May 25. If ever a couple seemed to have it made, they were that couple. Good looks, talent, big money, promising future, exciting and satisfying work—they had it all. Little wonder they rushed back to New York after their Syracuse wedding. Their life was a honeymoon.

Apparently Bunny was unaware of, and untouched by, the deepening economic depression. His recording activities continued at a fruitful pace. On June 18, he recorded eight titles with Ben Selvin and the Columbia Record Company house band. This is probably the first time Bunny recorded with Benny Goodman. Two days later, Benny used Bunny on four titles issued under Goodman's name. On this session, Mannie Klein and Bunny split the trumpet solo work.

In September, Bunny made a decision that might have damaged his career. The Dorseys had arranged to get a job leading the orchestra for a new show produced by Jacob and Lee Shubert, the brothers who had such impact upon American theater. This show, *Everybody's Welcome*, was a musical based on a comedy hit from the previous year, *Up Pops the Devil*. The show was to open in Philadelphia at the Forrest Theater, play there for several weeks, then open in New York. Bunny could not resist the temptation of the offer from the Dorseys, especially considering the other players who were involved. He vacated his prime spot with Fred Rich's CBS band, incurring Rich's wrath.

Everybody's Welcome opened in Philadelphia in late September. It starred Frances Williams, Oscar Shaw, and Bonnie Lake's sister, Harriet Lake (who became Ann Sothern in Hollywood), and introduced the song "As Time Goes By," later immortalized in the 1942 film classic *Casablanca*. In New York, the show opened at the Shubert Theater, 44th Street west of Broadway, on October 13, closing 137 performances later, on February 14, 1932. Contrary to normal practice, advertising for the show credited the Dorsey Brothers band. Among those joining Bunny and the Dorseys in the band were trumpeter Mickey Bloom, pianist Chummy McGregor, and trombonist Teagarden. The personnel changed slightly through the runs in the two cities, but the nucleus remained. Teagarden and Miller joined Tommy Dorsey in the trombone section. It alone was worth the price of admission. The close-knit group of musicians gave new meaning to the word *players* as they drank their way through the engagement.

Teagarden and others readily acknowledged the alcoholic aspect of the experience.[5]

Bunny finished out the year of 1931 and the run of the show still at top speed. Included among his recording and other free-lance work was his first session with the Boswell Sisters on November 5. The estrangement from Rich seemed not to have slowed his progress. He had come a long way from Fox Lake in a short time. In reviewing the last three records Berigan made with Kemp, Spike Hughes, the English jazzman and critic, noted in a timely issue of the prestigious *Melody Maker* magazine that "the new wonder, Barney Berrigan, [*sic*] is featured."[6]

5. Jack Teagarden, interview with Bozy White, August, 1959, in White Materials. Most information about Berigan with Fred Rich, the CBS band, recording sessions, and *Everybody's Welcome* from research by Bozy White, in White Outline.
6. *Melody Maker, ca.* May, 1931.

8

All Dark People Are Light on Their Feet

Song recorded April 1, 1937
by Bunny Berigan and His Orchestra

Racial attitudes in white America in the 1930s had changed little since Reconstruction days. Popular songs, such as "All Dark People Are Light on Their Feet," simply reflected prevailing sentiments and rarely attempted to make a statement. Goodman used the work of black writers and arrangers for his band from the outset. However, when he integrated his performing groups in 1936 by hiring two blacks, pianist Teddy Wilson and later, vibraphonist Lionel Hampton, he stirred a sensational controversy. Black and white musicians had long fraternized, principally in black clubs in Harlem and Chicago, and they had played together in some radio and recording studios. But integrated public performance was a commercial rarity. Goodman's bold move, based simply on choosing his musicians by the excellence of their playing, made its own strong statement and set a tone for the music industry that has been followed since, though erratically.

Shortly after Berigan's permanent arrival in New York, he made his first impression on the black jazz community. As Jimmy Dorsey told researcher Tom Cullen: "I took Bunny up to Harlem with me and he asked to sit in. He played just like he was colored. The hat-check girl and the ticket-takers came out to look. They couldn't believe it: 'Here's this white boy playing like one of us.' They dug him. The brother and I began to use him on every recording we could."

Bunny's friend Clif Gomon recalled a related incident that was told to him by drummer Zutty Singleton:

Zutty and Bunny knew each other, of course, and there was this little place in Boston, a black club where they'd have jam sessions. Each night would feature a different instrument, like Monday night would be saxophones, and Tuesday would be trumpets, and so forth. This trumpet night, Zutty took Berigan over to it. The way they did it, all the trumpet players would sit at the tables around the dining room and they'd start out a jazz tune. The trumpet player at the first table would play 'til he ran out of gas, then the trumpeter at the next table would take over, and that's the way they'd go. Well, a few of them played and it was coming up toward Bunny's table, and Zutty said, "Come on, Bunny, take out your horn and play." Bunny wasn't too enthusiastic about it, but Zutty talked him into it. Finally Bunny took his horn out and Zutty told me, "Bunny stood up and let loose; he really let 'em have it! When Bunny got done and sat down, that was the end. Nobody else would play!"

Bunny's early fixation on Louis Armstrong's jazz voice as the one that moved him the most, and Armstrong's later reciprocal assessment of Bunny, was an easy, honest attraction. Louis and Bunny often evidenced their mutual affection through the years; their irregular reunions invariably carried a festive tone. Bunny's friendships with Red Allen, Fats Waller, Cozy Cole, Zutty Singleton, Sy Oliver, Jonah Jones, Rex Stewart, and other prominent black musicians were equally relaxed. Bobby Smith, arranger-writer-saxophonist with the Sunset Royal Serenaders and later for many years with Erskine Hawkins, recalled meeting Bunny in the early days of the Bunny Berigan orchestra: "For some reason, Bunny and I just seemed to take a particular liking to one another. We'd go hear his band at the Savoy or the Apollo when we were in New York. He was such a beautiful man, such a lovely guy. I couldn't stay with him drinking, though. Sometimes we'd go out together. I'd stay at the Mariette Hotel, and more than once Bunny would end up sleeping in my room. He'd stay there 'til morning, then we'd have breakfast together—which was when he'd start his drinking for the next day."[1]

Bunny's sidemen expressed great pride in the band's performances at Harlem's Savoy Ballroom and the Apollo Theater. Pianist Buddy Koss and others have remarked that Harlem's patrons "loved Bunny." At the Savoy, acceptance was doubly difficult: the Berigan band found itself musically paired with or pitted against the resident black band,

1. Bobby Smith, interview with author, August 13, 1987, tape in author's possession.

often the Savoy Sultans, in a traditional "battle of the bands," and the white musicians needed a certain degree of showmanship to win over the crowd. A visiting band might not win the crowd's acceptance but, feeling that it had won musically, could salvage at least a partial "victory." Or the "challenging" band might win the crowd but know that it had not measured up musically. But reports of the Berigan band's visits to the Savoy spoke of total victory. Those discerning crowds and the ones at the Apollo liked Bunny's music, and they found, in his open, giving manner, something that resonated.

An appearance at Detroit's Graystone Ballroom was typical of Berigan's many bookings at black affairs. "Those Easter Monday—black Easter—dances at the Graystone were the biggest event of the school year," longtime Detroit resident Mary Thrasher recalled. "Black people couldn't attend on Easter Sunday; that was just for whites. So we'd all dress up for church on Easter Sunday and parade around most of the day in our high heels; then we'd do it again on Monday and go to the Graystone." Now a retired executive secretary from the Detroit school system, Thrasher fondly spoke of Monday, April 6, 1942: "I remember Bunny Berigan clearly at that dance. He was very popular with the black community, and there was a tremendous crowd there that day; we spilled into the Graystone Gardens, that inner area with the trees and plants. It was really exciting."[2] The reaction of Thrasher and that Detroit crowd is representative of Berigan's reception by blacks through the years.

The October 1, 1940, issue of *Down Beat* featured a photograph of Bunny with Eleanor Roosevelt, Frank Sinatra, Lionel Hampton, and Tommy Dorsey, taken when they appeared at a benefit in New York for the Bethune-Cookman College School of Music, a traditionally black school in Daytona Beach, Florida. (Fred Norman, the outstanding black writer-arranger, was part of the original photograph but has been cropped from most reproductions.) They were celebrating the sale of the first ticket for the event. Another simple gesture earned Bunny what must have been one of his few denigrating letters. The Chicago *Defender* newspaper had published a photograph of Bunny in the act of congratulating black winners of a popularity contest held in Chicago. The photo elicited this response, carried by *Down Beat* in

2. Mary Thrasher, interview with author, August, 1985, transcript in author's possession.

its "Chords and Discords" Section: "To the Editors: Find enclosed a newspaper clipping and picture of Bunny Berigan shaking hands with a few of his colored friends. We just thought we would drop you all Yankee cats a line telling you that we hereby fluff Berigan off for having such a picture taken. We all enjoy your sheet and think it is terrific. [signed] Carl Johnstone And his University of Miss. Ork."[3]

Many years after Bunny's death, Donna recalled some of Bunny's black friendships:

Bunny and Louis got along great. Each one thought the other was the greatest trumpet player. That meant a lot to Bunny because Louis had been his idol when Bunny was coming up. They had good fun whenever they could get together. A few years ago I was on a radio program hosted by [my present husband]. After he mentioned my name and that I'd be on the air for a while, it seemed that hardly a minute had gone by and there was Louis on the telephone. He was playing in town. We must have talked for half an hour or more. Cozy Cole was one of my favorites of Bunny's friends. He was a fine drummer and had a great sense of humor. You should have seen him the night at our place when I introduced him to our police dog that I named after him. He burst out laughing so hard! Fats Waller was a good guy and a good friend. He's the one who died on a train, just a couple years after Bunny died. Bunny cared a lot for his musician friends. I remember the night Chu Berry died; Bunny cried.

One does not readily think of Bunny as a social activist, but a story told by Jack Sperling, drummer with Bunny's last band in 1941 to 1942, reveals a side of the trumpeter not often seen:

We're traveling in the Deep South, and the band boy with us was "Holly" Caffey, a black guy who had been a schoolmate of mine. Late at night, we went into one of those all-night diners—complete with the "no colored allowed" signs. The band filled up the counter seats. The guy says to Holly, "I can't serve you; you can't eat here." Bunny says, "Why can't he?" The guy says, "He's colored; he can't eat in here." With that, Bunny reached out and took the top off the ketchup bottle. The other guys took his cue and took the tops off the salt, pepper, and sugar containers and, led by Bunny, walked the length of the counter dumping all over it. Then we walked out. Thank God there weren't any "good ole boys" there, because our asses would have been in a sling.[4]

3. *Down Beat*, VI (October 1, 1939), 10.
4. Jack Sperling, telephone interview with author, February 10, 1988, tape in author's possession. Subsequent quotations from Sperling are taken from this interview. Sperling is still highly regarded as a versatile player.

Bunny was friendly, outgoing, and fun loving; he associated almost exclusively with musicians; he treated his musician friends alike; he valued his colleagues' musical ability above all. He had little time for, or patience with, pettiness and exclusivity. Like many others, Bunny equated certain nonmusical personal attributes—in his case, enjoying a joke, sharing a drink, keeping cool, being honest, having some fun—with being a swinger. Bunny's approach to all people was egalitarian: "Does he swing?" This approach, plus his amazing ability to communicate real feelings through his music, endeared Bunny to black musicians and to throngs of black music fans and dancers.

9

Rendezvous with a Dream

Song recorded July 20, 1936
by Bunny Berigan and His Studio Orchestra
on Thesaurus Transcriptions

When *Everybody's Welcome* closed on February 14, 1932, in New York, Bunny's recording activity accelerated. Within a period of several weeks he made records with the Boswell Sisters, the Dorsey Brothers, the ARC Studio Orchestra, Connee Boswell, Bing Crosby, Smith Ballew, Victor Young, Bennie Krueger, and Abe Lyman, among others. Following custom, many of these recordings were issued under a variety of names. February 24, 1932, was not a typical day but serves to provide a feeling for the kind of schedule Bunny was keeping. A session with Eddie Kirkeby and his group took up the full morning and produced six masters. Several masters with an unnamed studio orchestra took up the entire afternoon and early evening. When Bunny finally packed up his horn after wrapping up a three-hour session with the Boswell Sisters, accompanied by the Dorsey Brothers, the day had stretched into February 25.[1] Even following a pressure-packed day such as this, Bunny probably grabbed his horn and hit one of the clubs to enjoy some companionship, some drinks, and possibly some jamming.

Bunny spent an extended period with the Smith Ballew orchestra in the spring and summer of 1932. Ballew was a popular singer in the New York area between 1928 and 1937. He associated himself with some of the hot bands of the day for recording purposes and some-

---

1. Brian Rust, *Jazz Records, 1897–1942* (5th ed.; Chigwell, Eng., 1982), I, 157, and White Materials. Rust's work is a nearly 2,000-page source of jazz record information from 1897 to 1942, including almost all personnel lists, dates, and other discographical data. While not perfect, these volumes are an invaluable tool for jazz lovers.

times fronted his own orchestra. During the period Bunny was on the stand, Glenn Miller was the band's actual leader. Bunny probably played with that group in Baltimore from May 8 through May 21 and at the Pavilion Royal on Long Island from May 27 through August 6. On July 6, Bunny played on a recording session with Ballew at ARC that produced several masters.[2] Also during the Pavilion Royal stand, on July 23, Patricia Berigan was born to Donna and Bunny.

A sampling of *Variety* articles from this period gives an idea of the kinds of news stories Bunny might have noticed: Guy Lombardo and his orchestra followed Ballew at the Pavilion Royal, receiving a Depression-reduced fee $1,250-per-week less than his previous engagement; singer Mildred Bailey left Paul Whiteman to go out as a single; Fred Rich was in Hollywood to serve as musical director for the film *The Big Broadcast;* Victor Young, "the most versatile of all modern musical conductors, composers, arrangers," was conducting for seven network radio shows and was also general musical director of American and Brunswick record corporations; Whiteman spent several days in Detroit working out details regarding his new position as adviser to General Motors in radio musical matters; weekly salaries paid to some of radio's top stars—Whiteman, $8,500, Kate Smith, $7,500, Rudy Vallee, $4,500, Boswell Sisters, $3,000; Lee Wiley began a program on a sustaining (unsponsored) basis on WEAF, NBC's New York station; Paul Whiteman's Orchestra played the fourth Experiment in Modern American Music concert at Carnegie Hall on November 4, 1932.

Artie Bernstein was one of the early converts to the string bass, an instrument that rapidly came into vogue, forcing out the tuba. He was the premier string-bass player on the New York radio and recording studio scene from about 1932 to 1935, and later joined the Goodman band to begin touring in 1939. With Tommy Dorsey as the unofficial leader, the unofficial "ARC House Band" included Bunny Berigan, Tommy Dorsey, Jimmy Dorsey, pianist Fulton McGrath, guitarists Eddie Lang and/or Dick McDonough, bassist Bernstein, and drummer Stan King. These musicians made literally hundreds of records in the early- to mid-1930s at the ARC studios on 57th street and Broadway. Many of the recordings were done on electrical transcriptions

2. White Materials.

(ETs) and were for radio play only. Often, records were released crediting people having nothing to do with the music. Little did the instrumentalists foresee that these records and ETs, representing as they now do an important part of the history and development of jazz and swing, would become coveted by discographers and other collectors. At the time, they were viewed largely as an avenue to a good payday and only incidentally as a musically rewarding experience; that they were also musically rewarding was a welcome bonus.

Director Victor Young allowed Tommy Dorsey and the other regulars to work out the details of the music themselves. They would arrive at the studio cold, knowing neither which tunes they would play nor which singers they would accompany. Usually, publishers gave them stock arrangements that the band would proceed to cut, charting the introductions, changing keys, blocking in solos, setting a coda. Then they would run through a song once or twice before inscribing it on a master. Young exerted more control over the band members when they played with major artists such as Bing Crosby and Connee Boswell than when they played with the next echelon of singers such as Chick Bullock and Dick Robertson. Apparently Young recognized—even facilitated—the trend from song to star in the recording and radio industry. The Boswells, in particular, loved to work with this elite group, since they would arrive at the studio without instrumental arrangements. Bernstein says the sisters knew the bandsmen would always work out some innovative accompaniments for them. The other local musicians paid close attention to the record releases of these players; new ideas and "licks" were fair game to emulate. A brief stint with leader Abe Lyman in the fall of 1932 preceded another major move in Bunny's career.[3]

Perhaps because of his mother's influence, Bunny had long held an ambition to play with Paul "Pops" Whiteman's popular orchestra. The desire might have been related to his admiration for Beiderbecke, a Whiteman alumnus. Dubbed the "King of Jazz," Whiteman was hardly that, but his large aggregation enjoyed tremendous popularity and a reputation for playing "jazz" and other new sounds. Whiteman staged lavish shows featuring vocal and instrumental music, plus

3. Artie Bernstein, interview with Bozy White, February, 1961, in White Materials, copy of transcript in author's possession; additional information on Bernstein, Victor Young, the ARC bands, and Abe Lyman from research by Bozy White, in White Outline.

other acts. He was able to attract outstanding talent, and as indicated in the sample of *Variety* notes (above), "Pops" played in the big leagues. The Whiteman orchestra had been playing at the Biltmore Hotel in New York City since June, 1932, in addition to broadcasting a weekly radio program. At some point late that year, after the brief Lyman gig, Berigan became a member of the Whiteman orchestra. This move took place as Whiteman was playing a series of Carnegie Hall concerts. A Whiteman discography printed in the July 1, 1940, issue of *Down Beat* confirms that Bunny recorded on a Whiteman session at Victor on November 17, 1932, that produced seven masters. Bunny also almost surely appeared on recording dates with Whiteman on November 25, December 2, and December 8, 1932.[4] The orchestra still performed at the Biltmore and doubled at the Capitol Theatre while keeping up its radio schedule at this time. This was the kind of schedule Bunny thrived on and loved. He probably began his full-time association with the Whiteman orchestra shortly after that November 17 recording date. Barely twenty-four years old, Bunny enjoyed an enviable position: a recording and radio career bringing in good money; growing esteem of fellow musicians and the public; the honor of occupying the chair in the Whiteman orchestra that was once Bix's. On December 20, 1932, the magnificent Radio City performing complex opened and promised, in spite of the pall of the Depression, an even brighter future for those in the right place at the right time. Bunny was one of those.

Bunny's friends and admirers wondered at his eagerness to join the Whiteman troupe. A jazz band it was not. Bix had known this too, and many felt that Bix's alcoholic demise was hastened by his struggle against the constraining, straitjacket style of Whiteman, who increasingly played highly arranged and polished music and edged out individual creativity. And while Whiteman did extend himself financially to help Bix in his waning months, many observers agree that he never offered the great cornetist a truly nurturing musical atmosphere. In writing about Bix, Ralph Berton says of Whiteman:

That a man who was never himself a jazzman, and couldn't have swung a single bar of music to save himself from the electric chair, should have become known to the general public as the "King of Jazz," tells us a great deal about both Mr. Whiteman and that public. The fact that, as Marshall Stearns

4. White Materials.

correctly reports, the title was invented and conferred upon Whiteman by his own press agents, is incidental; what is significant is that the public enthusiastically accepted it, like bubble gum and Billy Graham; obviously it struck them as exactly the right note.

I would go further, and assert that there was even a kind of inevitability in such a choice, as symbolically appropriate as the choice, by the mob, of Barabbas instead of Jesus as the man to rescue from execution on the cross. Given the unerring instinct of the public in matters of art, it would have been surprising—the student of our life & times would feel distinctly taken aback—if in the so-called Jazz Age the populace had been found calling an actual jazz genius like Louis or Bix "King of Jazz" rather than some self-promoting purveyor of musical chewing gum, without, so to speak, a jazz pore in his entire body, like Whiteman—somewhat as though the national thirst were suddenly to choose fresh fruit juice instead of Coke. Once we understand that, there is no real irony in the fact Stearns rightly noted, that it was Whiteman—"of all people!"—who most visibly "advanced the cause of jazz." Who else indeed? What other sort of man could as effectively capture the ear of such a public—a public that, interestingly, has year by year increased its per capita consumption of sugar (it is now roughly 125 pounds for each man, woman, and child); could have calculated so nicely how much real jazz it would tolerate in its normal diet of musical syrup? Mr. Whiteman, I presume, had no trouble at all; he had only to consult his own infallible taste buds.[5]

Whether Berigan knew fully what lay in store for him in the Whiteman experience is doubtful. Certainly he encountered some of the same frustrations and artistic constrictions as Bix, but Bunny's extroverted personality seems to suggest that Bunny was somewhat better able to cope with these problems. Beiderbecke biographers Richard Sudhalter and Philip Evans downplay the negative side of Bix's treatment by Whiteman, stating that Bix appreciated the encouragement he received with Whiteman, particularly in developing his interest in modern classical music. Their position seems to be supported by trombonist Bill Rank, who played in the Whiteman band with both Bix and Bunny.[6] Bunny's experience with Whiteman was probably

5. Ralph Berton, *Remembering Bix: A Memoir of the Jazz Age* (New York, 1974), 367–68. Berton's caustic assessment of Whiteman, no doubt correct in thrust, was colored by an incident between his brother and Whiteman. Vic Berton was an outstanding drummer of the day and had served a tour of duty with Whiteman in 1927, a tour that was aborted by a bitter fight between Vic Berton and "Pops." This incident accounts for some of the venom in Ralph Berton's words, but does not negate the essential truth.

6. Richard M. Sudhalter and Philip R. Evans make this point in several places throughout their authoritative work, *Bix: Man & Legend* (New York, 1974); Chilton and Sudhalter, *Bunny Berigan*, 14.

more satisfying on a personal level than was Bix's. For one thing,
Bunny was more outgoing than Bix during their respective Whiteman
years. He and Whiteman struck up a friendship that included several
invitations to the Whiteman "ranch" in New Jersey. Further, Whiteman frequently exhibited some visible appreciation for the great
talent that Bunny brought to the orchestra. Gomon, Bunny's fellow
trumpeter from the Chanticleer days in Madison, remembered the
Whiteman troupe's appearance, during their massive 1933 tour, at the
Oriental Theater in Chicago: "Whiteman introduced a fine black tap
dancer . . . and Bunny stood up and backed the dancer, just him and
the rhythm, with two or three choruses of jazz. Whiteman stood at
the side of the stage and looked only at Bunny during the whole
act. At the end," Gomon concluded, "Paul applauded and bowed in
Bunny's direction." Finally, during his Whiteman stint, Bunny was
able to squeeze in musically satisfying recording dates and jam sessions with some regularity.

The headline in Bunny's hometown newspaper proudly declared:
"Bunny Berigan gets Position with World Famous Orchestra." The article went on to report, "You can hear him play Monday nights on the
Buick program from New York with the Paul Whiteman orchestra and
on Thursday evenings with Rudy Vallee on the Fleischmann Yeast
Program. . . . A week or so ago he was engaged by Paul Whiteman
to play in his orchestra at the Biltmore Hotel in NYC."[7] The pride
shown in the local paper honestly reflected the feeling of nearly
everyone in Fox Lake. Local boy was indeed making good, and even
the most tone-deaf of the citizenry were claiming they always knew
that boy would go far.

The program played by Whiteman at the January 25 Carnegie Hall
concert indicates the type of modern American music Whiteman presented: "Tabloid," Ferde Grofe's four-part suite about a newspaper;
"Night Club," six impressions for orchestra, with three pianos; "Land
of Superstition from Africa"; "Concerto in Jazz" by Robert Braine;
and two movements from Grofe's "Grand Canyon Suite." The next
day, perhaps as a purge, Berigan recorded "My Honey's Lovin' Arms"
and "I've Got the World on a String" with Bing Crosby and the Mills
Brothers.

7. Fox Lake *Representative*, January 12, 1933, in Cullen Materials.

On February 28 the Whiteman troupe closed at the Biltmore Hotel and took a break for nearly four weeks. Whiteman went to Florida, returning to New York each Monday, as did the orchestra members, for the Buick program's rehearsal and broadcast. Bunny kept himself extremely busy with recordings and other radio work. In addition to recording with the Whiteman orchestra, Bunny worked on records with Chick Bullock, Lee Wiley, the Dorsey Brothers, Mildred Bailey, Victor Young, the Boswell Sisters, Connee Boswell, and two popular members of the Whiteman organization, Ramona [Davies] and Roy Bargy. Some of Bunny's work during this time caught the attention of noted jazz critic Hugues Panassié, who wrote: "The Dorsey Brothers had at their command a first class rhythm section . . . as well as a very brilliant soloist, Bunny Berigan, with Glenn Miller, arranger. 'Shim-Sham-Shimmy' is certainly the finest performance of the band."[8] This flurry of recording activity preceded a long road trip that awaited the orchestra after their break.

In mid-April the Whiteman orchestra began a one-week run at the Earle Theater in Philadelphia that kicked off a long and successful road trip. Closing at the Earle on April 20, they traveled in three well-used Pullman cars to open in Memphis. The troupe included the Boswell Sisters, a sensational comedy team, Jack (The Baron) Pearl and Cliff (Sharlie) Hall, Ramona, and the New Rhythm Boys. Performing two shows a day, the troupe embarked on an itinerary that took them to twenty-three cities, the first twenty of which were consecutive one-nighters stretching from Philadelphia to Houston and from Minneapolis to Memphis. During a three-day run in Cleveland, Sophie Tucker was added to the bill. When the tour concluded with two weeks at Chicago's Oriental Theater, George Burns and Gracie Allen joined the show. The opening of the Chicago World's Fair also heightened the excitement of this stay. At the conclusion of the Oriental stand, the orchestra took a much-needed break.

At the beginning of the tour, Bunny enjoyed a serendipitous reunion with his old friend "Curly" Roberts. The two had not been in contact, save for an occasional card or two, since Roberts had helped

8. Hugues Panassié, *Hot Jazz: The Guide to Swing Music*, trans. Lyle Dowling and Eleanor Dowling (Rev. ed.; New York, 1936), 271. This early French jazz critic initially considered jazz to be the almost exclusive province of black musicians. His praise for white players came grudgingly at first.

pave the way for Bunny to join the Kemp band. As Roberts recalled, "The next time I saw Bunny I was with the Nash Motor Company. Whiteman was coming to town. I could look out the window of my room and see the North Station in Philadelphia, and I saw Berigan get off the train. About thirty minutes later the phone rang, and I knew who it was before I picked it up. Sure enough, it was Bunny!"

Bunny enjoyed another happy reunion when the Whiteman troupe played Madison's Capitol Theatre on May 8. The Fox Lake and Beaver Dam contingent appeared—relatives, friends, and fans. And so did a similar group from Madison itself. Don Berigan recalled: "About thirty of us showed up at the theater. After the show it was so crowded you couldn't get near Bunny's [the band's] dressing room. Afterward, we all met at my grandmother's house in Madison and had a party. Bunny was his old self. After the party we all went down to the Madison station and saw Bunny off on the midnight train."[9]

Donna Berigan had taken their young daughter, Pat, not yet a year old, to Fox Lake to stay with Bunny's parents during the tour. This began a relationship that seldom ran smoothly. Donna found the small-town atmosphere restricting, at times almost stifling. Bunny's parents could not understand the young mother's wanting to go "out with the kids," as Donna phrased it years later. Going out with the kids included a certain amount of dancing and drinking at one or more of the many places that offered such diversions. While this activity might have been perfectly normal behavior in New York, it was cause for social censure in Fox Lake. The mix was poor: beautiful, blonde New York show girl turned young wife and mother visiting and meeting family for the first time and unwilling to sit at home; small-town, German-Irish parents cast as parents-in-law and grandparents; hometown hero on the road with famous orchestra; some local residents envious and uncharacteristically inhospitable. As Bunny's friend and neighbor Emerson "Diver" Litscher remembered it, "I met Donna quite a few times. At first she seemed kinda high kaflootin', but she conducted herself like a nice girl. She came up to Casey's a lot. The townspeople accepted her as Bunny's wife. I couldn't say she drank a lot; she never got rowdy."

Acceptance of Donna by the Fox Lakers was marginal, never uni-

9. Wilson, "Beauty, Drive, and Freedom," 20.

versal, and was not something she found in any great measure within the Berigan household. These feelings muted what could have been joyful reunions when Donna met Bunny in Madison and later in Chicago as the Whiteman tour was winding down. Further clouding their happiness was Donna's ill health throughout most of her stay in Fox Lake. She consistently lost weight, a trend that did not reverse when she joined Bunny in Chicago near the beginning of that run. The tour over, Bunny and his young family returned to Fox Lake, where Donna's health problems persisted. Bunny and Donna remained there for nearly three weeks, the rest period marred by Donna's physical problems and her less-than-cordial relationship with her in-laws. Not comfortable with relative inactivity, Bunny kept his playing in shape by sitting in with bands in the Madison area and jamming for fun.

Donna remained in Fox Lake with Patricia when, on June 21, Bunny returned to New York, where he and his fellow Whiteman bandsmen immediately resumed the work tempo of a few months earlier. The Whiteman orchestra launched a series of one-nighters up and down the East Coast, from Maine to South Carolina. The band's best source of income, and certainly their most important source of exposure, was the new Kraft radio program. The sponsors and the Whiteman organization launched big plans to upgrade the program's popularity. *Billboard* announced: "Paul Whiteman gives up Chicago booking to resume in NYC for Kraft-Phenix Cheese program (NBC). Al Jolson to assist on kick-off broadcast. Chicago offer was $4,000 a week but Pops figures he can do better than that in NYC with broadcast and dance dates."[10] Station WEAF in New York carried the show's full two-hour program. A limited network of East Coast stations carried one hour. Jolson and Deems Taylor joined the regular Whiteman cast. The orchestra played such fare as Grofe's "Grand Canyon Suite" and George Gershwin's "Rhapsody in Blue." On July 31, the sixth and last of these Monday night programs was broadcast, this one pared back to one hour. Three days later Whiteman signed a new contract that specified a payment of $4,500 for each program in a series of twenty-four Thursday night broadcasts. Jolson and Taylor were retained when the program moved to Thursdays. While continuing to play one-night dance jobs, Whiteman conducted the Phil-

10. *Billboard*, June 23, 1933.

harmonic Symphonic Orchestra at huge Lewisohn Stadium in August. For this and a similar program with the Metropolitan Orchestra at Madison Square Garden on September 10, he augmented the ensemble with some of his regulars.

As if to demonstrate its versatility, the Whiteman band played a "breakfast dance" at the famous Savoy Ballroom in Harlem less than a week later. After playing a dance at the Biltmore in Westchester that ended at 1:00 A.M., the group earned $1,250 for playing at the Savoy from 2:30 to 3:30 A.M. The one-nighters ended on October 13 with a much-publicized opening of the Whiteman orchestra at the Paradise Restaurant, one of New York's biggest, most glamorous night spots. An enthusiastic *Variety* article conveys some of the flavor of this important opening:

> Paradise Restaurant and Hollywood set pace in Nitelife Struggles. . . .
> Band battle between Paul Whiteman and Rudy Vallee who are otherwise good friends, and have the same radio show agency, J. Walter Thompson, and who share a common rehearsal studio Thursday all day, prior to their common Thursday nite broadcast periods.
> Vallee opened Wednesday (11th) and Pops gala was Friday (13th). Vallee and the Connecticut Yankees with Alice Faye, vocalist, on twice nightly . . . at midnight and 2 a.m. Vallee band has undergone big change since it was last at Penn Hotel.
> To augment the Whiteman engagement the Paradise has gone to plenty of expense for its most lavish floor show yet. Girls, talent, class, color, nudity, and a general alluring show. It seems under a continental aura, such a show, as in Paris, would have the American tourists limp. It's the last word in lavishness and is blended into a brilliant ensemble. . . . As for the Whiteman orchestra, that is a show in itself.
> Whiteman's opening was made on an international broadcast gala by NBC. Rudy also came over for a gracious tribute to Whiteman, having announced the competition maestro's debut from the Hollywood floor at the Dinner show. Tariff at both places about the same: $1.50 to $3.00 per person.[11]

Donna and Patricia returned to New York on about August 17. Donna's health provoked further concern at about this time when she learned that she was pregnant. Donna's illness during her largely unhappy stay in Fox Lake might have been caused in part by the stress of the situation in which she found herself; it might have been pregnancy-induced. What followed her return to New York was almost

11. *Variety*, October 17, 1933.

certainly caused by her weakened physical condition. Three weeks after Whiteman's opening at the Paradise, on November 2, 1933, Bunny's twenty-fifth birthday, Barbara Ann Berigan was born at Sydenham Hospital. She did not live out the day. Cause of death was listed as "prematurity."[12]

Conflicting versions of Bunny's reaction to this personal tragedy cloud the facts. Some have been quoted as saying that Bunny became deeply depressed and embarked on a severe bout of drinking. However, Donna recalled no big reaction on Bunny's part: "He kept his mind occupied. He never said too much about it." While Bunny was sociable and extroverted in some ways, while he was at ease in the public eye, while he was always ready to give or receive a quip or the latest joke, he was, in fact, a private person. Very few, if any, knew him well. He only discussed one subject in seriousness with his peers: music.

The Whiteman orchestra played its regular radio show on November 2 and the next day recorded four titles, including "Smoke Gets in Your Eyes." Differing stories and failing memories do not help to establish whether Bunny played on one or both of these dates, which immediately followed the death of Barbara Ann.

Many years later, Donna summed up her feelings about that first Fox Lake experience:

I'd been in Fox Lake when I was pregnant with Barbara, only I didn't know it at the time. I didn't get along with them very well and I was a nervous wreck. I lost weight instead of gaining. Bunny wanted me to live in Fox Lake, but I wouldn't have it. I couldn't get along with them. Oh, with Mayme it was all right, but Cap was hard to get along with. He was bossy and money hungry. He didn't want me to go out with the rest of the kids. Being Pat's mother, I guess I wasn't supposed to have a good time.

Of necessity, Bunny's recording and radio studio activities were interrupted while he was on tour and during the Fox Lake visit. Some discographers erroneously credit him on recordings, principally with Freddy Martin, made in his absence. When the Whiteman one-nighter schedule permitted, Bunny lined up radio and recording sessions with other groups, including one with the Victor Young orches-

12. Fox Lake *Representative*, August 17, 1933, in Cullen Materials; New York State Standard Certificate of Death #23519, for Barbara Ann Berigan, November 2, 1933, copy in author's possession.

tra on the Friday *Ponds Playhouse* radio program, which regularly featured up-and-coming Lee Wiley as vocalist. Because Whiteman's Paradise booking provided stability and regular hours in New York, Bunny's recording activities again blossomed. More and more, Bunny was deriving his musical "kicks" from record sessions, principally those with the Dorsey Brothers and Mildred Bailey in October and with Adrian Rollini in October and November. Even the one-nighter dance jobs with Whiteman provided some room for jazz solos, but the show music at Whiteman's Paradise booking left Bunny little room to stretch his fertile imagination and creativity. The Whiteman orchestra uniform was pinching more and more. When Jolson left the Kraft show temporarily in mid-October to go to Hollywood for some movie-making, more of the show's burden fell upon Whiteman's ample shoulders. However, he was not disposed to putting out real jazz over the NBC "Red" Network, which included at least twenty-three cities from New York to Omaha. November trade publications listed a pop-oriented Rudy Vallee program as Number One in the East, the Midwest, and the Pacific Coast region, with the Whiteman show eighth, seventh, and ninth in the East, the Midwest, and the South, respectively. No—more jazz would not be Whiteman's response.

Some time between the last week in November and mid-December, Bunny joined the band of Abe Lyman. Perhaps financial reasons prompted the change. One rumor suggested that Whiteman fired Bunny for drinking. This does not seem likely, since many of the Whiteman troupe have indicated that Bunny's playing and behavior on the stage were never a problem. Whiteman himself told one writer, "Yes, Bunny took a drink, but you've got to remember, we were all pretty wild in those days. If you weren't pretty wild you were pretty square." [13] Bunny, unsquare, ended his association with Whiteman.

Bunny's Whiteman year, 1933, was not without drama and excitement on other fronts. Franklin D. Roosevelt became the thirty-second president of the United States, and he caught the nation's ear with his fireside chats. His March inauguration ushered in the Hundred Days, a period of sweeping changes designed to lead the country out of the crushing Depression. His New Deal package included such

13. Wilson, "Beauty, Drive, and Freedom," 20.

programs as the Emergency Banking Relief Act, the Economy Act, Civilian Conservation Corps, Federal Emergency Relief Administration, Agricultural Adjustment Administration, Tennessee Valley Authority, National Recovery Administration, Public Works Administration, and Federal Deposit Insurance Corporation. New York City elected Fiorello LaGuardia as mayor. Adolph Hitler was appointed chancellor of Germany, and his Nazi party, which won a majority of seats in the Reichstag, immediately outlawed freedom of the press, all labor unions, and all rival political parties. Joseph Stalin began his great purge of the Communist party in the Soviet Union, imprisoning and executing many old revolutionary loyalists. In Hollywood, filmmaker Busby Berkeley introduced the lavish "production number" and invited audiences to dance their way out of the Depression. Gertrude Stein offered *The Autobiography of Alice B. Toklas*, and James Hilton's *Lost Horizon* met with public approval. Book burnings of all Jewish and non-Nazi writing became one of Hitler's policies. FM radio broadcasting began. The Nobel committee awarded the prize in physiology and medicine to Thomas Hunt Morgan for discovering the role of chromosomes in heredi y; in physics, the Nobel prize went to Erwin Schrodinger and Paul Dirac for developing useful applications of the atomic theory. Jerome Kern and Otto Harbach wrote "Smoke Gets in Your Eyes." Voters repealed Prohibition. The American League beat the National League, 4–2, in the first All-Star Baseball game, played at Chicago's Comiskey Park. The Chicago Bears beat the New York Giants, 23–21, in Chicago, for the first national Professional Football League championship. Because of the Depression, 2,000 rural schools did not open for the fall semester; 200,000 teachers were out of work; 2.3 million children were not in school; many colleges and universities closed. And Bunny Berigan played his trumpet better than anyone.[14]

14. Much information about Berigan's association with the Whiteman orchestra from research by Bozy White, in White Outline.

10

In a Mist

Song recorded November 30, 1938
by Bunny Berigan and His Men

On November 30, 1938, barely two months after surviving a hurricane and a broken leg, Bunny recorded "In a Mist" and three other compositions by Bix Beiderbecke, adding one more Bix tune the next day. "In a Mist," written for solo piano, continues to be played both as a solo and in larger settings and is generally regarded as Bix's classic composition. This tribute to cornetist Beiderbecke and his writings ranks with the richest of Berigan recordings. As with the "Mahogany Hall Stomp" tribute to Armstrong recorded by Bunny in 1937, the arrangements and Bunny's playing evoke the feeling and the spirit of a musician Bunny admired, without in any way being imitative. This session is described by Albert McCarthy:

Late in 1938, a nine-strong section of the band [including Joe Lipman, Gus Bivona, George Auld, Ray Conniff, and Buddy Rich] went into the recording studios and made versions of Bix Beiderbecke's four piano pieces *In A Mist, Flashes, Candlelights,* and *In the Dark,* and his *Davenport Blues.* Beiderbecke's introspective and impressionistic piano compositions are not all that easy to transcribe into orchestral arrangements, but Joe Lippman's [*sic*] scores are intelligently conceived and he makes use of a number of individual voicings. The performances are very much governed by the arrangements, with solos generally of short duration and forming an integral part of the whole. *Candlelights* and *In the Dark* are probably the most successful titles, as they capture the emotional climate of the numbers well. Berigan subordinates something of his own musical personality during these performances, while remaining tonally quite distinctive; he manages to convey an impression of the unique lyricism that suffused Beiderbecke's own playing without ever attempting to directly copy him. The wistfulness of Berigan's playing during *Candlelights*, for example, is not recreated on any other of his recordings.[1]

Leon Bix Beiderbecke and Bunny Berigan, decades after their deaths, remain two of the major voices on cornet and trumpet in the history of jazz. Each was influential in shaping jazz, not only for the players who were their contemporaries, and not only for cornet or trumpet players, but also for those who have followed, irrespective of instrument. These two major artists' lives share many parallels; important differences divide them as well.[2]

Both—for sake of convenience, let us call them trumpeters—came from the Midwest. Bix was born in Davenport, Iowa, a Mississippi River port city, in 1903, five years before Bunny's birth in rural Wisconsin not far from the Wisconsin River, which feeds into the Mississippi north of Davenport. Bix's parents were both German, his mother a prize-winning pianist and piano teacher. Great-grandfather Beiderbecke had been an organist in Germany, and his son had led the Dutch-American choral society in Davenport before 1900. Bix's "Uncle Olie," actually his mother's cousin by marriage, was leader of the town band and a cornetist. Bix's older sister, Mary, was a semi-professional pianist at age twelve. As was the case with the Berigans, the Beiderbecke family contained enough musicians to enable them to form an ensemble of some skill. Young Bix was looked upon as a prodigy, able before age seven to replicate by ear complex melodies on the piano. Called "Bickie," a diminutive of his father's name, Bismark—the son's middle name is officially Bix—he received much the same kind of fawning attention accorded Bunny. While Mayme Berigan reveled in the story of Bunny's vocal debut at age eight, Bix's mother treasured the Davenport *Daily Democrat* article about her "Seven-Year-Old Boy Musical Wonder." Whereas Bunny early proved to be an instantaneous reader of music, Bix, perhaps because of his great imitative capacity, only late in his career attained barely adequate reading ability. Formal musical training seemed wasted on Bix; Bunny thrived on it. Bunny's teacher, "Professor" Wagner, is matched by Bix's Professor Charles Grade who, though he lived forty

1. Albert McCarthy, *Big Band Jazz* (New York, 1974), 209.
2. Biographical information on Beiderbecke in this chapter is drawn from Sudhalter and Evans, *Bix: Man & Legend*, and Berton, *Remembering Bix*.

miles from Davenport, was engaged as the best possible instructor for her budding prodigy by Bix's mother. Ultimately, Bix's insistence on playing by ear, and his imitation of the professor's rendering of each practice piece, including errors, caused the teacher to quit in defeat.

Both trumpeters' parents shared the frustration of trying to force a formal academic education upon their sons. At age eighteen, Bix was enrolled in the tenth grade at Lake Forest Academy, a private school about thirty-five miles north of Chicago, much as Bunny was later sent to Madison. In neither case did the move work out as the parents had hoped. Probably this was due less to the youngsters' lack of ability to learn than to lack of interest in the things school sought to teach. Whereas young Bix constantly filled his spare moments playing the piano, and later the cornet, in a manner that the family regarded as aimless, Bunny busied himself in purposeful practice and playing on his trumpet, thus earning parental approval. Both boys experienced serious illnesses. Bunny's burst appendix at about age twelve finds a parallel in Bix's earlier bout with scarlet fever in 1911 at age eight. Bix's illness caused him to miss most of the third grade and finally to drop out of that school year. Whether these illnesses contributed to the boys' school difficulties is not established. Bix's formal education ended in much the same way as Bunny's did, an incomplete year at the academy dovetailing with the more-or-less formal beginning of his professional musical career. Undoubtedly, in each case the move from home facilitated the entry of the trumpeters into music as a full-time endeavor, providing as it did almost unlimited exposure to playing opportunities, new sounds, and the momentum that comes with success.

In an economic sense, the background of the families of the trumpeters differed greatly. Bix's mother and father were of the privileged middle class of Davenport, with a rich cultural background and an emphasis on education as the key to success. Bix's father was co-owner of a successful coal company, which made Bix's private academy education a financial possibility. The family employed a maid and perhaps considered other domestic help to be essential as well. Bunny's salesman father was never financially successful. Bunny frequently sent needed money home, even later in his career when money became a problem for Bunny himself. While music was important in the Schlitzberg family, and to some degree with the Berigans, a broader cultural involvement in literature, art, and politics does not seem to have been present in Bunny's home as it was in Bix's background.

Bix's first contact with live jazz came from listening to the riverboats that docked not far from his home. Bunny's initiation took place at local dances. Bix's older brother, Charles, brought home a Columbia gramophone in late 1918 after being discharged from the army. Included in some of the records he bought were "Tiger Rag" and "Skeleton Jangle" by the Original Dixieland Jazz Band, featuring D.J. "Nick" LaRocca on cornet. This music hooked Bix, just as Armstrong records later captured Bunny. Both spent entire days playing along with records, and the Beiderbecke family feared that Bix's playing disturbed the neighbors—a fear Bunny's family later experienced. Esten Spurrier was Bix's friend when both were young cornetists in Davenport. He developed a style similar to Bix's, much as Clif Gomon did when Clif and Bunny were playing together in Madison. Spurrier's description of Bix's listening habits, and how he drew from several players, closely parallels Gomon's story of how Bunny developed through the use of recorded music: "Sure—Bix plucked the best from what he heard, saved it, and dovetailed it into a distinctive style. But it was his own."[3] Neither Bunny nor Bix, after their earliest excursions, slavishly copied what they heard.

Through their school years, and as both trumpeters grew toward manhood, they shared many qualities. Both were deemed good looking and they both attracted girls. Bix, contrary to legend, was outgoing and witty and loved a good time, as did Bunny. Bix played on the Lake Forest Academy baseball team, only one manifestation of his love of sports, a love also shared by Bunny. Later in life both men were attracted to carnivals and the games found there. Bix was almost addicted to Ski-Ball, a form of miniature bowling. Bunny liked bowling but preferred pool and golf. Bix played golf with more enthusiasm than skill. Each earned the admiration of peers with his even-tempered nature. Each accepted his own musical talent with easiness, without displaying an air of superiority.

One interesting coincidence is that Bix's first playing job of consequence was on the riverboat *Majestic;* Bunny sailed for Europe on the

3. Sudhalter and Evans, *Bix: Man & Legend,* 49.

British liner *Majestic* shortly after joining the Hall Kemp orchestra, his first major exposure.

Clothing and its care did not represent high priorities in the lives of Beiderbecke and Berigan. Bix, especially, was notorious for never having the proper uniform. Usually he was forced to borrow one or more parts of the requisite tuxedo, often showing up for a job in pieces of clothing that matched neither each other nor the garb of the other players. Bunny exerted somewhat more care about his apparel, but often displayed cigarette burns in his jackets and trousers. Late in his career he required the assistance of his manager or sidemen to maintain an acceptable appearance.

Although eager to provide the best piano teaching available, Bix's parents balked at lessons on the cornet because to them the instrument represented a much less desirable and acceptable form of music—jazz. As a consequence, Bix was self-taught on the cornet. He invented a fingering system for the notes he heard. Many of Bix's discoveries are taught as alternate fingerings, but they are normally much more difficult to use, especially in passages with many notes. However, in some instances his fingerings are easier than conventional ones, but they present serious intonation problems and must be compensated with the lip and a great ear. Since Bix enjoyed perfect pitch, the correction of intonation irregularities posed no great problem for him. His unique fingering also added two particular characteristics to Bix's sound: a decidedly personal vocal quality, and a "popping" sensation when some of the notes were articulated. Bix used these "wrong" fingerings throughout his career, frequently astounding many traditionally trained players, who recognized the difficulty of his technique. Bunny, on the other hand, received correct teaching from the outset and relied on it as one of the solid bases of his magnificent technique. Frequently in the upper reaches of his range, however, Bunny employed his great lip control and used fingerings not written in method books.

A comparison of Bix and Bunny cannot be made without mentioning their battles with alcohol abuse, beginning for both at about age twenty. Evidence indicates that Bix began drinking about the time he entered the Lake Forest Academy, when he was playing for many dances on and off campus. As with Bunny's beginnings with alcohol, Bix was away from home for the first extended time. The same Prohibition-induced excitement of trying something risky possibly came into play for both. The drinking exploits of these two musicians receive heavy emphasis in the legends that surround them. Benny Green touches on aspects of this legend as it applies to Bix. Many of Green's points apply as well to Bunny:

The Bix legend goes very briefly as follows—"Innocent young white boy with jazz gift. Becomes recognized and records masterpieces in the Big City. Starts to drink. . . . Sells his soul to commercialism. Falls ill. Half-recovers. Dies. End of life, beginning of legend." It will be perceived that this framework leaves convenient gaps for the insertion of gangsters, the Right Woman, the Wrong Woman and the rest of the clumsy farrago which takes the music for granted and delivers a kind of affectionate rap on Bix's posthumous knuckles for being naughty enough to join a band as corrupted as Paul Whiteman's, a band whose only contribution to jazz was the money it poured into the pockets of those who sat in its elephantine ranks. . . .

The Artist-Who-Sold-His-Soul-for-A-Hip-Flask theory is useful in one way, because it is so completely, utterly, hopelessly wrong that all one has to do to get to the truth of the matter is to reverse all its main propositions. After all, the man who is consistently wrong is just as sure a guide to conduct as the man who is consistently right.[4]

Alcohol consumption shortened Bix's and Bunny's lives, and it sometimes adversely affected their playing. But to argue that either of these players sold his soul to commercialism for any reason is ridiculous. This part of the legend is but one more example of the analogous aspects of the lives of these jazz pioneers.

Sudhalter and Evans discuss Bix's drinking pattern during 1928, when he played with the Paul Whiteman organization. These writers point out that Bix, like almost all musicians, drank because it was an important social factor in his life, in spite of (or perhaps partly because of) Prohibition. They do not identify exactly when he went beyond "the point of conviviality on [his] headlong plunge into excess and, finally, addiction." But it was clear to all who cared to observe that Bix had a seemingly unlimited capacity for booze while ostensibly remaining in command of his horn. The toll of this imbibing on his health was apparent to even his protective fellow musicians when he returned from the lavish Whiteman tour of 1928.[5]

Sudhalter and Evans go further, dispelling the notion that Bix was

4. Benny Green, *The Reluctant Art: The Growth of Jazz* (New York, 1962), 23–25.
5. Sudhalter and Evans, *Bix: Man & Legend*, 254.

driven to drink because of alleged frustration imposed by the un-swinging Whiteman band. In their book, they point out that, contrary to the view espoused by Ralph Berton, Bix felt that he had learned a great deal and improved his reading ability while in the Whiteman orchestra and that he met challenges in playing that satisfied him. Bix particularly appreciated the exposure he got in Whiteman's band to the harmonies of some of the newer classical music, toward which he had long demonstrated a true appreciation and affinity. He expressed great joy at being able to play and record the trumpet solo in Gersh-win's "Concerto in F." Further, Bix was encouraged to explore his continuing interest in the piano while with Whiteman. By contrast, Bunny was not deeply interested in the same musical genre during his own Whiteman stint; further, Whiteman had begun to lean far more heavily on playing straightforward popular music while Berigan was on the band. Essentially a *player* and a jazz soloist, Bunny rarely spent his efforts writing or arranging. Bunny did listen to some classi-cal music, as classical quotations in many of his solos attest, but not with the ardor or consistency Bix showed. Bunny probably felt the musical pinch of the Whiteman band far more than Bix had before him. However, to claim that an unsatisfactory experience with White-man should bear the responsibility for the alcohol addiction of either Bix or Bunny would be specious.

At certain points in their careers, both Bix and Bunny endured, and probably enjoyed, a playing schedule that was physically de-bilitating. For Bix, the period from early March to mid-September, 1929, provides a good example of the kind of schedule he was keep-ing. Bix rejoined Whiteman's orchestra on March 4, immediately after a six-week period of rest and recuperation in Davenport. The rest pe-riod had been necessary near the end of one of Whiteman's triumphal tours of the country, a tour of more than four months' duration that had, in turn, been preceded by a flurry of recording activity in New York. When Bix returned to the Whiteman bandstand in March, the orchestra performed weekly on the Old Gold radio program, mas-tered a series of recordings, appeared regularly at the New Amster-dam Theater or the Pavilion Royal, rehearsed for another California trip, and played selected one-nighters. In addition, Bix recorded sev-eral sessions with Frank Trumbauer. Beginning on May 24, the or-chestra worked its way to California and back with a series of one-

nighters and week-long stands in various major cities, ending back at
Long Island's Pavilion Royal on August 31, all the while maintaining
the schedule of Tuesday broadcasts for Old Gold. Two weeks later,
Bix returned home to Davenport, on full pay from Whiteman, for another mandatory period of recuperation.

A comparable period for Bunny would have occurred after he returned to New York following his tour with the Goodman band. After
a stopover in his home town, Bunny wasted little time reestablishing
his radio and recording studio schedule at the beginning of 1936. Either of these activities would have provided an excellent income and
ample musical satisfaction for most people. At the end of February,
however, Bunny joined with Eddie Condon, Red McKenzie, Joe
Bushkin, and others in making up the house band at the Famous
Door nightclub. Later they moved to the 18 Club. Then Bunny began
rehearsing a big band with which he played a few dates. And on June
13, Bunny headlined a new radio program series that most people regarded as the best jazz program ever offered, the *Saturday Night
Swing Club*. During most of a six- to eight-month period, calculations
indicate, Bunny's trumpet was pointed at either a microphone or a
live audience for at least seventy hours per week.

Still more parallels between Bix and Bunny assert themselves.
Each suffered with persistent tooth problems. Condon tells of an
upper pivot tooth that frequently fell out of Bix's mouth, rendering
him incapable of playing his horn. The sight of Bix's bandmates on the
floor looking for the tooth was not uncommon. A particular challenge
faced them one morning in Cincinnati when the tooth fell into a fresh
snowbank. Condon claims, "It was natural for Bix not to get the tooth
permanently fastened; he couldn't be bothered going to the dentist."[6]
Similarly, Bunny never sought proper attention for his uneven teeth
or for a dead, discolored front tooth.

Like most of the early jazz musicians, Bix and Bunny reveled in jam
sessions, impromptu playing marathons that could break out at almost
any time and in almost any place where two or more players
gathered. The participants themselves were often a session's only audience; sometimes a few fortunate nonmusicians shared the experience. Given the right mix of musicians and conditions, the resulting

6. Eddie Condon, *We Called It Music: A Generation of Jazz* (New York, 1947), 121–22. Bix
finally had the tooth fixed late in his career.

music could leap from the realm of the ordinary and propel those present into a state of euphoria. Particularly in Bix's and Bunny's era, the early decades of jazz, while the musicians were still discovering the identity of their music and themselves, jam sessions were commonplace and seminal. Especially in New York, musicians would gravitate nightly to known hangouts to hear and to share the latest innovations of rhythm, harmony, and line.

Bix and Bunny shared a high regard for Louis Armstrong. Bunny's early affinity for Armstrong and his abiding allegiance to Louis are well known. Armstrong was not Bix's earliest model, but close associates of Bix have attested that the mature Bix regarded Louis as the only player he would go out of his way to hear. Bunny played with both Bix and Louis; Bix played with both Bunny and Louis. Bunny and Louis recorded together; Bix recorded with neither Bunny nor Louis.

A billing of Bix and Bunny on the same bandstand is almost too exciting to consider. The imagination runs wild with expectation; the facts are more prosaic. The two trumpeters played together on three occasions in the spring of 1931, a matter of weeks before Bix's death in August.[7] By 1931, Bunny had asserted himself among musicians as *the* new voice on jazz trumpet. Bix was newly returned to New York following a three- to four-month stay in Davenport that afforded very little playing. He had gone home after collapsing in the middle of a solo during a radio program with Whiteman. His wasted, frail body, rebelling from years of abuse and neglect, balked at the demands Bix was requiring of it.

The first job they shared was at Amherst College in Massachusetts on March 14. The thirteen-piece Dorsey Brothers Orchestra also included Glenn Miller, Arthur Schutt, and Carl Kress. Musicians who were in attendance indicate that Bix's lip sometimes betrayed his layoff and that he displayed some jealousy at sharing the solos with Bunny, the new, exciting trumpeter who played mostly lead that night. A small group within the band combined to back Bix in a feature of many of his famous recorded selections. The Amherst College newspaper sang Bix's praises in its next edition, indicating how he was still able to captivate college students. Two other dates brought

7. Sudhalter and Evans, *Bix: Man & Legend*, 398.

Beiderbecke and Berigan together, May 8 at Princeton and May 15 at Yale; each involved about ten musicians under the leadership of the Dorsey brothers. Bix experienced a problem with blood circulation on the way home from Princeton and required help in getting to his room. Bix's sure ear remained intact; it would not deceive him. It surely told him how much his own playing had deteriorated and how near he was to relinquishing his leadership to a younger player. Bix's decline saddened Bunny. While Bix had never influenced Bunny as Armstrong had, Bunny's admiration for Bix was of long standing nevertheless and had been made known on many occasions.

As players, Bix and Bunny repeatedly transformed some of the dullest songs, some of the most pedestrian arrangements, some of the most prosaic vocal performances, into records worth hearing and having. Given as little as four or eight bars of solo space or ad lib accompaniment, Bix and Bunny could breathe life into an otherwise hopeless performance. Both trumpeters performed on a large number of records that have little intrinsic worth, yet these musicians often rose above their material. This talent is demonstrated in Bix's case on the recording of "Sweet Sue" made with the Whiteman orchestra on September 18, 1928. Benny Green describes the effort: "Every indelicacy that might conceivably be crammed into a four-minute performance is included in what the sleeve notes . . . describe with some restraint as 'a real period piece.' . . . In the midst of this farrago, the listener may discover a single chorus by Bix Beiderbecke which momentarily dispels the nonsense as though by magic. There is no clucking interference from the rest of the band. The rhythm section merely accompanies Bix for thirty-two bars, and everyone else, from Whiteman to the lowest menial on his orchestrating staff, leaves it to him."[8] Green then describes in detail how Bix's instincts led him to deliver a logical musical statement in a relaxed and intuitive way.

A similar quality in Bunny's playing is exhibited on dozens, perhaps hundreds, of such records. Eight of the most telling bars of evidence beg for escape from an April 16, 1931, record by Freddie Rich and his orchestra. The recording's personnel are the regular Rich CBS group, the arrangement and the vocal are as dated as spats, and the tune, "Now You're in My Arms," possesses quality in neither the melody

8. Green, *Reluctant Art*, 39.

nor the lyric. The tune's slurpy, syrupy first chorus gives way to a muted trumpet solo for eight bars of straight melody—definitely not Bunny. The reeds lead into the bridge of the second chorus, and then it happens! Bunny, also muted, bursts into a solo that, while following the melody rather closely, recasts the feel from society orchestra to swing band, from 1931 to today. The rhythm section, catching the spirit, comes aboard instantly. One can imagine the knowing smiles or glances that bounce between the other musicians. For eight delightful bars they share the experience of creating something that will have lasting validity.

Even within the demanding and difficult world of jazz, where lives burned out swiftly, the careers of both musicians were disappointingly brief. Because of the placement of those careers, so very near the beginnings of jazz, and because of the volatility of the emerging art form, the seemingly insignificant five years' difference in their ages is magnified greatly. The jazz that Bix heard on the riverboats as a sixteen-year-old in 1919 when he first met Louis Armstrong was quite different from that heard by Bunny at the dance halls and on record when he was sixteen in 1924. In those five years, jazz not only developed as an art form and increased its repertoire, but also ceased to be an insular, unknown entity. The music had invaded large and smaller cities and captured the ears and the efforts of an increasing number of players. Jazz was no longer a totally improvised, black-only art form as it burst into the consciousness of white America in the mid-1920s. Written arrangements demanded more schooled playing technique, a movement in which many blacks took the lead. Further, in those years technology surrounding musical performance underwent refinement, the electrical recording emerged, and the acoustic method disappeared. As inaccurately as some of the electrical recordings of the 1930s and 1940s represent the live sound of the artists, nonetheless they stand as a vast improvement over their acoustic predecessors.

The recording careers of Bix and Bunny overlap just barely. Bix made his last recording on September 15, 1930, with Hoagy Carmichael and His Orchestra. Bunny debuted on record with Hal Kemp on May 14, 1930, only four months earlier. The inherent sound quality on Bix's early records and Bunny's middle and later ones is quite different because of constantly improving recording methods. "Enhanced sound" reissues are, at best, a mixed blessing, boosting certain segments of the sound spectrum and filtering others. Very recent improvements in recapturing the original fidelity of sound in older records through digital remastering and other technology offer promise in this area. For now, however, comparing the two trumpeters through their recordings remains difficult. Nevertheless, evaluations can be made.

Bix and Bunny were breakthrough trumpeters. Bix took in the raw, powerful sounds of the riverboat players and transformed them into something quite different. Throughout his recorded music, Bix exhibits a fluid, legato style, one that Sudhalter likens to a vocal quality. Much of the difference between Bix and his predecessors lies in his harmonic approach to playing. His ear heard, and his horn played, notes that were substantially different from the norm. He played elegant, graceful lines that danced in and out of the melody. In those instances in which he accompanied another soloist or vocalist, Bix displayed a beautiful, almost baroque complementary counterpoint that, instead of repeating a stated melody, spun a harmonic framework for it.

Bix's cornet tone was pure, warm, flannel. It possessed a matte, rather than brass, finish. Rarely venturing outside the middle range of the horn, Bix relied on his choice of notes and skillful sense of dynamics, often creating interest within a single measure by varying from loud to soft, or soft to loud. Each solo, however brief, stood on its own as a complete musical statement and offered its own sense of musical logic. Once Bix had played a jazz solo he frequently disowned it, eschewing requests to repeat it as recorded and looking for a new means of expression the next time around. Individual notes were most often attacked in soft, legato manner, rather than percussively. Bix's solo playing is relaxed, laid-back, unhurried, exuding a sense of control. One of the rare exceptions to this is in Bix's recording of "Goose Pimples" with Bix and His Gang in 1927. Here Bix cuts loose with a powerful, driving, uninhibited out-chorus that lifts the whole performance from something good to something extraordinary.

Bix served as an inspiration to the players in every group with which he played. They looked to him for musical leadership and for a sense of dignity in their music to counteract popular notions of jazz as a rough, unworthy stepchild of "real" music. More than that, they regarded Bix as a hero, protecting him from his own weaknesses when they could and wringing their hands in helplessness when they could not. Playing with Bix was considered a delight and an artistic privilege.

Bunny, too, heard the raw, powerful sounds of the riverboat players and transformed them. While he eliminated some of the rough edges in the transformation, he lost none of the raw power, compromised none of the uninhibited drive. Bunny's sound never lost its element of primitivism. His musical voice owed its characteristics to a unique blending of physical attributes, all enhanced by a classic technique. This remarkable combination—the embouchure, the lung and abdominal capacity, the digital dexterity, the sure ear—allowed Bunny to play almost anything his fertile imagination could conceive. He was equally at home playing driving, cohesive lead parts or carrying entire tunes as a soloist. He could play blues choruses that were black or straight melody on a ballad. He could trade explosive four-bar phrases that could fill a room with frenzy or tastily back a vocalist with a choice of softly muted counterpoint. He could read a complicated score with little or no preparation or fake any tune in any key. Bunny could, and often did, shout; but he could also whisper. His attack on notes could be vicious or surreptitious. He could growl or weep, but always he sounded like Bunny.

Of Bunny's trumpet tone, Irving Goodman, Benny Goodman's brother and a member of the trumpet section in Bunny's band, said: "Listen to that tone. It was massive, top to bottom. Even bigger than it sounded on the records. No microphone could capture it."[9] If Bix's tone was pure, Bunny's was pulsating. If Bix's was warm, Bunny's was hot. If Bix's was flannel, Bunny's was silk. Bunny, too, told a story with each solo, no matter its length. Multiple recordings of the same song, combined with air checks of live performances, afford the opportunity to compare Bunny's solos. Often he follows a similar pattern for a solo, varying only some parts of it while playing some phrases note for note as he recorded them. This was standard procedure at the time and should be attributed, not to lack of imagination, but to the expectations of his audience. Even so, alternate takes and mul-

9. Irving Goodman, quoted by Richard M. Sudhalter in the jacket notes for RCA 5657-1-RB, *The Complete Bunny Berigan, Vol. II*. Goodman played trumpet in Berigan's band from approximately June, 1937, through December, 1939.

tiple air checks of the same tune sometimes reveal vastly different solos.

The testimony of Bunny's bandmates confirms that he not only inspired them but drove them to play in ways they had not imagined. More than one player has attested that no band was the same without Bunny, whether he was playing that precise, compelling lead or astounding his compatriots with his inventive, self-challenging solos. As with Bix's colleagues, Bunny's fellow musicians surround him with an aura of awe and protectiveness. And, finally, comes the realization by Bix's and Bunny's peers that they have been witness to the genius and the fallibility of these two jazz brass masters.

11

Whatcha Gonna Do
When There Ain't No Swing?

Song recorded August 27, 1936
with Frank Froeba and His Swing Band

      Moving to the Abe Lyman band at the end of 1933 could scarcely have cured Bunny's longing to play good jazz, by whatever name it might be called. Of the many records made by Lyman between 1923 and 1942, only a few might be considered to have any significant jazz interest. On none of these does Berigan appear. His stay with Lyman was short. During 1934 and the early part of 1935, Bunny was concentrating his efforts at the CBS radio studios and the ARC recording studios. This appeared to be a period of consolidation for Bunny. He continued to establish himself within the music fraternity, demonstrating his virtuosity as a quick study on written or blocked-out arrangements while at the same time providing some of the most crackling, exciting jazz solos to be heard anywhere.

      Just as Whiteman would not feature more pure jazz in his broadcasts in an effort to capture a larger "share" of the audience, so recording companies refused to release much pure jazz. The Depression drastically reduced record sales in general, and jazz certainly did not escape this economic fact. From approximately 1931 to 1934, those jazz recordings that were released concentrated on larger groups and more tightly arranged selections rather than on mainstream, small-group jazz. And while many of the finest jazz musicians were indeed entrenched in the recording studios, too often their tasks were to back a poor singer singing a poor song, to make him or her sound good, and to do so quickly. Free-blowing, small-group sessions were a rarity, and only a relative handful of such recordings survive.

Once such gem is a two- or three-day session with the so-called Bill Dodge All-Stars that produced twenty-four tunes. Made as electrical transcriptions (ETs) especially for use on radio, these sides feature Benny Goodman and Bunny and provide an excellent example of the powerful styles of both players at that time. Chilton's notes sum up Bunny's recording activities of the period:

> While he was with Whiteman, Berigan had cut more than 100 sides with several pickup studio bands and had even appeared as the leader on a few of the various labels under which they were issued. The other musicians on these dates were mostly journeyman players, the tunes were generally evanescent pop stuff, and the results, except for an occasional flash of the Berigan horn, were far from notable.
> Starting in 1934, however, Berigan began appearing with increasing frequency on records whose line-ups included some of the cream of jazz-minded New York studio men: the Dorseys, guitarist Dick McDonough, saxophonists Frankie Trumbauer and Bud Freeman, drummer Ray Bauduc and clarinetists Artie Shaw and Benny Goodman. In this stimulating company Berigan produced some brilliant performances that enhanced his already considerable stature in the jazz community.
> By now he was also much in demand as an accompanist for singers, probably as a result of his superb playing on recordings he made with the Dorseys, backing the Boswell sisters. Few of the other vocalists he later supported were as musical as the Boswells, and the trumpeter's sensitive fills and brief solos frequently added a much-needed touch of artistry to some otherwise routine performances.[1]

The music business' general health at the beginning of 1934 was succinctly caught by a trade paper sub-headline that proclaimed, "2000 unemployed union musicians ask Local 802 to call strike in legit houses unless Equity lifts its Sunday ban—managerial interests address meeting."[2] Another battle being waged by the American Federation of Musicians was the growing use of ETs, rather than live musicians, on radio programs. A later January *Billboard* issue listed twenty-five separate laboratories that were engaged in the manufacture of ETs. The radio networks were intimately involved in the decisions about the transcriptions, as were major and minor recording companies. Early in the year CBS decided not to manufacture ETs; its counterpart and chief rival, NBC, made the opposite decision.

1. Chilton and Sudhalter, *Bunny Berigan*, 14–15.
2. *Billboard*, January 13, 1934.

By early spring, CBS claimed a total of ninety-four stations and affiliates, covering every area of the country. CBS leadership, spearheaded by William Paley, seemed to be banking on live music to help them in their battle with NBC for listeners. By midyear, CBS absorbed Moss-Hallett Enterprises, and Harry Moss joined the CBS bureau as a staff member who specialized in college dance bookings. Thus in 1934, CBS employed four men who worked exclusively on band bookings. They booked the popular Fred Rich band on a busy two-week tour of the Northeast. Under exclusive CBS management were such musicians and other popular entertainers as the Boswell Sisters, Morton Downey, Arthur Godfrey, Mark Warnow, Kate Smith, Colonel Stoopnagle & Budd, Howard Barlow, Ray Block, Benny Carter, Andre Kostelanetz, and Leith Stevens. The Fred Rich Orchestra on CBS supplied the radio music for such stars as Will Rogers, Georgie Jessel, Bing Crosby, Morton Downey, Helen Morgan, Fanny Brice, and Sophie Tucker. In June of 1934, NBC reported revenues of $2,174,000—the largest for any month in its history. No doubt CBS was doing as well. Considering the state of the general economy, this was an impressive figure for the up-and-coming industry.

Radio had become a magnetic force and, therefore, was getting a larger share of the entertainment dollar as compared with record sales. Not surprisingly, Bunny was spending increasing amounts of his time in the radio studios of CBS, which carried a nucleus of about fifty musicians on staff during 1934 and 1935. Bunny was assigned almost exclusively to the "morning band," which played all manner of musical programs and fill-ins during the morning and afternoon hours. At least three small, jazz-oriented instrumental groups, all featuring Bunny, evolved during this period: the Captivators, the Instrumentalists, and Bunny's Blue Boys. Each of these groups drew upon the same core of musicians; each was scheduled irregularly for varying periods of broadcast time. Their programs would last from a few minutes, strictly for fill-in, to as much as half an hour. The first listed date for Bunny's Blue Boys was May 14, 1935, but undoubtedly they had been announced as such somewhat earlier.[3] Bunny did not like

3. Most information about Berigan's association with CBS from research by Bozy White, in White Outline; New York *World-Telegram*, May 14, 1935, and radio broadcast information from research by Tom Cullen, also in White Outline.

Early photo of Bunny Berigan, *ca*. July, 1929. Probably while with Joe Shoer band in Lexington, Kentucky. *Courtesy Madeline Troisi*

Berigan with other members of the Hal Kemp band, *ca*. 1930. *Courtesy Madeline Troisi*

Sketch, taken from damaged publicity photo, of Donna McArthur, *ca.* 1930. *Original sketch by Stan Hench, 1990. Original photograph lent by Norm Krusinski*

EVENING, MAY 25, 1931.

Syracuse Dancer and Musician Wed at Church

Bernard Roland Berigan, left, son of Mr. and Mrs. William P. Berigan, of Fox Lake, Wis., and Donna Madeline McArthur, daughter of Mr. and Mrs. John J. McArthur, of 130 State Fair Boulevard, who were married at 9 o'clock this morning in St. Patricks Church. The Rev. Henry F. Curtin, pastor, performed the ceremony. Attendants were Beatrice Sullivan and Leland Whalen. The bride and groom left immediately for New York City. Mr. Berigan is a trumpeter with Freddy Rich's Orchestra and Mrs. Berigan is a dancer, a protege of Sonya Marens. She has appeared in Syracuse in adagio and ballroom dancing with her brother, Darrell McArthur, and has also been presented on the RKO Keith circuit several times.

Newspaper photograph and caption of wedding photo of Donna and Bunny, Syracuse, New York, May 25, 1931. *Courtesy Madeline Troisi*

Berigan and the Paul Whiteman trumpet section: Bunny, "Goldie" Goldfield, Nat Natoli, *ca.* 1933. *From the Duncan P. Schiedt Collection*

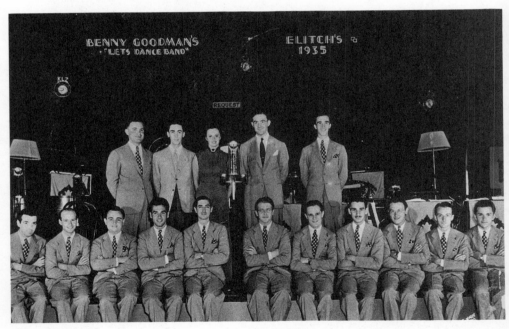

Benny Goodman Band in Denver, *ca.* August, 1935. *From the Duncan P. Schiedt Collection, courtesy Ralph Muzzillo and Bozy White*

The Famous Door Gang, 52nd Street: Forrest Crawford, Red McKenzie, Mort Stuhlmaker, Eddie Condon, Bunny Berigan, Joe Bushkin (seated), *ca.* early 1936.
Photo by Charles Peterson. From the Frank Driggs Collection

Berigan with Gene Krupa and Jimmy Dorsey, probably from *Saturday Night Swing Club* broadcast, *ca.* 1936–37. *From the Duncan P. Schiedt Collection*

Berigan publicity photo, *ca.* 1937. *From the Frank Driggs Collection*

DEC. 1937

Metronome

MUSIC AND ITS MAKERS

25 cents

Greetings

Bunny Berigan

NEW USES FOR MUSIC — SWINGING "JINGLE BELLS" — CESANA ARRANGING COURSE
NEWS, VIEWS AND REVIEWS OF BANDS, RADIO AND RECORDS

Cover of *Metronome*, December, 1937. *From the Frank Driggs Collection*

The Berigan rhythm section, *ca.* April–May, 1937: Tom Morgan, Arnold Fishkind, George Wettling, Joe Lipman. *Courtesy of Tom Morgan(elli)*

Publicity photograph of the Berigan band, *ca.* 1937. *From the Frank Driggs Collection*

Relaxing between sets, *ca.* 1937: Berigan, Joe Whelan, Lee Wiley, and her sister Pearl. *From the Frank Driggs Collection*

Tom Morgan and Berigan, *ca*. 1937—38. *Courtesy Tom Morgan(elli)*

the name, but the public did. Such was the quality of the music they played that in spite of irregularity of schedule, these three combos and their individual members built up a faithful cadre of eager listeners. Berigan was the spark plug of each group as it jammed its way through whatever music was selected, and the projected joy was caught by the audience. As satisfying as these groups were, however, they accounted for only a fraction of Bunny's playing time in the studios. Many of his assignments allowed no space for jazz, but Bunny was equal to the task.

One of the regular programs during this period was the *Kate Smith Matinee Hour,* which started at 3 P.M. Neither Smith nor her manager, Ted Collins, was well liked among the inner circle of studio musicians. Donna recalled that Smith's undisciplined eating habits alternately brought forth jokes and expressions of disgust from the instrumentalists. Both Smith and Collins presumed to know more about music than they actually did, which, according to the musicians, was little and nothing, respectively. Nevertheless, Smith and Collins both offered frequent suggestions-cum-orders to the professional musicians, including the orchestra directors. One such occasion involved Bunny in a battle of wills.

Bunny was known for his easygoing manner and generally light-hearted approach to life. Clif Gomon recalled that the only time he ever saw Bunny angered was at Madison's Chanticleer when one of the musicians was deliberately playing poorly on a tune he thought was inferior. "Bunny really got on him," Clif recalled. "He told this horn man in no uncertain terms that any piece of music could be played in such a way to make it sound good, and that he wouldn't accept anything less. He took his music seriously." In the rehearsal studio, Kate Smith provoked Bunny's anger about another musical matter. Smith began berating Bunny for playing what she perceived to be a wrong note. In the exchange that followed, Bunny responded heatedly, telling the portly star to go to hell. Smith or Collins tried to persuade CBS to fire Bunny, but the next day Bunny offered some measure of apology that resolved the clash.

In recalling the incident years later, Donna remarked, "Bunny wasn't a braggart and he wasn't a big talker. He knew he was good, but he let his horn talk for him. However, he wasn't going to let someone like Kate Smith tell him how to play his trumpet. How would she know?"

In most respects the "morning" assignment suited Bunny just fine. While much of the music he was called upon to play was pedestrian, the hours permitted him, with or without Donna, to explore the myriad offerings of New York City. For Bunny, this often meant bowling, pool, and, on days when the CBS schedule permitted, golf. In addition, rumors of Bunny's "one-night stands" of the nonmusical kind abound. Women found Bunny attractive for a number of reasons. The handsome, successful, fun-loving musician was at first surprised by, but later took in stride, the ease with which he could become acquainted with desirable women. Donna lived through a period of many months when she was not physically strong. The temptations and the opportunities for sexual exploration were certainly present for Bunny. The degree to which he took advantage of these opportunities is open to question. Donna professed knowledge of only one such encounter, and it was definitely not of the one-night variety. Whether Donna might have accepted any such casual encounters as simply "part of the business" is not established.

Invariably, Bunny's friends and music business associates refer to him as fun loving, happy-go-lucky, full of jokes, easygoing. Practical jokes abounded in Bunny's world and he eagerly participated in a variety of them. Drummer Johnny Blowers recalled a typical incident:

We finished this dance job outside Harrisburg and had a long jump to the next one. Bunny told the bus driver, "All the guys want a drink, so pull into the first bar you see." We were happy, and in we go into this empty place and the bartender's delighted to see us. All the guys were ordering two or three drinks. I was a Scotch drinker like Bunny, and when it came my turn to order, Bunny says to the bartender, "You aren't doing your job here. Look at this guy; he's too young to drink." The bartender asks me for identification, and I haven't got any ID on me; it's all packed away in my things on the bus. These guys are all drinking like crazy and all he'd give me was a Coke. Finally Bunny called the bartender over and told him he was only kidding. I had him set me up five drinks. Bunny wasn't mean enough to let me suffer.[4]

4. Johnny Blowers, interview with author, June 26, 1985, and by telephone, May 20, 1985, and from subsequent correspondence, all in author's possession. Subsequent quotations from Blowers are taken from this material. Blowers played drums for the Berigan band between Dave Tough and Buddy Rich. After a successful career as a studio player, Blowers is still active as a drummer at jazz concerts and parties.

Another drummer, Jack Sperling, told of a favorite trick of Bunny's, used more than once when a new female singer joined the band or when a sideman's new girlfriend began hanging around with regularity:

Bunny would sort of play the role of the father-figure and tell the girl, "Listen, you're with the band now, and with musicians around you're likely to hear quite a bit of rough language. So just to get the embarrassment out of the way, to sort of break the ice and get it out of our system, let's do this: On the count of three we'll all yell "fuck" just as loud as we can. Then you've heard it, we've heard it, and nobody'll be offended." Then he'd count—one, two, three—and you know what happened! The girl shouted out "FUCK" and everybody else was silent. Bunny liked that trick.

Sperling also recalled that Bunny would invite him to come to Bunny's room at all hours of the night. "He liked to tell me stories and make me laugh. I was a good laugher, I guess, and he needed company. Yes, and he'd slip in and out of his W. C. Fields voice so naturally. And on the street sometimes he'd just go up to a stranger and talk to them in double-talk, you know, so they couldn't understand him. If they asked him what he said, Bunny'd say, 'Your ass!' and walk away. Even though these tricks might seem unkind, the word I think of when I remember Bunny is *gentle*."

Nonetheless, another ungentle antic remembered by several of the sidemen from his last band was Bunny's purchase of an air rifle. Sperling characterized it as "a lot of craziness going down. We all thought it was smart. At two or three in the morning Bunny'd take out that rifle and shoot at clocks in little town squares."

Many have expressed surprise to learn that Bunny was attracted to games of various kinds. Photographs of the trumpeter from 1933 to 1935 suggest a somber demeanor: conservative three-piece suit, upright stance, wire-rimmed glasses, serious facial expression. Such photographs belie the facts. Bunny loved jokes and stories. Friends could double him up in laughter with bawdy limericks. In addition to using his W. C. Fields imitation with regularity, he loved the "scissors-paper-rock" finger game, as well as making little bets for drinks after a gig and flipping coins. Jess Stacy, among others, characterized Bunny as "a *good* pool player." Joe Dixon remembered Bunny as "very much like a child. He loved to go to amusement parks. He'd ride the roller coaster and merry-go-round and have a great time. And he was quite a golfer."[5]

Many of his associates remember Bunny the golfer. One publicity release credited him with a low golf handicap. Paul Weston, a premier arranger with the Tommy Dorsey band, recalled his golfing experience with Bunny: "He was a fine athlete, and one sad recollection I have is of playing golf with him at Van Cortlandt Park in New York. This was around 1937, and I was pretty naive at that time and didn't realize what was going on. After pars and birdies on about the first six holes, Bunny got progressively worse (he had a jug in his golf bag) and we had to quit before we finished eighteen holes."[6] Several of Bunny's colleagues remember playing golf with Bunny while on tour and in Fox Lake. All considered Bunny a fine golfer, as long as he didn't combine the game with drink.

Donna also called Bunny a good golfer, though she could not precisely recall his scores. She said they enjoyed "a lot of bowling and golfing" and skied on one occasion:

We were up at Lake Placid on the only real vacation we ever had during our married life. We were skiing, which neither one of us really knew how to do. It was a laugh, I'll tell you. Bunny had on a pair of skis that were straight— they didn't turn up much at the ends. Well, he came down this one hill and tried to go back up the other side, only he didn't go up. His skis just stuck their points in the snow and he was skewered there. They also had a beautiful ice-skating rink there and we decided to try that. Both of us had done some skating when we were young. I came out of the ice house holding onto the rail because I knew I needed it. Bunny just came out thinking he remembered everything. Well, he went flying on his butt and slid halfway across the rink.

When we were living in Rego Park we used to go horseback riding. Nat Natoli and his wife, Dorothy, and Bunny and I would go riding all the time.

5. Jess Stacy, interview with author, August 13, 1987, and by telephone, August 15, 1987, tapes in author's possession. Stacy played with Berigan only during Bunny's stint with Goodman in 1935 but kept abreast of his playing thereafter. Joe Dixon, telephone interview with author, July 14, 1986, tape in author's possession. Dixon played reeds with Berigan in the Tommy Dorsey band in 1936 and 1937. He played on some record dates with Bunny but is best remembered as a reed player, especially solo clarinet, in the Berigan band from approximately May, 1937, until September, 1938. Dixon continued to play professionally through the 1980s and taught jazz studies at Adelphi College through the late 1980s.

6. Paul Weston, to author, August 25, 1985, in author's possession. Weston's personal and professional relationship with Berigan began when Weston was an arranger with the Tommy Dorsey band in 1937. Later married to Jo Stafford, a premier Dorsey singer in the 1940s, Weston has had a successful career as writer, arranger, and leader in the Los Angeles and Hollywood music scene.

One . . . time Bunny was on this horse and after they got out so far, the horse decided to hurry on back to the barn. Well, they were coming fast when they got to the corral, and the horse just jumped the fence and kept heading for the barn. If Bunny hadn't ducked in time that overhang would have taken his head off!

You know what else we used to do? We'd get into a town and go get something to eat, and if it was early enough we'd head for the golf course, usually with a couple of the boys from the band. We'd play eighteen holes of golf, then go back to the hotel and rest until show time. If it was morning when we got in it was golf, but if we arrived when it was dark then we went bowling. Sometimes we'd bowl for hours.

In spite of these happy memories of time spent at games, Donna did not consider Bunny to be a very good athlete. She thought him "clumsy" rather than well-coordinated. Perhaps this is the perspective of the graceful professional dancer, or perhaps his actual lack of coordination could be traced to the protectiveness of his family when Bunny was young and not allowed to engage in some of the usual sports activities. Bunny was, nevertheless, an enthusiastic participant in a wide variety of games. Donna further recalled that in baseball Bunny played catcher "becaus⸜ he couldn't run very well."

Softball was quite the rage among big bands of the day, with competition, bragging, and betting sometimes reaching wild proportions. During an extended Astor Roof stand, Tommy Dorsey's band played regular Wednesday afternoon games in Central Park. An extant scorecard shows the results of a game between teams representing the Jimmy Dorsey and Tommy Dorsey bands on July 10, 1940, during Bunny's second stint with Tommy's band. This 12 to 10 victory against his brother's band carried special significance for Tommy. According to *Down Beat*, the contest

featured much baiting and little brilliant playing by the leaders, with TD's lads finally recovering from their leader's costly outfield blunder and capturing the game with a ninth inning, three run splurge. Despite their gaudy uniforms, Jimmy's boys found Chuck (Pied Piper) Lowery's pitching difficult and though they connected for 13 hits were unable to score in the pinches. Jimmy himself drew three free passes, the first of the season that didn't come from song-pluggers. Featured on the T. Dorsey team were Bunny Berigan's energetic catching plus his uncanny ability to stretch every triple into a single.[7]

7. *Down Beat,* VII (August 1, 1940).

The accuracy of the last statement can scarcely be doubted, given Bunny's general physical condition at the time and the fact that he would certainly have required several trips to the "drinking fountain."

Bunny had a home life, too. He and Donna tried to provide for their daughter Patty as normal an existence as a show-business life would allow. Donna, still weakened in 1934 by her difficult pregnancy and their infant daughter's subsequent death, needed some assistance with her housekeeping duties. On a visit to Fox Lake in 1934, Bunny hired one of the local girls, Eunice Sheskey, to join the Berigan household in New York as housekeeper. Eunice's brother Joe recalled some of the circumstances:

Eunice was a good singer, and she had this desire to go to New York and audition, thinking someone would hear her and give her a job. They worked it out so that she would go work for Bunny and his wife. He came out to the house in his new '34 Ford. I remember shaking his hand. Eunice would write once in a while. I remember she talked about them having a big police dog, and that there were lots of parties. I don't think she ever got to sing for anybody. She mentioned those parties a lot, though.[8]

Beguiling as these diversions were, they could not hope to compete for Bunny's sustained attention. To borrow a phrase from Duke Ellington, music was his mistress. Joyously, Bunny sought out places where he could play his horn freely, and that meant jam sessions.

In the 1930s, jam sessions frequently meant the Onyx Club. When Joe Helbock's new speakeasy opened at 35 West 52nd Street, it enjoyed almost immediate success with the "in" musicians. (The exact date of opening is in question. Although widely reported as July 30, 1930, Helbock disputes this. "I was on 52nd St. before Leon & Eddie's. I was there before 21 came over from 9th St. in 1930." He has stated that he launched the Onyx in 1927.)[9] On break time during the day, the instrumentalists would rush over from 485 Madison Avenue (CBS) or 711 Fifth Avenue (NBC) to satisfy their thirsts. Helbock was an enthusiastic host, one who appreciated the men who created the most exciting sounds of the era. At night he paid Joe Sullivan union scale to play his great swing piano by the hour. Sullivan had become a favorite of the studio musicians and others, and at night they would

---

8. Joe Sheskey, interview with author, May 18, 1986, tape in author's possession.
9. Arnold Shaw, *The Street That Never Slept* (New York, 1971), 52, 54.

flock to the Onyx with their horns, gaining entrance with the password "Local 802."

Nightly, jam sessions would build to a peak as more and more of the players joined in after finishing their paying jobs for the night, ending only when exhaustion sent them home. "It never ceased to amaze me," Helbock said, "how they would come in complaining about how some leader kept them for rehearsals ten minutes longer than expected. Then they would stay in my place playing all night long—for free."[10] Regulars included Tommy and Jimmy Dorsey, Jack and Charlie Teagarden, Art Tatum, Benny Goodman, and, of course, Bunny Berigan. In the relaxed atmosphere of the Onyx, these professionals could stretch out and try things that would not be permitted on the airwaves or in the dance halls—at least, not until they were perfected. These and other influential musicians such as Carl Kress (who later became part owner), Joe Venuti, Mannie Klein, Eddie Lang, Frank Trumbauer, Arthur Schutt, Roy Bargy, and Dick McDonough were virtually the only audience; they were critical only in the finest sense of the word.

Among them the listening was as intense—and as relaxed—as the playing. Arrangers and other players were not above making a mental note, or a written one, of a particularly arresting new lick or harmonic sound. Some little-known performers came to the Onyx in the hope of getting a chance to be heard. For more than one this exposure resulted in a record date or a chance at a radio appearance. "We started with some pretty good talent at the Onyx, and the Onyx started some pretty big careers," Helbock recalled. "Performers like Art Tatum and Maxine Sullivan and Joe Sullivan and the Spirits of Rhythm and John Kirby and Louis Prima and Stuff Smith."[11] After Joe Sullivan went to Hollywood, mainly for the purpose of accompanying Bing Crosby, the piano chair was assumed first by Charlie Bourne and later by Art Tatum. With the end of Prohibition in 1933, the Onyx traded in its role as a "private" club for the musicians and those on Radio Row; on February 9, 1934, Helbock opened a new Onyx across the street. Featuring the Spirits of Rhythm, it quickly became *the* place to go for the public. Upstairs, spillover crowds reveled in the playing of the master, Art Tatum.

10. *Ibid.*, 60.
11. *Ibid.*, 56.

The Onyx was by no means the only place where kindred spirits could gather to jam, but it certainly was preeminent during the seminal years of swing. Other clubs sought to duplicate the Onyx's post-Prohibition success. To varying degrees they were successful in attracting the players and the audience, some of whom were there because they truly appreciated the music, others because of curiosity or because it was a fashionable place to be.

For the players, however, scenes like the Onyx, Plunkett's, and the Clam House were the *only* place to be. It was there—playing their instruments, talking their craft, extending their capabilities, testing their instincts and their ears, feeling a part of something real, sensing the acceptance of their peers, directing the surge of creativity—there they felt most alive. Almost nightly, Bunny and Tommy and Jimmy and Jack and Benny and Frank showed up at the Onyx or elsewhere to place their musicianship—their lives—on the line, jamming with comrades. Anything else just didn't swing. And swing was the thing!

12

With Thee I Swing

Song recorded November 3, 1936
with Dick McDonough and His Orchestra

Benny Goodman was regarded as the epitome of the studio and jazz musician by the beginning of 1934. About six months younger than Bunny, Goodman early displayed a flair for leadership never really shown by Bunny. The clarinetist had gone to New York from Chicago in 1928 and, like Berigan, had established his reputation quickly with a combination of impeccable technique, reading ability, and jazz character. Unlike Berigan, he just as quickly began recording extensively as a leader with such players as Tommy Dorsey, Glenn Miller, Jimmy McPartland, Fud Livingston, and Ben Pollack. Most of the earlier recordings made as a leader were with small or midsize bands. But by 1934, Goodman was bitten by the big-band bug and by midyear, with a thirteen- or fourteen-piece band, had led recording sessions and personal appearances. This activity accelerated for Goodman as 1934 drew to a close. The personnel of his band shifted constantly, depending in large part on the availability of the musicians, not surprisingly drawn from the ranks of the recording and radio studio elite. The fit of the players, their ensemble sound, was becoming increasingly important to Goodman as the band began playing highly sophisticated arrangements such as those by Fletcher Henderson, Benny Carter, and Deane Kincaide.

Pianist, author, and *bon vivant* Oscar Levant introduced Goodman to Billy Rose, the noted impresario, who was in need of a band for the March opening of his new nightclub, the Music Hall. The band and the job were a poor match; Rose expected the band to accompany the entire show, a star-spangled vaudeville extravaganza featuring every kind of act. Since Goodman had carefully selected the band basically as a jazz unit, their failure to please either Rose or their leader in backing the show must have been due in large measure to their lack of enthusiasm for the task, rather than to lack of ability. Even when Rose relieved the group of its show responsibilities, they failed to please as a dance band. The type of audience attracted to the popular new nightclub was not ready for the kind of music Benny Goodman prepared his first big band to provide.

Both Goodman and Berigan were working in their separate radio studios by day, playing a variety of jobs at night, sometimes recording together. Despite the discouraging experience with Billy Rose, Goodman continued his efforts to put together a big band that would find acceptance, and on his terms. His break came in December, 1934, when NBC decided to broadcast a unique program, *Let's Dance*. Goodman later described the band's tense audition for *Let's Dance* and the equally disquieting lapse of time before Goodman learned of the decision: "The call came when I had just about given up hope of hearing from them. NBC was going ahead with its 'Let's Dance' program, featuring the bands of Kel Murray (for sweet music), Xavier Cugat (for Latin American) and—Benny Goodman!"[1]

On this Saturday night program each of the bands played for alternate fifteen-minute segments from 10:30 P.M. to 1:30 A.M. Generally, West Coast listeners heard the third hour first when they joined in at 9:30 local time. Back in New York the bands continued to play through 12:30 A.M. Pacific Standard Time, repeating the first two hours and signing off at 3:30 A.M. eastern time. Other affiliate stations across the country joined in at various times. Beginning on the first Saturday in December, 1934, the program, sponsored by the National Biscuit Company—Nabisco—ran for twenty-six weeks through May 25, 1935. In time for the inaugural program Goodman added two key players to the band, Berigan and drummer Gene Krupa. *Let's Dance* also gave Goodman the resources to hire bandleader and arranger Henderson, who contributed significantly to the Goodman book. Goodman recalled:

1. Benny Goodman, with Richard Gehman, "That Old Gang of Mine," *Collier's*, January 20, 1956, p. 28. Goodman earlier collaborated with Irving Kolodin to write similar recollections in *The Kingdom of Swing* (New York, 1939).

The first problem was to get some arrangements. The great Negro leader Fletcher Henderson had more or less broken up his band the year before. He was looking for work, and was only too happy to begin developing a book for our band. He charged us only $37.50 per arrangement! As I recall, the first things he did were "Sometimes I'm Happy" and "King Porter Stomp." We also got some other arrangements, but Fletcher was the man who really made our band, by arranging popular tunes in the same style he used for hot numbers, which we called killer-dillers.[2]

This time the fit was right, both within the band and between the band and its audience. Goodman never doubted the music community's appreciation but could not predict the public's response. Their acceptance of Goodman's sound was immediate and enthusiastic, as letters that began pouring into NBC attested. With public support, the band became tighter and more assured each week. Edgar Sampson, a fine arranger from the Chick Webb band, prepared fresh numbers for the book, not the least of which was "Stompin' at the Savoy." Goodman and his sidemen entertained a cautious optimism as their engagements increased and the band's personnel stabilized. More and more, the men were making a commitment to the band, sometimes turning down other work; together they began to forge an identity.

One element did not fit. From the beginning, Bunny's association with the Goodman band could be characterized as sporadic, at best. Goodman knew perhaps as well as anyone how Bunny could, through his brilliant lead trumpet playing and his exciting solos, lift a whole band's performance. Goodman also knew that he could not—at least, not in the beginning—hope to match the money that Bunny was able to earn by taking on all the studio work he could command. Goodman knew one thing further: Bunny Berigan was not above drinking on the job, and if he drank a lot, anything could happen.

Bunny played on some of the early *Let's Dance* programs with the Goodman band. Air checks—recordings of on-the-air broadcasts—of most, if not all, of the series are becoming increasingly available. The air check for the program of January 5, 1935, reveals slurred playing, a clear sign that Bunny had been drinking a generous amount of Scotch that night. Goodman was incensed. Either during or immediately

2. Goodman, "That Old Gang of Mine," 28.

after the show, Goodman fired Berigan. Soon Pee Wee Erwin took over Berigan's chair in the trumpet section.

Erwin was a masterful trumpeter, much in demand. Shortly after Erwin replaced Bunny, George Simon wrote a most favorable review of the BG band, citing Erwin for outstanding trumpet work. *Metronome* listed Erwin's schedule over a three-day period when he was playing with both the Ray Noble and the Goodman bands:

Friday AM—Electrical Transcriptions—Noble
Early PM—Traveling to Amherst, Mass.
 9 PM to 3 AM (Sat.)—Amherst College Dance—Noble
 3 AM to 10 AM—return to NYC
10:00 to 12:30 PM—Rehearsal and Trans-oceanic program—Noble
 3:00 to 5:00 PM—Rehearsal—Goodman
 6:00 to 8:30 PM—Playing Roosevelt Grill—Goodman
 9:00 to 9:30 PM—RCA Victor Program—Goodman
10:00–4:30 AM (Sunday)—"Let's Dance"—Goodman[3]

Meanwhile, Bunny's playing on CBS was drawing more attention. All three of his jazz groups—the Captivators, the Instrumentalists, and Bunny's Blue Boys—enjoyed separate listings in the radio sections of the city newspapers by early- to mid-1935. Unfazed by Goodman's temporary rejection, Bunny was keeping a schedule that was perhaps equally as demanding as Erwin's. On January 25, 1935, Bunny cut four titles with the Red Norvo Swing Octet in a memorable session at Columbia. Reviewer Warren Scholl proclaimed, "Bunny Berigan, who has been making records with a number of swing combinations is in his best form and confirms my opinion by his playing here, that he is now the leading white hot trumpet player."[4] On April 25, Bunny and a carefully selected group cut the first recordings of the Glenn Miller Orchestra. This was essentially the same personnel that composed the Ray Noble Orchestra, a band of Radio Row musicians assembled, rehearsed, and led by Miller but fronted by the Englishman, who had brought only a drummer and vocalist with him across the Atlantic. On May 9, Bunny recorded with a pickup group, the Mound City Blue Blowers, and on May 13 recorded a session with

3. *Metronome*, LI (June, 1935), in White Materials.
4. *Down Beat*, I (October 1, 1934).

Gene Gifford and His Orchestra that featured the vocals of Wingy Manone.

As the end of his twenty-six-week *Let's Dance* contract neared, Goodman was shocked to learn that Nabisco did not intend to renew its sponsorship. Booker Willard Alexander rushed to set up a massive cross-country tour for the band and arranged a stint to begin at the end of May at the Roosevelt Hotel's Grill in New York City. This room had long been the "property" of Guy Lombardo, leader of the quintessential sweet band. As expected, the customers received Goodman's swinging organization, with its uninhibited rhythms and assertive brass, in much the same manner as they would have welcomed more bad news from Wall Street. Somewhat unnerved, the band continued at the Roosevelt until about the last week of June or the first week of July. On June 6, while still at the Grill, the band took part in what is probably the most monumental recording session in history, cutting *fifty* titles for NBC on ETs.

George Simon's long, laudatory review of the Goodman band's Grill performance stated: "This is the band about which all the musikers have been raving—raving plenty, and rightfully so. Even with one or two minor defects, the outfit is the closest to perfection this reviewer has heard in many moons."[5]

Near the conclusion of the Roosevelt engagement, Bunny Berigan reappeared with Goodman's band, doubling from his CBS studio work. On June 25, Bunny made his first recordings with the band, cutting four titles at the Victor studios. Bunny cut four more titles with Goodman on July 1 when his trumpet solo was etched into recording history as the band immortalized "King Porter Stomp." Bunny was devoting as much of his time to the Goodman band as his CBS commitments would allow without jeopardizing his steady studio pay. Most Goodman bandsmen, in fact, banked as many dates as they could in preparation for a trip that could offer only uncertainty and excitement.

Critical acclaim for Bunny's playing continued to roll in. French critic Hugues Panassié cited "King Porter Stomp/Sometimes I'm Happy" as "undoubtedly the best record ever made by a white orchestra of fourteen musicians," and Simon revisited the Goodman

5. *Metronome*, LI (June, 1935).

band in his "Pick-ups" column: "Band was caught at rehearsal on its last visit to New York—picked up if that's possible. A great improvement in the brass—credit to addition of Bunny Berigan, considered by most to be today's greatest hot white trumpeter. . . . Finally a nice toast to another CBS studio outfit—Bunny's Blue Boys—They're mornings usually—Sound like seven men—Nothing but jam—They seem to be having the time of their lives—so did this listener."[6]

Goodman hardly needed the accolades of these writers to tell him what he already knew: nobody could make a band swing like Bunny. Clearly, Berigan would be making the trip to the West Coast, not Erwin. For his part, Bunny knew that he would be sacrificing money on Goodman's West Coast tour, even though, as Jess Stacy recalled, the trumpeter was the highest-paid member of the band at $200 per week.[7] Bunny could not resist the prospect of playing with such a unit, thinking that the musical experience and the trip west would provide a welcome break from the New York grind. Perhaps, too, the decision was colored by his late-May studio clash with Kate Smith. The pact was made; Bunny was hired to join the Goodman band on tour as soon as he was able.

Goodman's first stop was a five-day stand at the Stanley Theater in Pittsburgh. Some eventual band members did not play the Pittsburgh date. Trade journals still listed the Goodman band at the Roosevelt Grill as late as July 8, indicating a possible overlapping contract. With perhaps a one-nighter in between, the Goodman band in its full power assembled at the Valley Dale Ballroom in Columbus, Ohio, in mid-July. On this date Bunny, Krupa, and pianist Stacy all probably appeared together for the first time. Stacy came from Chicago to replace Frank Froeba, who was forced to leave because of family illness. Stacy's recollection was that he first joined the band at Jackson, Michigan, a few days later.[8]

Goodman recalled the early days of the trip:

Despite the Roosevelt fiasco, we started out on the road tour Willard had arranged. Because we weren't prosperous enough to afford a bus, we traveled in three or four automobiles. The first stop was Pittsburgh, for a week's engagement at a theater. The reaction was fair. In Columbus, Ohio, we did

6. Panassié, *Hot Jazz*, 252; *Metronome*, LI (July, 1935).
7. Stacy telephone interview.
8. *Ibid.*; Jack Smith research from Bozy White Outline.

a little better, but not much. I began to wonder what had happened to all those radio listeners who'd written us fan letters. None of them seemed to turn up, either, in Toledo, or at a couple of Michigan dates [at Walled Lake Casino and Jackson] we played. We had two good days in Milwaukee, principally because it was handy to Chicago—which has always had its jazz fans. But even Milwaukee was not very good.[9]

The band's Milwaukee appearances at the Modernistic Ballroom were on July 21 and 22. Reviewer Helen Oakley's comments about the Milwaukee appearances catch the essence of the impact Berigan had on the Goodman band:

Bunny Berigan was a revelation to me. Never having heard him in person before, even though well acquainted with his work on recordings, I was unprepared for such a tremendous thrill. The man is a master. He plays so well I doubt if I ever heard a more forceful trumpet, with unending ideas and possessed of that quality peculiar to both Teagarden and Armstrong, that of swinging the band as a whole at the outset and carrying it solidly along with him, without a letup, until the finish of his chorus. Bunny is, I believe, the only trumpeter comparable to Louis Armstrong.

(When read this statement during an interview more than fifty years later, Helen Oakley Dance, long an established jazz presence, would change little of her original assessment, nor was her enthusiasm for Berigan's playing dimmed.) The local newspaper noted Berigan's visit to Fox Lake on July 22, stating that Bunny was on a western tour with "an orchestra." "Then came Denver, and near desperation," recalled Goodman.[10]

The desperation was well-founded, and quickly found. As Goodman remembered, the booking called for four weeks at Elitch's Gardens, probably the largest, best-known dance emporium in the Rockies. Within moments of the band's beginning number on opening night, the manager burst out of his office complaining about all the noise. Customers were demanding their money back. This was not dance music as they knew it. Goodman characterized the first night as one of the most humiliating of his life. The audience and the manager wanted waltzes. Goodman improvised a solution: a rhythm section comprising vocalist Helen Ward on piano, Krupa, Harry Goodman on

9. Goodman, "That Old Gang of Mine," 29.
10. *Down Beat*, II (August 1, 1935); Fox Lake *Representative*, July 25, 1935, in Cullen Materials; Goodman, "That Old Gang of Mine," 29. Other details about the Goodman tour have been drawn from this article.

bass, and Allan Reuss on guitar, accompanied Bunny in playing a set of waltzes, rendered with as much schmaltz as anyone could hope for. This pleased the customers; it did not please the manager. He was paying for a full band and wanted it all!

Goodman quickly bought some stock arrangements, and the band limped through the engagement playing these stocks and as many small-ensemble waltzes as they could sneak in; their spirits sank with each night. Goodman was ready to quit, but Stacy and others encouraged him to "hang on until we get over the mountain." The contract for the Denver engagement probably guaranteed two weeks, with an option to extend. No extension was offered.

The next stop on the tour was a mid-August one-nighter at Grand Junction, Colorado. Several members of the band recalled that this was the date the world found out about the deaths of Will Rogers and Wiley Post, who had been flying in Alaska. Stacy recalled this gig as a poor one; he remembers that a net had been set up in front of the bandstand to catch the empty bottles that the audience might launch. The band pressed on to an engagement the next night in Salt Lake City, Utah, after a long, sleepless night of driving. The Coconut Grove ballroom there attracted the largest crowd of the tour thus far, and a more receptive one.[11]

Several of the musicians drank regularly as they traveled in the caravan of private automobiles. The most notable drinkers, as Stacy recalled, were Bunny and Nate Kazebier. These three rode in a car with Goodman and Mort Davis, the road manager. Only Stacy, Goodman, and Davis assumed the driving duties.

Two nights after Salt Lake City, after motoring 752 miles, the motley travelers arrived at McFadden's Ballroom in Oakland, California.[12] Goodman related:

> As soon as we got in sight of the place, I knew there'd been a mix-up in our bookings. The street in front of the auditorium was soldily packed with people. I was utterly disgusted, and was all set to send [booker] Willard [Alexander] a furious wire about the mix-up. "Imagine him making a mistake like this," I muttered.
>
> A guy was shaking my hand. "How do you like our turnout, Mr. Goodman?" He was the manager.

11. Stacy telephone interview; details on Goodman performances in Grand Junction and Salt Lake City from Bozy White interview with Goodman band member Dick Clark.

12. White Materials. White's meticulous research contradicts the memories of some that Sweet's, a better-known ballroom, was the locale for this date.

It was impossible for me to believe that so many people had come to hear us—I was still sure they had us confused with some other band. We set up our instruments sort of warily, half expecting the other band to walk in the door.

When the manager finally opened the doors to the public, the crowd surged inside and jammed up tight against the bandstand.

I thought: **If it's a mistake, it's a mistake. I might as well make it a real mistake.**

I called for "King Porter Stomp," one of Fletcher's real killers.

That number started off with Bunny Berigan playing a trumpet solo, the saxophones and rhythm behind him. Before he'd played four bars, there was such a yelling and stomping and carrying on in that hall I thought a riot had broken out. When I went into my solo, the noise was even louder. Finally the truth got through to me:

We were causing the riot.[13]

Other versions of this rite of swing's birth assign to Krupa a plea that if the band was destined to flop in Oakland, they should at least go down playing their own kind of music. Regardless, the crowd's reaction provided a much-needed elixir, albeit short-lived, for the weary Goodman players. The next night found them at Pismo Beach, 245 miles from Oakland and worlds away in terms of receptivity to the band. A gun-shy Goodman band then trudged to the Palomar Ball-room, Los Angeles, to begin a four-week engagement on August 21.

The scene at the Palomar resembled the one in Oakland. Goodman started the band out cautiously, recalled Krupa, who eventually petitioned the leader to allow the band, if necessary, to go down in a blaze of rhythm and brass and saxophones. When Goodman agreed and Berigan started out with "King Porter Stomp"—or "When Buddha Smiles," as Goodman averred—the audience responded wildly, catapulting the Goodman band into musical history and in the same instant crowning the new "King of Swing." Most of the audience stopped dancing and began to crowd around the bandstand, pressing ever closer, cheering, shouting, hailing this tired troupe in a manner normally reserved for conquering troops. Musicians were a large part of that crowd, and they made their appreciation known to the members of the band by their rapt attention as much as by their vocal support. As Jess Stacy remembered of the Palomar crowd: "They ate it up! There must have been ten thousand people there. Every musi-

13. Goodman, "That Old Gang of Mine," 30.

cian in L.A. was there. They loved it; they all stood in front of the bandstand. They were a little more dignified than the rest of the crowd, but they were *really* listening."[14]

This Palomar band, one of the most celebrated in jazz history, lined up in this way: Goodman, clarinet and leader; Ralph Muzzillo, Berigan, and Kazebier, trumpets; Jack Lacey (later replaced by Joe Harris) and Red Ballard, trombones; Hymie Shertzer, Dick Clark, Bill DePew, and Art Rollini, saxophones; Stacy, piano; Reuss, guitar; Harry Goodman, bass; Krupa, drums; Helen Ward and Harris, vocals. The unrestrained reception accorded the band by local musicians greatly excited Goodman's band; the wild public reaction was a total surprise. As this reaction grew to general frenzy in the succeeding months, the "swing era" dawned, its heat and light intensifying by the week. The West Coast's wild, enthusiastic acceptance of Goodman's music is generally attributed to the unique scheduling of Goodman's pre-tour *Let's Dance* broadcasts. On these, Goodman had deliberately saved the band's hottest numbers for the program's last hour. In the eastern time zone, only devotees who could stay awake were still listening at 1:30 A.M. In the Pacific zone, this third hour segment aired during prime time, and the entire show was heard early enough to develop a broad-based audience, but with a heavy concentration of young listeners. In addition, in the Los Angeles area, and particularly in Hollywood, a large music and jazz community was growing, its development due in no small measure to the increasing role of music in film. Recognizing the great fascination the Goodman band provided for the local musicians, the Palomar management designated Monday nights as "musicians' nights" at 3rd and Vermont. They extended Goodman's four-week engagement to seven, during which all attendance records were broken. Goodman's band probably drew more than 200,000 listeners and dancers for the seven weeks.

One further reason helps explain the Goodman band's wild acceptance on the West Coast. Given the quality of sound-reproducing equipment in the mid-1930s, the difference between a radio broadcast and a live performance could be measured only in titanic terms. Microphones were primitive and failed to gather all of the sound emanating from the instruments. Cross-country transmission lines were

14. Stacy telephone interview.

crude, and over a distance they often delivered as much static and other noise as they did music. Further, 1935 radios, even when receiving a good signal, boasted neither the circuitry nor the speakers to reproduce sound with fidelity. The same limitations applied to recorded music. What the California fans had been hearing on the *Let's Dance* broadcasts was but a feeble approximation of the thrilling sound of the Goodman band. When that live sound, complete with Goodman's stiletto-like solos, Berigan's fiery, searing tones, and Krupa's pulsating rhythms—when that *live* sound burst upon the Palomar patrons, they could not restrain themselves. As they crushed ever closer to the bandstand to get inside the music, as they yelled and screeched their delight, many knew they had discovered something new and important. Most knew that this music made them *feel* different, more alive. They may have sensed that they were witnesses to, and participants in, the making of musical history.

Many of the band members took advantage of the ambiance provided by California's climate. As he had in Denver, Bunny played a lot of golf in Los Angeles, frequently with Muzzillo, sometimes with Shertzer, Davis, Ballard, or Lacey. Connor says that on September 25, Lacey returned to New York to resume his studio job, thus missing out on the first BG recording date to that time in Hollywood, on September 27.[15] Harris took over Lacey's trombone chair for that session. One of the tunes recorded at that session was Gordon Jenkins' beautiful "Good-Bye," which Goodman adopted as his closing theme. Berigan's plaintive, muted trumpet, heard in an answering figure to the main melody, makes this recording memorable.

Within a few days of the recording date, Berigan said good-bye to the Goodman band permanently and flew to Wisconsin, meeting Donna and Patty in Fox Lake, where he remained for about two weeks. Various stories exist explaining how Bunny transported his trumpet back to New York. Connor and others are convinced that he mailed it in an unlocked case to a friend in New York, calmly arriving after the Fox Lake sojourn to reclaim his horn and his place at CBS.[16] Harry Geller, a Los Angles trumpeter, took over Kazebier's third chair after Kazebier moved into Bunny's "hot" chair. This arrangement prevailed as the band finished out its Palomar run on October 1,

15. D. Russell Connor, *Benny Goodman: Listen to His Legacy* (Metuchen, N.J., 1988), 54.
16. *Ibid.*

played some one-nighters, winged through a short stay at the Paramount in Los Angeles, and then moved to a celebrated eight-month stand at the Congress Hotel in Chicago that brought them more adulation from the public and the music fraternity. Taking over once more the chair that had been Bunny's, Erwin replaced Geller in Chicago.

Thus ended the formal Berigan-Goodman relationship. At bottom, they greatly admired one another's musicianship. Each was able to ignite the other, and those around him, in a musical setting, providing an exhilaration seldom found elsewhere. Beyond that, the men were quite different. Goodman was organized and purposeful; Berigan made little attempt to influence events. Goodman became a strong, often difficult leader; Berigan was ever the sideman, the players' pal. Goodman put business first, pleasure later; Berigan's business *was* pleasure. No one but Benny played solo clarinet in Goodman's band; all musicians were given solo space in Berigan's band, including many fine trumpeters. And, of course, Goodman did not punish himself with alcohol as Berigan did.

Stacy summed up the Berigan-Goodman relationship in this way: "Berigan didn't like Goodman at all; in fact, you could say he hated him. Benny put up with Bunny because of the way he played."[17]

Goodman was parsimonious with praise through the years, doling it out as though only a finite supply existed. This seems especially true regarding Bunny, and the paucity is the more striking considering their musical affinity. Perhaps Goodman felt disappointment when he contemplated Bunny's wasted potential, a reaction shared by many. In his *Collier's* article, Goodman did slip in a description of Bunny Berigan as "one of the all-time greats on trumpet." Perhaps Goodman's trumpet-playing brother, Irving, best expressed the leader's feelings: Berigan "was with Benny only a short period, but *whenever he was present it was another story* [emphasis added]. There haven't been that many guys could electrify Benny, but Bunny was certainly one of them."[18]

In the short time they were together in this context, Goodman and Berigan collaborated on several memorable recordings and a number of air checks, fortunately preserved. More than that, Berigan truly

17. Stacy telephone interview.
18. Stanley Dance, *The World of Earl Hines* (New York, 1977), 196.

helped to propel, not only the Goodman band, but the whole country into the swing era. Again quoting Stacy: "Bunny was the mainstay. With his reputation and ability he helped sell the band. He played first trumpet as well as solo. He was something else!"[19] Berigan's role in the Goodman band's success and the mania it created can scarcely be overstated.

19. Stacy telephone interview.

13

Night Song

Song recorded November 28, 1938
by Bunny Berigan and His Orchestra

Following the sometimes-grueling, sometimes-exhilarating trip with Goodman, Bunny's stopover in Fox Lake once more failed to provide him with the relaxation that might have been helpful. Donna's relationship with the Berigan family, never good, had deteriorated further when she had again stayed with them while Bunny played the Goodman tour. Bunny arrived home on about October 1. Ever the player, Bunny borrowed horns and sat in with a few bands in Madison before returning to reclaim his studio position. He, Donna, and Pat left for New York on about October 16, 1935.[1]

Bunny wasted little time getting back into full circulation. He began working again at the CBS radio studios, principally with the early shows. CBS reactivated Bunny's Blue Boys and gave them a regular time slot. Bunny also rejoined the Instrumentalists almost immediately. On December 4, he recorded with Bud Freeman's Windy City Five, a session that produced four sides that are still highly treasured. Soon thereafter he backed a session with Mildred Bailey that included Johnny Hodges on alto sax, Teddy Wilson on piano, and Grachan Moncur on bass. They recorded four titles, among them "Honeysuckle Rose" and "Downhearted Blues." On December 13, Bunny Berigan and His Blue Boys cut four titles at the Decca studios for EMI, marking the first time Bunny had recorded as a leader. Among these cuts were "Chicken and Waffles" and "I'm Coming, Vir-

1. Fox Lake *Representative*, October 17, 1935, in Cullen Materials. Information on recording dates given below from research by Bozy White, in White Outline.

ginia." These eight sides find Bunny in excellent, relaxed form, obviously enjoying his playing companions.

Bunny returned to an exciting New York nightclub scene. Red Norvo and Roy Eldridge were alternating at the Famous Door, sometimes abetted by Mildred Bailey's vocal sitting-in. The Onyx Club—called the "rich man's Plunkett's" by Eddie Condon—featured the wacky duo of Eddie Farley and Mike Riley on trumpet and trombone, respectively. Actually decent musicians, these coleaders felt it necessary to throw pies, disrobe one another, and engage in whatever bizarre behavior might attract business to the club. At the Hickory House, trumpeter Manone and his group performed. Before the end of the year, Norvo and Manone changed places, and Teddy Wilson moved to the Famous Door as intermission pianist.

As his recording activities in the first five or six weeks of that year indicate, 1936 might well be regarded as Bunny's optimum year. He began on January 3 with a session for Red McKenzie and the Mound City Blue Blowers, producing "The Broken Record" and a cover for the runaway Riley-Farley hit, "The Music Goes Round and Round." Recording again with the Blue Blowers on January 8, Bunny participated in what *Variety*, in its February 5, 1936, issue, chronicled as a record-setting session: four masters in two hours and fifteen minutes. On January 15, Bunny cut four titles that featured vocalist Bob Terry and harpist Casper Reardon. On January 18, Bunny's trumpet voice was prominent and potent on four sides with Chick Bullock as vocalist, and two days later he recorded two more sides with Red McKenzie designated as leader. On January 22, he was probably present for four titles with Jack Shilkret as leader, and on January 24, Bunny was in the orchestra to record accompaniment for Harry Richman, a popular vocalist. The next day, Dick Robertson was the vocalist-leader as Bunny played on six masters. One day later it was Bob Howard's turn to serve as leader and vocalist for the four titles recorded. Included in this band were Artie Shaw, clarinet, and Babe Russin, tenor sax. On January 29, Dick Stabile, alto saxist and leader, employed Bunny in backing vocalist Billy Wilson for four titles.

Bunny reached a career milestone when, on February 4, he recorded two sides with his mentor, Louis Armstrong. Louis sang on "I'm Putting All My Eggs in One Basket" and "Yes, Yes, My, My." The use of an all-white backing for Armstrong drew comments in the trade journals. A February 5 *Variety* article cited Berigan and the In-strumentalists as "standouts for the noon hour." The next day, Bunny played on four sides with McKenzie and with Dick Robertson. February 10 saw Bunny making two more sides with Bob Howard.

A new phase of Bunny's career began at about this time, probably on Monday, February 10, when he began playing at the Famous Door. *Variety* covered the event:

> Chicago Reunion—Red McKenzie/Eddie Condon, the team that made history in Chicago for OKeh records in 1927, are cutting riffs and licks at the Famous Door, NYC. This six piece outfit headlines Bunny Berigan, king of the Cornet, with Paul Ricci on Tenor, Joe Bushkin on piano, Stoolmaker [*sic*] slapping the bass. For their latest specialty, Berigan steps back to allow Joe Bushkin to trumpet and vocalize in "I'm Gonna Sit Right Down and Write Myself a Letter." A bunch of musicians' musicians, McKenzie and Condon are bringing back the old days when the professionals flocked to the Door.[2]

McKenzie was a St. Louis native, a former jockey (by virtue of having broken both arms in that pursuit), a virtuoso of the paper-covered comb, a part-time singer, part-time fast-talking entrepreneur, and the organizer of several versions of the Mound City Blue Blowers. He and Condon, a banjoist, guitarist, promoter, part-time singer, and fast-talker, had met in Chicago in 1927. Almost by accident, McKenzie had arranged for Condon and cornetist Jimmy McPartland, saxists Frank Teschemacher and Bud Freeman, pianist Joe Sullivan, bassist Jim Lanigan, and drummer Krupa to cut some records. Instantly successful, the early sides propelled this group of relative unknowns into the consciousness of listeners who were even mildly interested in jazz. McKenzie took his Mound City Blue Blowers to New York, followed soon by Condon and most of the others. They began playing at the Onyx with Riley and Farley. Condon tells of his disgust with the pie-throwing antics of Riley and Farley, which he considered demeaning to the music he respected. When he refused to take part in the circus, Condon was fired. He related: "McKenzie and I moved to an opposition club across the street, the Famous Door. It occupied the old quarters of the Onyx, with a down-stairs room added. Billie Holiday, the singer, had preceded us, with Teddy Wilson on piano."[3] When Condon and McKenzie moved to the

2. *Variety*, February 12, 1936, in White Materials.
3. Condon, *We Called It Music*, 240.

Famous Door in 1936, Berigan beat as the club's musical heart. Any recognition that Bunny had not already garnered within the music community quickly came his way now. Joe Bushkin, a brash, street-wise New Yorker, had made his record debut only a month earlier; as a relief pianist, he quickly commanded peer and public attention. For nineteen-year-old Bushkin, the opportunity to play at the Famous Door came about unexpectedly:

It had to be January, February of 1936; I remember it being cold. My dad had a barber shop up in East Harlem, and the pay phone rang. I had been playing around town, different gigs, and had just made a recording with Art Karle, Frankie Newton, and Mezz [Mezzrow]. George Zack, a pretty good pianist who had great big hands like Fats [Waller], got drunk and fell apart on Bunny's opening night at The Door. Anyway, my dad answers the phone—he's working late in the shop—and it's Eddie Condon calling for me. He says, "Can you get your ass down here in a hurry?" I says, "I'll get there as soon as I can," and I asked my Pop to drive me down there. So he just slapped a note on the door and just closed the door. In those days no one ever bothered locking the doors. What are they going to steal, a barber chair? It was a different world then, and maybe that's why the music came out the way it did. There was a basic honesty and openness. It still exists in some places. Anyway, dad got me down to the club and I played the gig. I guess they called me because I had been playing intermission piano in some of the places and they were pretty sure I'd know the tunes. And that's how I began playing with Bunny.[4]

Bushkin and Condon had become good friends, and while Condon sometimes became defensive about the pianist's lack of technical and reading skills, he never had to apologize for Bushkin's innate swinging ability. Bushkin related:

At the beginning I was having a little trouble and Bunny says to Eddie, "He plays the middle part of 'Talk of the Town' on 'Please Don't Talk About Me when I'm Gone.' There's a little confusion goin' on here; you better straighten it out. We better get a guy who can keep track of the tune we're playing." And Eddie tells Bunny, "No, Bunny, this guy's all right. The *time* is there. We'll straighten the chords out." But what had happened was that Bunny's playing was so sensational—you know, this heavy company I was thrown in suddenly—it rattled me. I was tryin' to be so careful, and some-times tryin' doesn't help. But Eddie stuck with me and he worked with me. I

---

4. Joe Bushkin, interview with the author, June 26, 1985, tape in author's possession. Subsequent quotations from Bushkin are taken from this interview. In addition to playing this stint on 52nd Street, Bushkin made several recordings with Berigan. He also played in Bunny's big band through most of 1938–39. They were reunited briefly with the Tommy Dorsey band in 1940.

wanna tell you: anybody who comes up to me and puts down Eddie Condon as a guitar player, they get a battle from me. Eddie knew his stuff. Eddie Condon is the one who set up the chord changes for "I Can't Get Started," the turnaround and the ending chord changes. The night we tried that tune out, it didn't have that setup.

For a while I was playing intermission piano, too. Then after a while they got Teddy Wilson to play intermissions. The place had two floors, with no business on either floor. Upstairs they had people like Billie Holiday and Roy Eldridge. Imagine what went on. Sunday afternoons we had jam sessions—Fats Waller, Bessie Smith—it was absolutely unreal!

Condon takes up the narrative:

The club took its name from a small door made of plain wood on which visitors scribbled their names. The signatures I remember as memorable were those of the musicians who came to the jam sessions we held on Sunday afternoons. We didn't charge admission; the audience sat around buying drinks while the best jazz men in the country played for their own amusement. Bessie Smith was in town for a while; she came over and sang: "Baby Won't You Please Come Home," "Mama's Got the Blues," "I'm Wild About That Thing," "The Gin House Blues," "Dirty No Gooder's Blues," and "Nobody Knows You When You're Down and Out." She was still the great Bessie; hearing her magnificent voice complain about the sadness of living made life a lot easier to bear. On that Sunday afternoon Bessie seemed immortal; she had one more year to live. Mildred Bailey was there that day but she refused to sing. She was right; no one could follow Bessie. . . .

We used a saxophone and string bass and got along without drums. Lee Wiley, a girl from Oklahoma, dropped in to sing occasionally. The manager, Jim Doane, liked our music and let us play it without interruption.[5]

Reports of Bunny's tasteful, muted accompaniment to Smith's blues singing fanned outward, enhancing his already-solid reputation as a player who could enliven any jazz session. But the strain of his schedule was beginning to tax Bunny despite his cast-iron lip and hearty physique. CBS studio work occupied his mornings and afternoons, beginning at about 10:00 A.M. And Bunny continued to record with a variety of groups at Decca. Increasingly, Decca and Vocalion organized recording sessions around Bunny, specifying him as the leader; representative of this recording era is the February 24, four-title inaugural session of Bunny Berigan and His Boys.[6] Additionally, the Famous Door required a forty-two-hour-per-week schedule, including

5. Condon, *We Called It Music*, 241, 240.
6. Rust, *Jazz Records, 1897–1942*, I, 122.

the Sunday jam sessions. *Variety, Metronome,* and *Down Beat* carried numerous reviews and laudatory comments about the Famous Door's McKenzie group and usually singled out Bunny for special praise. One *Metronome* article warned, however, that because of his heavy schedule, Bunny occasionally played less than his best.[7]

In addition to radio studio work, recording sessions, and the Famous Door job, special events claimed pieces of Bunny's time and talent. At one such event, the Advertising Club of New York sponsored a February 21 dance at the Hotel Shelton, featuring the Red Norvo and McKenzie groups and other jazz stars. On March 12, Bunny played a "What Is Swing?" broadcast. It featured Marshall Stearns, the president of the United Hot Clubs of America, an umbrella group for the various local clubs with a jazz interest. He joined with K. K. Hansen in an attempt to discuss examples of swing in a scholarly fashion. Berigan led the group that provided the examples. This broadcast may be best remembered for the pretentious explanations and for those musicians who did not appear. Louis Armstrong and Mildred Bailey backed out at the last minute; Nat Brusiloff, who had rehearsed the house band, became ill just before air time, and Gordon Jenkins was called to step in. The music was nonetheless creditable, as an aircheck recording demonstrates.

The Famous Door group played another notable special gig on March 15 at Hoagy Carmichael's wedding reception; they were hired because the groom thought they were "the best band in the country." George Gershwin graced the guest list and played a special musical part, as did Carmichael's mother. Bushkin recalled some of the celebration's details:

It's an afternoon wedding. We show up—the party was right opposite the Blackstone Hotel on 52nd Street right near Lexington. Davie Tough played it with us; Davie and Bud Freeman, Bunny, Morty Stuhlmaker, Eddie Condon, and myself. We're waiting in front of Hoagy's house for the wedding to end, and we can't get in. Davie's got all his drum stuff there, and the guests are starting to arrive from Saint Bartholomew's. Finally, Hoagy shows up in a hansom cab with his bride. He very grandly gets out of the hansom cab, and as he extends his hand to his bride, the driver gets out of the cab too. Then the fuckin' horse took off with the bride in it. That horse is now on Third

7. *Metronome*, LII (April, 1936), 21.

Avenue someplace. Now a bunch of the guests are running down to Third Avenue with the bride standing in the cab yelling, hysterical! They finally nail this fuckin' horse and walk him back to the apartment.

Now we get in and set up our instruments, and when the couple comes into the room we're swingin' "Here Comes the Bride," and everybody's laughing in a hysterical mood. We played all the Gershwin tunes and Hoagy's songs. Gershwin—I can still see his face right in front of me—he couldn't believe what he was hearing. We did "They Can't Take That Away from Me," "Strike Up the Band," " 'S Wonderful." We were swingin' that party backwards. He came over to me and said, "By God! I never heard my music played that way." That was a hell of a compliment. . . .

Then people asked him to play, and he said he'd do some things from his new show. He played "Bess, You Is My Woman," "Porgy," and "Summertime" and knocked everybody on their ass with this stuff. He looked to be in great shape, but it wasn't much more than a year when that brain tumor cut him down. It was something to hear him play his own stuff! We didn't let Hoagy play, 'cause he couldn't play shit on the piano, as good a songwriter as he was. But Hoagy's mother—he should have inherited her piano talent— she played great! Hoagy's dad was sick and back in Indiana. They called him up and she played "Maple Leaf Rag" for him over the phone, and the band did one number for him.

Hoagy paid us for the gig; you know we were playing for food on the table. But what a party. He had a bar from here to First Avenue. With Berigan there! Hoagy was tuned in to Bunny and Bud and our kind of music and he stayed with it through the years. He was a great fan.

At about the time of the Carmichael wedding in mid-March, Bunny decided that he could not continue his pace and maintain all his musical commitments. Seven thousand New York musicians were out of work, but Bunny had the luxury of deciding which of his jobs to relinquish. He left the CBS studios. The unhappy task of filling Bunny's chair there fell to trumpeter Gordon "Chris" Griffin, long a Berigan admirer, who felt that he had some large shoes to fill. Bunny's longtime "ace in the hole," the solid financial underpinning that CBS provided, became a part of his past.

Recording and club dates now occupied Bunny's professional life fully. In the April 4, 1936, *Billboard* listing of top records, Berigan's name dominated the first three places. The first two were by Bunny Berigan and His Boys: "It's Been So Long" and "I'd Rather Lead a Band." Third place was claimed by "Don't Count Your Kisses," a tune that Bunny recorded with McKenzie. On April 3, Bunny waxed the first of three different recordings of the song with which he is permanently associated, "I Can't Get Started." This recording bore the Red McKenzie imprimatur and featured Red's vocal, backed by Berigan, Al Philburn, Frank Signorelli, Carmen Mastren, Stan King, Sid Trucker, clarinet, and Pete Peterson, bass. Just ten days later, Bunny assembled the Famous Door crew, plus—probably—Artie Shaw on clarinet and Dave Tough on drums, and recorded the same song as part of a four-tune session of Bunny Berigan and His Boys, this time with Bunny himself on the vocal. Using the Condon chord structure Bushkin alluded to, this version featured Bunny's trumpet in a precursor to his classic August, 1937, recording. This second version received immediate critical acclaim, earning a "Best Sides of 1936" designation by *Metronome*.[8]

Two of Condon's more vivid recollections of the Famous Door days involve Berigan. Condon delights in retelling the story of his burst pancreas, an affliction that was nearly always fatal at that time. Bushkin and McKenzie nursed him for several hours before physicians completed their diagnosis and attempted risky surgery. After the operation, a fever of 106 degrees and problems with blood transfusions complicated his recovery. Condon continued:

The fever lasted for three days and three nights. I was rubbed with whiskey and wrapped in hot blankets. When McKenzie found out about the whiskey massages he brought a bottle from the Famous Door.
"What's that for?" Miss Roach, the nurse, asked.
"It's to rub Mr. Condon with," Mr. McKenzie said.
Miss Roach sniffed. "We only use bonded whiskey!" she said.
McKenzie stared. "To rub a guy with?" he said.
He opened the bottle and he and Berigan and Bushkin drank it.
Later, after leaving the hospital to convalesce, we stopped at the Famous Door to say good-by to the boys. Tommy Dorsey, Bud Freeman and Dave Tough were there; as we came in they were sitting in with the band, tearing the clothes off "Dinah." [A friend] was fascinated. "I've never heard music like that," he said to me. "What is it?" I told him. It's amazing how many North Americans have never heard jazz, I thought.
Berigan came over and put a twenty-dollar bill in my hand. "I owe you this," he said. "I thought if I kept it until you got out you'd have a better chance of making it." I thanked him. I was broke, as usual. "This is the best hypodermic I've had in three weeks," I said. Bunny smiled. "Someday I may

8. *Metronome*, LIII (January, 1937), 23.

be in the same spot myself," he said. He was. A few years later he died in [the same hospital].[9]

Donna gave birth to a second healthy daughter, Joyce Berigan, on April 22. Meanwhile, trade journal articles reported that business at the Famous Door had improved during the McKenzie group's tenure. On May 9, Condon and Bushkin arrived at the Door as usual. As Bushkin recalled: "Eddie used to like to stay with me. I was still living with my parents on 103rd Street on the East Side, and he loved my mother's cooking. In good weather we'd walk to work—from 103rd to 52nd Street. We'd put on our tuxes and start out early, about 6:30. Those were great walks. We got a lot out of those times, all the talking and the therapy. I'll never forget it. We walked to work this night and get to the Famous Door and there's a sign on the door, with a chain: closed by sheriff." Because of a lack of paying customers, the establishment ended in bankruptcy. Undaunted, the musicians merely reconvened within about a week at the 18 Club, across 52nd Street.

At about the same time, on May 24, the new Onyx Club, at 72 West 52nd Street, sponsored a concert at the Imperial Theater. Billed as the world's first swing concert, the printed program listed Red Norvo and His Swingtette, with Mildred Bailey; Stuff Smith, the hot violinist, and His Onyx Club Swing Gang, with Jonah Jones on trumpet and Cozy Cole on drums; Bunny Berigan and His 18 Club Swing Gang, which included Artie Shaw on clarinet replacing the ill tenorman Forrest Crawford; Casper Reardon; and Tommy Dorsey and His Clambake "7," with Bud Freeman, clarinetist Joe Dixon, trumpeter Max Kaminsky, Dave Tough, Carmen Mastren, bassist Gene Traxler, pianist Dick Jones, and vocalist Edythe Wright. The standing-room-only crowd also heard segments by Artie Shaw's unique string ensemble, a Paul Whiteman group, and a closing set by Louis Armstrong. Adjudged a financial, artistic, and critical success, this huge concert pioneered a method of marketing jazz music that is still observed in the jazz festivals of today.

Bushkin remembered that some of the 52nd Street gang would sometimes try to get Bunny interested in smoking "tea" rather than drinking. While this did not have any lasting appeal to Bunny, sev-

9. Condon, *We Called It Music*, 244, 245–46.

eral musicians remember that Bunny did, indeed, make a concerted effort (or perhaps several abortive ones) to curtail his drinking and smoking. At about this time, John Hammond wrote as part of an assessment of Berigan's playing, "The wagon *agrees so well with Bunny* [emphasis added] that he is becoming increasingly more consistent."[10] Whether moved by the added responsibility of a second child, or frightened by observing some of the obvious physical consequences of his smoking, drinking, and fast pace, or inspired to preserve his health for trysts with singer Lee Wiley, or persuaded by common good sense—whatever the motivation, Bunny did make at least a passing attempt to curtail his two-to-three-pack-a-day smoking habit and his alcohol intake. In any case, this attempt at exercising control evaporated into the fast flow of events as Bunny's career raced forward.

The success of colleagues such as the Dorseys, first collectively, then individually, and of Goodman and Miller in fronting their own bands caused Bunny to visualize a Bunny Berigan Orchestra. Why would Bunny be tempted to forsake both the financial security and the musical satisfaction he had attained? Perhaps he heard from those around him or from his inner voice: "Those guys are no better musicians than I am. In fact, if it wasn't for me, Benny's band might have folded. I helped Miller get started on records. I've had all the studio experience, know all about making records. Lots of guys would like to be in a band I front. Lots of bands out there can't hold a candle to some of the stuff we could do. Not to brag, but I can play hot trumpet with anybody out there, and I know what to do with a ballad too." This dream received encouragement from some of those same leaders but apparently not from Donna, who was emphatic: "I didn't want him to have his own band. No. I wanted him to stay where he was. He made more than $500 a week in the studios, and the recording— he made good at that. We'd been married five years when he decided—they talked him into getting his own band, and I didn't want him to. I figured if he did—I could sort of feel those things. I just thought something's going to happen." Perhaps during the last part of the McKenzie Group's Famous Door run, certainly during its stand at

10. *Down Beat*, III (May 1, 1936).

the 18 Club, and despite Donna's foreboding, Bunny began rehearsing a full band that bore his name.

In the same article cited above, Hammond reported an important Berigan career milestone:

Bunny Berigan is now rehearsing a big band of his own, under the sponsorship of Artie Michaud, who was Benny Goodman's first manager. Most of the guys are young and unknown, but the names of Irving Goodman, Joe Lipman, Bob Flanagan, Tom Fellini and Bollinger [Art Drelinger?] may be familiar to some of you. Bunny recently made some more Vocalions, best of which is a Vernon Duke tune from the current follies, "I Can't Get Started," in which he plays magnificently and sings surprisingly well. . . . If there are any better trumpet players in the world I'd certainly be surprised. He deserves either to have or be in the greatest band in the country.[11]

Hammond's announcement in this article proved accurate, and while this first edition of a Berigan big band survived for a relatively short time, it did thrust Bunny into the role of leader. The band played a few club dates and some dances, perhaps at nearby colleges. Its members served as the nucleus of Bunny Berigan and His Studio Orchestra on July 20, when that group recorded twenty tunes on ETs for Thesaurus Transcriptions. Also that summer Bunny found time to play for about a month in the big band of Red Norvo at the Commodore Hotel.

On June 13, what is widely regarded as the most influential—certainly the most venturesome—jazz radio program of all time made its debut. The *Saturday Night Swing Club* (SNSC), broadcast over WABC from 8:00 to 8:30, represented a bold move by CBS. Its premise was simple: present the best available jazz musicians in an unsponsored, relaxed half hour of pure music, making the program available to the widest possible audience of musicians and jazz listeners. The printed program commemorating the first anniversary broadcast provides further insight:

Back on June 13th, 1936, when the so-called swing craze was already doomed by critics, when a song was being published called "The Death of Swing" . . . the Columbia Network went on the air with the first weekly session of The Saturday Night Swing Club. The avowed intention of these weekly sessions was to bring to the large audience of musicians and swing

11. *Ibid.*

fans of the country, music of known and unknown swing artists playing in the informal atmosphere of a musician's own swing session. How "large" this audience really was, constituted the grounds for considerable skepticism on the part of many. Tonight's anniversary celebrates a year of weekly sessions unashamedly devoted to hot music, during which listeners from not only the United States, Canada and Mexico, but short wave enthusiasts from England to New Zealand have indicated their enthusiasm in such fashion that no longer does there exist any doubt as to how "large" an audience good swing enjoys.

Our premiere session, June 13th, 1936, went on the air with Frank Trumbauer, Lee Wiley, Red Norvo and Bunny Berigan as featured soloists and with Paul Douglas as swing commentator. Subsequent sessions, featuring Berigan as trumpet soloist brought such names as [a list of seventy-one individuals or groups, representing the epitome of then-current jazz artists, followed here. See Appendix A.]

To these talented musicians and vocalists who have enthusiastically contributed their time and talents, The Saturday Night Swing Club owes whatever success it enjoys.

Jazz, played by talented performers, has proven its permanency as a form of valid American musical expression. We like to think of "swing" as a present day style of jazz interpretation. As long as real artists in the medium are allowed to interpret it, swing, or some more advanced style, will permanently serve to retain the jazz idiom . . . and as long as there are fans like yourselves who want to hear it, The Saturday Night Swing Club hopes it will be able to do its part.[12]

The SNSC did its part every Saturday night until 1939. A full studio band, comprising the usual excellent musicians, provided the backing for the unending parade of jazz greats. From the beginning, Bunny was the impelling musical force behind the show, also serving as a magnet attracting other top players and singers. At least one publication credited Marshall Stearns and the United Hot Clubs of America with exerting considerable pressure on CBS to convince it of the viability of such a program.[13] Several outstanding leaders served as musical director for the show as it ran its course: Leith Stevens, Mark Warnow, Fred Rich, Lud Gluskin, and Johnny Augustine. Mel Allen also served as "swing commentator."

The first anniversary show, on June 12 to 13, 1937, featured Duke

---

12. Jacket notes, Soundcraft LP-1013, *The Saturday Night Swing Club—On the Air*. This is a recording of the June 12–13, 1937, first anniversary broadcast of the *Saturday Night Swing Club*. These notes reprinted the program from that historic broadcast.

13. *Billboard*, December 26, 1936.

Ellington, Casper Reardon, the Raymond Scott quintet, the Adrian Rollini trio, Kay Thompson, Berigan's band, remote from the Hotel Pennsylvania, Glen Gray and the Casa Loma Orchestra from the Palomar in Los Angeles, Les Lieber, and the Quintet of the Hot Club of France, featuring Django Reinhardt and Stephane Grappelly, via short wave from Montmarte, Paris.[14] It is preserved on record.

Concurrent with the first SNSC broadcast, Bunny returned to the CBS studios, forsaking his gig with the McKenzie group at 18 Club. Stu Pletcher, previously with Red Norvo, assumed Bunny's club chair. Whether the advent of the SNSC and Bunny's rejoining CBS represented more than coincidental timing is not known. It is certainly possible that with the SNSC program pending, studio executives were able to attract Bunny with a good offer. His was an increasingly recognizable name (albeit still frequently misspelled), and the knowledgeable audience CBS sought for this show wanted to hear Bunny. Unquestionably, Bunny's appearance on the new show assured its artistic success. Further, the pay at the 18 Club could in no way match that at CBS, though Bunny's total earnings must have been more than adequate. The nightclubs' assets—the embracing live audience and the opportunity to play the kind of jazz Bunny loved—had been somewhat devalued by nearly a half year of the punishing schedule of 52nd Street life wedged in with the other activities. His reconciliation with CBS held the promise for Bunny of an increased number of musically satisfying radio shows.

Meanwhile, Bunny's recording activities continued richly. From the end of June to early January, Bunny participated in six excellent sessions led by Dick McDonough. On July 10, one day before her first appearance on the SNSC, Billie Holiday recorded the first sides on which she was designated as leader. On this session, and for her second session in September, Holiday chose Bunny as one of her accompanists. Perhaps this selection was made with the aid of Bernie Hanighen, a friend who was producing records for Vocalion.[15] Each session produced four masters, with "Did I Remember?" "No Regrets," "Summertime," and "Billie's Blues" providing the vehicles for the

14. Jacket notes, Soundcraft LP-1013.
15. Melvin Maddocks, *Giants of Jazz: Billie Holiday* (Alexandria, Va., 1979), 35. This is from the booklet accompanying the Time-Life album.

first session's great singing and sensitive accompaniment. Bushkin played piano on the July session:

I remember that one. It was hot and the Vocalion studio didn't have any air conditioning. Cozy Cole was sitting there in his—you'd call it a tank top today. We were all sweating—Shaw, Bunny, Dick McDonough, Pete Peterson, and myself—that was the band. The way the piano was located in the studio, Billie was facing me and had her back to Cozy. I remember being so intrigued by Billie. If I looked past her, I had a view of Cozy sitting there, and the sweat was just pouring off this man. It was like he was in a rainstorm all by himself in the corner of a studio on the eighth floor of a building. I kept thinking, jeez, it must be raining out. It was that hot. But we got through those sides, and they sure don't sound like we were suffering. They're played today and they sound very organized. By the way, that was one of Bunny's great talents: he absolutely had an arranger's mind when he played. For example, if he played something off the track of the song, his compositional mind would have him repeat the goof in several different areas or keys. He'd cover it up and make it sound planned.

SNSC earned favorable reviews in all the trade magazines and from those newspaper reporters who concerned themselves in any way with jazz. *Metronome* declared of four sides that Bunny made in a session with Frank Froeba on August 27: "This quartet of sides is notable if for no other reason than Bunny Berigan's best record playing in many months, if not of all time. That's especially so in ['Whatcha Gonna Do When There Ain't No Swing?']. . . . For sheer consistent brilliance it's Berigan who takes honors on all four sides."[16] In August, Lee Wiley became a regular feature on SNSC.

By September, Bunny was again rehearsing a big band, similar in instrumentation to the one he organized earlier in the year but with more carefully selected personnel. Joe Lipman, pianist and arranger for Shaw, was also doing arrangements for Bunny's band. At the same time, Bunny found himself dazzled by another prospect: motion picture director Vincente Minnelli had conceived the idea for staging and producing a lavish musical comedy featuring Beatrice Lillie, Bert Lahr, Reginald Gardiner, and Mitzi Mayfair. The music for *The Show Is On* would include songs by Rodgers and Hart, Dietz and Schwartz, the Gershwins, Harold Arlen, Yip Harburg, Herman Hupfeld, Carmichael, and Duke. For perhaps the first time ever, a stage show

16. *Metronome*, LIII (November, 1936).

would feature jazz. Minnelli selected Berigan, Sonny Lee, Cole, McKenzie, and clarinetist Milt Yaner as the starring jazzmen. Bunny was to be heavily featured in one of the show's big numbers, and his name received prominent display in the advertisements preceding the show, which was scheduled to open in Boston before its debut in New York. Technical difficulties caused Boston's Shubert Theater opening to be postponed. Although reviewers spoke favorably of the show, they deemed it too long. Perhaps more important, Minnelli's grand scheme for Bunny's featured number never worked as envisioned. After a few performances, Bunny and the entire jazz contingent found themselves back in New York, out of the show.[17]

Back at CBS, Bunny appeared as a guest on SNSC with some regularity, but rehearsals with a group of his own commanded much of his attention. On November 23, a small group cut three titles at Brunswick. This session involved the rhythm section from the clubs, with George Wettling replacing Tough—who had joined Tommy Dorsey—on drums. Altoist Toots Mondello, tenorman Babe Russin, and trombonist Red Jessup joined in what was to be a much more highly structured session than Bunny had ever led in the past. The arrangements Bunny had prepared for the session were somehow destroyed. One version quoted Bushkin as saying that one of Bunny's daughters took them to school. Since the elder, Pat, was only four at the time, this seems unlikely. Donna recalled that Bunny was angry at the girls for tearing up the arrangements while playing. Bunny directed the session without benefit of the written charts. In mid-November, another source of musical activity presented itself to Bunny: McKenzie opened his own jazz club on 52nd Street. Modestly named Red McKenzie's, or Club McKenzie, it featured Bushkin, Stuhlmaker, and the Marsala brothers—Joe and Marty—on reeds and trumpet, and sometimes Bunny.[18]

The prestigious British publication *Melody Maker* featured a major article about Berigan written by noted critic Leonard G. Feather. The laudatory piece reviewed Bunny's professional history and contained a lengthy analysis of Bunny's style, adding a rather complete selected discography. Feather began the article:

17. All information about the Minnelli production from research by Bozy White, in White Outline.
18. Chilton and Sudhalter, *Bunny Berigan*, 40; *Down Beat*, III (December 1, 1936).

Just about three years ago I listened, very impressed, to the lengthy and very original introduction on a Mildred Bailey record called "Is That Religion?" This introduction was played by [Bunny Berigan], said to be a rising star. Never having heard of him, I made a mental note to watch this youngster. It would have been just about as intelligent to visit Crystal Palace on the Fifth of November and make a mental note to watch the fireworks; for, since 1933, it has been impossible not to watch the rise and busy career of Bunny Berigan. His activities have bombarded me from all sides—records from every company; radio every Saturday night; and news items almost as regularly.[19]

Bunny was to be the subject of still one more news item in 1936. During Christmas week, he joined the Tommy Dorsey band, playing an engagement in Buffalo and then some one-nighters. This collaboration produced a chapter in jazz history that is marked by brevity, bombast, and brilliance.

19. Leonard G. Feather, "Bunny Berigan: Master of the Blues," *Melody Maker*, November 28, 1936, p. 2.

14

Me Minus You

Song recorded September 27, 1932
with Connee Boswell

Bunny's previous association with Tommy Dorsey had been as a member of the Dorsey Brothers Orchestra and as a fellow member of the studio orchestras that had churned out records by the hundreds. Almost without exception, Jimmy Dorsey had been an integral force at these uncounted sessions. As the end of 1936 approached, about two-and-a-half years had elapsed since Berigan had recorded with the brothers' orchestra. In the interim, that orchestra had undergone several important changes of musical direction.

The Dorsey brothers' more or less stable small group had been the accompaniment of choice for many of the top singers from the late 1920s until 1933, when the Dorseys transformed it temporarily to a full, embellished big band, then finally into the classic, eleven-piece Dorsey Brothers Orchestra that highlighted one trumpet and three trombones. This skillful group enjoyed great popularity; it featured George Thow as the trumpeter and Glenn Miller as one of the trombonists, as well as Bob Eberly as the band's new singing sensation. George Simon reported Eberly's recollections of Tommy:

He was doing everything—leading the band, making up the radio programs and all the things a leader does. He resented Jimmy for several reasons. For one thing, Jimmy was drinking quite a lot, and Tommy, even though he may have wanted to, didn't. That alone made him mad. But, then, Jimmy used to like to needle Tommy too. He'd just sit there in the saxes, and when Tommy was leading, he'd make cracks like, "Smile, Mac," and "You're the big star!" and that sort of thing. Tommy just kept on working harder. I remember how he used to drive himself. He never had more than five hours sleep a night, and every evening, when we were finished work, he'd drive all the way home to Bernardsville, New Jersey, going ninety miles an hour on back roads. I know, because I lived with him.

Tommy, who had difficulty getting along with Jimmy and at times with the rest of the band, sometimes drove his car instead of traveling in the bus with the others. [Vocalist] Kay Weber recalls one time when Tommy passed the bus in his car, got out, signaled for it to stop, then climbed on board and, obviously very emotionally upset, blurted out, "Why don't you guys like me?" There was an embarrassing silence, then [drummer Ray] McKinley broke in with, "Tommy, you always say this was a band of handpicked musicians. Then why don't you treat us with respect? That's all we want." [1]

It was well known that in his eagerness to strive for perfection, Tommy frequently would berate musicians publicly. Although he would often later recognize how counterproductive this was, and though he could sometimes laugh at himself for such tactlessness, this complex man created many enemies in this way.

On what Eberly recalled as Decoration (Memorial) Day, 1935, following years of bickering, brotherly bitterness, and sometimes bullheaded brawling, Tommy Dorsey walked off New Rochelle's Glen Island Casino bandstand, horn in hand. Farewell, Dorsey Brothers; hello, Jimmy Dorsey Orchestra. Tommy did not return to the safety of the radio and recording studios that had been the source of at least the same level of income that Berigan had enjoyed. Tommy wanted to prove that he could lead a band that would exceed his brother's in musicality and popularity. Assuming the nucleus of his friend Joe Haymes's band—eleven players plus arranger Paul Weston, who had recently earned a Dartmouth degree—Tommy began to build a band intended to vindicate his pride. The Tommy Dorsey orchestra made its first recordings when Bunny was playing with the Goodman band in L.A.'s Palomar Ballroom. Simon describes some of the TD band's early troubles:

The band made its New York debut—in the Blue Room of the Hotel Lincoln. Tommy instituted numerous personnel changes, bringing in drummer Davey Tough and tenor saxist Bud Freeman. He also snatched three formidable talents from Bert Block's local band—trumpeter Joe Bauer, vocalist Jack Leonard and a young, flaxen-haired arranger who'd been known as Odd

---

1. George T. Simon, *The Big Bands* (New York, 1967), 145–46.

Stordahl but who, as Axel Stordahl, was to develop into one of the most sensitive and musical arrangers of all time, a man who was to contribute immensely to the success of Dorsey and, in later years, to the rise of Frank Sinatra. These three Block graduates, Leonard, Stordahl and Bauer, also functioned as a vocal trio, known as The Three Esquires.

Other important musicians soon joined. Tommy had played often with Bunny Berigan in the studios, and he persuaded the great Wisconsin trumpeter to join him. A young clarinetist named Johnny Mince, fresh out of Long Island, had been making some attractive sounds around town (he played for Ray Noble for a while). Tommy got him too, as well as Joe Marsala's guitarist, Carmen Mastren.

Actually, the band went through numerous personnel changes in its formative years—a procedure that continued to plague it through a good part of its early history. Tommy was a perfectionist, and if his men didn't measure up to what he expected from them, he'd let them know in no uncertain terms. It didn't matter who else was listening, either, so musicians with thin skins or tin ears weren't likely to last long in the band. Later, as he mellowed a bit, his musicians stayed with him longer.[2]

Constant motion, uncertainty, volatility: these were the qualities of a situation that seemed to attract Bunny, and they drew him into the Tommy Dorsey band in December, 1936. This was no blind attraction. Bunny and Tommy had been friends almost since Bunny's arrival in New York from Madison, a friendship bolstered by mutual musical respect. Tommy left little doubt as to who was his trumpeter of choice when he had a choice. Both Dorseys had recognized early what the public had just begun to learn: Bunny Berigan's trumpet was the one to listen to. The fact that voters in the *Metronome* poll for 1936 awarded the hot trumpet chair to Bunny and cast numerous votes for him in the lead chair as well certainly must have made Dorsey's choice even easier. For Bunny, however, playing with the Dorsey band in many ways echoed his Goodman experience. Tommy could tailor his professional actions to a specific goal; he could be totally single-minded. Perhaps unlike Goodman, he genuinely liked Bunny, and while he acknowledged that Bunny's resumed drinking could present problems, he felt that he could deal with this on a personal level. Bunny, on the other hand, relished being present at the birth of a new venture, but as he had done on other occasions, he hedged his bet. His commitment to the Dorsey band halted far short of total

2. *Ibid.*, 160–61.

dedication. Berigan continued to be heard on the SNSC as a regularly featured guest. He appeared frequently on the January through March broadcasts, all the while persisting in rehearsing a big band of his own. What would cause Dorsey, the perfectionist, to employ Bunny on these terms? For one thing, the changing personnel in Tommy's band had weakened its initial impact as, grasping for a hit record, the band struggled to attain an identity. It needed an inspiration, something to propel it. If anyone could fulfill that need, Berigan could. For another, Bunny's personal success, as measured by the polls in the trade magazines and the sales of some of his records, was viewed by Music Corporation of America (MCA) as bankable if he were to form his own band. Since MCA also managed Tommy's band, and since Tommy wanted to help his friend get his own band, and since Dorsey's manager, Arthur Michaud, expressed interest in handling it, a Bunny Berigan band seemed to be a natural move. And if, in the meantime, he could provide some of the spark needed by the Dorsey organization, so much the better. As Bunny moved back and forth between the Dorsey band and his own, MCA was served, friendship was served, Tommy's band benefited greatly by the well-timed injection of Berigan's musical energy, and Bunny's own band was safely launched in a nurturing atmosphere.

Within about a month of his joining the Dorsey band, Bunny participated in one recording session with his own band and three with Dorsey's band. The Berigan sparks that Dorsey sought ignited his band immediately. Several radio broadcasts in the first quarter of 1937 give testimony to the kind of focus the Dorsey band achieved, and the excitement that was generated, by both the lead and the solo work of Berigan. By mid-January, the band moved to the Meadowbrook in Cedar Grove, New Jersey, from which almost-nightly broadcasts emanated. Berigan was featured soloing on almost every tune, and his relentless, driving lead trumpet virtually *dared* his fellow sidemen not to swing, not to play at their most spirited level. The TD band's concentration on making exciting swing music was seldom more evident than during this period. This month of Dorsey-Berigan association culminated in the monumental recording date on January 29 that produced two of the enduring classics of big band jazz, "Marie" and "Song of India."

Certainly the arrangements for both these recordings must claim much credit for their lasting success, now of more than fifty years' duration. Some insight into their conception is given by Sudhalter:

Tommy Dorsey got the notion for his version of "Marie" while appearing late in 1936 at Philadelphia's Nixon Grand Theater in company with a black band, the Sunset Royal Serenaders. In their performance of "Marie," the Serenaders' vocalist took the melody while his mates filled in with antiphonal chanting between phrases. Fred Stulce, Dorsey's first alto man, worked up an arrangement using the same device, and the Dorsey band eventually made a smash hit of it. "That's all we took, that idea," said bandmember Carmen Mastren. "Later, when the Sunset Royals played the Savoy Ballroom in New York, they accused us of stealing their arrangement. But we didn't; the arrangement was all Freddy's."[3]

Arranger Weston recalled the particulars differently:

On "Marie" the whole appeal of the recording was two-fold: the lyrics, and Bunny's solo. Carmen is wrong on the lyrics. Freddy stood in the wings at Tommy's direction and copied them word for word when the Sunset Royal band played them. He later gave the band a couple of our arrangements to make up for it, but they needed our arrangements like a hole in the head. Later Tommy sent Bobby Burns (his manager) and me up to Harlem to buy their arrangement of "Who?" and they threw us out. We went back to the Commodore Hotel and Tommy said to me, "*You* write it!" And I did, plus some other similar type vocals later on. Freddie Stulce just wrote the instrumental part; the lyrics were all theirs.[4]

Bobby Smith, reedman-writer-arranger at that time for the Sunset Royals, supported Weston's recollection. With any possible animosity removed by the intervening years, Bobby could smile as he brought back the details: "Another guy did a few bars of 'Marie' for us, then I did the rest of the arrangement. Dorsey's guys were in the wings at the Nixon Grand just copying the thing. The crowds were eating it up. The next thing we knew, Dorsey had recorded it. We went down to Florida for a gig, and by the time we got back that recording was all over the radio. Of course, Bunny's solo didn't hurt their record. Before he died Tommy admitted he stole it."[5]

"Song of India" came about as an extension of Dorsey's penchant for recording adaptations of classical music themes. This was an approach

3. Chilton and Sudhalter, *Bunny Berigan*, 42.
4. Paul Weston, to author, June 3, 1986, in author's possession.
5. Bobby Smith interview. Because both Weston and Smith recall the incident in essentially the same detail, I am convinced that theirs is the more accurate account.

shared at that time by many jazz players, perhaps in an attempt to "legitimize" their music. Earlier in the month, Dorsey had recorded Anton Rubinstein's "Melody in F" and followed shortly with arrangements of Franz Liszt's "Liebestraum," Felix Mendelssohn's "Spring Song," and Johann Strauss's "Blue Danube." Again, Sudhalter quotes Carmen Mastren's recollection of the circumstances: "'Tommy had thought of the intro,' he said, 'and I'd sketched out the first chorus with Red Bone, one of the trombone players. Bud Freeman suggested a little sax section passage after the trombone solo. But you know, I'd forgotten all about the second part. The 'Song of India' has a second theme, a very beautiful one. But I'd left it out altogether. So I said to Red, 'Let's give it to Bunny as a trumpet solo.' I guess the rest, as they say, is history.'"[6]

Weston, again, remembered somewhat differently: "Carmen's memory on 'Song of India' is pretty confused. The arrangement was written and copied on the job at the Meadowbrook. Red Bone wrote some, Carmen wrote some, and I definitely wrote the sax section after the first strain (Bud did suggest the first line) and then I wrote the brass ensemble section that followed the sax passage. Bunny's solo did start out with the second theme, but whether someone suggested it to him or he did it himself, I don't remember."[7]

Weston's recollection seems precise and is backed completely by Smith's memory, but differences in detail notwithstanding, the musical harvest from January 29's four-hour, four-tune recording session (the other two tunes offer Jack Leonard vocals on contemporary ballads) remains one of the richest from the so-called big band era. Sudhalter's musical expertise serves well when he describes what happens during the playing of this dynamic duo. He writes first of "Song of India," then of "Marie":

Dave Tough opens this bit of history with a quiet tattoo on his tom-tom, joined first by reeds and then by brass in Dorsey's introduction. Dorsey takes the first chorus, tightly muted and supersmooth, the reeds backing him with a controlled, clipped little riff. They move out front for their own melody statement over a light two-beat rhythm before the ensemble swells up with a full, warm sonority but considerable rhythmic restraint. . . .

Then Berigan comes on and there is swing aplenty. He kicks off with a

6. Chilton and Sudhalter, *Bunny Berigan,* 41.
7. Weston, to author, June 3, 1986.

simple, attractive figure—an eighth-note triplet and three forceful quarter notes—as Dave Tough whacks his paper-thin splash cymbal and takes up the pulse on the big old Chinese ride cymbal that was one of his trademarks and on which he could generate the irresistible swing called for by Berigan's power and drive.

Berigan, having opened up with four bars of the melody in his middle register, bounds up a tenth to concert A above the staff to deliver a phrase full of passion and drama yet with no thinning-out of tone, no sign of strain or inaccuracy. He follows the natural slope of that first dramatic phrase downward to end his first chorus of the 12-bar strain, then vaults aloft again for further exploration.

In both of his choruses he stabs at the harmonic underpinning of the melody, making the most of its few variations and even, in the eighth bar, outlining a chord that is implied by the melody but not played by the rhythm section. His solo flight rings to an end with another annunciatory high-register phrase, and the ensemble caps it with a little triplet figure. Dorsey returns, still muted, to restate the original melody before Tough and the full band finish with a gently fading recapitulation of the introduction.

The no-frills ["Marie"] opening brings on Dorsey for the first chorus, taking the melody on open horn over a sax-section chord carpet with muted punctuations from the brass. His tone is beautiful, his execution faultless.

Vocalist Jack Leonard sounds every bit as smooth as Dorsey as he slides through the lyrics with band members chanting their contrasting interjections behind him. As they hit their final "Mama!" Berigan steps forward with two notes, a clarion F-to-high-F "Ma-RIE!" that sends him vaulting into his top register and instantly changes key, mood, intensity level, depth and rhythm. . . .

His solo here, pursued at a remarkably consistent level of inventiveness and execution, is more than just a piece of jazz improvisation. With its daring reaches into the topmost range of the horn, its imaginative, bold figures (like the triplets in bars 13–16 that plunge more than an octave down and straight up again), its heraldic, Armstrong-inspired *bel canto* statements (such as the last eight bars, beginning on a high concert E flat), it is a composition, a paraphrase and a development of the original. . . . It is still a standard of excellence.

Dorsey solos with more of an edge on his tone this time, and Bud Freeman contributes an especially witty half-chorus commentary. But Berigan has captured this moment with a gesture so eloquent, so sweeping, that all else seems diminished beside it.[8]

In his statement on "Marie," Berigan displays most of the characteristics of his playing that make it so endearing and enduring. His stamp is placed indelibly on both songs. For more than one genera-

8. Chilton and Sudhalter, *Bunny Berigan*, 41–42.

tion of careful listeners, and indeed for even casual listeners and dancers, "Marie" and "Song of India" *mean* the Dorsey versions, with Berigan. Indeed, Dorsey's full recognition both of this symbiotic relationship and of his public's demand for the Berigan solos led Dorsey to have both of them transcribed for full trumpet section when Berigan was no longer on the TD bandstand. The Dorsey band played these tunes this way for many years after Bunny's departure, as does the current TD "ghost" band.

The evolution and shaping of Bunny's "Marie" solo are well documented on the Sunbeam air checks from the broadcasts leading up to the January 29 recording. The song was played on a January 11 broadcast of the *Jack Pearl Show*, which featured the Dorsey band regularly. It was repeated on the January 18 broadcast because, according to the announcer, "after last week's program, everybody's been asking Tommy Dorsey to repeat his unusual arrangement of 'Marie.' So here it is with Jack Leonard and the boys singing." On each of these versions, Bunny stays in mid-range for a while before hitting the upper reaches of the horn. The solo on January 11 retains a definite relaxed feel throughout, displaying an almost casual comfort in execution unusual even for Bunny, especially notable since the arrangement's ink was probably still drying at the time. As with all Berigan solos, each of these is well shaped, a minor composition in itself, yet blending in perfectly with the ensemble writing. The solo on the next week's broadcast reveals a higher degree of intensity, with more upper range playing.[9] When, eleven days later, Bunny recorded the classic solo, all was in place. He had lived with the arrangement for a few weeks, had played the solo countless times. His opening two-note fanfare declares to the listening world that a master player and a piece of music have coalesced, that what follows is not to be missed.

The source of Bunny's seemingly boundless energy for playing remains a mystery. His schedule during the first three months of 1937 continued to be extremely taxing. In addition to playing dance dates with Dorsey, Bunny played with that band on five recording sessions and a weekly radio show. Additionally, he was featured almost weekly on the SNSC; led January 22 and February 17 recording sessions with his own orchestra; spent considerable time and effort rehearsing a

9. Sunbeam SB-235, *Rare 1936–1937 Broadcast Recordings: Tommy Dorsey, Vol. II*.

band; and, with his fledgling band, auditioned for (and secured) a regular spot on an upcoming new radio program, the Tim and Irene Admiration Shampoo show. On February 17, Bunny recorded both with his own band at Brunswick and with Dorsey at the Victor studios. His band also won a February 3 to 16 engagement at the Meadowbrook, replacing the Dorsey band with whom he had played the previous engagement there. Existing recordings from air checks confirm some of the less-than-flattering critical opinions about the quality of Bunny's band at this time. The group that played at the Meadowbrook was comprised largely of free-lance players who could remain near New York. Matty Matlock on clarinet was the strongest jazz player aside from Bunny. Hymie Shertzer, the fine lead alto player, was available only for recordings. While Bunny could always assemble a reasonable group of studio friends and free-lancers for any given gig, the resulting band lacked suitable arrangements and, partly because of a lack of adequate rehearsals, never jelled. Unable to attract bookings, it was disbanded following the February 17 recording session at Brunswick. Bunny played record sessions with Dorsey on February 17 and 18 and rejoined the Dorsey band—if he can be regarded to have left it—as it began an engagement at the Commodore Hotel on February 19.

Veteran Clyde Rounds, whose friendship with Bunny was growing at that time, remembers performing in the Dorsey reed section during these eventful months. Rounds recalled how hard Dorsey was driving the band, wanting it to be perfect. The reedman claimed that one night Bunny hit a loud "clinker." Dorsey protested loudly, and in the ensuing argument Bunny just walked out.[10] Shortly thereafter, two important resources fell into place: the beginning of the already secured Tim and Irene Admiration Shampoo radio show, with broadcasts over the full Mutual Network, and the signing of a recording contract with Victor records. With this, Rounds, trumpeter Steve Lipkins, and reedman Joe Dixon joined forces with Bunny.

The bandstand clash between Berigan and Dorsey by no means ended their musical or personal relationship. They appeared together

---

10. Bozy White Outline; Clyde Rounds, interview with Tom Cullen, May, 1960, in Cullen Materials, copy of transcript in author's possession. Rounds played in the Berigan band from April, 1937, through December, 1938, and was a friend of the Berigan family offstage.

on the renamed *Swing Club* on March 6. A few weeks later, Fats Waller, Dick McDonough, George Wettling, Dorsey, and Berigan were all recording at the Victor studios on different sessions. Somehow they came together and began jamming to kill time; an alert recording engineer, Eli Oberstein, who later supervised most of Bunny's recorded material for Victor, suggested that he record what they were doing. The result is a historic recording session, the "Jam Session at Victor," with Waller's "Honeysuckle Rose" and "Blues" paired in performances that are prized by collectors. Furthermore, Dorsey and Berigan continued a relationship that, though sometimes stormy, was always based on mutual respect, musically if not personally.

Donna Berigan expressed dislike of Tommy Dorsey for decades after Bunny's death. Whether her feelings reflected Bunny's regard for the man with whom he spent so many hours in the recording studios cannot be known. The men were vastly different in the way they treated their sidemen. While it was virtually impossible for Bunny to criticize a musician publicly, such ridicule was an important part of Dorsey's leadership arsenal. Donna certainly heard reports of this from Bunny; perhaps she reacted more intensely to these railings than did Bunny himself. It may be that Donna possessed no more insight into the complex relationship between Bunny Berigan and Tommy Dorsey than did other, less subjective observers.

While the paths of Berigan and Dorsey crossed many times again, their 1937 activities formed the core of their artistic partnership. Orrin Keepnews and Bill Grauer, Jr., sum up succinctly the Berigan-Dorsey association just before Bunny finally launched his big band: "Bunny Berigan, perhaps the most talented trumpet man of this era, was with Tommy Dorsey only briefly, in 1937. But his work included the memorable recordings of 'Marie' and 'Song of India,' so that in retrospect he remains permanently associated with the band."[11] This is a perceptive statement about a band that established strong roots in the 1920s, began under a gifted, driving leader in the 1930s, and continued as a major force in the music business well into the 1950s. The Tommy Dorsey band launched the careers of Frank Sinatra, Jo Stafford, and uncounted musicians and arrangers. Although Bunny

11. Orrin Keepnews and Bill Grauer, Jr., *A Pictorial History of Jazz* (New York, 1955), 171.

Berigan mainly performed with the Dorsey band for only the first three months of 1937, and later for about five months in 1940, and though the band featured a succession of marvelous soloists on trumpet and other instruments, nevertheless the association remains a permanent one. And as the Dorsey band adjusted to performing minus the inspiration of Bunny Berigan, Bunny tried to adjust to a new role, minus the security of a lucrative studio job and minus the strengths of a leader like Goodman or Tommy Dorsey. [12]

12. Information about Berigan's work with the Dorsey band, his own band's engagement at Meadowbrook, and the *Swing Club* broadcasts from research by Bozy White, in White Outline.

15

Patty Cake, Patty Cake

Song recorded March 15, 1939
by Bunny Berigan and His Orchestra

Bunny Berigan ascended rapidly, dizzyingly to a position of prominence in the New York and national music scene: a free-lancer, rushing from one studio to another and from the studio to a jam session somewhere; the ultimate swing musician, the man whose playing was idolized not only by the knowing musicians of Radio Row and the other professionals but also by a growing number of "hep" listeners and budding musicians in schools; a handsome, fun-loving, never-a-serious-thought habitué of New York's night scene, the un-crowned king of 52nd Street; one of the champion consumers of il-legal-turned-legal beverages, whose drinking feats and defeats were already becoming legend; an attractive and desirable public figure with a sometimes-roving eye; a man who rarely worked at only one job and who, when his band became his only job, found it consuming most of every day. This Bunny Berigan was also, in fact, a pretty good part-time family man.

Throughout his life, Bunny maintained close ties with his mother and father, Mayme and Cap, and made frequent visits to Fox Lake and to the Madison area. His boyhood neighbor and friend, Jack Smith, recalled one of the methods Bunny used to keep in touch dur-ing his early studio days in New York. "I worked in the telephone office on the night shift," Smith related.

Bunny's folks didn't have a telephone in their home, so his dad used to come up to the office. Once a week, at about 2:00 in the morning, Bunny would call. He'd ask for the operator and I'd talk to him first, and then his dad would take over. This started about the time he was playing with Paul Whiteman and Rudy Vallee. I can remember once Bun said to be sure to tell his brother "Tony" to have his Ma teach him to read music, because Tony was a good drummer and if he could read, Vallee would be sure to hire him.

Although the upright piano in her house remained untouched from the mid-1930s on, Mayme continued to play the organ until near the time of her death. Each Sunday she played for mass at Saint Mary's Church, a service that paid her twenty-five dollars per month. Aside from this, Mayme performed very little publicly and rarely taught piano after Bunny left the Madison area. Arthritis in her hands became increasingly painful, severely restricting her piano playing and interfering with her favorite hobby, crocheting. Mayme's other principal diversion was playing cards with "the club." Cap, so called because he was captain of his bowling team, pursued no other major interests. He persevered in his territorial sales job, driving a small, enclosed truck with "Badger Tobacco & Candy" lettered on its sides, to all the nearby towns. Only when Cap entered Wisconsin General Hospital in Madison for the last time did he relinquish his six-days-per-week route.

Whenever booking schedules permitted trips to Chicago, Milwaukee, or Madison, Bunny automatically sought contact with his family, meetings that, at least during the early years, proved joyous. Sometimes, as with the celebration in the middle of the Whiteman tour, a group of family and friends would drive to attend a performance, coupling the enjoyment of the music with a brief reunion. When possible, Bunny would squeeze in side trips of varying lengths to visit with his parents and friends in Fox Lake. On at least two occasions when Bunny and his band were playing at the Fox Theater in Detroit, the leader made arrangements for family members to visit him there. In 1938, Bunny's brother, Don, married Loretta Reichenberger, a young and once-aspiring singer who, worn down by the nightclub grind in Chicago, had relocated to rural Wisconsin. In mid-July, shortly after Loretta and Don's wedding, Bunny's band played Detroit's Fox. As a wedding gift, Bunny provided the couple with a honeymoon trip to Detroit. Much has been written and said about Don's claim that when Bunny greeted Don in Detroit with a handshake, he left two hundred dollars in Don's hand. Loretta maintains that Don informed her the gift was fifty dollars.

Loretta Reichenberger, singing under the name of Rich, had performed mainly blues, mainly in Chicago. She met Don, many years older than she, on a trip to Fox Lake to visit the mother of a friend. When she became disillusioned with what she considered to be unsavory associations that came with success in the nightclub jazz scene, she turned her back on some of these seamier aspects of the music business and opted for the quietude of the small town, making her home with her Fox Lake friends. To her surprise, she found herself living next door to the Berigan family. A jazz fan, she had admired the trumpet playing of their younger son for a long time. After a courtship of only a month, Loretta and the older son, Don, were married in Beaver Dam on July 3, 1938, and a few weeks later accepted Bunny's wedding gift by traveling to Detroit. Don, the self-acknowledged hellraiser, was able to control his behavior only until about the following January, when his drinking resumed. Their son, Kaye, was born on July 17, 1939, but the responsibilities of fatherhood did not for long alter Don's conduct. Don and Loretta lived in several homes in the Fox Lake and Beaver Dam area, often with the senior Berigans sharing the quarters. Don sometimes lived away from home, attempting to establish a stable barber shop. Cap and Mayme Berigan welcomed living with Loretta and Don, an arrangement that prevailed until Mayme's death in 1944. This roughly coincided with Loretta's separation from Don, and subsequent divorce, after which Loretta moved to Milwaukee.

Loretta's relationship with her in-laws proved to be amicable; she was accepted as a part of the family and has stated, "They were wonderful people and will always be like Mother and Dad to me."[1] Nevertheless, during the three and one-half years she lived with them before Cap's death, the elder Berigans evidenced little mutual affection. Loretta characterized it as "not a particularly outwardly loving relationship; just a tolerating situation of a marriage. They were both quite opinionated, but not bossy. They weren't very demonstrative, and you had to 'read' how they felt about you."

---

1. This quotation from Loretta Berigan and all those from her throughout the book are taken from an interview with the author on May 21, 1985, and from other formal interviews that followed. In addition, Mrs. Berigan and the author have carried on a regular correspondence, some of which is also used in quoting Loretta Berigan. Tapes and correspondence in author's possession. Since she lived with Bunny's parents for a number of years, her perception of Bunny and his family situation is valuable.

Loretta confirmed that the Berigans treated their sons differently. "When it came to Bunny, of course, it was all smiles because they were so proud of him. Where Don was concerned, there were so many problems he created that they felt they had nothing to be proud about. But Don never discussed that, never complained that he felt he received unequal treatment. I think Don was always proud of his brother, although this came out more in later years." When asked on how many occasions she had been around Bunny, Loretta responded quickly and specifically:

Five. Of course, the first time was on our honeymoon trip in Detroit. After that, it was always when he came to Fox Lake for some reason, usually with the band nearby. There was a kind of air about Bunny that a few people didn't like—maybe it was a false assurance that so many performers carry. But he was a lovable, likable guy. I fell in love with the man immediately when I met him. You couldn't help it; he was so likable, really. He was a good guy all the way around. If anybody needed money, he gave it to them. He sent his father hundreds, maybe thousands of dollars. His father always needed money.

Rural Wisconsin struggled with economic depression, as did every part of the country. By 1938, midway through Roosevelt's second term, the federal government had implemented some actions for crop insurance and other aid to farmers through legislation such as the Agricultural Adjustment Act, and the general economy's resuscitation had begun. However, Little Fox Lake, like most rural towns, lagged far behind in the recovery. Nevertheless, the reasons for William Berigan's perpetual lack of money are difficult to pinpoint. While his sales job was never especially profitable, it should have provided a reasonable sustenance. He often claimed that his customers defaulted or were slow in paying for the goods he left in their stores. Mayme's small stipend from the church, and later a thirty-dollar monthly pension, helped, but the household often struggled to pay the fifteen-dollar monthly rent. To whatever degree he could, Bunny provided financial assistance. In November, 1941, Bunny, in poor shape himself, both physically and financially, left his band on the East Coast and made a quick trip to Fox Lake for his father's funeral. He assured his mother, who was left without funds, that he would take care of Cap's funeral expenses.

In spite of his apparent devotion to his parents, Bunny appeared to derive very little succor from them on his later trips home. Donna's relationship with the Berigans was far from ideal. They viewed her as a poor partner for Bunny, and when she was in Fox Lake with them, they criticized Donna's method of caring for her children. Her in-laws accused Donna of going out drinking and "carrying on" when she was there without Bunny. Mayme was uncharacteristically outspoken in her criticisms of Donna, her less-than-model behavior, and her seeming neglect of Patricia and Joyce. This concern lay at the heart of the senior Berigans' rejection of Donna. Further, both parents expressed the view that Donna was the major reason behind Bunny's drinking. Burdened with all this strong feeling, and complicated by the overlay of Cap's own unstable financial situation, Bunny's home visits were often punctuated with argument and recrimination.

At least one of these combative scenes was brought about by Bunny's own actions. Through the years he had maintained contact with a woman in Madison to whom he felt attached. He would visit her whenever he was in the area, including well after his marriage. Loretta remembers when Donna found out about these clandestine visits: "Donna was very upset about it, and they had some battles because of it. The ironic thing is that fairly recently I met [a friend of a friend] who knew who I was. She said to me, 'You know, I *almost* became your sister-in-law.' She was the one Bunny dated and knew all those years in Madison! I asked her why she didn't marry Bunny and she just said she couldn't see herself as the wife of a bandleader." Patricia's recollection of her mother's discovery is quite specific: "When Dad's band was in Chicago something was going on with another woman. Everything was running along pretty smoothly. Then there was some arguing, and the next thing I knew, my mother was gone."[2]

Bunny's success as an acclaimed musician brought great pride to Mayme and Cap. He had learned his music lessons well and had exceeded the dreams Mayme had permitted herself when her son was just beginning to learn about music from her. But the gnawing problems associated with Bunny's drinking would not disappear, and they became a source of deepening dismay. Increasingly, his trips home

2. This quotation from Patricia Berigan Slavin and all those from her throughout the book are taken from a telephone interview with the author on June 14, 1988, and from an interview, also with the author, on August 10, 1988, tapes and transcripts in author's possession.

were punctuated with extended bouts of drinking at Casey's bar or at one of the resort clubs or simply around the house. Some of the industry rumors about Bunny's unreliability had begun to filter back to Wisconsin and were supported by the first-hand observation of his parents. For several months in early 1939, both parents ventured east to join Bunny, with Cap serving as a kind of manager, ostensibly to help with the finances. Donna was suspicious of her father-in-law's motives in placing himself near the source of the money; others questioned Cap's qualifications to serve as a manager. After several months, Cap and Mayme returned home to assist Loretta around the time of Kaye's birth. Cap went east a second time, alone, mainly to monitor Bunny's drinking; the financial considerations were by then mainly a subterfuge.

When William Berigan returned home the second time, defeated in his purpose of helping to curtail Bunny's drinking, one of the people he confided his disappointment to was his bowling partner and neighbor, Jack Smith.

When Cap came back [Smith recalled], he was really disgusted with Bunny. He cursed him and said that Bunny was throwing his life away. He told me about a time in Philadelphia with a full house when Bunny was just so "stewed" the two Negro valets ["Little Gate" and "Big Gate"] could hardly get him dressed. Cap said, "I was so mad I grabbed him and pushed him out on the stage and told him to make a fool out of himself in front of all those people instead of in front of me all the time. You know what, he straightened out and played OK." Cap had tears in his eyes when he told me that his son was drinking three quarts of White Horse Scotch a day. I felt sorry for him.

Bunny's daughter Pat was five years old before her father formed his own band. For most of those five years, Bunny's main activities centered around New York's Radio Row. Joyce, on the other hand, was born while Bunny was doubling in the studios and on 52nd Street, a demanding period that coincided with Bunny's ill-kept secret affair with Lee Wiley and ended with the formation of his band. Since fronting the band involved almost constant travel for Bunny, the children experienced different degrees of contact with their father in their early years. Pat remembers that her father traveled a lot. "I had an unbelievable number of dolls. Everywhere he went Daddy would bring me a doll. And I had lots of clothes; I was always dressed to the hilt." Pat especially bears out the statements made by friends of

Bunny that he loved his children dearly and was devoted to them. "When Daddy came home it was always good. We'd have friends up to the house—mostly show business people—and I would help serve them. It was a help to my Mom, but I did it because I could hear everything, and I wanted to be where my Dad was."

Notwithstanding the hours that he could not be with his family because of travel and performance schedules, Bunny, characterized by many as a "big kid," provided good companionship for the youngsters. He initiated rough-and-tumble play and other kinds of active games with the girls. He truly enjoyed being with them and playing with them. While Joyce can recall little detail of this period, she firmly states, "I always had warm feelings about Bunny as a father. I still have parts of a scrapbook that I began as a teenager. All of my feelings about my father are good."[3] Again, Pat's recollections are more specific:

We used to go out to Long Island a lot with Nat Natoli and his wife, and sometimes some other couples. We'd go to Ronkonkoma Park on a Sunday. Dad would pack a picnic lunch. There'd be a few couples and all the kids and we'd have a very pleasant Sunday afternoon. The guys would throw the softball around, and Dad would swing me. He'd get on the swing himself and scare us to death that he was going over the top and all the way around. He'd laugh and laugh! There was a period when Sunday ball games with the band were very important. Daddy would insist that the guys come out on Sundays and play softball, even if they were hung over. He'd call them and make them come.

And Daddy was the one who taught me to swim. I was afraid of the water, but he assured me, and pretty soon I could do the dog paddle. I think that was at the Sherman Hotel in Chicago. One time on my birthday, Mom had blown up what seemed like hundreds of balloons of all colors. Dad came home before the party and right away he got this idea, and he went and got us each a pin. I said Mom would be mad, but we went and pricked them all! Mom was mad.

Dad was a very sensitive person. I can remember being terrified of rain, thunder, and lightning. I'd run and hide and cry. Mom never knew what to do; she'd just tell me to be quiet. This one time Dad was home as it started to get very dark. I remember him picking me up and getting this great big, fuzzy quilt and carrying me into the living room. Then he got this big, old chair and sat it by the open window and wrapped the quilt around me. Then he began to explain to me about the thunder and the lightning—what it was,

---

3. This quotation from Joyce Berigan and all those from her throughout the book, are taken from an interview with the author on May 14, 1988, and from subsequent correspondence. Tape and correspondence in author's possession.

how the rain came and washed away the tears of all little girls. He spoke in this low, soft voice about the love of God, and that the rain was God's crying for children who are unhappy. By the time he was finished it was thundering and lightning and we were both all wet, but that's how he helped me get over my fear of storms. That's the way Dad was.

"We lived in some nice places in Queens," recalled Donna. "Rego Park, Elmhurst, Jackson Heights, Sunnyside. Rego Park was the last place. We had a big, beautiful home there. Unfortunately, Bunny was always on the go; he didn't spend much time at home. Before the kids started school I used to catch the subway in and see the shows. We always had a housekeeper. We had the kids with us, and my sister Madie—we brought her up from the time my mother died. It was real family life, you know; no wild stuff," Donna added. "He was a good daddy. He loved his kids and the girls liked him. When we lived on 86th and Central Park West, Bunny'd have the boys up. Pat would serve the boys just like a little waitress."

Donna delighted in recalling a happy incident with little Joyce:

Bunny had Jo come up to the bandstand one time when she was about six years old and handed her the trumpet. He said, "Now play it!" She tried and, boy, she came out with a darn big sound out of it. I couldn't get a squeak out of it myself. When Jo was about six years old, she only wore a size-three dress; she was real tiny. She had long curls, way down her neck, down her back. When she got up there with her cute little dress and patent leather shoes and grabbed that horn—she'd do anything her daddy told her to—when she blew that horn, it amazed the audience. I think that was at Jacksonville.

Guitarist Tom Morgan(elli) remembered a show at New York's Paramount Theatre in 1937 attended by Donna and five-year-old Pat: "Bunny wasn't at his best for that show, and as the stage lowered at the end, Donna and his daughter came toward Bunny. The little one says to Bunny, 'Gee, daddy, you didn't play so good today.' He really felt bad about that."[4] Pat did not recall this particular incident but thought it quite likely. "Daddy would often ask, 'Princess, how did

4. Tom Morgan(elli), telephone interview with author, April 10, 1988, and from subsequent correspondence. Tape and correspondence in author's possession. Subsequent quotations from Morgan(elli) are taken from this interview and correspondence, unless otherwise indicated. Morgan played guitar with Berigan bands from approximately January, 1937, through March, 1938.

Daddy play tonight?'" Pat recalled. "It was natural for me to tell him. If he asked me how he sounded, I'd answer honestly."

Loretta recalled that during one of Bunny's visits home, the family discussed the formal adoption of Donna's sister, Madie. Loretta's impression remains that Bunny favored taking this legal step. For whatever reasons, Bunny and Donna did not adopt Madie, but while conditions permitted, they provided her with a home, from about 1933 to 1940. Loretta further remembered Bunny's tender feelings expressed after her son Kaye's birth:

Bunny was so thrilled about it. He had tears in his eyes as he stated over and over again how he wished he had a son. I'm sure it was his greatest regret, although he loved his girls and Patty was his number-one favorite. He doted on those girls, but he wasn't hesitant to discipline them if necessary. Bunny told Don in front of me to take good care of our boy. At the time of Kaye's birth, Bunny had promised to come to Saint Joseph's Hospital in Beaver Dam to visit us, but he didn't. Don explained to me that Bunny and Donna had had a battle with Mayme and Bill about not spending enough time at home and being out drinking far too much. The battle was mainly against Donna. Bunny and Donna left way ahead of their plans, but Bunny always had a soft spot for Kaye, the son he never had.

I was devastated when Bunny didn't come to the hospital, because he had promised and because I had him sort of on a pedestal. He was loved by all the musicians he had in his band, all the ones he ever played with. He was so easygoing, happy, smiling, always the jokester, the comedian. Really, that man should have been an *actor;* he had all those qualities. He was a lousy business man, yes, but that's beside the point. He paid men to do that job, to be trusted, though they took advantage of him. I will always admire and love Bunny. He was truly a superb person and musician, giving all of us fans who love jazz or trumpet playing far more than we even deserve. As to his inner self, it is impossible for anyone to be able to please every other human being.

When met with the suggestion that she married the wrong Berigan brother, Loretta smiles and does not deny that she, too, has harbored this thought.

In fact, Bunny and Donna's marriage was not a smooth one. Before marriage, Donna had concentrated her attention on her development as a dancer. Bunny's rise to the top of his profession preempted all of his time and efforts, and music-related activities encompassed virtually his entire world. Acquaintances characterized both Donna and

Bunny as living in a fantasy, removed from the real world and not capable of solving—nor interested in confronting—the problems and makeup of the world that existed outside the entertainment business. Removed from that narrow range of interests, their thoughts were unsophisticated, their lives largely unexamined. Both Bunny and Donna seemed content to be swept along by the tide of events that surrounded them. Bunny and Donna's household accommodated, at various times, a sizable extended family. In addition to Madie and a housekeeper, several pets inhabited the Berigan home or apartment. Donna loved dogs—at one time the Berigans shared their then-modest apartment with five puppies—and only gave up their companionship when circumstances required. She sadly remembered giving her favorite Boston terrier, Zozo, to Cap to take back to Fox Lake during a period when the dog became an encumbrance.

Madie recalled Bunny as fun-loving and kind, but she said she was used "constantly" as a baby-sitter when she lived in her sister's household. She also remembered that it was a period filled with "*frequent* arguments."[5] Arguments were a regular part of the Berigans' existence. "I'm sure you've heard before about their arguments," Pat offered. "I can remember some good times with my mother, and especially good times with my father, but not good times when they were together, as a family. Two of their arguments stand out still. Once, I was playing a wind-up phonograph and kept playing 'Ja-Da' over and over. Mom went crazy. Dad tried to talk her out of it and have her let me play it. They went into the kitchen and argued. Pretty soon Dad came back into where I was and asked me quietly to turn it off."

The other memorable argument ensued on an occasion that Pat attributes to her parents' drinking together. "Mom got real bad when she drank. Jo and I would go hide. One time they got to arguing, and Mom went into the kitchen and came out with this big butcher knife. I told Jo to stay in bed, and I came out to tell them to stop it. Daddy was standing there saying, 'Go ahead!' I warned my Mom, 'Don't you ever hurt Daddy!'" To this day, Joyce—only a toddler at that stage—professes a profound aversion to arguing and loud voices.

5. Madeline "Madie" Troisi, to author, October, 1987, in author's possession.

Pat is an accomplished artist, working mostly in oils. She credits some of this interest and talent to early experiences with Bunny. "I was just a little one when I drew some 'people' for my Dad. They were the typical round faces with feet and arms attached. Daddy sat me down and showed me how to draw faces. He drew a funny picture of Paul Whiteman. He was actually teaching me caricature. He'd say, 'Pick out one thing about that face and draw just that. Make it funny.' Then he'd show me. I wish I had those drawings of his now."

One of the activities associated with the 1920s and 1930s entertainment business, and with the jazz-music business in particular, was drinking. A good companion was someone who would drink with you. At some point, Donna passed her companionship test and moved beyond that into her own battle with alcoholism. Friends, fellow musicians, and family confirm that Donna consistently drank generous and regular quantities of alcoholic beverages over a period of years. Donna's drinking unquestionably influenced Bunny's own drinking problem and exacerbated some of the other disturbing elements creeping into their marriage. At times when Bunny was not drinking or was making some attempt to limit his alcoholic intake, Donna would begin drinking in his presence and encourage (some say allow) Bunny to join her—never a difficult bit of persuasion in either case. When the Berigans could no longer afford a housekeeper, the condition of the Berigan apartment deteriorated. Even the most casual visitor noticed litter and other signs of neglect. While Bushkin expressed surprise at finding a fairly normal home life in the household of the hard-living man he knew, he also witnessed some shortcomings: "One night Bunny and I went back to the apartment they had on Central Park West. This was after we had busted our ass and played five shows at the Paramount. I remember dinner being the lousiest fuckin' hamburger I ever ate, with some canned peas. If that's the way you treat Bunny Berigan, who just played five shows at the Paramount. . . . I remember the time he broke his leg playing with his kids. He was playing skip rope or something in the apartment. He would bust his ass to make life good for those kids." Pat could not clearly recall Bunny's breaking a leg, but she remembered playing with Bunny in the snow, probably on a steep slope in Syracuse. She thought he might have injured himself at that time.

In spite of their parents' sometimes-successful attempts at providing a normal home life, both daughters share abiding memories of living with a series of temporary, "foster" parents during the times when Donna would accompany the band on the road, and also when Bunny and Donna were separated. Actually, these were persons paid by the Berigans to take care of the girls for extended periods. Their quality ranged from "Aunt Iona," fondly remembered by both girls, to a home where, Pat recalled, "we were subjected to cruelty and child abuse. Joyce was beaten badly. We went through a lot of traumatic experiences there. I finally got hold of Kay Altpeter—I can't remember how. I told her about some of the things that were going on. She contacted Dad. Dad came racing in and took us right out of there."[6]

Donna's poor health, particularly during the period surrounding the birth and death of the infant Barbara, presented yet another difficult hurdle for the young couple as it sapped vitality from the agile former dancer. The association between Donna and her in-laws, begun with mutual reservations, deteriorated over the years, aggravating the troubles between Bunny and Donna. Bunny worked odd, often extended, usually topsy-turvy hours, constantly in the spotlight's glare. He may have lost sight of matters beyond the stage. While Donna entered eagerly into marriage, giving up her promising show career, her adjustment to the new role was difficult. She clearly resented having the responsibility of raising two young daughters. Her handsome husband's popularity grew, and he continued to be admired, and perhaps desired, by a wide range of women both inside and outside of show business. For Bunny, the opportunity for new attachments was always close at hand. One woman, in particular, enjoyed Bunny's reciprocal attentions.

6. Kay Altpeter and her husband, trombonist Larry Altpeter, were friends of the Berigans.

16

Somebody Else Is Taking My Place

Song recorded March 11, 1942
by Bunny Berigan and His Orchestra

Joe Dixon: "He probably should have married her. She was the love of his life. She would call my wife-to-be and leave messages for Bunny there."[1]

Sue Mitchell: "She was always around the Penn Roof, even in the short time I was with the band."[2]

Donna Berigan: "I hated her, that snake eyes!"

Musician's wife: "She sucked men dry—financially, physically, and psychologically. Everybody knew about her. The sad thing is that she ruined some wonderful men. She had good taste."[3]

Joe Bushkin: "If that's the way you treat Bunny Berigan, who just played five shows at the Paramount, I wouldn't blame him for wanting to be with Lee Wiley."

Tom Morgan(elli): "That Lee Wiley used to drain him dry, you know."

At age fifteen, Lee Wiley ran away from home in Fort Gibson, Oklahoma, and she rose to almost instant prominence in Chicago and New York clubs before she was twenty. In the early 1930s, her work, which included a long and close association with CBS orchestra leader Victor Young, leaned more toward popular songs. As her career progressed, she gravitated toward jazz stylings of standards, and at vari-

---

1. Joe Dixon, telephone interview with author, October 23, 1986, tape in author's possession.
2. Sue Mitchell, interview with Deborah Mickolas at the request of Bozy White and based on his questions, September 10, 1975, copy of tape in author's possession.
3. Musician's wife who asked anonymity.

ous times she recorded top-quality work with Condon, Max Kaminsky, Bushkin, and Waller. During the 1940s, when she was married to Jess Stacy, she traveled and sang with his big band. According to Leonard Feather, "Lee Wiley's is one of the few completely distinctive feminine voices in jazz. There is a husky, erotic warmth to her work, in which her wide vibrato is the most recognizable quality; combined with her ability to select superior tunes and interpret the lyrics sensitively, her unique characteristics have produced many memorable, timeless records."[4] The superior tunes leaned heavily toward composers Rodgers and Hart, Gershwin, and Cole Porter. Wiley is said to have been Porter's favorite interpreter for his songs.

Wiley was quoted on her own singing by John S. Wilson: "I don't sing gut-bucket. I don't sing jazz. I just sing. The only vocal trick I've ever done is putting in the vibrato and taking it out. I don't believe in vocal gimmickry and I had never had the commercial instincts to concentrate on visual mannerisms. I always sang the way I wanted to. If I didn't like something, I just wouldn't do it. I'd take a plane to California and sit in the sun."[5]

Wiley's looks and her voice seemed perfectly matched. Hers was a compelling, magnetic beauty. Her almond-shaped face, framed by corn-colored, simply styled hair, exuded sultriness, sensuality. Wiley was tall and sinuous, and her Cherokee heritage was evident in her bronze skin and high cheekbones. Her kinetic warmth—her heat—seemed masked, kept under rein by a sophisticated coolness.

Bunny Berigan, as a member of the Dorsey Brothers group, backed Lee Wiley on March 7, 1933, on the first records she made under her own name. Not released until much later, the two tunes recorded were "You've Got Me Crying Again" and "I Gotta Right to Sing the Blues." Wiley remembered first meeting Bunny on the Ponds radio broadcasts on CBS. Since Bunny was on tour with Whiteman during the middle of 1933, the earliest he could have taken part in those broadcasts would have been mid-October, when Whiteman began a long run at the Paradise Restaurant. She probably did not notice the

4. Leonard Feather, *The New Edition of the Encyclopedia of Jazz* (Rev. ed.; New York, 1960), 461–62. Additional information about Wiley on the Ponds show from Bozy White Outline.

5. *New York Times Biographical Service*, VI (December, 1975), 1630. This obituary entry was written by John S. Wilson, veteran New York *Times* jazz writer and critic.

new trumpet man at the time of the March, 1933, recording date, but that oversight had changed drastically by the time Bunny, who was by then certified star material, headlined the SNSC broadcasts beginning in June, 1936. Wiley appeared as a guest on the first show and many times thereafter.

Walter Gross was on the SNSC inaugural broadcast as a pianist and played with the show almost without interruption before taking over as the show's director when it had become well established. He praised Bunny for his great versatility, his ability to fit into a symphonic setting as easily as a jazz mode: "Bunny read well. He always held his own in a legit[imate] brass section. When we combined the smaller groups to form the CBS Symphony, usually under Howard Barlow, we used Bunny many times." Gross recalled that in those days, Bunny was having great trouble with his teeth, and he attributed much of Bunny's drinking to this fact. Further, he remembered that Bunny and a well-known female singer were seeing a lot of one another at that time. He asserted that together, this singer and alcohol negatively affected the trumpeter's musical performance and his life. By early or mid-1936, the relationship between Bunny Berigan and Lee Wiley was common knowledge, at least among the music community. Questions about Bunny's marital stability reached print in the trade press, with one observing, "The local rags are reporting the trumpeter's domestic harmony is hitting clinkers. . . . (Aside to BB—she's sewed up solid by a West Coast movie maestro. . . .)"[6]

Guitarist Tom Morgan(elli) was one of the early sidemen Bunny selected when he began to form his band. He remained with Bunny through March, 1938. Of Wiley, Morganelli recalled:

She was a character. She used to follow us around a lot. When we played at Valley Stream, Long Island, she was there *every night*—every night. Bunny'd go out in the car with her between sets and when he'd come back he'd be . . . spent. After he was with her he used to fold up sometimes.

We lost that job on account of her. It was a beautiful job there at the Pavilion Royal. The boss finally told Bunny, "Look, either she goes or the band goes." Bunny said, "Well, the band goes!" Oh, my God! Everybody was real unhappy with Bunny. The job was so good, and we had to go out on one-

6. Walter Gross, interview with Tom Cullen, September, 1952; *Down Beat*, February, 1938. Since the Berigan-Wiley liaison was so well known as to reach print, one finds difficulty in understanding Donna's claim that she was surprised by Nat Natoli's later revelation.

nighters and crap like that. He wasn't thinking of the guys in the band that time. But we wouldn't fool with him; he could be a thickhead at times too. We were frustrated because there were no bookings; we had to scramble around.

After forty-eight years, Donna's recollection of the situation was still clear, still painful:

The only time I was really hurt was when Bunny was playing at the Paramount Theatre and he was running around with this dame—what was her name—you know, "snake eyes"—yeah, Lee Wiley! He was running around with her and I found it out. The person who told me what was going on was one of Bunny's best friends, Nat Natoli. I'm not a jealous person, and I never had reason to suspect that anything was wrong. Nat didn't like what was happening. He loved my kids and he liked me, and he didn't appreciate it that they were carrying on. He came home one night and said, "You'd better get down to the club and see what's going on." They were just switching from [the Paradise] to the Paramount. I told Nat I didn't believe it, and he said, "Take my word."

So I came down from Rego Park. I decided I would go and see what was going on. He had to make up his mind one way or the other and not embarrass me by cheating on me. My bringing up was pretty straitlaced, even though I was in show business. The doorman let me in, and I went to the dressing room; he was on the third floor. I knocked at the door. He told me, "Wait a minute." I waited. He let me in. I said, "I can't go on this way. You're either going to be right with me or you're not—one or the other. Do you want her or do you want me?" He stopped . . . and he thought . . . and he said, "I'll take *her*."

I walked out and shut the door and went downstairs. All the boys were sitting around on the next floor. . . . I told them what had happened. I said, "So that's the end of that. I quit." I turned around and went downstairs and took a cab back to Rego Park. That was the first time Bunny'd ever cheated on me—well, it was the *only* time that I know of—and I was *terribly hurt*. Oh, I knew that some of the women were attracted to Bunny. A couple of his singers were—how shall I say it?—on the make for Bunny, but nothing ever came of it.

Following this revelation, and Bunny's jarring renunciation of her, Donna left New York as quickly as she could. Taking the children and her sister, she returned to Syracuse, where her father lived.

My dad had remarried and had three kids. He found me a house up by the university, a beautiful place of about eight rooms. It had four bedrooms upstairs, and a fireplace. I stayed all winter in Syracuse, but I began to have trouble. Bunny's dad was working for him then as a sort of manager. All of a sudden I was having trouble paying my rent, buying groceries, and everything. Finally I called, and called, and called. At last I got Bunny and told him. He said, "What! You're supposed to be getting a hundred dollars a week! What's happened?" I said, "A hundred dollars? I've only been getting fifteen dollars a week. I can't live on that with buying food, paying the rent and utilities." Bunny was surprised. He said, "I'll have to find out about that." Bunny really thought he was sending me a hundred dollars a week. The old man was giving that money to his girlfriend. Bunny didn't know. Well, he fired the old man when he heard about it. Then I started getting my right money.

This was the beginning of a fairly long period of separation, punctuated by intermittent, brief reconciliations. One took place at the time of Loretta and Don's honeymoon trip to Detroit. "We knew before the trip that they were separated," recalled Loretta.

At first Donna was not going to be there. Then she decided to come, apparently to put up a united front and welcome me as a new family member. This seemed very important for Bunny. At first it was very strained; Don and I both sensed it. Then things began to loosen up. Bunny and Donna had a few drinks, and he started teasing and joking with her. She couldn't keep from laughing. It ended up that we all had a good time. I remember wondering at the time if there was ever any down-to-earth conversation between them. It was all fun and games. But I was aware many times that they were separated.

The separation lasted until approximately the early months of 1940 and ended when Bunny rejoined Tommy Dorsey for a five-month stint. Jack Maisel, an occasional drummer and manager with Bunny's band, and a highly talented music copyist, played a part in the reconciliation. As Donna related:

I guess Bunny had thought things over and knew how things were going, how they'd been with me. He and Jack came down [to Syracuse] and asked me to come back. Jack was a good friend. I said, "No, I'm not coming back to the same stuff I just went through. I've been too hurt." And Bunny said, "It won't be that way." So they convinced me, and I went back to New York.

That's when Bunny was having trouble with Tommy Dorsey. He went bankrupt. I guess that's the reason he came up to see me. We moved into a hotel and he went to work for Tommy, I guess because he owed Tommy some money. Tommy would take most of the money that he owed him out of his salary, and that hardly left us any money to live on with the kids and all. I had the kids and five puppies all in the hotel, the Maryland Hotel on 49th Street. We were eating corn on the cob for our supper, which we were not used to. That's when they talked him into taking out his other band. He started over again with Don Palmer as manager.

Donna's understanding of Bunny's financial troubles at the time of their reconciliation was, of necessity, incomplete.

You see, I didn't hear all that stuff that went on, especially when I wasn't with him. I know he went bankrupt, and there was talk of trouble with Petrillo [James C. Petrillo, longtime president of the American Federation of Musicians], but I don't know what all that was about. Anyway, our whole separation was brought about by that Lee Wiley dame.

I hated her. You know, when Bunny was playing in the club on 52nd Street with Red McKenzie, she was always there. There was only one time I got a kick out of running into her. We were in the [Paradise Restaurant] one night—we used to go there almost every night and get a broiled steak and all—and she was standing at the bar. She had an evening gown on with the back cut way down to her waistline. Jerry Colonna was there. He was always a comedian, funny all the time. He didn't like her because of what she was doing to Bunny. So he walked over to her and said something to her. She just looked at him with her snaky eyes. Jerry said—you know how he talks with those big eyes and that moustache—"What's the matter, don't you like me?" He just took his drink and poured it right down her back.

At least it wasn't a lasting thing. She was the type of woman who would run from one bandleader to another and had a bad reputation for it, too. In fact, every bandleader she ever contacted, she practically ruined. That's what they tell me.

Anonymous musician's wife: "Victor kept her for years. Apparently he was able to put up with her antics with other men."

Anonymous Berigan researcher: "She was considered bad news by the boys in the band."

Anonymous Berigan scholar: "What she did to poor Jess Stacy was terrible. He wouldn't talk about her after they divorced."

Donna Berigan: "Snake eyes!"

17

I'd Rather Lead a Band

Song recorded February 24, 1936
by Bunny Berigan and His Boys

The Bunny Berigan Orchestra, as it is now remembered, came into existence on April Fools' Day, 1937. Prior to April 1, Bunny had been rehearsing a band as diligently as he ever did, working with the band by day, then rushing them to play one-nighters in the Boston–New York area. *Metronome* carried an article announcing that Bunny's band would be returning to Danny Duggan's in Worcester, Massachusetts, on March 31 because it had made such a marvelous impression at the second-floor dance hall during an earlier appearance. Instead, on April 1 Bunny gathered his musicians for a four-title recording session at RCA Victor that ushered in twenty-two separate sessions there stretching through 1939.

For this session, Bunny showed more care in his selection of sidemen. The nucleus of the thirteen-piece band included Steve Lipkins on trumpet, veteran reedman Clyde Rounds, exciting new tenor soloist George Auld, Joe Lipman, a solid pianist and burgeoning arranger, Tom Morgan(elli) on guitar, and George Wettling on drums. This group established the Bunny Berigan Orchestra, though as with all new bands, turnover proved inevitable. Certain changes made in the next two or three months added strength to Bunny's band. Irving Goodman came in on trumpet; the great Sonny Lee and Morey Samel entered on trombones; Joe Dixon's stylish clarinet and alto playing, plus Mike Doty's alto, solidified that section; Hank Wayland joined on bass. For several months of 1937 and in early 1938, this group represented the most stable band Bunny ever fronted, and except for regular appearances on *Swing Club*, Bunny was devoting full time to the band. Their debut was impressive.

Following the April 1 recording session, they played Easter Sunday, April 4, at Reade's Casino in Asbury Park, New Jersey. In early April, Bunny's band played a "battle of the bands" with Artie Shaw at the Roseland State Ballroom in Boston. This type of event was a regular feature at the Roseland and at other ballrooms during the early swing years. This particular "battle" was remembered as a special occasion by several of the band members. On April 18, the first *Fun in Swingtime* program, with comedians Tim and Irene, debuted over WOR, the first of twenty-six broadcasts that ran until October 10. April sizzled to a climax as the new band opened an extended stay at New York's top-drawer Madhattan Room of the Pennsylvania Hotel.

Perhaps no new bandleader ever enjoyed such an auspicious first month. Not Goodman. Not Miller. Not Ellington. Not Basie. Not J. or T. Dorsey. Not Kenton. So important did the Penn Hotel gig loom that Bunny did not line up any one-nighters for about two weeks before the Penn opening. This permitted the band to rehearse intensively at the Nola studios, one of the prime locations for such a purpose. Bunny wanted the band to be ready not only for the Penn opening but for one May and two June recording sessions scheduled, as well as for the move to the Penn Roof at the beginning of June. He continued to make some personnel changes, so that the band was nearly set by the time of the move to the Penn Roof. Lipman, Abe Osser, Larry Clinton, and probably Fred Norman and Dick Rose were busy whipping arrangements into shape as quickly as possible.

Reviews of Bunny's records, his radio program, and the band's Penn Hotel opening appeared lavishly throughout the general newspaper columns as well as in the usual trade papers:

Metronome, May, 1937—"'All Dark People are Light on Their Feet,' Victor, shows the Bunny Berigan band at both its musical and recorded best."

Variety, April 21—Bunny's radio music is "snappy but commercial. Famed around 52nd Street 'cats' as very swingo, he wisely modified his stuff for home consumption."

The Jersey Journal, (Jersey City, N.J.), April 28—"Mutual's new Sunday nite Radio Show 'Fun In Swingtime' features Bunny Berigan who tops his rise to popularity when he takes his 14-piece band into

Hotel Penn to succeed his old orchestra-mate Benny Goodman. Unknown until he was on a sustaining program a few months ago, this show gave him a buildup and a recent eastern tour added to his popularity. BB's success with the 'Fun In Swingtime' left the door wide open when the Hotel was casting about for a successor to Benny Goodman who will go to the coast."

Nick Kenney in the New York *Sunday Mirror*, May 2—"Bunny Berigan gets his big chance when he opens at the Penn Hotel on Thursday night (April 29th) following Benny Goodman. Things are just starting to break for Bunny and it's about time. Only a week ago he started a new WOR-MBS program. They call Bunny 'The Son of Swing.' His engagement should prove that swing isn't on the way out as critics claim. Betcha Tin Pan Alley turns out."

Malcolm Johnson in the New York *Sun*, May 8—"Bunny Berigan doing well at the Madhattan Room of Penn Hotel and he and his band will be downstairs in the hotel till 1 June and then go up on the Roof, the grill closing for the summer. The roof is really better since the low ceiling downstairs allows occasional suggestion of blasting. There is almost a constant double audience—dancers and those who pause to watch the band as they dance by."

Metronome, May, 1937—"That Bunny Berigan man has finally landed himself a big spot for his band. He's now ensconced in the bandstand, warmed for him all winter long by Benny Goodman's boys, in the Madhattan Room of the Penn Hotel. The Big, Bouncing, Blasting Bunny boy now has a new outfit that's not only larger, but definitely a good deal better than his earlier venture. He has a tough spot to fill—following Benny, but that trumpet of his should help mighty much to make this easier."

Not every review read favorably. *Metronome*'s June issue gave poor marks to vocalist Carol McKay for her performance during one of the live broadcasts from the Madhattan Room. Her efforts on two vocals on the first recording session reveal reasonable phrasing and a semblance of vocal personality asserting itself. Her handling of lyrics and her voice quality are more or less typical of the emerging "girl" band singer of the day: not remarkable, but certainly not unpleasant. When McKay suffered a throat ailment on the eve of the May 13 recording session, Sue Mitchell replaced her for three vocals. Since the poor *Metronome* review covered the May 12 broadcast, either McKay's throat problem had manifested itself during the broadcast or Mitchell had stepped in on that evening. Mitchell's singing, with its throaty, grating, yet somehow little-girl quality, deserves a poor review. Mitchell's stay was brief, terminated by McKay's temporary return. McKay, in turn, left the band at about the time it moved to the Penn Roof at the beginning of June.

Ruth Bradley, at twenty-two a veteran reed player and singer in "all-girl" bands, was appearing with the Ruby (not a girl) Newman band at the Rainbow Room of Radio City Music Hall when she heard that Berigan's vocalist spot needed filling. Bradley had sung and played clarinet and sax with Ina Ray Hutton and others, and the instrumental training revealed itself in her vocal work. Her phrasing was sure, her pitch secure, and the voice quality benefited from proper placement and proper breathing. Bradley held forth as the Berigan vocalist through the June and early July stand at the Penn Roof and through the first month of an extended stay at the Pavilion Royal. Reluctant to go along on a series of road stops that would follow the Royal engagement, Bradley left the band near the beginning of August. She was replaced by Gail Reese. Although Reese recorded some interesting sides during her nearly yearlong association with Bunny's band, she lacked the musical assurance and voice quality that set Bradley apart from other Berigan vocalists.

At the start of his career as leader, Bunny experienced little difficulty staffing his band. He enjoyed almost universal recognition among the music fraternity as a great technician and as the most exciting of the instrumentalists. His outgoing personality and friendly approach to everyone drew positive responses. The leader's enthusiasm for playing was contagious. His relationship with the bandsmen was less that of the leader-employer and more that of fellow sideman, though as Morgan(elli) observed, "he could be a thick-head at times." Bunny was one of the early charismatic figures in jazz. According to Dixon and Lipman, Bunny would not hire anyone he did not like. To some degree, he enjoyed the pick of the better musicians around New York. Naturally, many of them would not leave their steady, well-paying studio positions for the lower pay, risk, and road time that were part of the band business. But for a large number of musicians, the opportunity to play with Bunny Berigan was akin to dream-fulfillment.

Bunny's roster also benefited from trouble in the Tommy Dorsey band. Onetime Dorsey sideman Dixon recalled: "I was sick and in bed on doctor's orders. Frank Langone was sent to fill in as a sub for me on a recording session. Dorsey screamed and threw a fit. He wouldn't accept my word that the doctor ordered me to bed. It turned a lot of the guys off. I left as soon as I could for Gus Arnheim's band. Bunny kept calling me when he got his band formed, and as soon as I could I joined him." Rounds confirmed that he and several other Dorsey sidemen became involved in the Dixon issue and gave their notices to quit. When Bunny asked him the next night to join his forming band, Rounds agreed.[1] Lipkins also shifted to Bunny's band in time for the April 1 debut recording date. Dave Tough, another of those present at the unpleasant Dorsey incident, took over Bunny's drum chair within several months. Bunny discovered the young Canadian George Auld playing at Nick's in Greenwich Village; Auld eagerly responded to Bunny's offer. Sonny Lee, an old Berigan colleague from the studios and from Bunny's ill-fated stage venture with Minnelli, agreed to come on the band when Bunny could assure him that it offered enough security—an assurance that came with the recording contract and the radio program.

Bunny considered personal compatibility to be the most important ingredient in his selection of prospective band members. For the most part, the band's harmonious blend extended beyond their performances. In fact, except for one serious breach in this area, pianist Lipman would later recall the group as a "love band." The breach involved Lipman and drummer Wettling, viewed by most of those on the scene to be more of a problem drinker than Bunny. As Dixon related: "We always had trouble between Lipman and Wettling. They were always in fights. When Wettling got drunk he was like a raging bull. One time he sent Lipman to the hospital. It was a shame, and not only personally. We felt it in the rhythm section that they couldn't get along. The guys were glad when that combination was split up."[2] Morgan(elli) said the most serious fight was in Harrisburg, Pennsyl-

1. Clyde Rounds, interview with Tom Cullen, September, 1960, in Cullen Materials, copy of transcript in author's possession. The White Outline has also provided many details about this period in Berigan's life and changes in his orchestra.

2. Joe Lipman, telephone interview with author, January 20, 1985, tape in author's possession. Subsequent quotations from Lipman are taken from this interview. Lipman, chief arranger and frequently pianist with the Berigan band from 1937 to 1938, arranged "I Can't Get Started"

vania, and thought that Lipman's arm had been knocked "out of joint" and that a substitute pianist was needed. He affirmed the difficulties experienced by the rhythm section while Wettling and Lipman were in it together.

Not surprisingly, the piano and drum chairs saw frequent replacements during the first year. Lipman, Fulton McGrath, Graham Forbes, Lipman again, and finally Bushkin recorded on piano with the band during its first year or so. Lipman's role as arranger accounted for some of the personnel changes on the piano bench. Wettling, Tough, Blowers, and Buddy Rich variously served as drummer through about the same period. Only Bunny's trombone section experienced as much turnover at this time, with Al George replacing Samel, then Nat Lobovsky and Ray Conniff replacing Lee and George. "George Auld and I had to convince Bunny that it would be OK to hire Conniff and Rich," Dixon remembered, "because he didn't know them and wasn't sure how they'd fit in. *He had to like you.* If he didn't like you personally, he didn't want you in the band. He genuinely liked his musicians. We were *his boys!*"[3]

As leader of this new musical venture, Berigan found himself at the vortex of a whirlwind of musical activity, a position he truly seemed to enjoy. In the several months surrounding the band's formation, Bunny conducted rehearsals, selected tunes, sought out arrangements, held informal business meetings, conducted auditions, and drank. Lipman observed, "Bunny always had a mike in front of him, and when Bunny saw a mike, it was 'Let's go!'" Bunny was indeed seeing a mike almost constantly during those months: one-nighters; the extended stands at the Penn and at the Pavilion Royal, both with regular radio broadcasts; the Tim and Irene *Fun in Swingtime* weekly broadcasts; sound checks at rehearsals; appearances on *Swing Club*; and, of course, the recording dates.

During its first nine months, the band recorded thirty-seven sides at nine sessions, played for dancing and listening in uncounted ballrooms and auditoriums in nine states, and broadcast twenty-six commercially sponsored half-hour radio programs and a minimum of

---

and many of the tunes recorded by the Berigan big band, including the Bix Beiderbecke tunes with the reduced band; Joe Dixon, telephone interview with author, December 1, 1986, tape in author's possession.

3. Dixon telephone interview, December 1, 1986, tape in author's possession.

forty-one regularly scheduled sustaining radio shows, mainly from the Pennsylvania Hotel and the Pavilion Royal.

The band's early recording dates consisted mostly of current songs, mainly from films. Many were the products of notable composers and lyricists such as Al Dubin and Harry Warren, Richard Rodgers and Lorenz Hart, Rube Bloom and Johnny Mercer, and Charles Kenny, Nick Kenny, and Norman Ellis. None of these teams, however, contributed a song to the original Berigan book that can be considered a standard. Rather, the three early recordings that hold enduring appeal are arrangements of tunes from other eras: "Swanee River" (May 13, 1937); "Frankie and Johnny," and "Mahogany Hall Stomp" (June 25, 1937). Not until the Berigan band's fifth recording session (August 7, 1937) did the group record what could be considered a hit and a survivor. This, of course, was the date Berigan immortalized "I Can't Get Started," the Vernon Duke–Ira Gershwin tune from the *Ziegfeld Follies of 1936.* Backing this twelve-inch gem was an arrangement of an unlikely tune for a swing band, "The Prisoner's Song." With rueful humor in his voice, Dixon tells of how this side came to be:

Dick Rose came in to Nola, or one of those studios on Broadway where we rehearsed, one day with this arrangement. I don't know if he'd been invited in or if he just walked in. Anyway, Bunny said, "Pass it out." Bunny would always say, "Pass it out," and then he'd sit there and listen. So Dick Rose kicked it off and when we got through playing the thing Georgie Auld and I went over to Bunny and said, "This tune is a pig; we don't want this." And Bunny says, "Aah, it isn't that bad." Then Bunny gets the idea for the introduction, with the tom-toms and his growling with the plunger. The funniest part of it is, it became a hit. So we were wrong![4]

At that August 7 session, Reese served as vocalist for her first of several sessions that, except for the December 23 recordings, are represented by only two songs ever heard today: Duke Ellington–Juan Tizol–Irving Mills's "Caravan" and Larry Clinton's "A Study in Brown," both recorded on August 18. One of the strangest of that session's offerings features Bunny singing "Mama, I Wanna Make Rhythm," a silly-sounding, throaty vocal surrounded by a decent chart and good playing. On December 23, the band's final recording session of the year contained all winners: "In a Little Spanish Town," "Black Bottom," "Trees," "Russian Lullaby," and "Can't Help Lovin'

4. *Ibid.*

Dat Man." Like most performers, Bunny and his men responded more positively to superior material. Perhaps surprisingly, the least satisfying tune of this group is the elegant Kern-Hammerstein evergreen, "Can't Help Lovin' Dat Man," which receives a punchy, uptempo treatment. Although Tommy Dorsey and others had found success in marketing swinging arrangements of classics, that formula does not work here. Bunny's own playing on this session ranges from outstanding to sensational, and the band performs tightly as a unit. This is not to say that the other recordings from these 1937 sessions are without merit. Most of the arrangements far outstrip the compositions. All of them boast solos worth hearing and ensemble work that gets better with each session, as the band begins to tighten and take on personality brought by improved players. Bunny's solos on every tune are worth hearing as he fights to imbue them with quality. And his lead playing is impeccable and inspiring, as always.

Bandleader Berigan's enhanced reputation prompted commercial concerns to offer him financial compensation in return for product endorsements. The Selmer instrument company ran a series of advertisements featuring Bunny and his musicians. Dixon confirmed the accuracy of the advertisements, stating that Bunny and his entire sax section played Selmer instruments.[5] Later in his career, Bunny similarly lent his name for product endorsement with perhaps less concern for truth.

During a November stand at the Fox Theater in Detroit, Bunny's parents visited from Fox Lake for a few days. Their pride in the success of their son's new band was evident. This feeling was shared by friends and neighbors, who read about him in Fox Lake *Representative*, where he was still referred to as "Bernard." (Singer-pianist Bobby Short, while in Detroit for an appearance at the newly restored Fox in January, 1990, remembered this show as his first Detroit appearance. "It was the biggest theater I ever played in my career. The star was Bunny Berrigan [*sic*], the trumpet player. . . . The Fox was *very* glamorous."[6] Dixon remembered that during this stand, Bunny pulled one of his wackier surprises on some of his bandsmen:

When we were in New York, Bunny didn't go out after the jobs and jam and drink with the guys, but on the road he did. We were playing the Fox in

5. Dixon telephone interview, July 14, 1986.
6. Detroit *Free Press*, January 18, 1990, Sec. D, p. 2.

Detroit and staying up the street at the Hotel Detroiter. After the last show one night Bunny says, "Get some broads and a bottle and come on up to my suite,"—Bunny always had a suite of two rooms. We go up and he's there in his shorts. It's about 2:30 in the morning, and Bunny's got the window open and he's hitting golf balls. With his eight and nine irons he's practicing chip shots out onto Woodward Avenue! Bunny did crazy things like that. He loved to play around.[7]

A three-week booking at the Paramount in New York during late November and early December represented another great showcase opportunity for the band. Bunny's band followed Tommy Dorsey's run there. Frances Langford, referred to in newspaper advertisements as "Hollywood's greatest singing star, making her first Broadway appearance in four years," starred in the stage show.[8] (At least one band member recalls that Langford had some pitch problems, and the reedmen in the band purchased extensions for their mouthpieces to lower the pitch of their horns so that they could provide accompaniment that would match her pitch.)

When asked about Berigan as leader and taskmaster, his sidemen call forth somewhat differing memories. According to Rounds, Bunny often overlooked fine details at rehearsals, resulting in a relaxed style in person that sometimes sacrificed precision in the recording studio.[9]

Lipman offered a contrasting view:

Bunny was pretty much in charge of rehearsals. At rehearsals all arrangers take over; it doesn't matter which band you're in. Even in studio work, it's the arranger who rehearses the band, then when the conductor takes over he might make a change or two. That's par for the course; it's not a thing that's contrived. The conductor wants to get used to the arrangement. After all, the arranger has lived with the arrangement for days or weeks maybe; he knows every note of it. The leader has to listen to it, get the feel of it. Then he might make some changes; generally they're minor. Bunny was particular about musical detail like most good musicians are. He didn't hop on any of the guys for making mistakes because he knew they'd rectify them. They wouldn't be there if they wouldn't do that. There was an awful lot of pride in those Berigan bands. [Like most of the groups of that day,] we wanted to be better than anybody. I don't remember anyone ever being fired in Bunny's bands. . . . [T]he sidemen supplied their own discipline quite well.

7. Dixon telephone interview, December 1, 1986.
8. See New York *Times*, November 16, 1937, p. 27.
9. Ian Crosbie, "Bunny Berigan," *Jazz Journal*, XXVII (September, 1974), 9.

Dixon agreed in some respects: "We wanted to play well. The band had fantastic élan. Playing *live* in a dance hall there was no way any white band could touch us. The recordings weren't as good. Tommy Dorsey wasn't demanding—he was *impossible!* The same for Miller and Shaw. That's why their bands didn't swing; they were regimented and overrehearsed. That's one reason why Bunny's band was so terrific, especially when *he* was 'on.'"[10]

Bushkin remembered that Berigan ran his big band very much as he had the small swinging group on 52nd Street. Like Dixon, Bushkin contrasted Tommy Dorsey's approach to leadership with Bunny's style:

At the rehearsals, Bunny'd always have whoever had done the arrangements rehearse the band. He'd come in and play his parts like one of the guys in the band. Bunny wasn't tough, not like Tommy. Tommy would *lean* on you. He was a taskmaster. If you played three extra notes, he'd ask you what's the big panic all about. He'd say, "I don't want to hear all those runs, Joe; it's gettin' in the way." Then if I played too little he'd say, "What're you doing, getting lazy on me?" There was no way to get in the middle with this guy.

Albert McCarthy summed up Berigan's leadership style rather succinctly: "Holding a big band together and maintaining high musical standards is an arduous job; it is noticeable that most of the really successful leaders of the swing era were men with an element of iron in their souls. Tommy Dorsey, Benny Goodman and Jimmie Lunceford, to name but three, were known as strict disciplinarians, something which Berigan palpably was not."[11]

Dixon adds some perspective and insight with his comparison of the rehearsal styles of Berigan and Duke Ellington:

In the fifties I was doing quite a bit of recording at Columbia. A few times I got permission to sit in on Ellington's rehearsals, just to listen. Perhaps surprisingly, Ellington ran his band pretty much the way Berigan did. For example, a trumpeter or someone else would come in early and Duke would say, "Here, try this." One difference was that Ellington was a writer, as Bunny was not, and also Ellington had Billy Strayhorn. And Duke was a classic—America's musical gift to the world. But Ellington did basically what Berigan did. The men he chose were the men he wanted, and he wrote for his men. Jazz being primarily a players' art—this is a very important point— once the thing was set, Ellington never bothered his men. He never over-

10. Dixon telephone interview, December 1, 1986.
11. McCarthy, *Big Band Jazz*, 207.

rehearsed his band. Bunny wanted that same looseness and freedom. I could never have worked for Miller, Shaw, or Goodman, and I'll tell you why: as Dave Tough put it, by the time they got through rehearsing a piece, it was antiseptic. It took all the kick out of it. Jazz is a loose thing. You have to allow the players room to let their creativity come through.[12]

On at least one matter Bunny's former sidemen agree completely: Bunny was not a reliable conductor for shows. As good a reader as he was, and in spite of having played on hundreds of stage and radio shows, Bunny had neither the interest in nor the knack for such conducting. Dixon claimed Berigan "couldn't throw a down beat," and thus Rounds often assumed such duties on shows. Additionally, Bunny's associates during his band years unanimously agree that he never demonstrated any business sense and, further, that he had no real appreciation for money. Even during the band's crucial early months he just could not be bothered with the myriad details associated with running a band. He put his faith in his managers and in MCA. More than one sideman has stated with conviction that Bunny's treatment by the managers and by MCA, as well as by some of the club and theater owners, was simply not fair, and some aver that Bunny was cheated. Most agree as well that as a new bandleader, Bunny spent personal money lavishly—and perhaps wastefully. These opinions are bolstered by documented evidence that Bunny preferred expensive Chrysler automobiles and custom-made clothing, the latter usually selected by Donna or by some of his more devoted sidemen. While some anecdotes portray Berigan as overly extravagant when giving gifts or tipping service workers, Bushkin denies that Bunny was a spendthrift, preferring to characterize his mentor this way: "He paid generously for personal service. He was a generous man. Bunny was a *giver*, not a user."

At the end of what had been an eventful, successful year, and following a series of one-nighters that brought the band back to New York, Bunny treated the band members to a festive holiday party and presented gifts to all. Gail Reese received a traveling case. The white gold pocket watches the sidemen received bore individual inscriptions—"To Joe from Bunny—1937"—and in place of the maker's

12. Dixon telephone interview, December 1, 1986.

name on the face, "Bunny Berigan" was inserted. From the band he received a set of luggage. He gave Donna à fur coat.

During the party, this happy group might have reflected upon some of the noteworthy events that surrounded them in 1937: the United States Supreme Court upheld the Social Security Act; Neville Chamberlain, the new British prime minister, attempted to achieve peace in troubled Europe through appeasement of Hitler; John Steinbeck's *Of Mice and Men* became a hit; Grote Reber built the world's first radio telescope, which from Earth read radio waves in the cosmos; German engineer Walter R. Dornberger directed the construction of the V-2 rocket; auto workers organized a sit-down strike that established the UAW as a bargaining agent; President Roosevelt restricted munitions trade with Japan; Anastasio Somoza became president of Nicaragua; the Marx Brothers starred in *A Day at the Races*; J. R. R. Tolkien's *The Hobbit* reached publication; Edwin H. Land established the Polaroid Corporation; San Francisco opened its Golden Gate Bridge; Japan apologized for bombing and sinking the U.S. gunboat *Panay* in Chinese waters; dramatist Clifford Odets offered his play *Golden Boy*; Dimitri Shostakovich's Fifth Symphony premiered; Dow Chemical began manufacturing polystyrene plastic products; the German dirigible *Hindenberg* exploded near Lakehurst, New Jersey; Japanese troops seized Peking, Tientsin, and other Chinese cities, including Shanghai; Walt Disney's feature film *Snow White and the Seven Dwarfs* illuminated screens nationwide; anthropologist Franz Weidenreich discovered the skull of prehistoric Peking Man; Joe Louis won the heavyweight boxing championship; Benito Mussolini visited Libya and was proclaimed protector of Islam.

Following a brief year-end respite, the Berigan band began 1938 at Philadelphia's Earle Theater, one of the choice road stops.

18

There'll Be Some Changes Made

Song recorded March 15, 1939
by Bunny Berigan and His Orchestra

        In contrast to the sensational successes sustained by the
Bunny Berigan band over 1937, the new year began less auspiciously.
After closing at Philadelphia's Earle Theater during the first week of
1938, the band was idled by illness in the Berigan household. Bunny
contracted a severe case of flu, and one of his children—Madie recalled it was Joyce—became afflicted with what *Billboard* called a
"critical illness." In mid-January, the band reunited to tour New England. The physical violence between Wettling and Lipman that had
precipitated Wettling's departure had drawn notice in the press. Rollo
Laylan had filled in the vacant drum spot for only a brief time before
the magnificent Dave Tough replaced him for the New England tour.
Lipman, in turn, stayed on in New York to concentrate on arranging
as veteran Fulton McGrath briefly joined the band on piano, replaced
after about a month by Graham Forbes. In spite of the band's promising beginning, Bunny's weaknesses as a leader began to seed doubts
in the minds of some of his strongest players.
    Annual polls by the music magazines did not treat Bunny as kindly
as they had in previous years. *Down Beat* readers placed Bunny second to Harry James, who had become a very hot item with the Goodman band, as favorite trumpeter, just ahead of Louis Armstrong. "I
Can't Get Started" did no better than tenth in the year's record rank-
ing, and the Berigan band rated only thirteenth among swing bands.
Martin Block's *Make-Believe Ballroom* contest placed Bunny's band
tenth. Goodman and Tommy Dorsey headed the list, with such sweet
bands as those of Guy Lombardo, Horace Heidt, Sammy Kaye, Hal

Kemp, Eddie Duchin, and Shep Fields ranked ahead of Berigan. Nevertheless, reviews of the band live and on record continued to be primarily laudatory. Tough deserved the praise he drew at this time for helping to create stability and drive within the band.

Stability was not to be found, however, in the band's managing and support functions personnel. Arthur Michaud of MCA continued to be Bunny's personal manager, securing bookings and overseeing the financial operation, but other backstage positions turned over with regularity. From the band's inception to the end of 1938, Mort Davis and Jerry Johnson were two among many who served as road managers. Meanwhile, Bob "Little Gate" Walker, who had served as "band boy" almost from the beginning, became ill and was replaced in March by Bernie Mackey. Mackey's official duties included driving the band truck, handling the instruments and library, helping to set up the band before jobs, and reversing the process afterward. Later a guitarist with the Ink Spots, he would take over for Bunny's guitarist on occasion and would sometimes sing with the band, as he did on two recording sessions in June and September. When Walker rejoined the band after his illness, he and Mackey worked together— "Little Gate" and "Big Gate."

Michaud, already manager for Tommy Dorsey and Berigan, seized an opportunity to expand his influence and his pocketbook. In one of the never-ending moves made by band personnel, Krupa left Goodman to form his own band in March; Michaud landed him as a client. This combination of events affected Bunny's band in at least one direct way, and probably in other ways indirectly. Goodman was left in need of a top-flight drummer. Dave Tough was the one BG wanted; Dave Tough was the one BG got. After completing recording sessions with Berigan on March 15 and 16, the diminutive drummer began making his big sounds with the Goodman band. At the same time, Michaud, in adding Krupa to his stable of stellar instrumentalists/ leaders, devoted even less of his time to serving as Bunny's personal manager. He concentrated the bulk of his efforts on promoting Tommy Dorsey, Goodman's chief rival for the hearts and the dollars of listeners and dancers. He expended his leftover promotional energies, in the previous year devoted to Bunny, on Krupa's new band.

The Berigan band's first extended stand of 1938 was a two-week engagement at the Arcadia-International Restaurant in Philadelphia beginning on February 24. *Billboard* devoted much space to a review and information about the band's appearance:

One of the most successful bands molded in the Benny Goodman groove to come along since the swing craze is Bunny Berigan's (WABC, ARCADIA-INTERNATIONAL RESTAURANT, PHILLIE). Bunny himself is tops for hot trumpeteering and band as a whole has the same pounding drive as BG. Arrangements are strictly jive, giving every instrument a chance to take a bow with a hot lick and giving Bunny a chance to take a sultry solo in brass on every number. . . . A loud, youthful band, strictly for the junior jitterbugs, it has built up a tremendous popularity with the swinging kids by slanting its stuff for the jive market. Band stresses the hottest standards but keeps their music-pluggers happy. Gail Reese sings some pops in a capable manner, con expressivo. . . . Should be a sock in ballrooms and theaters. For radio their roughness could probably be polished up except that the outfit can better be sold on a blazeroo angle. . . . In selling the Bunny Berigan opening at the heretofore staid Arcadia-International Restaurant to the college and high school crowd, he invited the editors of the school papers to meet the maestro at a cocktail party. Best interview or story of the party printed will get a prize of $25.00.[1]

A follow-up article the next week indicated that Bunny's crew drew an excellent crowd for its stand, surpassed by only four of the major sweet bands and far above the room's average.

Graham Forbes took over the piano seat during the Arcadia engagement. He recalled that the band when he joined was "playing great. Bunny was on the wagon [not drinking] at that time, and so was Davie Tough. Both of them were just at the top of their playing. It was a great band. I'm quite sure that Johnny Blowers replaced Davie while we were still at the Arcadia."[2] Actually, Blowers played some one-nighters with the band after the Arcadia closing on March 9 and before Bunny's group began a long and celebrated run at the Paradise Restaurant in New York. Blowers says his own diary indicates that he permanently joined the band on March 17 at Rochester, New York, and photographs verify his presence on the stand the next night in Buffalo.

"I first met Bunny in Philadelphia at the Arcadia-International, just before I joined the band," Blowers recalled.

1. *Billboard*, March 5, 1938.
2. Graham Forbes, interview with Tom Cullen, *ca.* September, 1960, in Cullen Materials, copy of transcript in author's possession.

When Krupa left Benny Goodman, Benny hired Davie Tough. Red McKenzie called Bunny in Philadelphia, and Bunny came down to Nick's in the Village, without my knowing it, to listen to me play. He hired me after I sat in with the band in Philadelphia. Of course, Red and Bunny were friends, and for some reason Red had taken me under his wing. Red told me, "You know, Johnny, if you stay here, you'll become a drunk like the rest of us." I'd have been happy to stay at Nick's with those guys, but Red urged me to go with Bunny and get more exposure. Nick was mad as hell because he had gotten me my [union] card. Bunny's was a great band. We did some one-nighters before opening at the Paradise Restaurant in New York, right at 49th and Broadway, on March 20th. I made my first records with Bunny on my birthday, April 21st.

Blowers admitted to having had some reservations about replacing Tough. "He was the most emaciated guy I ever saw, but my God, he had such tremendous power. I don't know where it came from. He was just a marvelous drummer. Later on, Davey and I became good friends, and I had occasion to sub for him a number of times with [Tommy] Dorsey and with Woody Herman because he continued to have health problems."

The Berigan band enjoyed the distinction of being the first jazz band booked into the prestigious Paradise, the same restaurant graced earlier by Paul Whiteman when Bunny was still a member of that organization. The advertisements of the day lured customers by announcing three shows a night, 7:30 P.M., midnight, and 2:00 A.M., and heralding "Bunny Berigan, the Miracle Man of Swing, and his Orchestra." Bunny and his band played, not for the shows, but only for the dancing preceding each show. Dinner, including show and dancing, cost $1.50 on weeknights, $2.00 on Saturday. Jam sessions, featuring Gene Krupa, Joe Marsala, Maxine Sullivan, and others, maintained the pace on Sundays. Columnist and celebrity Walter Winchell proclaimed, "Broadway is raving." Almost from the beginning of the run, station WOR broadcast half-hour or hour programs of Bunny's music at least twice a week, at times almost nightly.

A rotating stage at the Paradise enhanced the show's visual appeal and slick production and sometimes abetted comic relief. As Blowers recalled:

The Paradise was some showcase! The combination of their regular show and Bunny's band was terrific. Wow! What business they did. That stage rotated. At the finale of the show, as that was ending and the girls were going off stage, the stage started to spin. As it did, now we're coming on the scene and Bunny's playing the theme, "I Can't Get Started." The people are screaming and applauding. It was *very exciting!* We played for dancing, alternating with the shows. The girl dancers were hanging in the wings and going crazy because we were the first jazz band to play there. We turned that place upside down.

At the Paradise they had two kinds of girls: the showgirl, the tall one who wore very little clothes, and showed mostly body. All she does is [pose and stand around]. Then they had the ponies, the ones who did the dancing. None of them had ever heard a band like ours. They were just hanging in those wings in amazement, watching Bunny. They were crazy, dancing there after their show without even changing their costumes. Most of our band's clothes were made at Leeds over on 48th Street. Bunny had this one double-breasted, powder blue jacket that was very good looking and very long. One night about two weeks into the gig, we're playing this nice ballad and all the broads are [peeking out from the wings]. Bunny's got his back to the audience. He turns sideways like this and opens up his coat and he's got himself all exposed, hanging out. The gals all screamed, "Oooh!" and the band broke up; the guys were dropping their horns. Those broads went crazy! I wouldn't be surprised if Bunny tried out every one in the joint before we left the Paradise.

Dixon remembered that pianist Oscar Levant was a regular patron and a big fan during the Paradise nights. "I wouldn't be surprised," offered Dixon, "if Levant put Bunny up to the flashing bit. He was always fooling around. He wrote 'Wacky Dust' for us."[3]

At the time of the Paradise run, guitarist Dick Wharton replaced Tom Morgan, doubling as vocalist. Surprisingly, in view of the quality of the gig at the Paradise, trombonist Sonny Lee began to feel that the force behind the Berigan buildup was waning. Perhaps this veteran virtuoso, several years older than his fellow sidemen, had access to information denied most journeymen, or perhaps Lee had developed the ability to sniff out changes in the wind. Shortly after Lee recorded with both the Berigan and Jimmy Dorsey bands on March 15 and 16 (as with Tough), he accepted an attractive offer from the latter, raising his pay to an unusually high level.[4] About the first of April, Nat Lobovsky replaced Lee in Bunny's Paradise band.

One of the common practices among bands at this time was the "impromptu" jam session in which prominent leaders miraculously

3. Dixon telephone interview, December 1, 1986.
4. Dick Wharton, interview with Tom Cullen, *ca.* September, 1960; Sonny Lee, interview with Tom Cullen, February, 1961. Both in Cullen Materials, copy of transcripts in author's possession.

appeared at the site of another leader's gig to join with his band in a free-blowing session. While the appearances were seldom spontaneous, the playing often reached exciting levels, both for the musicians and for those lucky patrons who happened to be in attendance. In Philadelphia, just before the conclusion of Bunny's Arcadia stand, one such session drew the official wrath of A. A. Tomei, president of Philadelphia's Local 77 of the American Federation of Musicians. Philadelphians were offered the chance to choose among the music of the bands of Bunny, Benny Goodman, both Dorseys, Larry Clinton, and Claude Hopkins. Krupa must have been nearby as well, for he and Tommy Dorsey appeared at the Arcadia for a hot session with Bunny. Tomei reacted with this proclamation in *Billboard:* "I don't care what they call it now, but there's always been a strict union rule about free playing, and that's what jamming is. It's not going to get any leeway here." The *Billboard* article continued: "Tomei made this blast when he heard [of the appearance of Dorsey and Krupa at the Arcadia last week]. The Arcadia patrons went wild; nothing like it has ever been seen here." The article went on to say that Tomei would take action to prevent the three instrumentalists from carrying through on a planned jam session on the radio.[5] Patrons who enjoyed this session were probably unaware that manager Michaud's strategy lay behind the seemingly spontaneous jamming.

During Tommy Dorsey's run at the Paramount in New York, one of Michaud's planned promotional sessions redefined *spontaneity.* Advertisements appeared in at least two New York papers announcing with straight face the "impromptu jam session" to be held during Dorsey's last show on April 14. In addition to Berigan and Krupa, whose new band was to open on April 16 in Atlantic City, Jimmy Dorsey joined with his brother in what amounted to a promotional affair for the new Krupa band. At about this time, Michaud instituted another innovation whereby he would partially refund to club owners his bands' advance fees if attendance at their events indicated that the "front money" was out of line. Michaud envisioned this as an incentive to club and ballroom owners to book his bands, but it might have opened the door to falsification of attendance figures and reduced fees paid to the performers. Several of Bunny's musicians remember that

5. *Billboard,* March 12, 1938.

Bunny frequently argued with Michaud and others regarding "short counts" on attendance and pay figures. Some have bluntly stated their conviction that Bunny was cheated out of significant sums of money. Most of these musicians, justifiably or not, lay the problem squarely at the feet of Michaud. Indeed, such an arrangement would place temptation in the way of the agency and the ballroom owners, who could agree to report low attendance figures and then benefit by splitting the resulting refund if a band did not appear on paper to have met its agreed-upon minimum gate.

The Berigan crew's reception at the Paradise was so positive that Bunny was rewarded with an extension of the contract from the original three or four weeks to seven, ending on May 6. But personnel continued to turn over at a disturbing rate. Lipman returned to the band on piano but was replaced by Bushkin before the end of the run. Andy Phillips joined Lipman in turning out suitable arrangements. In yet another key move, Ray Conniff replaced Al George, joining Lobovsky in the trombone section. Whereas Lee had played both lead and jazz trombone, Lobovsky was less the jazz player but was very strong on lead. Conniff's youthful verve complemented his partner's strength, and additionally, Conniff began to contribute some arrangements to the band's book. In another personnel change during this run, Ruth Gaylor replaced Gail Reese as female vocalist. Despite this spate of personnel moves, the band was playing magnificently. More convincingly than the records produced at this time would indicate, the generous number of available air checks from the Paradise attest to the band's usually clean, always exciting playing. Auld and Dixon continued to churn out their brand of swinging solos. The young Blowers can be heard improving his feel for the band on almost every broadcast, becoming more relaxed, more swinging. Bushkin's solo piano added a dimension that Lipman admittedly had not provided. The ensemble work in the reed, brass, and rhythm sections was tight, belying the claims of some that this band played sloppily or carelessly. True, its great strength lay in its ability to swing mercilessly, but its treatment of the obligatory ballads that were the meat and potatoes of a dance band's repertoire was consistently respectable, sometimes inspired. Unquestionably, this was a band that loved to cut loose, to take chances, and it was led by perhaps the most visceral, the most audacious of the player-leaders. When that band got going in front of an audience, players and listeners seemed to energize one another. Bunny would call for chorus after chorus of solos from not only Auld, Dixon, Bushkin, and Conniff, but from anyone who felt moved to try out his creative ideas. But on virtually every tune Bunny's commanding, high-tilted horn—sometimes muted, sometimes hatted, but mostly open—dominated the music.

"We probably hit our peak as a band in the summer of 1938," reflected Dixon. "I would remind some of the critics that we were a very young band, but we had more élan than any band in the country. That band was self-propelling. There was no white band that could go against us toe-to-toe."[6] Renowned Berigan discographer Bozy White essentially agrees with Dixon in pinpointing the band's peak:

This [Paradise Restaurant period] was perhaps the zenith for the Berigan band. Never again would it play a major job of any length in the "Big Apple" nor would it again have a network radio wire for such an extended period of time. Nor would as many top sidemen grace the Berigan band again. The band broadcast almost nightly and these air checks feature plenty of solos by [Auld, Dixon, and Lee]. The sax section, led by Mike Doty and anchored by Clyde Rounds (both very underrated musicians) was at its peak and the rhythm section had good drive with Hank Wayland on bass the standout. . . . Bunny blows happy, driving horn and the band seems relaxed and really swings on the up tempo tunes. This was the band that "cut" the Artie Shaw band in a "battle of music" in New England around this same period.

White more recently stated that he considers the band's peak to be in late 1937; he also places the time of the Shaw-Berigan battle in April of that year.[7]

It was at about this same time also that a complaint surfaced concerning the quality of the tunes assigned Bunny's band to record. The band was recorded with reasonable frequency in 1938, but very few of the tunes carry a pedigree. "Outside of Paradise," "Rinka Tinka Man," and "Round the Old Deserted Farm," for instance, qualify as mongrel examples of the "real dog tunes" often referred to by Dixon. Victor records claimed under contract the three big money-makers of the time—Goodman, Tommy Dorsey, and Shaw—as well as Berigan.

6. Dixon telephone interview, December 1, 1986.
7. Bozy White, jacket notes for Shoestring SS-100, *Bunny Berigan—Vol. I (1938–39)*— White also produced these records; Bozy White, to the author, March 15, 1988, in author's possession.

This situation, coupled with diffused managerial interests, gave Berigan a disadvantage when the distribution or assignment of tunes from publishers took place. The better choices almost invariably went to Goodman and the others among the swing bands. The major sweet bands, such as those in the Martin Block poll, also commanded preferential treatment in the assignment of good tunes to record. Continuing the pattern set earlier, most of the best material recorded by the Berigan band is the result of Lipman arrangements of non–Tin Pan Alley songs such as "The Wearin' of the Green." Often, Lipman and the other arrangers were given little lead time before a recording date. The quality of the charts and the playing under these circumstances speaks to the musicianship and the spirit of those involved.

In 1938, the Berigan band cut forty-four sides for Victor, culled during eleven recording sessions: January 26, March 15, March 16, April 21, May 26, June 8, September 13, October 14, November 22, November 30, and December 1. The last two sessions featured a reduced band playing Lipman arrangements of Bix Beiderbecke compositions. In addition, Bunny scheduled lengthy and prolific sessions on June 27 and August 9 for Thesaurus Transcriptions under the name of Rhythm Makers Orchestra, with vocalists Dick Wharton and Ruth Gaylor identified as Bob Brown and Elsie Wright, and Bernie Mackey identified as Burt Victor. These dates resulted in twenty and sixteen sides, respectively, and, as with all transcriptions, were intended solely for radio broadcast.[8]

In supporting his view that the Berigan band of this era was loosely disciplined, critic Leonard Feather cited the band's forty-one takes required to arrive at a satisfactory pressing of "Down Stream" on the March 15 session. In fact, manifest sheets from the RCA Archives show that the band completed three selections in four and one-half hours that day and three more in four hours and forty-five minutes the next day. While these times are not fast for big band recordings, they do not seem excessive, particularly in view of the probability that several of the charts were new to the band. By comparison, taskmaster Tommy Dorsey's band committed four tunes to record on the historic January 29, 1937, "Marie" session; these required four hours. Other comparable sessions confirm similar performance data, calling

8. Rust, *Jazz Records, 1897–1942,* I, 124–26.

into question Feather's observation. One participant in the "Downstream" session labeled Feather's assertion "bullshit!" and added that nobody would be allowed forty-one takes at RCA.[9] Bunny's band was able to complete sixteen and twenty transcription sides in single sessions, and on at least one of those dates the session preceded a regular evening gig at the Steel Pier in Atlantic City. These figures indicate instead an admirable level of discipline, whether self-generated or imposed by the leader.

The band had only four days between the May 6 Paradise closing and the beginning of another important gig. As was customary, they filled the interval with one-nighters in the area around New York City before beginning their one-week stand at the Paramount on May 11. It was during this stand that Donna confronted Bunny about Lee Wiley. Yet publicity photographs of Bunny clowning with Cass Daley, a dancer and comedienne who shared the stage bill with Bunny, do not reveal any personal problems. Gene Raymond, a popular movie singer and actor, headlined the stage show.

Following the Paramount stand, the band embarked on another series of one-nighters, completed two recording dates, and made a few radio guest appearances, including one June 26 on *Magic Key* with Bob Hope. In early July, the band played a week at Manhattan Beach, New York, a large amusement park next to Coney Island with an open-air bandstand. During this stand, drummer Blowers left the band to join Ben Bernie; he later went on staff at CBS. Blowers recalled with mixed feelings the going-away party Bunny threw for him in Boston: "They got me so loaded that I passed out and missed the train. I almost didn't get the job with Bernie. I called and asked them to make any excuse for me." Auld and Dixon persuaded Bunny to hire the young Buddy Rich out of the Joe Marsala band at the Hickory House as Blowers' replacement.

Bunny's band opened for a week's engagement at Detroit's Fox Theater on July 15, the week during which newlyweds Don and Loretta arrived as guests and Donna and Bunny temporarily reunited. Closing at the Fox on July 21, the band played a one-nighter two days later in Syracuse, New York, Donna's hometown. The band then had an engagement at the Steel Pier in Atlantic City during which they par-

9. Chilton and Sudhalter, *Bunny Berigan*, 23; RCA Archives, New York City, personal research conducted June 28, 1985; Dixon telephone interview, December 1, 1986.

ticipated as the third in a series of top bands featured on a trans-Atlantic broadcast by the British Broadcasting Corporation. Before opening at the Steel Pier, however, the band drove to New York City, arriving at 4 A.M., so that they could participate in a rehearsal for an important show at Billy Rose's Casa Mañana, a potential two- or three-week engagement slated to begin the next week. The rehearsal on July 24 was a mess. Jimmy Durante, Benay Venuta, Pat Rooney, and John Steel were on the bill, and the show required precision cueing for this mixture of singers, dancers, and comedians. Bunny could not cue well, and his key rhythm players, Bushkin and Rich, read with limited ability. Various participants reacted with ill temper. After the rehearsal, the band played a five-day engagement at the Steel Pier, cutting two days off the customary week to allow for additional rehearsal at the upcoming Casa Mañana. When the band returned to New York to prepare for the opening, probably set for Saturday, July 30, they were told of a revised scheme for the show. In the end, Bunny, guitarist Wharton, Rich, and Bushkin did not play the stage show. Instead, Bunny and the full band played his theme and an introductory number, after which the four musicians were replaced, probably by Durante's regular pianist and drummer, another guitarist, and an experienced show conductor. Following the show, the band played for dancing. While this seemed a good compromise, some time during the first week Bunny and entrepreneur Billy Rose argued about something relatively minor, and Rose immediately hired the band's replacement.[10]

With a resulting hole in the middle of its peak summer schedule, Bunny's organization scrambled for one-nighters and second-rate engagements. On August 14, they began a week or more at Cincinnati's Coney Island Moonlight Gardens, followed by a week at the Stanley Theater in Pittsburgh beginning on August 26 and a week at Detroit's beautiful outdoor ballroom, the Eastwood Gardens, ending on September 9. The events of Sunday, September 11, made big news:

BERIGAN'S CORRIGAN ACT GIVES HUTTON 7 'C's—One of the biggest mixups in memory occurred [at Bridgeport, Conn.] Sunday at . . . Pleasure Beach Ballroom, where Bunny Berigan was booked to play the closing dance of the season. Berigan, giving a Corrigan twist to the directions, went up to

10. Cullen Materials; Dick Wharton, interview with Tom Cullen, *ca.* September, 1960, in Cullen Materials, copy of transcript in author's possession.

Lake Compounce Ballroom, Bristol, Conn., instead. Berigan's boys had their equipment set up after arriving there early when in walked Gene Krupa and his men who were booked there. Hurried explanations followed, with Krupa staying and Berigan packing quickly and hurriedly getting underway for Bridgeport where they arrived several hours late. Meanwhile Pleasure Beach had turned out the lights and those who didn't return home went over to the Ritz Ballroom where Ina Ray Hutton was holding forth.[11]

The difficulties continued. At a "Millionaires' Party" the next night on Long Island, so-called because of the privacy of the setting and the apparent affluence of the guests, both Bunny's band and a Meyer Davis sweet unit were engaged. In a rare display of bad temper, Bunny refused to play sweet music and waltzes as requested. His frayed temper that night may have been attributable to the presence on the stand of two new reed players, brought about by the defection of both Dixon and Mike Doty.

Dixon and Doty had served notice to Bunny about three weeks earlier, having become convinced that the band's generally poor management, and especially Bunny's self-destructive drinking, would not improve. Many incidents combined to lead Dixon and Doty to their decision. Early in the summer, the trade papers carried stories of an upcoming Palomar Ballroom engagement in Los Angeles for the band. This never materialized. At about the time of the *Magic Key* broadcast with Bob Hope, serious talk surfaced about the probability of Bunny's band being selected for the projected Bob Hope radio show, to originate from Hollywood. This opportunity also disappeared. Among the bands that did play Hope's show were those of Stan Kenton and Les Brown, the latter serving as Hope's accompanist for more than a quarter of a century, and still counting. Dixon and Doty determined that they had been patient enough. One day during a series of some one-nighters in Ohio—Dixon remembered jockeying between Youngstown and Akron—Bunny, having had some drinks, called an unannounced rehearsal. Both Dixon and Doty missed the call.

We were out shopping or something [Dixon recalled] and when we got back to the hotel someone asked us, "Where have you been? Bunny's sore as hell."

11. *Billboard,* September 24, 1938. The "Corrigan twist" refers, of course, to the 1938 flight of Douglas "Wrong Way" Corrigan, who, ostensibly headed for Los Angeles, landed in Ireland instead.

We found out we'd missed a rehearsal, so we went to find Bunny in a saloon behind the theater. We walked in there and Bunny really ripped into us. This is the first time I'd ever seen Bunny read me down; I never heard him do this to anybody. Mike and I walked into his dressing room later; Donna was there. Both Mike and I told him we were quitting. "It's not because of what happened today; we know you just lost your temper," we told him. "This band just isn't going anywhere." Bunny tried to talk us into staying, but it was no go. He said, "We're going to California, Joe. We're going to do the Bob Hope show. You'll be able to get married, like you want." I told him flat out that he wasn't going anywhere because he was drunk all the time. I had already turned down too many good opportunities. [12]

George Bohn replaced Doty on lead alto, and Gus Bivona took over Dixon's jazz clarinet and third alto chair. Incredibly, following the all-night party, the band, replete with the new reed men, recorded six tunes the next day in a five-and-one-half-hour session that began at 1:30 P.M. New vocalist Jayne Dover and band boy Bernie Mackey provided the vocals on four of the sides. Perhaps, as the relatively efficient use of studio time suggests, Bunny had used the party as a rehearsal opportunity for the recording session. Press reviews of this session were mixed.

The next important booking for the Berigan band was at the Hotel Ritz in Boston for two full weeks, beginning Monday, September 19. On September 21, a hurricane smashed Boston and large areas of New England, causing an estimated 460 deaths and property damage of approximately $460 million—and ending a prime engagement for the Berigan band. Apparently the Ritz agreed to a settlement with Michaud that gave the band partial compensation for the two weeks, in spite of a clause in the contract that made this unnecessary. Trumpeter Johnny Napton was to join the band at the Ritz, replacing mainstay Steve Lipkins. His initiation into the band proved to be more than the nineteen-year-old had counted on. Jazz writer Ian Crosbie has recounted trumpeter Napton's experience in trying to join the Berigan band while traveling on a train turned on its side by the forces of the hurricane. [13] So extensive was the damage to the Ritz that its outdoor terrace bandstand was never again used.

12. Dixon interview, July 14, 1986.
13. Ian Crosbie, "Bunny Berigan," 10.

Picking up the pieces presented even more problems for Berigan, as reported shortly after the devastating incident:

The Bunny Berigan Orchestra picks up where it left off after being blown out of a two-week date at the Ritz Hotel, Boston, by the recent hurricane, starts four successive Wednesday evening one-nighters at the Roseland Ballroom, N.Y., tonight. . . . Berigan capped a string of hard luck, which included loss of the Boston date, smacking up his own car in an auto crackup, ditto fate with his instrument truck among smaller things, with a sprained ankle Sunday making it necessary for him to stay off his feet until the last minute prior to going into the Roseland.[14]

The four Wednesdays at Roseland turned out to be only two. Milton Schatz replaced George Bohn on lead alto, and Wes Hein, who replaced Nat Lobovsky on lead trombone, was himself soon replaced by Andy Russo, with Conniff moving to lead. The "breaks" continued. Some time in early to mid-October, Bunny's sprained ankle may have received a jolt and become broken while Bunny was riding on the band bus. Dick Wharton, Gus Bivona, and Bushkin all recall with certainty that Bunny had a broken leg at about this time. Bushkin maintains that it was broken while Bunny was at home playing with the children. Eventually, Bunny's right leg had to be rebroken and set in a cast for several weeks.

One buoyant piece of news for Bunny came from the publication, in the October *Down Beat*, of the results of the second annual All American Swing Band Contest. Listed as trumpet winners: first— Harry James; second—Bunny Berigan; third—Louis Armstrong. The band's general pattern of unrest continued, however. In late October or early November, Bushkin left the piano bench, and once again it was occupied by Lipman, who continued to provide arrangements; Bob Jenney, the much-less-experienced brother of the magnificent Jack Jenney, replaced Russo on trombone; Kathleen "Kitty" Lane entered as vocalist in mid-November; and Murray Williams took over the lead alto chair from Schatz before the November 22 recording session. About a week later, during the November 30 to December 1 recording sessions that produced the Beiderbecke compositions, Auld gave his notice and within two weeks had joined the Artie Shaw

14. *Variety*, CXXXII (October 5, 1938).

band.[15] Don Lodice took over Auld's chair. One final personnel change remained for 1938: Bunny severed his often-stormy relationship with personal manager Michaud. Jerry Johnson, the husband of singer Kathleen Lane, took over Michaud's responsibilities during Christmas week and served for a time as road manager as well.

Throughout the fall and early winter of 1938, the band played mostly one-nighters in places like North Adams, Massachusetts, Savin Rock, Connecticut, Lawrenceville and Princeton, New Jersey, York, Pennsylvania, Ithaca, New York, and Riverside Plaza, New York City. On November 19, Bunny played one of his many guest appearances on *Swing Club*, sharing the billing with Lee Wiley. Even the most ardent Berigan fan must cringe at hearing Bunny's reading of this version of his famous theme, minus the vocal, on this air check. He sounds much like a caricature of his recording, converting runs into cheap glissandi, pinching his normally exalted tone in places, slurring simple passages, missing notes, and quivering his way through the low-note passage after the final bridge. Whether from drink or exhaustion, Bunny was not in control.[16]

Billboard's article on December 31 heralded a new format for the Berigan band. Bunny's Beiderbecke sides, recorded with reduced instrumentation a month earlier, had been released to great critical acclaim and enjoyed an encouraging sales spurt. Buoyed by these results and his separation from Michaud, whom Bunny had considered a major cause of his ever-growing problems, Bunny announced that he would begin operating with a slimmed-down, nine-piece band that he viewed as swing's equivalent of chamber music.

15. George Auld, interview with Tom Cullen, n.d., in Cullen Materials, copy of transcript in author's possession.

16. Much of the information about activities of Berigan's band during this period from Cullen-White research, in Bozy White Outline.

19

Keep Smilin' at Trouble

Song recorded December 4, 1935
with Bud Freeman and His Windy City Five

Perhaps the first change in 1939 was a reversal of Bunny's announced intention to pare the size of his band, if indeed this ever was his intention. Personnel changes in the big band continued at a furious tempo rivaling that of their rendition of "The Prisoner's Song" on a good night. In either late December or early January these shifts took place: Buddy Rich out on drums, followed briefly by Phil Sillman, then on January 19 by Eddie Jenkins; Dick Wharton out on guitar and vocals, replaced on guitar by Tom Morgan, but only for occasional gigs in or near New York City; Danny Richards in as vocalist on January 25; Jack Koven added as a third trumpet; Irving Goodman out on second trumpet; George Johnston in on Goodman's chair; Bernie Mackey out as assistant band boy–guitarist-singer. In one of the most significant moves, Bunny's good friend and anchor of the sax section, Clyde Rounds, vacated his position on January 1. His chair was assumed by Larry Walsh. Bushkin returned on piano.

The early days of 1939 must have been an emotional, musical, managerial roller-coaster ride for Bunny. On January 8, the city of Bridgeport, Connecticut, beckoned once again. This was the location of the previous September's infamous "wrong turn," when the band failed to show up for the gig at the Pleasure Beach Ballroom. When Bunny arrived in January, at the right place at the right time, he was greeted by the city comptroller and the sheriff. They demanded and received, before the band was allowed to play at the Ritz Ballroom, a payment of $117 to the City of Bridgeport, which owned Pleasure Beach. Bunny had promised earlier to make good the lost expenses incurred by the city; the sheriff's presence ensured that payment. All of the trade papers carried articles detailing the incident.

Four days later, Bunny participated in a recording session with the 1938 *Metronome* All-Star Band, a session that was the brainchild of *Metronome*'s editor, George T. Simon, and the forerunner of similar sessions held over the course of a number of years. Sudhalter's notes describe the scene well:

Simon . . . resolved to do something more with his magazine's annual popularity polls of jazz musicians than just print the results. Why not assemble an all-star band of winners and make a record? Victor recording supervisor Eli Oberstein agreed, and in the early hours of January 12, 1939, a select group of musicians gathered at Victor's 155 East 24th Street studios to record two titles, one to be led by Benny Goodman, one by Tommy Dorsey—provided that these bitter rivals could keep their tempers. They did, possibly because neither could bear to miss the chance of recording with a dream band like this one. Flanking Goodman were his longtime alto saxophonist Hymie Shertzer (second place in the latest *Metronome* poll behind Jimmy Dorsey, who could not attend) and tenor stand-by Art Rollini. Tommy Dorsey and Jack Teagarden were the trombones. From the Bob Crosby band came tenorman Eddie Miller, bassist Bob Haggart, pianist Bob Zurke and drummer Ray Bauduc, the latter two filling in for Teddy Wilson and Gene Krupa, whose Brunswick contracts kept them from recording for Victor. The trumpets included Harry James, Charlie Spivak, Sonny Dunham and the winner of the 1938 hot-trumpet poll, Bunny Berigan.

"All the musicians worshipped this guy," said Simon. "That night he was in fine shape. No problems at all. He just pitched in—and played great." No problems in the studio, that is; in the real world outside, where his band was plagued with personnel turnovers and dreary one-night bookings, the future looked dim.

But this was a night for high spirits and good music. Dorsey even asked the incredulous Goodman to kick off the tempo for the number the trombonist was supposed to lead, "Blue Lou." "You're up front," he called from his station back in the trombone section. "They can all see you. I'm just a trombone player back here." So Goodman kicked it off and settled down to play second alto on a borrowed horn. After a couple of tests and a first take, the men had felt their way into the piece and produced a fine second take.[1]

On January 16, Bunny's parents left Wisconsin to live in New York with Bunny, a move Cap and Mayme viewed as possibly mutually beneficial. By this time Donna may have rejoined the household, at least temporarily for appearances' sake. Serious financial restrictions

1. Chilton and Sudhalter, *Bunny Berigan*, 47.

added to Donna's and Bunny's strained partnership. On the positive side, a late January to early February stand at Boston's Southland was a record-breaking engagement for the Berigan band, complete with radio broadcasts. As for the Berigan sidemen, they continued to change. Vic Hauprich, a reedman from the Madison area who had played there with Bunny years before, took over the lead alto chair sometime in February. Within about a month, Henry Saltman replaced Hauprich, with Bivona probably moving to the lead chair. Arranger Andy Phillips occasionally played guitar with the band after taking rudimentary lessons from Allan Reuss. At a recording date on March 15, the band produced six sides in five and one-half hours, their efficiency no doubt abetted by prior rehearsals. Reuss sat in on guitar for this recording session only. Before the end of March another of Bunny's Madison friends, "Doc" DeHaven, replaced Saltman on alto. Hank Wayland created a major void at about the same time when the showy bassist, a member of the rhythm section almost from the band's inception, gave notice. He was replaced briefly by Sid Weiss; then bassist Mort Stuhlmaker, Bunny's friend from 52nd Street days, took over the rhythm keeping.

Berigan's 1939 band followed a grueling road schedule. According to a log kept by drummer Jenkins, from mid-January to mid-April the band played nearly sixty ballrooms, hotels, theaters, armories, clubs, auditoriums, halls, pavilions, casinos, and academic institutions from Massachusetts to Florida, from Michigan to North Carolina, and appeared in Ontario on three separate occasions.[2] The early part of the band's 1939 schedule was undertaken, of course, during the most difficult part of the winter, complete with snowstorms and dependent upon the reliability of mid-1930s automobiles on 1939 roads. After a gig in Lorain, Ohio, on January 24, for instance, the band members took to their cars in a blinding blizzard to make a January 25 date in Bradford, Pennsylvania. During the all-night caravan, one of the band cars was involved in an accident in which Bob Jenney and another musician were injured. The band played four shows at Bradford's Shea's Theater with new vocalist Danny Richards doubling on trom-

---

2. Jenkins' log was made available in Bozy White's research and was later published (see Jerry Kline, ed., "Touring with Bunny," *Mississippi Rag*, X [February, 1983]). Information and quotations in this paragraph and the following one are taken from this log.

bone to fill in for Jenney. On a late January drive to Boston, the band was likewise endangered by a severe blizzard. They were engaged for eight days in Boston, but Massachusetts "blue laws" prohibited night-clubs from operating on Sundays. Thanks to the profit-paramount booking practices of MCA, the musicians found that Sunday, February 5, was filled with a date in Newark, a particularly difficult round trip from Boston. This treatment from their bookers provoked the band's anger during an otherwise buoyant engagement at Boston's Southland.

Some of Jenkins' comments in his log are illuminating. When the band hit New York City on several occasions, he welcomed the oppor-tunity to sleep in his own bed. During the Southland engagement he met Avedis Zildjian, noted manufacturer of drum cymbals, and toured the factory "through an introductory note from my drum dealer in N.Y.C. I selected several marvelous cymbals with the understanding that I was to pay for same through my dealer in New York. Mr. and Mrs. Zildjian came to the Southland to hear the band one night soon after my visit to his plant on February 2, and Bunny called me over to their table to inform me that the cymbals were a gift to me." Jenkins also expressed great pleasure at meeting Mr. Slinger-land, manufacturer of the drum set he was using. On March 26, after playing a full show at Brooklyn's Riviera Theater, the band swung through a "Battle of Music" at Harlem's famed Savoy Ballroom. The band of Erskine Hawkins, dubbed the "20th Century Gabriel," pro-vided friendly competition. Jenkins notes, "We cut him. Wonderful crowd, wonderful music! I played a hole right through the bass drum (first and only such occurrence)!"

Through the years of performing in public, Bunny had developed a number of musical and visual gimmicks designed to please an adoring public. One particular favorite, maintained almost throughout his band-leading days, became a patented ending to any dance or con-cert. Upon completion of the closing theme, Bunny would take his horn from his lips and, sometimes still facing the audience with his back to the band, throw his trumpet with apparent carelessness to-ward the back of the bandstand. Usually "Little Gate" appeared ser-endipitously from the wings to catch the horn. Sometimes the drum-mer or a trumpeter carried this responsibility. Once Bunny misfired and struck one of his players in the face with the trumpet. Bunny apologized and suggested, "Why don't you sue me?" Gene Kutch, the pianist-arranger for Bunny's last band, remembered, "Bunny was a terrible clown with his horn. He'd twist around and heave the thing after we finished the theme. One night he throws it to [drummer] Jack Sperling and it dropped! And bent the valve casing. I play trumpet too, and I carried my horn with me. I had the Conn Coprion model, with the copper bell, just like the ones Jimmy Lunceford's trumpet section used. Bunny liked my horn and used it for quite a while [after his was damaged]. He used it for the picture *Syncopation*."[3] Another of Bunny's tricks with the closing theme was to arrive at the final, majestic high E-flat and then turn the playing of that note over to another pianist who played trumpet. Bushkin could play some acceptable blues on the horn, and even showed further versatility by singing an occasional song, but he did not have the lip to negotiate the theme's final note. He would contort his body, turn purple in the face, and fail, much to the delight of the paying customers. After Bushkin left the band, Bunny would vary this routine by announcing to the crowd just how easy it was to finish off the theme. Buddy Koss recalled: "Bunny would play a dirty trick on his trumpet players. As you know, his theme is very difficult. He'd say, 'Just to show you that it's not that hard, every one of my trumpet players is going to do it.' These guys would struggle, their eyes would bulge. I really don't know why Bunny would do it; it was kind of a mean trick."[4]

On April 23, Eddie Jenkins was replaced by Paul Collins as the drummer while the band was filling in a Tuesday-Thursday-Saturday schedule at Cleveland's Trianon Ballroom through May 4 with a pattern of one-nighters in "nearby" spots like Detroit, Ontario, West Virginia, and Pennsylvania. Before the end of the Trianon residency in Cleveland, the band added, besides Jenkins' replacement, Tom Moore on guitar, Charlie DiMaggio on alto sax, and a new third trumpeter, George Johnston. Toward the end of the Trianon run, Kitty

3. Gene Kutch, interview with author, June 25, 1985, tape in author's possession. Kutch later played with the band of Tommy Dorsey and others. Kutch shared information during this interview and in subsequent conversations and correspondence. Subsequent quotations from Kutch are taken from these conversations and the correspondence.

4. Edwin "Buddy" Koss, telephone interview with author, March 13, 1988, tape in author's possession. Koss was Berigan's pianist on two different stints during 1940 and 1941. He has shared information in subsequent telephone conversations and correspondence with the author. A taped interview of Koss was also conducted on July 28, 1978, by Deborah Mickolas, who lent it to the author.

Lane was given her notice of termination. Wendy Bishop assumed Lane's duties, probably during a May 6 and 7 stand at Coney Island Moonlight Gardens, in Cincinnati, Ohio. The Berigan band attracted nearly five thousand paid admissions for these two nights, a season high. At about this time, Bunny's father began traveling with the band and tried to assume some of the functions of road manager.

Departing Ohio temporarily after some one-nighters, the band landed near Pittsburgh for a two-week run at the Dance Pavilion at Kennywood Park. What purported to be an attractive gig, complete with regular radio broadcasts, was marred by a demanding, out-of-character schedule and an incident of some meanness. The Kennywood manager expected nearly *continuous* music, seven nights a week, plus weekend matinees, and lots of waltzes. This was hardly the format to cheer the hearts of a band that loved to swing. Bushkin recalled the scene:

It was one of those nickel- or dime-a-dance places. They didn't want you to play more than a chorus or two, then you'd stop. You'd start a new tune and then stop. You're not allowed to do it for more than two minutes or they're losing money. We get a break this night and we go to a bar and we're having a beer or something. There's a bunch of tough guys there—maybe a local baseball team—and somebody makes a move on the guitar player's wife. Naturally we're going to step in, and now there's some heads that are going to be busted. And naturally Bunny is in the middle of it. There's a lot of punching and shoving going on, but it breaks up.

Then after work when we get through playing and we're coming out of the ballroom, there's about twenty guys there with lead pipes and broomsticks and baseball bats. They're going to break all our heads. Bunny's father was a big, huge guy—I loved him—and he got in the middle of this fuckin' fight. Small as I am, I gotta fight because there's lots of heat on us. When he saw all those guys out there the manager of the ballroom figured he'd better get the police department. "You guys can't walk into this and get killed," he says. So he got the police and they escorted us to our rooming houses. We didn't stay in a hotel because this was a small steel mill town outside of Pittsburgh.

Police continued to escort the band for a few days after the incident, probably until the conclusion of the engagement on May 30. This respite from the incessant one-nighters proved to be less a restorative than an irritant.

Summer bookings promised needed relief from the band's punishing schedule of the first half of 1939. Regular radio broadcasts highlighted the band's week at Detroit's Eastwood Gardens in early June.

According to saxist Walsh, on this gig Berigan and Conniff angrily parted, leaving both the lead and jazz trombone responsibilities vacant.[5] Jimmy Emmert, who had been playing in the Bob Crosby band, came in on lead trombone, and Bob Jenney, still a relative novice on the instrument, became the jazz player.

Following a one-nighter in Grand Rapids, Michigan, Bunny sent his band back to Detroit to await him while he snatched a few days' visit to his hometown. Mayme had preceded him, arriving in Fox Lake to attend Loretta in the birth of her expected child. In Mayme's wake, Donna and her two children also traveled to Fox Lake, intending to remain there throughout a long job the band was soon to begin in Chicago. While Donna and Bunny were not really reconciled at this stage, small-town expectations played a part in convincing Donna to help maintain the outward appearance of marital unity. A week's lull in schedule may have benefited the band's and Bunny's physical condition, but financially it created further hardship. Nonetheless, Loretta recalls this visit by Bunny, her second meeting with him, as one filled with lots of fun and good conversation. While Bunny relaxed in Fox Lake, band members Bushkin, Lodice, and Koven discovered vocalist Ellen Kaye in Detroit's Shamrock Club, located in the Irish section of the city near the Detroit Tigers' home ballpark. When Bunny returned to Detroit, he quickly auditioned Kaye and hired her to replace Wendy Bishop as vocalist. The band resumed working in Detroit, this time at Westwood Gardens, with nightly broadcasts June 15 through 22. On the move again, they played a one-nighter at the familiar Valley Dale Ballroom in Columbus and two days at Madison's Orpheum Theater before beginning a historic Berigan engagement at Chicago's Sherman Hotel.

The Sherman's Panther Room provided a stylish showcase for Bunny's band from July 1 through August 11 that summer. Exposure afforded by the prestigious room was enhanced by nightly network radio broadcasts. In fact, both WMAQ (NBC) and WENR (ABC) listed half-hour programs for at least part of the engagement. Bunny's band played nightly for the broadcast, as well as for the stage show

---

5. Larry Walsh, interview with Tom Cullen, June, 1960, in Cullen Materials, copy of transcript in author's possession. Subsequent quotations from Walsh are taken from this interview.

and the dancing. The show's intermission band, Muggsy Spanier's Ragtimers, included stellar trombonist George Brunies and pianist George Zack, for whom Bushkin sometimes sat in. During the Sherman run, Ralph Copsy, a fine studio trombonist, replaced Bob Jenney, and Joe Bauer took over George Johnston's trumpet chair. When she replaced Ellen Kaye, Gail Robbins became another in the growing list of Berigan's female vocalists, but only for the duration of the Sherman engagement. Fox Lake's proximity to Chicago allowed Bunny and some of his bandsmen to motor there each week immediately after the Sunday-night closing, spend the typical off Monday in Bunny's hometown area, and drive back on Tuesday in time for the gig. Some of the musicians recall driving to Fox Lake for the weekends and sleeping in their cars, then waking up to pool their coins for breakfast and enough gas to make the return trip. Bunny's reputation in the Chicago area, extending as it did to patrons from Madison and Milwaukee, resulted in excellent attendance throughout the engagement. But the potentially idyllic Sherman run was tangled in a twisted financial morass.

Bunny's own lack of financial sophistication has been well documented. What descended upon him and the band in Chicago was the accumulation of months, if not years, of mishandling, misappropriation, and misfeasance. Probably several individuals played a part in the resulting mess. Leading up to the Sherman engagement, the musicians had been paid only partially—if at all—for a series of weeks. While on the tough string of one-nighters, Bunny appeared to be having as difficult a time financially as any, and no one complained. When they arrived at the Sherman, playing to good crowds, and the compensation still was not forthcoming, the simmering situation boiled over. As Bushkin remembered:

We hadn't been on location for a year. We've been killing ourselves on one-nighters. I've got my father's Pontiac and I'm driving. We haven't got any buses because Bunny's busted out. Sometimes we're playing ballrooms that haven't been open in twelve years and nobody knows we're going to be there that night, thanks to MCA. Do you love this? MCA and that asshole Arthur Michaud are busting Bunny's balls. At one point my father came to Chicago to get the car and I drove him back to New York; I wouldn't let him drive back by himself. I guess Muggsy's piano player sat in for me for a night, and I came back to Chicago on a bus. We hadn't been paid for about three weeks.

The guy at the saloon across the street from the Sherman—a big, heavyset guy named Freidman—was loaning us money, five dollars at a time so we could keep eating.

What had been happening was that sometimes when Bunny couldn't meet the payroll he'd been borrowing money from MCA. They'd loan it to him at some ridiculous interest rate and he built up quite a debit. Michaud was involved, and he's not coming up with any more money. The Sherman Hotel was paying MCA to pay Bunny, and instead of paying us they're keeping it, deducting against their debit. One night Bunny was stoned, and after the radio program he told the guys in the band, "When you get through playing come up to my room, I want to talk to you." We go up and he's in his bed, stark naked. We're all standing around in our band uniforms and there he is in that single bed, big as he was, with his arms draped over the edges. We'd never seen him flat on his ass before; we'd always seen him upright, with us praying for him to hit those high notes. He said, "Do me a favor. One of you guys go to Jimmy Petrillo at the musicians' union, not only for yourself for the weeks that we haven't been paid here, but maybe you can loan me a few bucks and we can keep this damn thing going." Isn't that sad? We don't have any money; we can't eat anymore. How can we come here and play every night? But we told him we don't want to go; still he insisted. Nobody wants to go, so we take pieces of paper and put an X on one and draw. Thank God I got a blank one. Johnny Napton the trumpet player got the X. He actually started to cry; he said "I'm not going." Bunny is telling him, "John, I'm sorry you got the X; you've got to go." So we all decided, OK, we'll all go with you. So the next morning we meet at 11 o'clock at the Sherman and we march down to Randolph Street like an army troop in our band uniforms to the musicians' union. It must have looked strange to the people on the street to see these guys marchin' down the street.

Bivona recalled some of the particulars differently, citing one of the newer members of the band as one who voluntarily called the union.[6] In any case, the ensuing meeting with Petrillo is a remarkable demonstration of a union boss's power.

Bushkin continued:

We sit down in Petrillo's office at a long table and he wants to know what's goin' on. We tell him we haven't been paid. He says, "What? That's ridiculous. How much you got coming?" So now we're all in the same room at the same time; we're finding out who's getting ninety, who's getting sixty-five, and who's getting seventy. Nobody's lying; we're lookin' right at each other! So Petrillo gets his secretary there to take notes on what's owed us. He calls MCA and talks to the person in charge—was it Jules Stein?—and says we have to have $6,300, or whatever the amount was, in cash. He says, right in

6. Gus Bivona, interview with author, August 14, 1987, tape in author's possession.

front of us, "Don't send any checks over here; we don't accept any checks on this basis. We only accept cash that can be disbursed to the members of the Bunny Berigan orchestra because they haven't been paid for three weeks. I don't know what you people think you're doin' over there, but if one of your guys in those shiny silk suits doesn't show up in the next hour with $6,300, there will be no music in the city of Chicago tonight. That includes the ballet, the theaters, and the hotels. This town will be silent!" They showed up with it and we got our money. I think I got $210, so I must have been getting $70 a week. Then we all went back to the hotel and chipped in and gave Bunny some money. Then we got paid every week, until we didn't have a job again.

As Bushkin further explained—and his statement is borne out by several others from various band members—"We were mad at MCA, not Bunny. We loved Bunny."

That was part of the story. Another aspect lay in the fact that Bunny owed $875 to the Greyhound bus company, a debt carried over since the previous fall. This was a bill that Bunny thought Jerry Johnson had paid before he left. Still another pressure for payment came from the owners of the Hotel Detroiter, where the band had stayed during its Detroit stop in June. Further, the trade papers reported a squabble between Michaud and John Gluskin over which agent had jurisdiction over Bunny's affairs. Bunny's ever-present debt to MCA—plus interest—continued to be taken off the top of his earnings. Finally, Petrillo summoned Berigan to his office for a hearing and "called Bunny every filthy name in the book," Bivona recalled.[7] One of the arrangements the union leader made was to have the Sherman pay the band's money directly to the union, which then paid the musicians. Bunny was fined $1,000 for "conduct unbecoming a member of the American Federation of Musicians," an amount that would likewise be deducted from his future earnings. With this, Bunny was forced to declare bankruptcy. A special affidavit issued by the Chicago district court allowed Bunny extra time to scrape together the $40 bankruptcy petition filing fee.[8]

7. Bivona interview.
8. *Down Beat*, VI (October 15, 1939); *ibid.*, September 1, 1939.

20

Gee, but It's Great to Meet a Friend (From Your Home Town)

Song recorded September 3, 1937
by Bunny Berigan and His Orchestra

Gee, but it's great to meet a friend from your home town.
What difference does it make if he is up or down?

When he takes you by the hand,
There's a feeling you can understand.

Oh, gee, but it's great to meet a friend from your home town.

This partial lyric from a song written in anticipation of the 1939 New York World's Fair, and given a decidedly unsentimental, swinging treatment by the Berigan band, provides a poignant backdrop for a simple incident that occurred during Bunny's troubled engagement at the Sherman Hotel. The trumpeter's broad shoulders had begun to sag beneath the weight of his proliferating problems. His marriage was nearly nonexistent. The woman he loved, Lee Wiley, who was one cause of Bunny's marital breach, began to spend more and more time in California, severing her association with Bunny. Although Bunny continued to make jokes about his drinking problem, it bore in on him. Every doctor he consulted confirmed alcohol's negative effect on his overall health. The business and financial burdens of the band, the shame of the bankruptcy, and the union's official crackdown were overwhelming. Yet in spite of these crushing pressures, most of the time Bunny maintained an air of equanimity and even good cheer on his weekend visits to Fox Lake.

Both Loretta Berigan and Art Beecher remember these visits.

He had that bad old Plymouth he drove back and forth from Chicago [recalled Beecher], and some nights we'd go out to the country club. It was real small then, just getting started with nine holes. He'd start at Casey's bar and then go out to one of the clubs. Then he'd get on the phone and call his friends. One time I went out to the country club and played suitcase drums with him because I'd left my drums on the job in Madison. Donna was always invited on weekends. She was definitely kinda lost. It was like New York against Fox Lake. They thought she was too wild. But Bunny was usually very happy-appearing when he was home—very up. If he had any real problems he might have told them to his cousin, the bar owner, Casey. They were very close.

Loretta, living then with Bunny's parents, agreed in general, but added, "He'd be happy at times, and then you knew he was dejected. He definitely had his ups and downs. But he was always the joker."

Although he had surmounted mundane and otherwise uninspiring conditions earlier in his career and had often turned them into showcases for his transcendent talent, Bunny now had become a performer in search of an inspiration. His night-to-night playing level, and thus the performance of the entire band, could be subject to a full range of factors, from the physical to the intangible. His bandsmen were acutely aware of the unevenness of Bunny's playing, and while most of them emphasize that Bunny "never played bad," they still savor the feelings of those nights when he caught fire. These were precious nights when somehow Bunny managed to cut through the enervating layers of nonmusical mire that engulfed him, driving his trumpet and his band onto a higher emotional plane.

His old friend and fellow trumpeter Clif Gomon fondly remembers one such night:

One night I've thought about several times was when I was in Chicago playing in Bobby Meeker's band, not on location, just jobbing. Berigan brought his band into the Sherman Hotel. He'd been there maybe a couple of weeks, and the nights we weren't playing jobs we'd listen to Bunny on the eleven o'clock NBC radio shot. I listened every chance I got and, I don't know, I got the feeling that there was something wrong. His playing was *not* the way I thought it should be or the way it used to be. On his choruses it just seemed like he'd lost all interest and he didn't have any inspiration. He'd take a jazz chorus and it was just a matter of routine, more or less. I couldn't figure out what in the world had happened, because always up until then whenever I heard him I liked very much everything that he played. But there was definitely something wrong there somewhere. The other trumpet player in the band I was playing with mentioned it to me two or three times. We lived in the same building in Chicago, and he was wondering about this too.

This went on for about three weeks, and one night I told my wife that I was going down to see Berigan. That evening about 9:30, 10:00, I walked into the [Panther Room] and went around the back of the dining room and sat down at the bar and listened. Not too much was happening musically. Right down at the edge of the bandstand was a large round table, with three or four of the bookers from the MCA office sitting there, and I knew them so I walked down that way. They asked me to sit down with them. Bunny was playing, and when they finished the set he turned around and saw me sitting there. I'll tell you, he just came off that bandstand—he just flew off there— and he grabbed me, and I thought he was going to break my back the way he was giving me a hug. He just seemed like he was so happy to see me; it was something else.

After we talked for a few minutes he said, "Come on upstairs." Up in his room we sat down and talked about old times—about mouthpieces, Madison, how I was doing, about playing in his band. I almost got the feeling that he would like to have me come on his band, but I think we both knew that it wouldn't work out because he played all the jazz [solos] and I like to play jazz too. We talked for quite a while and finally I asked him if he didn't have to get back to the stand. He said, "That's all right; let 'em go." A few minutes later he said he'd better go. When we got down in the lobby he said, "How about me buying you a beer?" I asked if he had time and he said, sure. We went across the street to a little tavern and each had one and talked some more; then he went back to the bandstand.

Brother, I want to tell ya, I never heard trumpet like he played from then on! It was just something out of this world. He *really* played. And these men from the booking office were sitting there going wild. They're asking me, "Hey, Clif, what's that high note he hit?—what's he doin'?—what's this?— what's that?" He did. He played just terrific! I never heard him play any more horn than he played. And he put on a half-hour broadcast on NBC that night that was really something too! The next day this other trumpet player from the band I played with saw me and says, "Hey, Clif, did you hear Berigan last night?"—meaning the broadcast—"Boy, I never *heard* such trumpet!" He was all enthused too.

I've thought about that many times since. It could have been that the band business was getting to Bunny, that it was more of a job than anything else. It becomes so much like business after while that you kinda forget the good musical end of it, to appreciate the good music you can play and hear. Maybe seeing somebody from home, a good friend that he'd been away from for a long time, brought back memories of the old times when we really used to enjoy playing, *really* playing that jazz. Maybe that kinda got him stirred up again, got him back on the ball.

> Gee, but it's great to meet a friend from your home town.
> What difference does it make if he is up or down?
>
> When he takes you by the hand,
> There's a feeling you can understand.
> Oh, gee, but it's great to meet a friend from your home town.

21

I Gotta Right to Sing the Blues

Song recorded March 7, 1933
with Lee Wiley
accompanied by the Dorsey Brothers' Orchestra

The potentially great Sherman run ended on August 11, 1939, after which Bunny spent a few days in Fox Lake before embarking on a spotty series of one-nighters as the band played its way back to New York. Bushkin recalled the financial situation during this period between the Sherman closing and the band's leaving for New York: "I remember looking so shoddy, without any clothes to speak of. My dad sent me fifteen or twenty dollars. I went into a tailor's shop and spent twenty-five cents of that and had my suit pressed while I stood in back of the shop. I had heels put on my shoes for twenty cents or whatever it was, and I gave Bunny five dollars of it. I'm not makin' myself any hero; he had two little kids. What else could I do? I knew he'd just run dry."

One of the oases, at least musically, was at the Savoy Ballroom on Chicago's South Side. Another was at Milwaukee's Modernistic Ballroom at State Fair Park, where the reception was outstanding, with the band and Bunny, buoyed by the cheering of the pro-Berigan crowd from Madison and Milwaukee, rocking hard. This experience recalled an earlier time in Baltimore when the band was ordered to change the way it played because of the high bandstand's precarious swaying. In spite of all the physical and fiscal troubles, the Berigan band, and its leader, could and did swing mightily.

Bunny, Donna, their daughters, and Cap Berigan left Fox Lake on August 18.[1] Mayme remained behind to assist Loretta with her new-

1. Fox Lake *Representative*, August 24, 1939, in Cullen Materials.

born. Donna probably returned to Syracuse at least temporarily; Cap stayed with the band. *Billboard, Down Beat, and Variety* each carried some coverage of the financial difficulties that had surfaced in Chicago. They were not yet at an end. On August 31, Bunny petitioned for bankruptcy in New York Federal Court, duly reported the next day in the New York *Times*. His liabilities were set at $11,353, of which $4,680 was owed to his musicians, $1,500 to MCA. Bunny's assets were listed at $100.

On August 24, the band opened a successful week's stay at Loew's State Theater, Times Square. Reed section mainstays Bivona and Lodice, sensing a lack of bookings, left the band at the end of the run. September proved to be a capricious month, both in terms of personnel and bookings, so that by the beginning of October, sweeping changes had created what amounted to a new band. Gone were pianist Bushkin, lead trumpeter Napton, trumpeters Bauer and Koven, and a trombonist, in addition to the reedmen mentioned above. Edwin "Buddy" Koss assumed the piano stool; John Fallstich, Karl Warwick, and Joe Aguanno were in on trumpet; Joe DiMaggio, soon replaced by Jack Goldie, and Stu Anderson became the new reeds; Kay Doyle came in on vocals. Trumpeter " 'Bama" Warwick may have been the only black musician to play regularly with the Berigan band. A trade journal carried an article in which Bunny denied any rumors of his disbanding. He was also quoted as saying, "The changes were for the betterment of the band. I have an entirely new band now, although only four changes have been made. It is softer, a little more restrained, and I am confident it will very shortly be the best band I ever had." Of Fallstich, who had never played with a bigtime band, Berigan added, "He will rank among the best after I get through with him. I've got three first trumpet men now."[2] Bunny may simply have been trying to convince *Down Beat*'s readers, or himself, that his band could stand so much turnover. They had to devote many September days to rehearsals while playing one-night jobs that were mostly dances. One exception was a longer stand at Boston's friendly Southland. Another, on September 26, was the Third Annual Martin Block WNEW Swing Session at Manhattan Center, featuring

2. *Down Beat*, VI (November 1, 1939).

both the Berigan band and Glen Gray's Casa Loma Orchestra. The latter group, featuring Sonny Dunham on trumpet and Murray McEachern on trombone, played a tribute to Bunny Berigan.

A brief southern tour began with some one-nighters, probably including Tampa, Florida, Starkville, Mississippi, and Gainesville, Georgia. *Billboard* made special note of Bunny's ill health in Starkville. The tour continued on October 2 as the band played the first of four dates at the Hall of Swing, a feature of the Southeastern Fair in Atlanta. The band jumped back to New York City by October 13, when they opened at the Mardi Gras Casino of the 1939 World's Fair, a run that took them through October 19. On the off Monday, Berigan's band shifted to the familiar and friendly bandstand of Harlem's Savoy Ballroom. Once again the band played the Southland in Boston, this time for about two weeks beginning on October 23. Pianist Koss conducted the band for the Southland floor shows, as he did whenever this was required. "Bunny really didn't like to conduct for shows," recalled Koss, "and sometimes he'd just walk off the stand and leave me to do the whole show." Leapfrogging around the Boston area, the band enjoyed the exposure of radio broadcasts on an almost nightly basis. On November 19, with Paul Whiteman, they inaugurated a name-band, two-a-day vaudeville policy at the Westchester County Center in White Plains, New York. Two dates at the Arcadia Ballroom in Providence, Rhode Island, preceded rehearsal dates in New York for a November 28 recording session, Bunny's first recordings since March 15, and his last session for Victor. By comparison, since March 15, Goodman—with his band or a small group—had led fourteen different recording sessions; Tommy Dorsey, sixteen. For his session, Bunny added two performers, Joe Aguanno on trumpet and Mark Pascoe on trombone. The four sides were not released until almost a year later. *Down Beat* made these comments in its review of two of the tunes, "Ay, Ay, Ay" and "Ain't She Sweet?": "Made over a year ago by Bunny's big band, these were never pressed until a few weeks ago. The reason for the delay must be most obvious to all who study these two performances closely. The band is unclean, Berigan's horn is inconsistent and shaky and the material he chooses is below mediocrity. Joe Bushkin's piano [*sic*] and Don Lodice's tenor [*sic*] aren't enough to overcome the many other faults. Only the rhythm section merits a listening." [3] Two months later, the other two concurrently recorded tunes received a similar review from *Down Beat*.

The band plodded through the balance of the year with yet another series of mostly one-nighters in and around the New York City area. A major exception was a full week in mid-December at the Apollo Theater, complete with the house's famous Wednesday night amateur contest. Bunny's band, the only white performers on the otherwise all-black show, delighted the critical audiences before bowing out on December 21. During Christmas week, Bunny sat in with Auld's new band, a friendly gesture tendered so that a young trumpeter, Bernie Privin, could take time off to get married. On Christmas Eve, Bunny's band opened a week's engagement at Newark's Mosque Ballroom, owned by Jean Goldkette, a pioneering bandleader with whom Bix had played. For a period of two weeks or more, Bunny had been plagued with a swelling in his fingers, knees, and ankles that he called arthritis. By year's end, Bunny was admitted to the hospital across from Madison Square Garden in a delirious state, his body wracked with acute, painful swelling. There he remained for approximately ten days while the band carried on without its charismatic leader.

Instantly, Wingy Manone came forward to front the Berigan band at the Mosque. Unable to read the arrangements, however, all Wingy wanted to do was jam some familiar Dixieland tunes, not the most satisfactory utilization of a fourteen-piece band. Jack Teagarden provided a more stable leadership when he took over for the remainder of the engagement. "Big T" was able to transpose Bunny's trumpet parts and solos to his trombone range, and the band could play the familiar charts. Since vocalist Kay Doyle's stint with the band had come to an end, Kitty Kallen, vocalist with Teagarden's band, sat in for at least one night at the Mosque. Tenor saxist Walsh remembered that Teagarden was rehearsing or re-forming his own big band at this point and that he offered some of Berigan's men a job. Walsh saw this not as an effort to steal Bunny's personnel but as an opportunity provided to them "just in case." In fact, when Teagarden's band was reviewed in *Variety's* January 10, 1940, edition, Fallstich, Goldie, and Walsh were on the band, and were so listed on a Teagarden recording date in early February.

3. Information on the band's southern tour in Cullen Materials; Koss interview with author; *Down Beat*, VII (November 1, 1940).

Trumpeter Napton recalled that for four or five weeks during 1939, Bunny had refrained from drinking. However, for the several months preceding his hospitalization, during the period his father had found so discouraging, Bunny had been consuming unusually large quantities of liquor. As Koss recalled:

Bunny always carried about six mouthpieces and two trumpets. Some nights he'd say, "This horn's no good; I'll play the other one. Yeah, this is better." But he always kept a bottle in each case. By now he was drinking a cheap rye whiskey. The only time I ever saw him get mad was when someone snorted on his whiskey one night; I guess they didn't leave him any. One of the band boy's jobs was to keep a Coke bottle filled with half booze. Sometimes on the stand Bunny would carry a flask in his inside coat pocket and stick a straw in it so he could drink without being noticed.

Bunny emerged from the hospital, perhaps as early as January 7, with the aid of a cane. Although his joints were still swollen, he was able to play. Several of his musicians felt that the hospital stay, with its enforced rest, balanced diet, and unavailability of alcohol, had truly helped Bunny. For a while after this illness Bunny drank little or no alcohol, and his playing responded. Koss remembered that he and Bunny would go jamming together after hours at Nick's on Monday nights. "Some nights he really played up a storm," Koss stated.[4] Word got around that Bunny was playing up to this old standards, and on one occasion Tommy Dorsey, Benny Goodman, and Artie Shaw all came by to hear Bunny. Once again illness interceded; the trumpeter could not play.

The first post-hospital jobs Bunny faced were an improvement over the steady grind of one-nighters. First came a week at the Century Theater in New York City, followed by two weeks with option at Boston's Hotel Brunswick. When the option was picked up, this stand ran from about mid-January through about mid-February, complete with radio broadcasts. However, even Bunny at his most optimistic could discern that the Berigan band was nearing the end. Bunny was unable to escape his lingering financial problems. Koss recounted that "sometimes the guys would gripe about underpayment. Bunny would toss all the money on a bed and say, 'Help yourselves.'"[5]

---

4. Johnny Napton, interview with Bozy White, *ca.* 1952, in White Materials; Koss interview with author.
5. Koss interview with Mickolas.

The band's personnel for the Brunswick engagement underwent still further changes. Even so, some writers praised the band:

Bunny Berigan, one of the leading exponents of the hot trumpeteering art, is surrounded by twelve versatile boys who dish out the jive in the approved manner that pleases both adults and juniors alike. The maestro handles his trumpet in a superb manner, playing in almost flawless tone. He fronts and vocalizes occasionally. Joe DiMaggio is standout of the group, alternating between saxophone and clarinet. . . . Arrangements are danceable and despite the fact they are swing, they do not cater exclusively to the jitterbug/exhibitionists. Standouts beside DiMaggio are Stu Anderson on sax, Mort Stuhlmaker on bass and the old hide-pounder, Paul Collins.[6]

The old hide-pounder gave his notice during the Brunswick run, joining Teagarden, while Bunny's band, with copyist Maisel on drums, lurched through an uneven group of one-nighters, ending up at Brooklyn's Saint George Ballroom during the last week of February. Bookings had simply run out. Unceremoniously, and probably without notice, the moribund band broke up; the players dispersed. Bunny and "Little Gate," the loyal senior member of the troupe in terms of service, together dismantled the "BB" music stands one last time. Nearby, a representative of the AFM made sure the musicians received their proper compensation. Within a week, Bunny Berigan was playing his trumpet from behind music stands displaying another set of initials.

6. *Billboard*, February 3, 1940.

22

Dr. Heckle and Mr. Jibe

Song recorded *ca*. February-March, 1934
with the Bill Dodge All-Stars

Bunny had launched his own big band at the Meadowbrook in Cedar Grove, New Jersey. Bankrupt and without a band to
lead, he rejoined the Tommy Dorsey band in the same ballroom on
March 3, 1940. *Down Beat*'s headline proclaimed, "DORSEY GETS
BERIGAN AS SIDEMAN," and the explanation followed:

Still juggling sidemen in the most sensational shakeup his band has yet
undergone, Tommy Dorsey astounded the entire music field early this month
when he persuaded Bunny Berigan to join his band. Bunny's band, rumored
on repeated occasions to be breaking up or about to disband, finally did
when the leader went over to the Dorsey clan at Meadowbrook. Berigan had
been a leader since 1937 and in all that time, despite a series of good recordings and much air time, never seemed to get set. Rather than continue struggling along unsteadily Bunny decided to sidestep leaders' headaches and return to Tommy, with whom he played in 1937 shortly before he organized his
own crew.

Some behind-the-scenes maneuvering among MCA, the AFM, Bunny,
and Dorsey may have contributed to working out such an arrangement. Dorsey's prominence had begun to wane, and he had, as a result, begun to lose certain band members. Bunny's financial condition
had worsened, but his improved playing following his hospital stay
gave Dorsey hope that Bunny could once again provide the spark that
the TD band sought. Dorsey asserted in *Metronome*, "This is just
the beginning of my answer to those who think my band can't swing."
The magazine editorialized: "We like Tommy Dorsey's move in taking Bunny Berigan into his band. We like it musically and logically

too. . . . Tommy's music obviously will benefit, and Bunny won't have to be tossed around with a little-more-than-fair bunch, hoping that some day he'll be able to make ends meet. . . . With moves like that, swing bands in general will benefit. There's more drawing card in a Dorsey band featuring Berigan than there is in a Dorsey band not featuring Berigan, and certainly more than in a Berigan band featuring only Berigan." All of the trade papers hopped on the Berigan-Dorsey story, and one of the common elements of the reporting concerned the arrangement's financial agreements. Bunny's salary, probably the highest accorded any sideman of the day, was paid directly to Local 802, the New York affiliate of the AFM. The union then skimmed off a substantial amount that went toward paying what Bunny owed to various sidemen. Other garnishments resulting from his bankruptcy action further eroded Bunny's paycheck. One researcher has stated that Bunny then received $45 per week from the union for his own living expenses.[1] Donna and Bunny, reunited after Bunny and Maisel's persuasive visit to Syracuse, lived in what one of their friends called a "cheap midtown hotel," probably the Van Cortlandt at 142 West 49th Street.

The volatile Dorsey appeared to be making an honest effort to help reestablish his old friend Bunny. Of course, the TD band had undergone almost total turnover in personnel since Bunny's departure in 1937. Only reedman Fred Stulce and some of the arrangers remained. Veteran bassist Traxler and Dorsey's old standby guitarist, Carmen Mastren, probably left the band just before Bunny's return. This band was not without Berigan friends, however. Tenorist Lodice, altoist Shertzer, and arranger Weston, as well as drummer Rich, whose popularity was skyrocketing, greeted Bunny on his arrival. Bunny's good buddy, pianist Bushkin, came in shortly after Bunny's arrival, as did bassist Weiss. Among the newcomers on the Dorsey band were two vocalists, Jo Stafford, who was at that time singing primarily as a member of the Pied Pipers vocal group, and Frank Sinatra. Dorsey— or the agency with Dorsey's approval—accorded Berigan featured billing on marquees and printed programs. New York newspaper advertisements proclaimed the band's opening at the Paramount in

---

1. *Down Beat*, VII (March 15, 1940); *Metronome*, LVI (March, 1940); *Metronome*, LVI (April, 1940); *Variety*, April 3, 1940; *Down Beat*, VI (April 15, 1940); Cullen interview with author.

Berigan playing at Lakeside Park, Dayton, Ohio, *ca.* 1939. *From the Duncan P. Schiedt Collection*

Berigan band at Loew's State Theater, New York, *ca.* August, 1939. *From the Frank Driggs Collection*

Berigan band at the Savoy Ballroom, Harlem, *ca.* October–December, 1939. *Courtesy Edwin "Buddy" Koss*

At The **125th STREET** **APOLLO** AMERICA'S SMARTEST COLORED SHOWS! THEATRE 125th Street Near 8th Av. Telephone fJn. 4-4490

PROUDLY ANNOUNCES A GRAND PRE-HOLIDAY
SHOW FEATURING "THE MIRACLE MAN OF SWING"
AND ONE OF AMERICA'S GREATEST SWING BANDS

ONE WEEK ONLY
Beginning **FRIDAY, DEC. 15th**

BUNNY
BERIGAN

AND HIS **BAND** with **KAY DOYLE,** RADIO SONGSTRESS **DANNY RICHARDS,** SONG STYLIST

AND A LARGE AND VERSATILE CAST
OF REVUE STARS HEADED BY

APUS and ESTRELITA

AL HYLTON TROUPE OF MAGICIANS

VIOLA UNDERWOOD

LONG and SHORT

THE APOLLO'S BROWNSKIN DANCING
GIRLS AND DASHING BOYS

WEDNESDAY NIGHT
AMATEUR BROADCAST
FROM THE STAGE

SATURDAY
MIDNIGHT SHOW
RESERVED SEATS NOW ON SALE

Handbill advertisement for Berigan band's appearance at Harlem's famous Apollo
Theatre, December 15–21, 1939. *Courtesy Edwin "Buddy" Koss*

Berigan at rehearsal with band, *ca.* 1939–40. *Courtesy Edwin "Buddy" Koss*

Berigan (upper left) with the Tommy Dorsey Orchestra, *ca.* summer, 1940. *From the Duncan P. Schiedt Collection*

Band boy Bob "Holly" Caffey and Berigan, *ca.* 1942. *Courtesy Gene Kutch*

Berigan and band at Roosevelt Hotel, Jacksonville, Florida, *ca.* November–December, 1940; Edwin "Buddy" Koss at extreme right. *Courtesy Edwin "Buddy" Koss*

Berigan band in a promotional photo, Buckeye Lake, Ohio, *ca.* autumn, 1941. *From the Frank Driggs Collection*

Berigan, suffering from the bus blues, in Pennsylvania, *ca.* 1941. *From the Frank Driggs Collection*

Leith Stevens, Berigan, and George Thow, on a Hollywood
sound stage for the film *Syncopation, ca.* January, 1942. *From
the Frank Driggs Collection*

Payday: Bunny's last band, *ca.* 1942: Berigan, second from left; manager Don Palmer,
foreground, with money; Jack Sperling, right. *Courtesy Gene Kutch*

Cover of Victor's memorial album, *ca.* 1943. *From the Frank Driggs Collection*

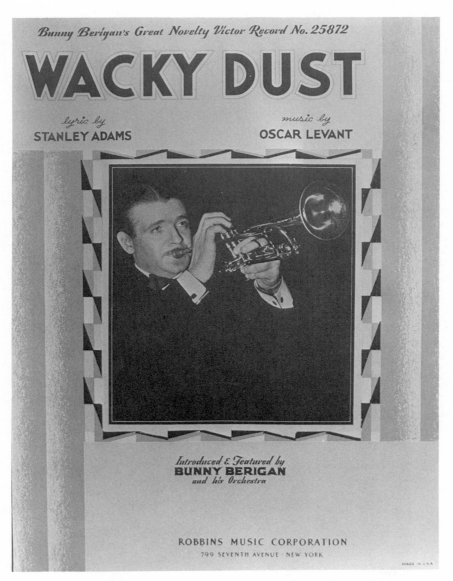

Cover for "Wacky Dust" sheet music, written for the Berigan band by Oscar Levant. *Courtesy Mike Montgomery*

New marker for Berigan grave site, Saint Mary's Cemetery, Fox Lake, Wisconsin, October 8, 1950. Attending the dedication were, from left, Tom Cullen, Merrill Owen, Ray Groose, Doc De Haven, and Art Beecher. *Courtesy Art Beecher and Norm Krusinski*

Welcome sign at entrance to Fox Lake, Wisconsin. *Courtesy Norm Krusinski*

Loretta Berigan at Saint Mary's Cemetery, Fox Lake, Wisconsin, May 1987. *From the author's collection*

Joyce Berigan in her home, with the author, May, 1988. Notice the large photograph of her father in the background. *From the author's collection*

Patricia Berigan Slavin in her studio, August, 1988. *From the author's collection*

March: immediately below the prominent layout for *Road to Singapore*, featuring Crosby, Hope, and Dorothy Lamour, is the announcement, "In person—Tommy Dorsey and His Orchestra; Bunny Berigan, Buddy Rich, Frank Sinatra, Pied Piper Quartette, Winfield and Ford; Extra Added Attraction—Red Skelton."[2] Air checks of the band's radio programs reveal frequent references to Bunny in the introductions and ample solo space for him, with appropriate credit. On occasion, Berigan was scripted in for some radio dialogue, a practice soon abandoned when Bunny consistently fumbled the parts.

The TD band welcomed Bunny enthusiastically. *Metronome* declared, "Bunny Berigan has made a whale of a difference, musically and psychologically, to Dorsey's band."[3] Asked about the quality of Bunny's playing at the time he rejoined Dorsey, Bushkin responded convincingly:

He was playing great, beautifully. On the records that he made at that time you can hear that he was the one guy you could count on to come up with the solos. On the jobs he was sensational, and he had so much pressure on him then. He owed everybody money; his salary was attached. But when it came to the music, he didn't sound attached. There might have been a collector in the audience, but damn it, he acted like they were collecting the music, not the money he didn't have. At the Astor Roof Tommy would come late and leave early, like Benny Goodman—a little power play going on there between those guys. Bunny would lead the first and the last sets. The band was very happy to see Dorsey leave and we were relieved he didn't show up for the first set, 'cause that's when we had fun. We were delighted to have Bunny on the band. Bunny got me the job with Tommy. I auditioned at the Meadowbrook and I joined at the Paramount Theatre.

Berigan and Sinatra established a friendship that was probably somewhat deeper than Bunny's relationship with some of the other sidemen. The young singer's taste told Sinatra that he was in the presence of a master. Besides, they mutually derived fun from their acquaintance, and both men loved to have fun.

Bunny reentered the recording studios just the day after joining Dorsey and, before again departing, participated in a total of eleven recording sessions that produced forty-two sides. Several of these sides featured a band-within-a-band, a common practice with many of the big bands. Dorsey's "Sentimentalists" were: Berigan, Dorsey,

2. New York *Times*, March 13, 1940, p. 29.
3. *Metronome*, LVI (April, 1940).

Bushkin, Weiss, Rich, Sinatra, Stulce, clarinetist Johnny Mince, and guitarist Clark Yocum. Regular Meadowbrook broadcasts commanded good coverage. As the youthful Sinatra polished his craft under Dorsey's critical eye, the singer began to attract adoring crowds of new fans. Buddy Rich, a scrappy showman, competed with Sinatra for the fans' attention, initially with some success. Dorsey featured Rich on such drumming *tours de force* as "Quiet Please," and every show became, in part, a Rich showcase. The stand begun on March 13 at the Paramount Theatre lasted four weeks, an engagement of unusual length.

One day after the closing, on April 10, Bunny, Bushkin, and Weiss engaged in dual recording sessions. RCA's archival records show that the first, with the Dorsey band, began at 9:30 A.M. and ran through 6:30 P.M. With an hour's break for lunch, the musicians were recording for eight hours. For the second session, at a studio across town, Wettling joined the three sidemen on drums as they backed Lee Wiley in recording four classic Cole Porter songs. Bushkin offered a description of the sessions:

We were at the RCA studios at 24th Street between Third and Lexington. It was a long day. Tommy Dorsey was a workaholic. We all got a guarantee, including Frank Sinatra, of $125 a week. After a late closing at the Paramount, we started at 9:00 or 10:00 in the morning and had a break for lunch, then worked through 6:00 or so. Then we had just enough time to get uptown and grab a sandwich or something—and in Bunny's case, a number of drinks. So we showed up at the second studio at about 8:00 in the evening and we played until about 1:00 or 2:00 in the morning. That means that Bunny Berigan's lip held up from about 10:00 in the morning until about 2:00 the next morning, with a lot of pressure on him, because there's no screwing around at RCA Victor with Tommy Dorsey. Obviously those were big band arrangements, and Bunny was playing lead a lot. He was a *tremendous* lead player.

One bullish review of the Dorsey records applauded Berigan's performance: "Bunny Berigan takes all sorts of ad-liberties and they're all good, through most of 'I'm Nobody's Baby' by Tommy Dorsey. Listen to him behind Tommy. . . . The bite and phrasing of the Berigan-led brass section on 'Buds Won't Bud' is also something."[4]

---

4. *Metronome*, LVI (July, 1940).

The TD aggregation, with vivacious Connie Haines added on vocals, played a week at Shea's Theater in Buffalo, New York, ending April 18. An April 23 recording session produced a classic Berigan solo as part of "East of the Sun" and a tasty Berigan-backed Sinatra vocal on "Head on My Pillow," as well as three rejected versions of "I'll Never Smile Again." Dorsey's fourth attempt at "I'll Never Smile Again," on May 23, resulted in one of the most beautiful, most popular ballad recordings of any era. It featured Dorsey's trombone, Sinatra, Jo Stafford, the Pied Pipers, and the orchestra, sans brass, in a smooth blending of textures and phrasing.

After taking a brief vacation and playing some one-nighters to fill out late April and early May, the band opened at the Astor Hotel Roof on May 21. During this fourteen-week residency the Dorsey band attracted sensational crowds, averaging more than 3,100 admissions per week. It was an engagement marked by achievement and acrimony, by welcomings and walkouts. Regular half-hour radio broadcasts bore witness to the momentum beginning to propel the band. On June 25, the Dorsey band replaced Bob Hope on the weekly Tuesday Pepsodent radio show.

Dorsey and Berigan joined with a truly all-star musical group on June 14 at the Apollo Theater in a "welcome home" concert for tenor saxophone giant Coleman Hawkins. Among those greeting "Bean" upon his triumphal return from several years in Europe were many of the major jazz stars of the day. *Swing* magazine's review of this concert reflected the general reaction:

They all came. Jenney, TD, Berigan, Eldridge, James, Krupa, Basie, Marsala, Mastren and Kirby. And people. In droves that really shook the rafters of the Apollo and set jumping and howling one of the greatest crowds ever. Such music as was played that day can only be described as great. With the collaboration of Coleman Hawkins, these stars played just as you'd imagine an all-star dream band would play. The solos flew fast and furious as one after the other of these giants stepped forward to blow great horn. The super-solid rhythm section kept things going superbly, Krupa, Kirby, Mastren and Basie shining by their steadiness and colossal rock under cramped conditions. Harry James arrived late. So he had to step forward before the curtain and play about six choruses unaccompanied. It brought down the house. You'd think that was enough. But these fine men were getting great kicks out of working together, so late that afternoon, most of them congregated again in the small WNEW studios whence originates Martin Block's famed "Make-

Believe Ballroom" and proceeded, once again, to fashion All-American dream music.[5]

Attempts to capitalize on Bunny's and the band's success included the promotion of a one-dollar booklet, *Modern Trumpet Studies*, featuring Berigan's picture on the cover and boasting, "studies in technique, phrasing and chords . . . also contains twelve complete Berigan solos." The band's records were selling well. As they played through their fourteen-week Astor Hotel stand, the band enjoyed a summer of Central Park baseball games against other bands, particularly the one between the teams of the Dorsey brothers that was reported so fully in *Down Beat*.[6] The Tommy Dorsey orchestra was making beautiful music; they were even winning ball games.

Backstage, and sometimes onstage, all was not smooth. Two members of the band continued to vie openly for recognition, and most of the trade magazines and newspapers reported what had been whispered about: on at least one occasion, Sinatra and Rich came to blows and had to be physically separated. Bunny's drinking pattern had resurfaced, reportedly at an accelerating pace, but by this time Bunny's body was less able to process the alcohol than it had been when he was younger. Colleagues noticed the effects of his drinking. Stulce and Weiss recognized the pattern from earlier association with Bunny. Bunny's drinking was definitely apparent to his boss. When Bunny fluffed spoken lines during air shots from the Astor or on the Pepsodent program, Dorsey flew into a rage. He heckled the trumpeter and tried to discourage Bunny's alcohol abuse through ridicule. On one occasion when Bunny weaved through the band to solo in front, Dorsey held up an advertisement for Calvert's whiskey, obviously a staged gesture. Probably no method existed that would have permanently aided Bunny in his perpetual battle, but Dorsey, ever the combatant, again chose exactly the wrong one. One frequently repeated Berigan drinking tale involves one night at the Astor when Dorsey, who paid Bunny's dinner bill, questioned the check's amount. Legend asserts that the disproportionate bill included one ham sandwich and as many as twenty-four single or double servings of Scotch. "He didn't drink any twenty-four Scotches!" protested Donna when

5. *Swing*, September, 1940.
6. This ball game, as reported in *Down Beat*, VII (August 1, 1940), is described in some detail in Chapter 11, p. 101.

asked about this. "He probably included me and half the band on the tab." That night, while attempting to play "Marie," Bunny allegedly fell from the stage.

Arguments between the leader and his star sideman erupted more frequently, provoked by Bunny's drinking and other issues. Dorsey was accustomed to being the preeminent musical attraction of his own organization; he felt his own popularity waning as credit for the band's new success went to Sinatra, Rich, Stafford, Haines, Bushkin, and a brilliant arranging staff. Bunny's major contribution also drew recognition and acclaim. As Dorsey's pride suffered, Berigan's even temper and uneven performance made the trumpeter the most vulnerable of the Dorsey stars. The more the leader felt that his success derived from the abilities of others, the more he vented his bitterness in taunting and criticizing his old colleague. Bunny typically responded with a quiet epithet, a muttered joke, a mocking retort, and then, frequently, consumed another drink. Occasionally he countered by arguing with Dorsey. More than once Dorsey shouted a dismissal, then retracted it. Finally, on August 20, the musical association between the volatile leader and the inspirational trumpeter came to an end. Dorsey fired Bunny; Bunny quit. Following some frantic behind-the-scenes machinations, Ziggy Elman, a powerhouse trumpeter from the Benny Goodman band, took Berigan's chair with Dorsey. The "Sentimental Gentleman of Swing" and the "Miracle Man of Swing" swung their separate ways.

23

Between the Devil and the Deep Blue Sea

Song recorded August 4, 1936
with Dick McDonough and his Orchestra

When Bunny disbanded, his music library had been almost entirely appropriated by Eddie Kirkeby, probably because Bunny owed him money for some of the arrangements. Kirkeby fronted a band for a time, using much of the material from Bunny's library. On his own again, and still faced with substantial debts, Bunny first organized a seven-piece group composed of such former colleagues as bassist Mort Stuhlmaker, trombonist Ray Conniff, pianist Buddy Koss, and drummer Jack Maisel, plus Andy Fitzgerald on tenor sax and Tom Moore on guitar. This group played for a few weeks in late August and early September, 1940, at the 47 Club in Manhattan before Bunny once again launched a big band, with MCA still serving as the agent. During this period immediately after leaving Dorsey, Bunny made several switches with Ziggy Elman that allowed Elman to acclimate himself to the Dorsey band before joining that group permanently. Jack Maisel's copyist skills came to the fore once more as he unearthed enough arrangements from his personal files to provide a nucleus of charts for Bunny's new band. According to those who knew Maisel, whenever he contracted to copy arrangements for others—these were copies written by hand—he made a separate copy for himself. This practice netted Maisel an impressive store of arrangements by some of the best in the business. Not all of the music was suitable to Berigan's needs, but if Bunny's new band sometimes played arrangements that sounded familiar to other bands, the reason was clear.

Setting out with three trumpets, two trombones, four reeds, piano, bass, and drums, the band was staffed by mostly new members, except for bassist Stuhlmaker, drummer Maisel, and pianist Koss, plus Danny Richards on vocals. Richards introduced Johnny DeSanto to the band, and he became its band boy and, later, its road manager. The Golden Gate Ballroom in Harlem provided the backdrop for this unit's debut on September 21 and 22. In late September and early October, the band played twice at the "Dancing Campus" of the Word's Fair. On October 17, it began a two-week stay at the Chatterbox nightclub in Mountainside, New Jersey, its first engagement of any length. Pianist Koss recalled that "at the Chatterbox, the first [extended job the reorganized band had, he quit drinking]. He was drinking Vichy water or something like that. He was trying to straighten out. But I think he had a feeling, like so many alcoholics, that he couldn't function and play, couldn't get through the day without booze."[1] Bushkin showed up for the opening at the Chatterbox and played some trumpet. More one-nighters took the band through November 17, when they began a southern tour at the Roxy Theater in Atlanta, sharing the bill with the Andrews Sisters. Some of the memories surviving from that week derive from the backstage Thanksgiving dinner arranged by Bunny for the band, the Andrewses, and the other performers. On November 27, Bunny and the band opened a four-week engagement at Jacksonville's Hotel Roosevelt. *Music and Rhythm* magazine for November, 1940, featured Bunny in a four-page article, complete with selected discography, photographs, and manuscript samples of Bunny's playing style. At the time of the Jacksonville run, the band's personnel was: trumpets— Ray Krantz, Jack Thompson, Frank Perry; trombones—Max Smith, Ernie Stricker; reeds—Frank Crolene, Andy Fitzgerald, Joe DiMaggio, Johnny Castaldi; piano—Koss; bass—Stuhlmaker; drums— Maisel; vocals—Richards; arranger—Fitzgerald. Donna traveled with the band on this trip. Some of the musicians recalled that she settled with the band members—cash in individual envelopes—on paydays.

Perhaps in an attempt to rekindle some of the magic of three years

---

1. Koss interview with Mickolas.

before, Bunny gave the band members inscribed traveling alarm clocks for Christmas. Although they lacked both the promise and the expense of the white gold watches of the earlier day, these gifts were an extravagance Bunny could ill afford, according to Koss, and Donna objected to the gesture because she knew they did not have the money for such generosity. Nevertheless, a four-week winter engagement in Jacksonville had induced in Bunny's optimistic mind visions of better, worry-free days.[2]

The band packed up to leave Jacksonville on New Year's Day, 1941. Two days later, they inaugurated yet another string of one-nighters in Philadelphia. This run of gigs, however, had many holes in it, and the band enjoyed playing dates on only about half the nights from January through June. Reedman Castaldi dropped out of the band briefly in this period, only to rejoin later. At about this time Bunny's powerful physique and handsome face were clearly betraying the years of neglect. He had begun to lose weight, and his stamina, once legendary, had faded. Looking at a crowd one night, Bunny observed to Koss, "Buddy, fifty percent of these people came to hear me play, and the other fifty percent came to see if I'm drunk."[3] Although still capable of making magnificent sounds, unevenness had become an accepted part of his playing. His marvelous sound-producing mechanism, the column of perfectly controlled air admired so much by Pee Wee Erwin and all trumpeters, was sometimes labored and unsteady. Nevertheless, a radio shot by the Berigan band on May 19 drew this review:

> To the jibes and accusations that Bunny Berigan couldn't get with his horn anymore, Bunny himself has the best answer. And that answer he gave conclusively, without any maybes, at Palisades Park recently. It was a date replete with all the elements of non-success—dismal night, a cold, stiff wind keeping the open-air casino well blown out, the guys playing with their hats and coats on, shivering spectators. But Bunny played, and played ravishingly, his low notes pouring out full and rich, his top notes soaring clean and round. And not a clinker in a hornload, all night. . . .
>
> The thrill of his amazing talent is not to be caught by mere words. For after all's said about Bunny, and about the band—its beat and blend, its push and persuasion—the only thing that really says it is Bunny's horn. His range,

2. *Ibid.*, and Koss interview with author.
3. Johnny Castaldi Diary, in White Materials; Koss interview with author.

his conception, his lip, and his soul, are without compare, and to hear him again is the kick of all listening kicks. . . .
[Hearing his theme] announces the return of one of the greats of all jazz—the return of Bunny Berigan in full glory![4]

That Bunny—and thus the whole band—could be terribly uneven is underscored by an article George Simon wrote at approximately the same time in the same magazine, a piece he later embellished:

The last time I heard the band was in a Connecticut ballroom during the summer of 1941 and, for one who admired Bunny's playing so tremendously and who liked him so much personally, it was quite a shattering experience. . . . The band was nothing and, compared with Berigan standards, Bunny's blowing was just pitiful. He sounded like a man who was trying to imitate himself, a man with none of the inspiration and none of the technique of the real Berigan. He looked awful too. He must have lost at least thirty pounds. His clothes were loose-fitting; even his collar looked as if it were a couple of sizes too large for him.

Apparently, though, he was in good spirits. He joked with friends and talked about the great future he thought his band had. But you had a feeling it would never be. And when, after intermission, Bunny left the bandstand, not to return for a long time, and some trumpeter you'd never heard of before came down to front the band, play Bunny's parts, and spark the outfit more than its leader had, you realized this was enough, and you left the place at once, feeling simply awful.[5]

July began well enough, with a promise of nearly full bookings, including at least two week-long dates in Trenton and Atlantic City. However, a combination of Bunny's own unreliability and still more financial problems, attributed at least in part to management, descended upon the leader and his players. Once again, promises substituted for cash as the band members were not getting paid properly. At about the time of the band's five-day stand at the Steel Pier in Atlantic City, money matters worsened, and most of the musicians quit after filing claims with Local 802 for back payment of wages. Koss reported that MCA eventually paid these wages.[6] Before long, leadership of the band was assumed by someone who was accustomed to following Berigan, Pee Wee Erwin. Bunny himself landed in an Atlantic City jail for accumulating a hotel bill that he could not pay. He

---

4. *Metronome,* LVI (June, 1940), 28.
5. Simon, *The Big Bands,* 91.

was bailed out by MCA agent Harry Moss. By July 29, Bunny Berigan was a leader without a band.

"Bunny and his band had played a carnival just outside Trenton for about a week, and I contacted his manager, Don Palmer, and asked if he would take one of my arrangements to Bunny to see if he would buy it," asserted pianist and arranger Gene Kutch, a Trenton native who was then playing with a local band led by Al Zahler.

Palmer said Bunny wanted some arrangements but explained that Bunny was short of funds, but, hell, I would have been glad just to have him accept the arrangements. I did an arrangement of "Maria Elena" and another tune for them, but then I didn't hear anything for about two weeks. Then I get a phone call at about two in the morning from Palmer. He says Bunny liked the arrangement and ordered six more. He also said that Bunny needed some band replacements and that they would be in Trenton in a couple of days. We happened to be recording with Zahler's band in a new studio without air conditioning. It was real hot, and we took a break and went outside to cool off. Here's Bunny in the car with Palmer with the doors open, and they'd been sitting there listening to us play. Bunny says to Palmer, "I like the band," and Palmer asks if anyone wants to meet Bunny Berigan. Naturally, we all rushed to do that. He's sitting there with a pint between his legs, and he says, "Hey, guys, you sound good. You want a job? I need two trumpet players, I need a piano player, I need a trombone player, I need a couple of saxophone players, I need a drummer and I need a bassist." Al Zahler is about to have a heart attack; he can see himself losing all his best players. Then Bunny wanted to hear us play with him, so we go to a restaurant in Little Italy that has a piano. We ask the owner if we can play a little and Bunny takes out his horn. We do "Honeysuckle Rose" and "I Surrender, Dear" and a blues. Then Bunny says, "I'm satisfied. We leave in the morning!"

Some of us had to go home and tell our mothers and fathers. We were just kids, barely out of school. It was amazing! We're getting our first big break by playing with Bunny Berigan!

We've got two or three dates before we get to a month-long gig in Ohio, one at Luna Pier, between Detroit and Toledo, and one at Dayton. Now we find out that Bunny hasn't got any book. His drummer had apparently supplied all the arrangements and when he took off he took the music with him. Bunny's got only a handful of charts—maybe twelve or fifteen tunes. I took

6. Koss interview with author.

arrangements of about thirty tunes with me, but just the scores, no parts written out. About the first three nights Bunny was fit to be tied. We sounded *terrible*. When we got to Buckeye Lake, Ohio, we stayed there from August second until the second or third of September.

It was a terrible job; ten cents a dance. Bunny and the manager of the Crystal Danceteria agreed that he would get about twenty or twenty-five stock arrangements, and we were cutting them in half. In the meantime, I was turning out charts as fast as I could. During the day we rehearsed. We lived in this boardinghouse, and outside there's a huge lifeboat that was overturned on blocks. I was upstairs copying arrangements, and as soon as I finished one I'd pass it downstairs on the grass and the band would run over it. It was wild! But the band began to get real tight, and Bunny was pleased.

Another of the musicians hired away from Trenton was alto saxist George Quinty. "It was terrible at Luna Pier that first night," recalled Quinty. "We had no rehearsal, no uniforms, and a big crowd on hand. We screwed up so bad! Bunny went into the dressing room and started to cry—real tears. But at Buckeye Lake we would rehearse from one o'clock until four or four-thirty in the afternoon on that upturned boat. By the time we left there we had both books under our fingers, the library that Bunny had, plus the things Gene Kutch was writing. And Bunny was playing so beautiful; it gave me goosebumps."[7] Others of the "Kid Band" who joined Bunny at Trenton were trumpeters Bobby Mansell and Arthur Mellor, saxists Walter Mellor and Wilbur "Weebie" Joustra, trombonist Charles Stewart, and a very young Jack Sperling, still highly regarded as one of the better big-band drummers. Mickey Irons also served as vocalist until Danny Richards could again rejoin Bunny. While at Buckeye Lake the band joined in a promotional stunt and grew beards, calling themselves the "Bearded Snake Hunters." A photograph of the band, taken near the end of the engagement, shows Bunny in apparent good spirits and good health.

Closing at Buckeye Lake on September 1, the band embarked for Jacksonville by private automobile, stopping only in Pulaski, Virginia, for a one-nighter at the Monticello Club. At this dance hall the band experienced a thrill, witnessing a reunion between Louis Armstrong and Bunny. This was a particularly emotional evening for Bunny be-

7. George Quinty, interview with Deborah Mickolas at request of Bozy White, with questions drafted by him, September 6, 1976.

cause of an article that had recently been a feature in *Down Beat,* an article that had reached Bunny before he left Buckeye Lake. In part it read:

Urged for several years by a *Down Beat* reporter to "come on and tell us which trumpet players you yourself like best," Louis Armstrong last week patiently and carefully typed out an answer between jumps on the road.

From Huntington, W. Va., came this answer directly from Louie, who typed his words out on yellow stationery bearing the single word "Satchmo'" in the upper left-hand corner.

Said Armstrong:

"Now this question about my opinion about the trumpet players that I admire—that is actually asking an awful lot of me. . . . Because there's so many trumpet players that I admire until there would not be room to mention them on this paper. And to only name six . . . well that is leaving me on the spot.

"But—as you wished—my friend I'll do my damndest so here goes. First I'll name my boy Bunny Berigan. Now there's a boy whom I've always admired for his tone, soul, technique, his sense of 'phrasing' and all. To me Bunny can't do no wrong in music."

Armstrong went on to name Harry James and Roy Eldridge among other favorites. In a companion article, the magazine printed Bunny's response:

Informed that Louis Armstrong had named him first among a group of his favorite trumpet men, Bunny Berigan commented to *Down Beat* here the other day:

"You can't imagine what a kick that is, especially when it comes from Satchmo', the King. All I can say is that Louis alone has been my inspiration, and whatever 'style' I play you can give Armstrong the credit.

"Why, when I was a kid back in Chicago, at night I used to sneak down to the Savoy, where Louis was playing, and listen to him night after night. Later I got one of those crank-up phonograph jobs and would play Armstrong records by the hour." [8]

Several of Bunny's band members confirmed that Bunny's spirits were buoyed by Armstrong's appraisal. Although Louis did not play with the band at Pulaski, the meeting provided another tonic for Bunny's mental and emotional state as the band headed for a month's engagement at the Patio Room of the Hotel Roosevelt in Jacksonville, where Bunny's earlier band had impressed the hotel's management so

8. *Down Beat,* VIII (September 1, 1941).

favorably. During this run several members of the band, led by road manager Don Palmer, began conspiring to reduce their leader's consumption of alcohol and to increase his intake of nourishing food. "Palmer really tried to take care of Bunny," recalled saxman Quinty. "He would do all he could to keep Bunny away from the booze, which wasn't possible totally. When Bunny would try to fool people by drinking his booze out of Coke bottles, Don would top them off with water. And we'd try to get Bunny to eat soup and things that were good for him. Sometimes Bunny would spike the soup, but we tried. Of course, he was Palmer's meal ticket—in fact, all of ours—so we wanted him to stay healthy. But it was more than that: he was such a great guy, very gentle and fun-loving."[9] Jack Sperling confirmed the conspiracy: "We all banded together. If Bunny asked for some booze we'd all say, 'Geez, I just ran out, Bunny.' And he was starting to eat some and get some color." By the end of the Jacksonville engagement, Bunny's spirits and physical appearance had improved noticeably. Gene Kutch recalled, "Bunny looked tremendous! He got a great tan, and he used to wear a white suit every night. He had his hair shampooed and we got his horn cleaned up. We used to go to the beach and have a great time playing around. We'd play baseball with a beach ball."[10] A home movie taken at the time by one of the bandsmen affords a peek at this happy group doing just that, with their leader sporting a potbelly but joining fully in the fun. Regular broadcasts emanated from the Hotel Roosevelt, and MCA's Moss, in charge of bookings, promised a long series of playing dates after Jacksonville.

That these dates were widely separated both in distance and in time, and that they were mostly one-nighters, was not revealed to the players until they experienced it. After closing at the Roosevelt on October 2, the Berigan troupe played the next night at County Hall in Charleston, South Carolina. Quinty remembered that the next booking was supposed to be in Richmond, Virginia, but that Bunny received a call from Moss while playing in Charleston telling him to have the band drive to Berwick, Pennsylvania, for an October 8 prom date, and then return for the October 10 date in Richmond. Drum-

9. George Quinty, telephone interview with author, February 9, 1988.
10. Quinty, Sperling, and Kutch, in separate interviews, confirmed the positive effects on Bunny's health and outlook brought about by the ever-improving quality of the band and by the stable, successful engagement at the Hotel Roosevelt. Coupled with the vigilance of the band members regarding Bunny's alcoholic intake, optimism about the band's future was growing.

mer Sperling characterized these as "the regular MCA screwed-up scheduling." Sperling continued:

We were just getting by. We'd look as neat and clean as we could. Sometimes we'd check into one hotel room and all of us would take a shower. Sometimes we'd go for a week at a time and not sleep in a bed. We'd clean up in the lavatories of the dance halls we played and sleep on the bus—that old beat-up school bus. We were always sneaking pillows out of hotels to pad up. Some of us would pool our money to buy a bottle of "Sneaky Pete" and drink ourselves to sleep. You'd wake up stiff and tired. My arms felt like *lead* some nights.

On November 4, the band took part in an unusual recording. With popular singer Georgia Gibbs, they cut a full-length band arrangement of a jingle for Pepsi-Cola, "Get Hep with Pepsi-Cola." While this record was not for sale, its recording did provide an extra payday. Paychecks came sporadically with such juxtaposed bookings as these: October 19, Fitchburg, Massachusetts; October 24, Boston, Massachusetts; November 7, Raleigh, North Carolina; November 14, Camden, New Jersey. At the conclusion of the Raleigh date, Bunny was called home to Fox Lake. His father had died.

The official cause of Cap's death was cardiac failure, with the contributing cause cited as generalized carcinomatosis, or, as Loretta Berigan described it,

spider cancer, all through his body. We were all hit hard by it, and when Bunny came home all that activity is somewhat of a blur. I've heard that his manager, Don Palmer, came home with him, but I remember Bunny being alone. He looked just terrible: he was tired and drawn; his face was full of grief; his hair was dyed; his teeth were stained; and he was drinking a lot. But none of us suspected that Bunny was really sick. His father died in the hospital in Madison and was laid out in the home of Bunny's uncle, Dave Schlitzberg. . . . Bunny hardly seemed to pay any attention to any members of his family; he seemed to be in a daze.

Orville Kratz, Fox Lake's funeral director, retains a similar memory: "Bunny came in—it was in the morning. It was hard to get information from him. He seemed to be off in a distance, fuzzy. He didn't look very good."[11]

Loretta continued: "His father died early in the morning on November 11, and the funeral was on the thirteenth. I just can't remem-

---

11. Orville Kratz, interview with author, May 19, 1986.

ber how Bunny came to town and how he left, but I'm sure he wasn't able to stay for the funeral service. And one thing I'll always remember: I was standing next to Bunny as he went up to view his father in the casket. He put his hand on him and said, 'Dad, I'll be there with you in six months!'"

After telling his mother that he would take care of the funeral expenses, Bunny rushed back to Camden's Convention Hall for a job on November 14. Ill and unable to play, Bunny remained in his hotel room that night as several old friends from the Artie Shaw band playing nearby came by to play, thus saving the job. Among those helping were Jack Jenney, Auld, Tough, and perhaps Shaw himself. The next night at Williamstown, Massachusetts, Bunny was well enough to play. On November 24, the Bunny Berigan band cut its first records in nearly two years. Eli Oberstein, who had overseen many of Bunny's sessions at RCA, recorded the band at the Imperial Record Company and distributed four titles, all Lynn Richards ballad vocals, on his Elite label. The year 1941 played out with a variety of one-nighters as diverse as the one at Boston's seedy Tic Toc Club on Pearl Harbor Day, a coveted December 27 Hotel Pennsylvania gig, and one on December 29 at Scott High School in Coatsville, Pennsylvania.

After playing a New Year's Eve job in Altoona, Pennsylvania, Bunny left the band for the month of January, when their only playing dates were at the El Rancho Club in Chester, Pennsylvania. This "engagement" consisted of three consecutive Saturday-Sunday dates beginning on January 10; Danny Richards fronted the band. As Gene Kutch's diary for January noted: "Checked in at Chester Arms Hotel (lousy hotel)."[12] Meanwhile, Bunny flew to California to record the sound track for *Syncopation*, a film starring Jackie Cooper, Bonita Granville, and Adolphe Menjou. Bunny's old friend Leith Stevens from *Saturday Night Swing Club* days was the musical director for the film, which purported to deal with the origins of jazz. As reported over a period of months in *Down Beat*, the concept of the film underwent many revisions between its inception and the final editing. The black cornetist Rex Stewart, who had been instrumental in acquainting Bunny with the Dorsey brothers on Bunny's arrival in New York, appeared in the film as a trumpeter. When it was Bunny's horn that

12. Gene Kutch Diary, January 10, 1942, copy in author's possession.

was heard for Stewart on the sound track, the studio was accused of racial discrimination and Bunny found himself caught up in a controversy he scarcely needed. Stewart himself bore no ill feelings, explaining that he simply was not available when the sound track recording was made.

Even musical satisfaction escaped Bunny on this second trip to Hollywood. Still grieving over his father's death and over the grim details of his own situation, and worn down by the endless one-nighters, Bunny sought relief in his usual fashion. Stripped of Don Palmer's monitoring, and away from the band's daily routine, Bunny began consuming alcohol totally without regard for its effect. The Tommy Dorsey band was performing around the Hollywood area while Bunny was there, and Bushkin, who was still Dorsey's pianist, recalls seeing Bunny:

We were playing a Sunday matinee at the Palladium. The place was jammed with people, and we look out in the audience and there's Bunny standing there. Tommy stopped the band in the middle of the tune. He said, "Ladies and gentlemen, a great personal friend and wonderful musician is with us today—Bunny Berigan." The audience went up in smoke, really excited. Tommy says, "Come on up and play something, Bunny." Bunny's already got his afternoon "load" on, and he says, "I haven't got my mouthpiece with me." Ziggy Elman offered Bunny his trumpet, and we were going to do "I Can't Get Started." He just started to play it, and I don't know if it was Ziggy's mouthpiece or what the hell it was, but he was in trouble. Bunny couldn't get through it. It absolutely tore us up, man!

And something happened on the film he was making.

In fact, Bunny had great difficulty playing some of the parts that the sound track required. The normal method for recording such passages was to record the music first, then to have the actors try to match their physical movements to the pattern of the music. For this film the sound of the studio band was recorded first, then Bunny, playing alone, dubbed in the trumpet solos for Stewart's and Cooper's roles. For *Syncopation*, Bunny was expected to watch the film and match his solos to the movements of Cooper and Rex Stewart. Bunny experienced particular difficulties with the longer passages; his cast-iron embouchure and amazing stamina had vanished. Trumpeter George Thow, one of Bunny's successors in the Dorsey Brothers band in 1934, also played in *Syncopation*'s studio band and was scheduled to dub in the trumpet part for one of the minor characters. To Thow additionally fell the unlikely jobs of filling in some parts for Bunny Berigan, playing the parts Bunny could not master, and redubbing some of the Berigan playing that proved unacceptable. Leith Stevens and the other musicians held Bunny in high esteem, so they exercised great patience with him. The film itself was a hodgepodge effort, not up to the standards expected of producer-director William Dieterle. Film critic Bosley Crowther termed it "a ponderous, unrythmical picture" that "turns out to be a lot of shoddy, stylized pretense."[13] Nevertheless, while much has been made of the backstage difficulties, a careful listening to the film's sound track reveals some good playing, much of it identifiably Berigan's.

While Bunny struggled on Hollywood's sound stage, his band played only the six dates at the El Rancho. After each weekend's playing they headed home, as they did whenever faced with brief layoffs, hoping to pick up a stray gig, or to at least save on expenses. In spite of continuing problems with bookings and with band finances, altoist Quinty remembered banking money while playing with Berigan. Much of the time his wife traveled with him, and through diligent planning and economizing, through sharing and pooling with other band members, through living simply and without indulging themselves, they survived reasonably well. Being a nondrinker helped. The men earned $10.00 to $14.00 a night at a time when, Quinty remembers, Trenton policemen earned $34.00 per week. Entries in pianist Kutch's diary indicate that hotel rooms ranged from $1.15 to $1.80 per night. At Buckeye Lake, a full, modest meal cost 35 cents.[14]

As with earlier Berigan bands, the members of this one recall frequent arguments with, and suspicions about, the honesty of club owners, Harry Moss, Don Palmer, and others about matters of finance. Again, the sidemen felt that they and Bunny were being cheated. Kutch maintained that "there was a lot of stealing going on." Palmer, who was highly regarded by Donna and who apparently did much to benefit Bunny, prompted the ire of some of the musicians, who, after military service, applied for compensation and discovered that Palmer had not paid their Social Security contributions. Sperling recalled this about the finances: "At first we were going nowhere. I would take only $15 or $20 that the manager—who I wasn't too sure

13. Bosley Crowther, Review of *Syncopation*, in New York *Times*, May 29, 1942, p. 13.
14. Quinty interview with Mickolas; Kutch Diary.

about—would give me. He'd say, 'Aw, c'mon, Jack, don't worry about it. Did I ever steer you wrong? I told your mom and dad I'd look out for you.' There was never any salary set. If my salary had even based out at $25 or $50 a week, I left with that band owing me a lot of money. But we all understood that Bunny owed a lot, and we were honored to be playing with him."

Despite the hardships of the road, the generally poor quality and spottiness of the bookings, and the unevenness of the pay, Bunny's band of musicians still speak of him fondly. "He was my first 'name' bandleader—and the best," declared Kutch.

He was generous with solos and kind to people. Bunny was good at working an audience. Depending on his mood, Bunny could be very funny and clown around. I only remember one time he got angry. One of the brass men made kind of a whimper of a mistake and Bunny yelled, "Goddamit, if you're gonna make a mistake, make a good one! Don't pull back." Later when I played with Tommy Dorsey we had the security of a year's contract, paid vacation, good locations and all, but it wasn't the same. Bunny's band was much more fun, and Bunny was very responsible. He felt the show must go on.

Quinty recalled getting an offer to leave Berigan and play with trumpeter Henry Busse's band:

I could have got more money, and Bunny encouraged me to take it. He wouldn't stand in your way if you could improve yourself. But I couldn't bear the thought of listening to Busse every night instead of Bunny.

I think Bunny kind of envied the happy marriage my wife and I had, and the fact that we didn't drink. We would talk with him a lot and try to get him to stay away from the booze. When we'd ask him why he drinks he'd always say, "Ask Jimmy Petrillo." Bunny had great magnetism; people loved to be near him. When he played that trumpet, he told a story. When Bunny wasn't with the band, like when he was out in Hollywood, people would come to hear us and it was like going to see the Yankees play, and Babe Ruth wasn't in the lineup.

Danny Richards adds: "What a leader! Bunny Berigan was one of the greatest inspirations of my life. All of my recollections of Bunny Berigan are the best."[15]

15. Quinty with Mickolas; Danny Richards, telephone interview with author, November 9, 1985, tape in author's possession. Subsequent quotations from Richards are taken from this interview. Richards was vocalist with the Berigan band from January, 1939, to April, 1942, with some interruptions.

"Babe Ruth" returned East on about February 1, warmly welcomed by his needy sidemen, who expressed concern at their leader's conspicuous decline. At this point, two months after Pearl Harbor, the United States was marshaling its military forces to join the Allies in fighting World War II. Every band struggled to maintain its personnel. A musician's 4-F draft status—an exemption from military duty that granted his ability to stay—could be as important as his ability to play. The Berigan band did not escape this new cause of turnover. After some rehearsing, they resumed their hopscotching schedule in Cincinnati on February 7. Fewer open dates made the travel even more rigorous because of the great distances that had to be driven between jobs with no dates off in between. On March 11, the Bunny Berigan band recorded its second—and last—set of four sides on Elite, with two vocals each taken by Danny Richards and Kay Little, the latter erroneously identified as Nita Sharon. A brutal schedule of widely separated one-nighters continued through February, March, and two thirds of April. One of the trombone players remembered sitting on the rented band bus during this period as Bunny finished up a bottle of some kind of liquor and began to sob, "I'm too young to die." On April 20, Bunny entered Allegheny General Hospital, near Pittsburgh, Pennsylvania, with a diagnosis of pneumonia.

24

Squareface

Song recorded May 13, 1935
with Gene Gifford and His Orchestra;
vocal by Wingy Manone

Old Squareface, old devil gin,
  what you lookin' at me for?
Ain't gonna lead me to sorrow and sin
  no more, no sir, no more.
Too many times you got under my skin.
  I'm through with you, old Squareface.
Ain't gonna get me again; no sir.
  Ain't gonna get me again.
Old Squareface, what you keep hangin' 'round for?
  What's that you sayin'? It's time to begin?
Well, just once more.
  Might as well bring those pink elephants in.
Man, I'm feelin' low, old Squareface.
  You know, you got me again. Yessir!
You *really* got me that time!

So sang Wingy Manone at a delightful, four-title, 1935 recording date. "Squareface" was a nickname for the gin bottle, but it also represented all kinds of alcoholic beverages. Prohibition, the so-called noble experiment, had ended ingloriously a year and a half before this recording session; Bunny's reputation as a heavy drinker had been building for six years. Gin was not his drink of choice; Scotch—preferably the good stuff—was. He drank his share of bathtub (homemade) gin during Prohibition years, but musicians around New York seldom went very long without their favorite Squareface contents. Like many other things about Bunny, his drinking habits and escapades have become legend, riddled with contradiction and inconsistency. Some have said that overstating Bunny's drinking capacity is impossible; others maintain that Bunny's dependence on alcohol is grossly exaggerated and that he only did what hundreds of his fellow musicians—and certainly uncounted others—did.

"It was a good band we had at Janssen's in Philadelphia. But this was where Bunny started drinking—unfortunately." Roberts, trombonist and Bunny's friend from the Madison area, remembers the 1929 experience: "[Two of the guys in the band were] 'weedheads' [a nickname for a marijuana smoker]. . . . They had played together earlier with the Dorsey Brothers and Nichols and Arthur Schutt and that gang. We were with a real fast group and Bunny started drinking with them."

Bunny's parents, William and Mayme, were not drinkers. Jack Smith, one of William's bowling partners, says he "never saw Bill take a drink." Mayme was known to have a glass of wine or a "pony" of beer on occasion, but nothing more. Mayme's father, John Schlitzberg, likewise rarely drank. Don, however, provided a poor example for his younger brother. Admittedly, he would drink and get into fights; drink and challenge the police; drink and take money and leave home; drink and wreck automobiles; later, drink and abuse his wife. Don was well into middle age before his physical condition forced him to quit drinking. In addition, two of Bunny's uncles, his father's brothers, are regarded to have been alcoholics. Further, two of Bunny's great-uncles, John and Pat Berigan, died at an even younger age than Bunny, twenty-eight and twenty-six, respectively. The causes of their deaths have not been established, but their early demise at least calls forth speculation about the passing on of genetic traits that muted Bunny's musical accomplishments much too bluntly.

On May 29, 1987, the American Broadcasting Company (ABC) telecast a documentary on their *Closeup* program, "Alcohol & Cocaine: The Secret of Addiction," which put forth a large body of the most recently established information about addiction. The program portrayed alcoholism as a disease urgently in need of further study and alcoholics as victims virtually crying for treatment. Any doubts in the minds of viewers as to the nature of alcoholism should have been dispelled. One of the points registered repeatedly was the scientifically accepted fact that the predisposition to severe alcohol addiction is inherited. In this connection, the point was clear: the *behavior* of the parents is less a factor in transmitting alcoholism than is genetics. Researchers know that the brain's natural chemistry regulates our sense of well-being, our energy, our sense of euphoria; it controls how we experience the thrill of competition, the feelings of pride, power, exhilaration, and excitement. It is in the brain's pleasure centers that alcohol (as well as cocaine and other substances) create addiction and change the brain's chemistry, offering exaggerated lows and false highs. Alcohol and cocaine *create* addiction in the same way: they *change* the brain *physically*, alter its *chemistry*, so that a user feels bad or hurt if he does not get more of the drug. They create a physical need that was not there before. The television program's consultants spoke of two different types of genetic alcoholism, one of which is much worse than the other. Type I is less severe and may be passed from either the mother or the father to either a son or a daughter. It usually begins after age twenty-five. The more severe Type II passes only from the father to the son and can begin as early as age eleven or twelve. Sons of Type II alcoholics are nine times more likely to become alcoholic than are sons of nonalcoholic fathers, and they show consistently greater brain abnormality—even those who never had a drink. This suggests a genetic link so strong that any contact they have with alcohol carries the threat of severe addiction. As biochemist Lawrence Lumeng recently demonstrated, 30 to 45 percent of Asians have a definite sickening response to alcohol that is traceable to one's DNA, "dramatic evidence that a bodily response to alcohol is genetically dictated—and is thus inherited as surely as eye color." In a related study, C. Robert Cloninger concluded, "What is inherited is not the fact that you are destined to become an alcoholic but varying degrees of susceptibility [to the disorder]." While some individuals encounter serious health problems in a relatively short time, others seem to have to drink for several decades before they begin to have problems. Most researchers now suspect that this may have to do with genetic transmission of these risk factors, and this may well explain why Bunny's dependence was so complete, his deterioration so rapid following his introduction to alcohol in 1929 at age 20.[1]

1. "Alcohol & Cocaine: The Secret of Addiction," *Closeup*, ABC-TV, May 29, 1987; Lawrence Lumeng and C. Robert Cloninger quoted in Charles Leerhsen with Tessa Namuth, "Alcohol and the Family," *Newsweek*, January 18, 1988, p. 66.

Reliable estimates place 7 to 10 percent of all Americans at high genetic risk for alcoholism. Alcoholism presently kills 98,000 Americans per year. It is estimated that as many as one in every two, three, or four hospital beds is filled by someone with an alcohol-related problem. One American child in every three is touched by alcoholism. A *Newsweek* cover story asserted that more than 28 million Americans have seen at least one parent struggle with alcoholism. Dr. Paul Dolmetsch concluded that alcoholism is an illness that affects, not livers, but families.[2] Surely, alcoholism affected Bunny Berigan's family.

Bunny's companions in the Madison area before 1929 seem to confirm that he did not drink. Erle Smith, coleader of the Smith-Berigan band, typified the responses of several who would know: "Bunny didn't drink then, but he did smoke."[3] Several who knew Bunny at the beginning of his career made references to his smoking "tea" or "weed," but this, if factual, was sporadic and probably occurred after his initiation in Philadelphia. Although it may seem a cliché, it would be accurate to say that the small-town boy went to the big city and picked up a bad habit. In the time between his first and second trips to New York, Bunny was probably drinking to some degree. Once he returned to New York to stay, a drinking pattern took shape that never altered as it led to his premature death.

Testimony drawn from a diverse group of Berigan's family, fellow musicians, and others represents the range of opinion and first-hand knowledge that many people are willing to share on the subject of Bunny as a drinker:

Joe Lipman, piano, arranger (most meaningful contact with Bunny from 1937 to 1938): "I never thought drinking got out of hand. Bunny always played well. Maybe it got to be a problem later in life for Bunny. There was a lot of pressure. There was always a microphone shoved in your face. I don't see on these network broadcasts how a man could get dead drunk and play that book, or any book, for that matter."

Danny Richards, vocals (1939; 1941 to 1942): "His drinking pattern when I knew him was quite steady. I'd try to tell him, 'Why don't you try cutting down?' And he'd say, 'I am, Danny.' Even if he seemed

2. Leershen and Namuth, "Alcohol and the Family," p. 62; "Alcohol & Cocaine: The Secret of Addiction."

3. Erle Smith, to author, June 5, 1985, in author's possession.

unable to play, he'd play around it. The man was a marvelous musician. The guys in the band didn't like him to drink. But he treated them like a gentleman, and they loved him. Was he on time for gigs and rehearsals? You bet he was!"

Pee Wee Erwin, trumpet (*ca.* 1935 to 1942): "What isn't generally in the books is that I used to try to outdrink Bunny. I couldn't do that, either. I could hold it better in the 1930s than he could. But eventually I had to either stop or die."[4]

Donna Berigan (1931 to 1942): "He was always on the go. He didn't spend much time at home. He wouldn't stop. That's what killed him—overwork. Of course, he liked to drink, a little. There's a lot said against him about his drinking which isn't all true. He worked too hard to be as bad as they said he was."

Joe Dixon, clarinet, alto sax (1937 to 1938): "Bunny was a great disappointment, especially to the younger guys. Just when we were about to make it big, he let us down. There were many nights when he couldn't come to work. We couldn't play without him. He was the center of the band. Part of the time I drove his car from job to job. He'd want to stop at bars along the way."

Johnny Blowers, drums (early 1938): "I never saw Bunny Berigan drunk—until many, many years later, after I left the band when Bunny became quite ill. I can't say that he overdrank. You can't stay drunk all the time and do your work, and believe me, Bunny had plenty of work to do. He was a very responsible guy. Every once in a while it got the best of him. He tried to quit. If AA had been started back then, I'll bet you Bunny would be alive today. When I roomed with him he'd start the day out with half a water glass full of Ballantine's Scotch."

Joe Bushkin, piano (1935 to 1936; 1938 to 1939; 1940): "Some of us in the band at the [Famous] Door were using pot. It was legal then, you know. We tried to get Bunny to smoke pot, but he preferred drinking. Eddie [Condon] and I would try to get him to light up so he would stay on the wagon. When he was on the wagon he'd eat a lot of candy and shit and ruin his teeth. Those guys taught me how to drink. I thought it was normal to wake up at noon and throw up. I remember when he had the big band and I was rooming with him, before we

---

4. Pee Wee Erwin, interview with Deborah Mickolas, October 30, 1977, copy of tape in author's possession. Subsequent quotations from Erwin are taken from this interview.

went to bed he would pour a half of a hotel water glass full of Ballantine's Scotch. I remember it was Ballantine's because I didn't like the stuff. Anyway, he would set it on the night table. He'd go take his shower and use a whole lot of talcum powder because he sweated a lot. There'd be a cloud of powder. He'd go to sleep immediately, then start snoring. In the morning when the wake-up call came, he'd sit up, down that straight Scotch, and answer the phone in that modulated voice, 'Good morning, this is Bunny Berigan.'"

Jess Stacy, piano (1935): "I helped drive [on the Benny Goodman band's tour West] because Bunny was stoned all the time. It seemed like every hundred miles we'd have to stop and buy a pint for him. When we first started out he was my roommate. I sort of had to take care of him. That wasn't an easy job because he was drinking so heavily. Sometimes he'd wake up at night screaming. He couldn't breathe; I guess the mountain altitude bothered him with that drinking. I'd put cold towels on him, and later he'd say, 'Jess, you saved my life.' I was glad we had separate rooms when we got to L.A."[5]

Hymie Shertzer, alto sax (1935; 1937): "I never heard Bunny sound bad because of booze."[6]

Donna Berigan: "What he used to do a lot—I forget where he started it. He was playing and hit the last note—way up there. Well, he took a step forward and kind of tripped and lost his balance. So he figured, 'Oh, well, what the hell! I'll make it good.' And he fell—flat on his face. So after that he'd reach that high note and take a fall. But he never hurt himself because he knew how to fall. He put it in the act for a while. I saw him do it; sure did."

Frank Langone, alto sax (1937): "Bunny would pick me up [on the way to the Pennsylvania Hotel job] and I was just a kid from the sticks. I couldn't talk to those guys. It was like they were on another planet. You know, they were on pot and booze. I thought I wouldn't last with the band because I was too square. Pretty soon I started to carry a jug and talk their language and started to loosen up. Bunny would ask me if I had a drink in the back seat. He'd take it and drink the whole thing. Many times he'd show up for the job loaded."[7]

5. Stacy telephone interview.
6. Hymie Shertzer, interview with Bozy White, *ca.* 1961, in White Materials, copy of transcript in author's possession.
7. Frank Langone, interview with Deborah Mickolas at request of Bozy White, with questions drafted by him, September 5, 1981, copy of tape in author's possession.

Buddy Koss, piano (1939 to 1941): "A lot of people say they saw Bunny fall off the stand. I never saw this. In all the time I was with him, I never saw him so bad. . . . [In the days leading up to the band's 1940 reorganization], I took Bunny to a doctor in New Jersey. He put Bunny up on a table. After examining him the doctor says, 'Bunny, you've got an enlarged heart, you've got the beginning of cirrhosis, you've got arthritis. If you don't quit drinking, you'll be dead.' I always kept a pint of booze in my car for Bunny, and Bunny says, 'I'm going to go out there and smash that bottle against a wall!' We get outside and he takes it, looks at it, and says, 'Gee, it's a shame to waste it.' Bunny went to priests, fortune tellers, hypnotists. Maybe if AA had been around, it could have saved him."[8]

Donna Berigan (*ca.* 1933): "We were up at Paul Whiteman's ranch; went to spend the weekend with him. The two of them got to drinking quite a bit. Well, Bunny got on this horse and fell right off. But after that, when we moved up by Rego Park, we used to go riding all the time."

Benny Goodman, bandleader (*ca.* 1935; upon being asked whether to begin broadcasts from the Los Angeles Palomar Ballroom at 11:30 or midnight): "I said we'd better start at 11:30 every night. After midnight Bunny was wiped out. Whatever, he was magnificent, truly."[9]

Pee Wee Erwin (*ca.* 1935): "Bunny started the *Let's Dance* series with Benny's band, and I concluded it. No, he didn't leave. They carried him out of the studio. Bunny was a very powerful man, very powerful, and there's an awful lot physical about playing the trumpet. Especially, Bunny had a very strong air column—until the booze cut him down."

George Quinty, alto sax (1941 to 1942): "Bunny would admire my happy marriage, and he seemed to envy the fact that I would only take an occasional beer. We often wondered why he drank so much. I think his wife was part of the problem. She was a lush. I don't think she helped him."[10]

Joe Dixon: "A doctor explained to me that Bunny was a [Type II] alcoholic. In the beginning, Bunny drank for exaltation. He'd go out with the boys and have a good time—jam, bowl, drink—like some

8. Koss interview with Mickolas.
9. Chilton and Sudhalter, *Bunny Berigan*, 16.
10. Quinty interview with Mickolas.

good old college boys. After while, after 'I Can't Get Started' took off, and he became successful—then he started drinking to put himself away. He didn't drink to have a good time; he just drank to get drunk and be out of it. Many a night he just couldn't get out of bed and come to work."[11]

Donna Berigan: "Bunny got mad at me once. We'd been out on a job or something, and he had a little too much to drink. Actually, he was mad because I wouldn't go to bed. He started chasing me around this camp we were in and I ran inside. Pretty soon he quieted down."

Jack Sperling, drums (1941 to 1942): "When his dad died, that did it! He was so hard back on the booze again. He'd have like hallucinations while fronting the band. He'd take his horn and swing it at something. People would be dancing in the middle of the floor, nobody nearby, and he'd swing his horn and curse or talk to them as though they were tugging on his pants and yelling for him to play 'Prisoner's Song.' We didn't even have that number in the book any more. We'd take him out and put him in [bassist] Tony Estren's trailer and talk to him a while and get him to cool down. Then he'd come back and be OK."

Berigan researcher (*ca.* 1937): "There's the classic story of the first time Bunny's band played the Paramount. They were just getting rolling; 'Started' was becoming a hit. A large group of bookers and agents and media people were scheduled to come to the second show of the day. During the first show, Bunny was playing spectacularly and the band had hit a groove where they would have won any 'battle of the bands' contest. They were all on cloud nine. After the first show, so the story goes, in came Lee [Wiley] with a fifth. The band's worst fears were realized. She starts feeding him tumblers full of straight booze and they go in a dressing room and 'socialize' and kill the fifth between them. All the bookers and agents had gathered for the second show. So Bunny got up and undid everything he had done in the first show—missing notes, missing cues, and visibly not too steady on his feet. All the bookers left in disgust. Then, as I was told, the guys in the band bring in some catered food and lots of coffee and straighten Bunny out, so that he's playing as well for the next show as he did for the first. But the harm had been done. On one of his first big bookings Bunny succeeded in starting a reputation for being unreliable

11. Dixon telephone interview, December 1, 1986.

and alienating some of the people who could have done him the most good."

Joe Dixon: "I don't remember that specifically, but Wiley was certainly around backstage a lot during that period. I also remember that Tommy Dorsey made a point of coming backstage to tell us how bad the band sounded."[12]

Tom Morgan(elli), guitar (1937 to 1938): "At the Earle in Philly one time he drank a fifth before the first show and couldn't get on. He was all wound up with the shakes and said bugs were crawling all over him—the classic DTs. Somebody played the theme for the first show, and he was able to get on stage for the second."[13]

Gene Kutch, piano, arranger (1941 to 1942): "The way Bunny was getting by, if he had a tremendous hangover, he just took a couple of blasts [of liquor] and he'd forget about the hangover. But at that stage his own work habits were good. He knew he had to toe the line. No play; no pay. The guys in the band got mad at Donna. She was encouraging him. They'd sit in the front of the bus and she'd wake him up to drink. From what I understand, Bunny really started to go downhill with the bottle the second time he was with Tommy Dorsey."

Jack Sperling: "I don't recall that she ever woke him for it, but Donna's traveling with the band created a bad scene. We were trying to keep booze from him and she handed it to him; she wouldn't say no to him."

Joe Dixon (*ca.* 1938): "Sure, it was at the Stanley Theater in Pittsburgh. Bunny went out bowling between shows with one of the girls who was a jitterbug dancer in the show. When he came back he was crocked, and we didn't know it. He walked out on stage and missed the microphone by two feet and fell off the stage. It was the only time that happened while I was with the band, but it cost us. Word got around. That's when Bob Hope canceled him. We thought we were on our way to California. I left the night of the 'Millionaires Party' and joined Fred Waring."[14]

Twenty-five thousand "eye witnesses" (1938): "I saw Bunny Berigan fall off the bandstand at the Stanley Theater in Pittsburgh."

12. *Ibid.*

13. Tom Morgan(elli), telephone interview with author, February 9, 1988, tape in author's possession.

14. Dixon telephone interview, December 1, 1986.

Patricia Berigan Slavin: "I never saw my father drunk. I know he got drunk, but I never saw him drunk. I saw my mother drunk many times."

Bunny Berigan (widely attributed, upon being asked how he manages, in spite of drinking heavily, to play so brilliantly and to pull off such technically difficult passages): "I practice drunk."

George Frazier accurately forecast soon after Bunny's death that legends would spring up about his life and his playing.[15] Predictably, some of his family and friends—and Donna in particular—became defensive when discussing the matter of Bunny's drinking. Many of his musical colleagues try to minimize the problem, perhaps in a self-defensive attitude about their own participation. This is typical behavior for family and others who are closely associated with alcoholics. No doubt some feeling that they might have contributed to his demise, either through actively encouraging him to drink or through not having done enough to reduce it, lingers in some of his drinking companions who have survived. Vernon E. Johnson is the founder and head of the Johnson Institute in Minneapolis, a treatment center for alcoholism. Dr. Johnson and other experts on alcoholism note that those close to alcoholics begin to feel that they are the *cause* of the alcoholism, thereby sharing in the blame and suffering the same feelings of low self-esteem as the alcoholic himself. In addition, in Bunny's not untypical case, genuine liking for the man prompted a desire to protect Bunny, to make it seem as though his self-destructive drinking was just a normal part of the high-pressure music scene of the time, to lump him as one of the boys, to excuse him somehow for squandering his unique talent. Almost without exception, his former colleagues and sidemen refer to Bunny variously as wonderful, funny, sweet, generous, modest, tops, the best leader they ever had, one of the boys. Apparently believing that alcoholism is something to hide, something to be ashamed of, and reluctant to appear to denigrate Bunny, they find great difficulty labeling as an alcoholic someone as lovable and as talented as Bunny. In Bunny's world—the New York music scene in the waning years of Prohibition and the early wet years—being able to handle your liquor was important. A generation later, only a "chicken" would refuse to drink with the boys; the present

15. George Frazier, *The One with the Mustache Is Costello* (New York, 1947), 248.

generation's reckless drinkers might be looked upon as "macho." For Bunny's peers to have said that Bunny had trouble handling his drinking would, somehow, have been almost the ultimate insult.

The fact that Bunny could initially not only handle it, but from all accounts play brilliantly as well, became a point of pride. Here was the precocious, handsome youngster from the Midwest who moved quickly into the rarefied strata of studio and jazz musicians in the toughest competitive arena possible. And as one of his admiring colleagues might have rationalized for Bunny and voiced it, "Look! Not only does he do it better than anyone else—he can even drink a lot and do it. Hell, he even plays *better* jazz when he's had enough to drink. It loosens him up, makes him freer. Have another drink, Bunny! You're no alcoholic." And Bunny bought it: the drink and the line.

The mechanism of alcoholism and the profiles of the various stages that alcoholics inevitably move through fit Bunny perfectly. Johnson's classic book on intervention for alcoholics provides excellent insight into the evolution of alcoholism, enunciating even the thought processes of an alcoholic as he or she moves through the clearly delineated phases of the illness. Johnson presents an overview of the treatment process as well. Much of what he writes, though a little preachy for some tastes, can be overlaid on the life of Bunny Berigan to reveal exact parallels. Johnson's description of the disease offers a good beginning:

This disease involves the whole person: physically, mentally, psychologically, and spiritually. The most significant characteristics of the disease are that it is primary, progressive, chronic, and fatal. But it can be arrested. The progress of alcoholism can be stopped, and the patient can be recovered. Not cured, but recovered. . . .

It is a myth that alcoholics have some spontaneous insight and then seek treatment. Victims of this disease do not submit to treatment out of spontaneous insight—typically, in our experience, they come to their recognition scenes through a buildup of crises that crash through their almost impenetrable defense systems. They are forced to seek help; and when they don't, they perish miserably.[16]

Johnson graphically describes the almost inevitable path followed by those afflicted by alcoholism. He points out that at the first stage,

16. Vernon E. Johnson, *I'll Quit Tomorrow* (Rev. ed.; San Francisco, 1980), 1.

ethyl alcohol use results in a feeling of euphoria, both for alcoholics and for other drinkers. The effect is a welcome one, such as Bunny felt in Philadelphia when he began drinking with the group at Janssen's. Initially, the degree of pleasant mood swing can be controlled by the amount consumed, and the drinker learns that it works every time. The relationship with alcohol is positive, and repeated experiences with booze prove it to be reliable in this regard. As experiences build up and solidify, Johnson explains, "the result is a deeply imbedded relationship which the drinker will carry throughout life." Social drinker and alcoholic alike then move into a pattern of programmed mood swings through the use of alcohol: celebrating the anniversary; the job promotion; for Bunny, perhaps playing on a successful radio show or record date—these and similar events provide reasons to drink and achieve euphoria. As Johnson further explains, "As our social drinker gets deeper into the chemical, getting drunk begins to have a very different effect, and the potential alcoholic is caught in an undertow which inexorably leads beyond social drinking. Paradoxically, the drinker thinks things are going along swimmingly, but an invisible line has been crossed into Phase Three, alcoholism, in which the former social drinker has become *harmfully* dependent on alcohol. *Why* we can't say. But *how* is thoroughly describable, both behaviorally and emotionally. . . . [A]nd yet the alcoholic remains unaware."[17]

Bunny, drinking with the "real fast group," inched drink-by-drink, totally unaware, to Johnson's Phase Three. His success gave him lots of reasons to celebrate; the camaraderie among the group of musicians with whom he was associating was itself almost a reason to drink in the early days of his climb to prominence. Drinking was "smart," and as many of that period's survivors have testified, its illegality enhanced the pleasure and joy of it. And Bunny had plenty of evidence to show that his drinking—at least according to his peers and nightclub patrons who were also drinking—had nothing but a positive effect upon his playing. Even such episodes as one Bunny had at the crucial time of the launching of his own band failed to have an impact upon his drinking pattern. In this instance, just before Goodman's band gave way to Bunny's at the Penn Hotel's Madhattan Room, Bunny appeared in the audience obviously inebriated. Tradition of

17. *Ibid.*, 12, 14–15.

the day dictated that a visiting leader be invited to sit in. Goodman recognized Berigan's condition but insisted that Bunny come to the stand and play. Since Goodman's quartet was on stage at the time, an idle Harry James lent his trumpet to Bunny, who proceeded to play very poorly.

Eventually—or, in his case, very rapidly, due perhaps to some additional complicating genetic legacy—Bunny was harmfully dependent on alcohol, and any gestures, absent a planned program, by those close to Bunny to help him arrest the disease were doomed to failure. Some incidents in Bunny's life provide nearly perfect illustrations of the profile of the alcoholic. For example, one characteristic of the alcoholic's enveloping problem is that he loses touch with reality. Ample evidence shows that Bunny had little sensitivity either to his own deepening dilemma or to the events in the wider world about him. His dependence upon alcohol effectively shielded him from a realistic view of his plight while keeping his thoughts turned ever inward, oblivious to local or world affairs, unable to face his own business affairs, and, only vaguely aware that alcohol might be a problem. This abnormality, an inability to respond normally, is known to researchers on alcoholism as anhedonia. Other facets of alcoholic behavior include an increasing emotional burden accompanied by a diminishing self-concept, characterized by severe mental mismanagement. This, as Johnson elaborates, "serves to erect a wall around the increasingly negative feelings [alcoholics] have about themselves. The end result is that they are walled away from those feelings and become largely unaware that such destructive emotions exist. . . . Because of this, judgment is progressively impaired—and impaired judgment, by definition, does not know it is impaired."[18] The alcoholic changes routines to accommodate his preoccupation with the use of alcohol, as with Bunny's habitually pouring his morning drink before retiring, and stashing alcohol in both trumpet cases and elsewhere. For promotional reasons, management at one point let it be known that Bunny was reliable and drank only Coca-Cola. Bunny's devious dodge was simply to replace the Coke bottles' contents with alcohol. Even toward the end, he spiked the nourishing soup or vegetable juice his guardians tried to coerce him to eat. His self-effacing

18. *Ibid.*, 27–28.

demeanor, in spite of his phenomenal beginning, and his failure to capitalize on his talent and achieve lasting success attest to the lowered self-esteem that fuels the alcoholic machine. Bunny's mismanagement of his time, his squandering of his talent, and his utter disregard for normal business routines all served to wall him off from reality. He could not find enough worth in himself to pay proper attention to grooming, to care for his teeth, or to wear the right clothes and keep them in good order, and his reckless inattention to business matters guaranteed the failure he saw within himself.

Johnson and other researchers of alcoholism treatment report that in order for an alcoholic to become arrested in his self-destructive behavior, intervention by family or close associates is essential. This intervention cannot be the kind of finger-pointing and criticizing usually offered by a drinker's family or close friends. Confrontation by loved ones must be carefully orchestrated, in concert with natural crises, in order to bring the alcoholic to a realization of his condition. In Berigan's era, successful alcoholism intervention depended upon luck rather than on today's wide body of knowledge, and other conditions were missing as well. For the alcoholic, associates in the workplace are often the last ones to know about the problem because the drinker protects that turf carefully; nonetheless, the threat of exposure or loss of employment can sometimes be the catalyst for successful intervention. In Bunny's case, two factors negated this possible avenue to intervention. First, Bunny was part of a culture in which drinking was an accepted part of the job. Second, Bunny was eminently employable; if he had encountered pressure to stop his drinking, he would simply have left and found other, perhaps more lucrative, more enjoyable, employment. He quit Hal Kemp; he quit Fred Rich; he quit Paul Whiteman; he quit Benny Goodman; he quit Tommy Dorsey. In each case he "bettered" himself. In this way, too, he effectively avoided crises. And yet Bunny had the same glimmerings of insight experienced by most alcoholics in the early stages of the disease: on several occasions he attempted to quit drinking, but without the necessary resources at hand these attempts were predestined to fail.

Individual tolerances for alcohol vary greatly and are genetically related to physical, chemical, and psychological predisposition. Several of Bunny's drinking buddies were able to drink with him, one for one, at some point in his progression toward becoming dependent upon alcohol. Some of them paid in the same way Bunny paid. Others—not true alcoholics—were able to cut down or quit drinking. This gives weight to a recent tenet in the scientific community: it matters not so much what or how much you drink, but *who* drinks. Many of Bunny's drinking cronies survive today, in retirement, in nonmusical employment, or still operating as successful professional musicians. That they survive may be simply due to a lack of all the necessary preconditions to alcoholism.

Bunny Berigan had them all. His alcoholism became an increasingly dominating factor in his life. From the early 1930s on, few notes that emerged with such compelling beauty from his trumpet bell were begun with breath that was free of alcohol. Further, while complications such as pneumonia, malnutrition, and overwork plagued him, the main cause of Bunny Berigan's death was cirrhosis of the liver, certainly hurried along by the primary disease, twelve years of regular, excessive consumption of alcohol. Since thirty-three is an especially tender age to succumb, one further factor may have been present in Bunny's case: another unidentified genetic quirk that made *this* alcoholic's body even more susceptible to the negative effects of that consumption.

Finally, when Johnson compares alcoholics with the New Testament's Prodigal Son, it is as if he had Bunny Berigan in mind:

[T]he chemically dependent person chases the rainbows of euphoria, seemingly heedless of the rising costs to himself and others. He is eternally hopeful that "the next time will be different." In the end, if it is allowed to progress that far, all resources are spent: health, wealth, feelings of self-worth, and all dear relationships. All he once had is laid waste; all he once was is gone. There is nothing left now but to crawl away and die. In its own way, his future role as he understands it is only to be a hired servant: for the rest of his days he will be at the beck and call of those he has hurt by his past behavior. He is to repay and repay his unrepayable debt.[19]

Joyce Berigan: "My father was an alcoholic. He did not die of pneumonia; he died of alcoholism. The family accepts that. I wish people could accept him as the artist. He loved jazz. He was a good and loving person who was dedicated to this music he loved. It was *in him*."

19. *Ibid.*, 117.

25

Someone Stole Gabriel's Horn

Song recorded September 24, 1932
with The Dorsey Brothers Orchestra

Donna Berigan: "He was in the hospital near Pittsburgh with pneumonia and the band was playing without him in Baltimore. Harry Moss of MCA called and said, 'Bunny's got to get to Baltimore to be with the band. He doesn't have to play, but he's got to be there.' He had no business leaving that hospital."

Artie Beecher: "I know that Bun was told in the hospital not to play his horn again—ever!"

George Quinty: "When he got out of the hospital [on May 8, 1942] he looked just terrible. His clothes just hung on him. You could put your whole hand inside his shirt collar it was so loose." [1]

Gene Kutch: "The day after Bunny went in the hospital we had a job at the Aragon in Pittsburgh. Claude Thornhill was playing with his band at a theater just around the corner. He came over and played for a few sets. What a nice gesture to help Bunny. Then we went on to the Summit in Baltimore for three whole weeks while Bunny stayed in the hospital. Harry Moss, the agent from New York, didn't believe Bunny was that sick. He told him to get on the job just as soon as possible or he would cancel all the remaining dates. Sonny Skylar, a singer from Vincent Lopez's band, was fronting for us. When Bunny joined us he looked awful! He had lost a lot of weight and was on a liquid vegetable diet. Two of us would help him get on the bandstand. We'd prop him in the curvature of the piano so he could support himself. He played, but it was pitiful—all shaky. We were told to watch

---

1. Quinty interview with Mickolas.

him so he wouldn't drink, but he brought up the small bottles he had the liquid vegetables in and poured whiskey with it."

Donna Berigan: "When Bunny heard that they didn't expect him to work, just be there, he insisted we take the train and go to Baltimore that night. He was awfully weak, but we got there and went to the club and sat at a table in front of the bandstand. We did have a couple of drinks, because he was weak and nervous, and he wanted to get up there so bad. He listened to the band and after an hour or so he said, 'I'm going to get up and play.' I told him he better not because he was still too weak. 'Yeah, I'm going to,' he says. And it was awful. The audience noticed it. He didn't have the wind, you know, but as he went on he kept improving, started to sound like his old self."

Pat Berigan Slavin: "Jo and I were both brought to the hotel [probably on May 16] to see Daddy after he got out of the hospital about a month before he died. We knew he'd been in the hospital, and we knew he was very ill. We were taken for an afternoon's visit but were told we could only stay a little while because he was so tired and weak. I remember *so distinctly* how very jaundiced he looked— although of course I didn't know that word. I asked, 'Why are you so yellow, Daddy?' He said he was going to be OK. It was at that time that he told me, 'Just in case, if anything should happen to me, your Mom can't take care of you guys. You're going to have to do it. I want you to take care of your sister for me.' And that was the last time I saw my Daddy."

George Quinty: "Bunny never complained. He stayed optimistic, but there were times when you knew he was in pain. He'd press his hand on his side or hold his back. Once he showed us this hard lump on his liver. Don Palmer said that it was hardening. But he'd sit on that Greyhound bus and smile as though nothing were wrong. I never saw him when he couldn't play. I never saw him when he could not make a job because he was drunk. I did see him when he couldn't make a job because he was sick. He made and played every job— even when he was in a lot of pain."[2]

Gene Kutch: "Bunny's work habits were good. He was on time for jobs and rehearsals. He never had trouble reading new stuff, and Bunny could still remember parts up to the end. He knew them or he

2. *Ibid.*

just faked them. His lip started to go, and that wasn't helped by something that happened to his mouthpiece. Bunny had this old unplated brass mouthpiece that he had had someone specifically put a groove in. It was on the bottom part, kinda like a grip. While Bunny was gone, Don Palmer took it and had someone smooth out that groove. When Bunny came back he picks it up and says, 'Who the hell has been screwing around with my horn? Who took the groove out?' And Don says, 'I thought it was just a dent.' Bunny says, 'Goddammit, don't do something like that on your own. Next time ask!' I guess maybe that's only the second time I ever saw Bunny get mad. But not having his favorite mouthpiece didn't help him."

Jack Sperling: "Yeah, I thought Bunny would kill Palmer when he screwed up his mouthpiece! But I was tired of the travel grind MCA was putting us through, and I didn't think Don Palmer was giving us a fair shake. I gave my notice to Palmer while Bunny was still in the hospital; I couldn't stand to see that man dying in front of us. It was awful. When he rejoined us after leaving the hospital Bunny would finish playing, then spit blood into his handkerchief. I left the last night of the three weeks at the Summit, near the Pimlico racetrack in Baltimore. Bunny tried to talk me out of leaving, but I knew I wasn't playing right and wanted to study. That last night Bunny came out to say good-bye to me and he fell down several steps. My father and I sort of caught him and picked him up. Bunny said, 'Gee, that was funny: my legs just lost their feeling, and I couldn't stand.'"

After closing at the Summit on May 13, the band played a United Service Organization (USO) benefit show in Aberdeen, Maryland, the next night, and on May 16, a single night at the Manhattan Center in New York City. Boston's Tic Toc Club provided the scene for some of the last great playing Berigan was to perform, during a week's run beginning May 17. Again, the recollection of Gene Kutch: "When we left Baltimore he got what they call that last surge of strength. We get to Boston and Bunny's playing his ass off. He sounds great! Everybody's saying, 'What the hell happened to Bunny?' But by now he's guzzling like mad. We're bringing him food and he thanks us, but he just isn't interested; he hardly eats anything. He's going on nervous energy now." During the Boston stand Donna despaired of keeping Bunny away from alcohol: "I tried everything I could, but he just kept drinking, so I just returned to New York. I couldn't stand it." It was during this Tic Toc run also that Henry "Red" Allen, an outstanding trumpeter often compared to Bunny, remembered catching the Berigan band. Allen was shocked to find his friend unable to stand for a whole set, sitting down for even his solos. He begged Bunny not to continue on with the band to Norfolk, but Bunny's stubbornness and seeming optimism prevailed. He assured Red that everything would be just great.[3]

Norfolk's Palomar Ballroom was the scene, during a three-night stand on May 25 through 27, of one of the most dramatic performances in the annals of jazz. Jack Pyle, a radio personality and a friend of Berigan's, was a spectator at the Palomar and wrote an account of Bunny's effort:

I had gone out front to watch the band when, after about an hour or so, Bunny walked over to the microphone and beckoned for attention.

"Ladies and gentlemen," he began, "I've had a lot of requests this evening to play our theme song, 'I Can't Get Started.' Well, you'll have to pardon me, but I just got out of the hospital a few weeks ago, and I'm not feeling up to par. Now, I'll tell you what I'll do—I'll try to play it for you. But remember, if I miss it's your fault."

The band broke into that old, familiar introductory strain. There, out in front, with his trumpet poised resolutely, stood Bunny Berigan, a man who, although his doctor had told him only a week ago not to play trumpet for some months, had the courage to attempt the toughest number in the books.

Bunny didn't miss. He played as I never heard it played before. You could see he was **working.** He went through the entire arrangement with flawless precision. When he pointed his horn toward the sky and hit a perfect F sharp [*sic*] above high C, the crowd rose to its feet in a tremendous round of applause which lasted five minutes.

And Bunny Berigan smiled.[4]

It is a strange coincidence, and somewhat ironic, that the Palomar ballrooms of Los Angeles and Norfolk were the sites for both the launching of the swing era by the Berigan-sparked Goodman band and the final electrifying performance by Bunny.

On May 28, the Berigan band played at Milford, Connecticut, and the next night at Scranton, Pennsylvania. "From Scranton University

---

3. Chilton and Sudhalter, *Bunny Berigan*, 26.
4. Pyle's account was first included in "A Tribute to Bunny Berigan," by Paul Eduard Miller. See *Down Beat*, IX (July 1, 1942), 14.

we headed for Sunnybrook Farms, a real nice place in Pottstown, Pennsylvania, for a Memorial Day date," recalled Gene Kutch.

The place was sold out. Our bus driver on this beat-up bus was a Hungarian fellow who spoke broken English. Usually Don Palmer sat up front with the maps and told him where to turn. Well, Palmer fell asleep, and before we know it the guy has made a wrong turn and we're at least a hundred miles in the wrong direction in upstate New York. Bunny and one of the trumpet players and a couple other guys had driven to Sunnybrook in a car, and they were there waiting for us. The owner has all that money in the till, and no band. I guess they tried to jam a little, but it was no go. By the time we got there it was 11:30 or midnight, and the owner had refunded all the money. We missed an hour's radio broadcast. Bunny had killed a whole bottle, and he was in the back room *smashed!*

To that account George Quinty could only add: "Palmer tried to hire a plane but couldn't. He told the driver to go as fast as he could, and we got some police escort, but it didn't do any good. It was all over when we got there. That really broke Bunny's back. When we headed for New York he was *sick*."[5]

The dance on May 31, in Manhattan Center, attracted an enthusiastic crowd, one clamoring to hear the leader. Bunny remained in the Van Cortlandt Hotel, his condition obviously very serious. Don Palmer scurried over to the Paramount Theatre to explain the situation to Benny Goodman. Goodman and five of his sidemen, including star tenorman Vido Musso and pianist Mel Powell—all the regular members of the BG sextet—plus vocalist Dick Haymes went to the Manhattan Center to palliate the customers by playing for about forty-five minutes. Convinced that Bunny would not be able to continue with the band for some time, Goodman, perhaps after prior consultation with MCA officials, worked out an arrangement on the spot for covering the Berigan band bookings. "We sat there right on the stage of Manhattan Center, and I heard Musso and Goodman and Palmer talking about it," recalled Quinty. "Vido says, 'Bunny's got to get well, man, he needs hospital attention. I'll tell you what I'm going to do, man. I'll go take the band over and I'll front it and take a hundred dollars a week—the same as I'm getting with Benny—and I want Bunny to get well, then he can take his band back.' Then Benny

5. Quinty interview with Mickolas. The same information was repeated in telephone interview with author, February 9, 1988.

says in that real low voice of his, 'Yeah, and you can come back on the band, man, soon as this is all over and you can get your old job back.'"[6] Kutch confirmed this account. Musso fronted the "Bunny Berigan Band with Vido Musso" for several months. Some insiders maintain that this was less an act of charity on Musso's part than the seizing of an opportunity to leave the Goodman band in good grace. A regularly featured number became Musso's solo on "The Man I Love," which he would dedicate to Bunny Berigan. Some time early on June 1, Bunny was removed to Polyclinic Hospital, hemorrhaging internally.

The June 1, 1942, *Down Beat* ran an article headed "Bunny Berigan Back, Blowing 'em Big." The body of the article stated: "Boston— Bunny Berigan, completely recovered from the pneumonia that kept him in a Pittsburgh hospital bed while Sonny Skyler [*sic*] fronted his band at Summit Inn, Baltimore, has been playing some one-nighters in this territory. The Bunn looks pretty hale, and is playing his head off."

On the morning of June 2, Bunny Berigan died.

"The night Bunny died I was sitting there at the hospital and the priest came in," remembered Donna.

They were having an argument, Bunny and the priest. Bunny was saying he wasn't Catholic. At one point he became Christian Scientist so as to convince people that he wasn't a drinker like they said he was. I told the priest that he wasn't a Christian Scientist, that he was brought up a Catholic, and so was I. So later the priest told me, "There's nothing more you can do for him tonight. You go on home, and if anything happens, we'll call you." I wanted to stay with him 'cause he looked so bad, and they didn't seem to think he was going to make it. I was upset because they sent me home. I went back to the hotel and sat on the couch. Nobody called. I had the radio on, and all of a sudden I heard, "Bunny Berigan just passed away." It was about four o'clock in the morning. I figured I'd get some calls, but *nobody* called—not Harry Moss, or Benny Goodman, Tommy Dorsey—nobody. Finally about six-thirty in the morning I heard a knock at the door and it was George Zack, the piano player. He said, "Where's everybody? You mean nobody's here! It's been announced on the radio; they know where you are." So he sat with me, went down and got some coffee and something to eat and brought up a drink, too. He thought I'd appreciate that; which I did. My girlfriend, Kay Altpeter, called me and came over.

6. Quinty interview with Mickolas.

The published obituary read, in part:

Bernard (Bunny) Berigan, 33-year-old orchestra leader and trumpet player, died early yesterday morning in the Polyclinic Hospital, where he was taken on Monday. He was stricken Sunday night with an intestinal ailment at the Van Cortlandt Hotel, 142 West Forty-ninth Street, where he made his home. . . . Don Palmer, manager of the Bunny Berigan band, said that in compliance with Mr. Berigan's wish his band will be kept intact under the Berigan name, that Mrs. Donna Berigan, his widow, will maintain his financial interest in it and that Vido Musso . . . will be the new leader. The band left last night to fill out-of-town engagements. . . . Besides his widow he leaves two daughters, Patricia, aged 10, and Joyce, 5, and his mother, Mrs. Mame [*sic*] Berigan, and a brother, Don Berigan, both of Fox Lake. The body will lie in state at Stafford's Funeral Parlors, 307 West Fifty-first Street, until 11 A. M. today, when a funeral service will be held at St. Malachy's Church, West Forty-ninth Street between Seventh and Eighth Avenues. Burial will be at Fox Lake.[7]

"Tommy [Dorsey] has said that he took Bunny to Fox Lake. He did like heck! They put me on the train and I took him there," Donna asserted, struggling both for recollection and for control. "This was a hard thing to do because I hadn't gotten over the shock yet. I got there, and his cousin Casey met me. He took me over to stay with Bunny's mother. I spent quite a bit of time talking to Don's wife. They took the body to his aunt Dais' house and had the funeral and everything. That was an awful trip," Donna continued, "and all the while I was traveling I kept thinking about what happened: with all the visitors who came to the apartment to see me before we left, someone stole Bunny's trumpet."

On June 6, 1942, Bunny Berigan was buried at Saint Mary's Cemetery in an unmarked grave.

7. New York *Times*, June 3, 1942, p. 23.

26

After You've Gone

Song broadcast on the Jack Pearl radio show
January 4, 1937
with the Tommy Dorsey Orchestra

"I had nightmares about Bunny's death and that trip to Fox Lake for about two years," recalled Donna. "I went back to an apartment in Harlem with the kids. I'd wake up screaming every night."

Loretta Berigan shared a room with Donna at the time of Bunny's funeral. Loretta remembered the numbing pall of those few days:

We stayed at Dais and Harry Timms's home. She was Mayme's second-oldest sister, Theresa. Bunny was laid out there. Don was drunk through the entire thing. Donna was practically incoherent with grief, and she was drinking quite a bit, too. We talked about many things, and Donna really poured her heart out. She was bitter about how they forced Bunny to work when he was too ill. She mentioned Harry Moss and James Petrillo. She was angry at them, as she had been with Arthur Michaud in some of the letters that Mayme had let me read earlier. Donna was quite a letter writer. I think she felt the most animosity toward Tommy Dorsey. She thought *he* had been taking money from Bunny's wages when he was with Tommy the second time. And apparently she and Tommy had had some confrontations. Donna told me that Tommy had called her "a whore, a tramp, and a no-good bum." She was concerned about money and how she would support the kids and herself. She said Don Palmer had helped Bunny pay back a lot of what he owed, but she was worried about what would happen with the remaining debts.

Berigan's financial situation at the time of his death received much attention in print. Tommy Dorsey has been credited with many acts of compassion in Bunny's behalf, some of which may be undeserved. One generally held belief is that Tommy Dorsey paid for Bunny Berigan's funeral. In fact, the Dorsey band was engaged at the Astor Roof when Bunny died. The Astor served as a collection point for a fund to pay necessary expenses and to assist Donna. Her recollection was perhaps colored by her feelings about Dorsey: "They started a trust fund at the Astor Hotel where Tommy's band was playing. The owner or manager . . . helped to set it up. I think the fund paid for getting Bunny's body and me to Fox Lake. Tommy no doubt put some money in, but it wasn't all his money. He didn't have control of it." This fund did pay for the expenses involved in the preparation of the body, the funeral service at Saint Malachy's, and the transportation to Fox Lake. From that point, the details ring clear in the memory of Orville Kratz, the funeral director for the burials of Bunny's parents and Bunny himself:

The body was shipped from New York to the Fox Lake depot, where I met it. I remember there was a young man who hopped off the train who was a fan of Bunny's. Bunny's mother—I admired her a lot—came to me and said, "First my husband and now Bunny." She knew that Bunny had assumed the responsibility for paying for his dad's funeral but that it hadn't been paid yet. I told her not to worry about it. She was grief-stricken. We had the service and the burial. Not long after that she came into our office—at that time our whole operation was in just a small corner of Jack Schlitzberg's furniture store—and told me about an insurance policy that had turned up. Somehow Bunny had this one that he hadn't converted the beneficiary from his mother's name to his wife's. Mayme came in and said, "I want to pay for Bill's and Bunny's funerals." That was a godsend for us; at that time every penny we could get a hold of was like a million dollars. I was *very appreciative*, and I took off something like $125 from the bill. I always said, "There's one lady who won't be buried as a pauper." Tommy Dorsey called us and said that the expenses in New York were all paid for, plus the transportation to Fox Lake. But Mayme paid us for the services here with that insurance policy.[1]

Ironically, Bunny's legendary poor business sense, here shown as neglect in updating the policy's beneficiary, had made it possible for his mother to pay for his father's funeral and his own.

Some claim that Tommy Dorsey kept Bunny on the Dorsey band payroll for a year after Bunny's death, sending the money to Donna. "Sent it to me! I never received a penny from him," insisted Donna. "I never heard from him either. He didn't even know where I was."

1. Kratz interview.

One article announced that "the action of Tommy Dorsey in placing [Berigan] posthumously on the band's permanent payroll" brought universally favorable comments. "He got credit for a lot of things he didn't do," maintained Donna. Another trade paper helped solicit contributions to the trust fund with this information: "Bunny Berigan friends have started a trust fund for the support of his children. It is an idea instigated by Tommy Dorsey, whose lawyer, William P. Farnsworth, is one of the fund's trustees. The other trustees are Bob Weitman, manager of the Paramount Theatre, Bob Christenberry, manager of the Astor Hotel, and Harry Moss of M.C.A."[2] One can speculate that Dorsey's manager would seize every opportunity to cast the leader in a favorable light.

"Jo and I were very angry at the time that they did not let us go with Mom to the funeral," recalled Pat. "We talked about it with 'Aunt Iona,' and she thought it appropriate that we go. I don't know who the 'powers that be' were who said no, but we were not allowed to go. . . . [F]or years, Jo and I thought Dad wasn't dead because we never saw him. He was just away on another trip. It created some confusion. We didn't want to accept the fact. We'd talk to each other. 'Watch: Dad's coming back from a trip; he's going to open that door and fool them all.' Nobody really dealt with our feelings."

"When I heard that Bunny died, I threw up," Bushkin confessed. "I was a dog-assed private in the army, the twelfth trumpet player in the Fourth Air Force band at March Field in California. I was on latrine duty, 'queen of the latrine' for the day, hosing off the place. I went to the day room to pick up the L.A. *Times,* and it says 'Bunny Berigan dead at 33.' I just threw up. It seemed a perfectly natural reaction for me. I got a beautiful letter from Jo Stafford describing the wake they had in New York. My dad sent Donna a hundred dollars for me."

Singer Danny Richards, who had been called into the army about two months before June 2, remembered receiving "a beautiful letter from Donna, telling me of his death and letting me know how highly Bunny thought of me. Let me tell you, boy, the tears flowed that day. I can't begin to tell you how I felt." Pianist Koss also recalled that he was in the army when Bunny died, and he happened to be in New

2. *Down Beat,* IX (July 1, 1942); *Metronome,* LVIII (July, 1942), 21.

York on leave. "I saw him laid out in this fleabag of a funeral parlor; I think it was on 7th or 8th Avenue. He was wearing the same beige suit he used to wear on dates. It had stains on it from the spit valve on his horn. It was very sad."[3] Predictably, the anguished members of the Bunny Berigan band were on the road doing one-nighters when their leader died. They learned about his passing while playing a job in Alexandria, Virginia, and their schedule was such that they were unable to pay formal tribute to their leader and mentor.

While Donna may have felt that Dorsey did not know where to find her after Bunny's death, Bunny knew where Tommy Dorsey was during the trumpeter's final hours. Along with Palmer, who had remained behind the band in New York, and probably Musso, Dorsey was sitting in Polyclinic Hospital, listening to the final measure of an up-tempo life, watching his friend die. On the June 3 broadcast from the Astor Roof, Dorsey offered "a little tribute to the memory of Bunny Berigan" and struck up "Marie." Harry James staged a benefit dance with his band on June 20 in Hollywood and sent the proceeds to Donna. Somewhat later, trumpeter Billy Butterfield recorded "I Can't Get Started" with his big band, earmarking the profits for Bunny's family. "Unfortunately," remembered Butterfield, "my own band collapsed and General Artists, my agents, seized whatever money or royalties there were to pay uncollected commissions."[4]

The trade papers featured tribute articles to Bunny, devoting lavish amounts of space to praising his abilities and expressing dismay at the deterioration and loss of such a talent. George Simon's tribute read in part:

> One of these years they're going to start talking about Bunny Berigan the way they now talk about Bix Beiderbecke. They're going to rave about his trumpeting feats; they're going to dig out his records, and they're going to play them for the next generation, pointing out this passage and that passage to prove that Bunny was one of the true Greats of All Jazz. . . .
> And now Bunny Berigan, like another great horn player with the same initials, is gone. Naturally, people are going to remark how great he was. And how right they are, too! There's too much proof to dispute the fact, recorded proof as well as the words of the many who heard him in person.
> And those who knew him, know what a great person they have lost, too. That goes not only for his wife, Donna, and his children, but also for men

---

3. Koss interview with author.
4. Billy Butterfield, to the author, May 7, 1987, in author's possession.

like the Dorseys and Goodman and Shaw and Glenn Miller and Mannie Klein and Carl Kress and Toots Mondello and Eddie Miller and Gene Krupa and Jack Teagarden and Jack Jenney and Charlie Barnet and Teddy Wilson and Red Norvo, and just about all the greats of jazz who some time or other played with and got to know Bunny Berigan.

Most of them will claim he's the greatest. If you asked Bunny, he probably would have called each of them the greatest, even though such appraisals of each would have been logical impossibilities. But Bunny always spoke well of everybody. You'd never hear him tearing down any musician. He'd build them up, whether they were already established stars, or whether they were discoveries of his, like Auld and Rich and Bushkin. . . .

Bunny is gone now. Fortunately, for most of us, he has left memories via the many phonograph records he made. Others of us, those who knew him as a person, don't even need such recorded evidence. We can remember Bunny Berigan, the person. You don't forget a man like that.[5]

Paul Eduard Miller had this to say:

Some day—and I have a profound feeling about it—we'll rate Bunny Berigan above Bix Beiderbecke. If quality of tone means anything (and it means a great deal to musicians), then it can truthfully be said that Bunny's tone was the biggest, the meatiest, and the strongest of any white trumpet player, living or dead.

The day Bunny died I talked to Cy Baker, himself an experienced first-chair and solo trumpeter of great merit, now with Bob Chester. Cy paid a tribute to Bunny which not only is a musically shrewd judgment, but one with which I am sure every musician in the country will agree.

"Bunny Berigan," Cy told me, "was the only trumpeter I ever knew who could play *good* spectacular jazz with a big, open tone. When he was at his best no one else could touch him. His recordings of 'Marie' and 'I Can't Get Started' will stand out as monuments to the beautiful quality of his expressiveness, his meaty tone—and his genius."

There is the core of Bunny's greatness. He combined expressiveness with a vigorous and dramatic tone. Above everything else he had "heart"—that elusive quality which musicians call "feeling" or "soul." . . .

[After his performance in Norfolk] was he philosophical enough to know that the end was near? I think he was. He had lived his life as he wanted to, expressing his whole life through his music. No man can do more. . . .

Let's not be fooled by a musician's economic struggles. The greatest jazz virtuoso in the world may be rendered temporarily "uncommercial," and drop out of sight completely except for scattered personal appearances.

It happened to Bunny Berigan. Even that does not alter the fact that

5. *Metronome*, LVIII (July, 1942), 20–21.

Bunny was one of *the* greatest. He lived and died with the soul of a sincerely genuine musician.[6]

Irving Kolodin's tribute introduced another facet. Kolodin focused on Bunny's work on the soundtrack for *Syncopation,* and while most listeners would dispute the writer's assessment of Bunny's playing on the film, he makes a valid point:

But, like the clown who got the greatest laughs while he writhed in genuine pain, Bunny's exit had an irony that was exquisite, and all its own. For the finest playing he has done in years and years—some would even omit this qualification—is being heard from the soundtrack of the film "Syncopation," which is currently making the rounds of the double-feature houses. It is even conceivable that the reclame from this film might have started Bunny back along the road he has traveled twice before. This time he might have made it. . . .

Thus it was that Bunny committed to celluloid what was truly a swan song to his public, but in a curiously opaque and grubby way that is hardly consonant with his great ability. To be sure, he earned some money, which was barely a consolation—for they will use it to bury him with, if it has not already gone to pay debts. Even the last solace—that he had done a job which people will admire him for, and credit him with—has been denied to Bunny for his playing in "Syncopation"—as brilliant as it is nameless.[7]

Down Beat declared, "Sentiments here about Bunny Berigan's death vary from extreme sorrow to a strange kind of irritation. Latter emotion was expressed by an office man who has been very close to Bunny for some years, pointing out that 'it was a crime to have talent like that wasted for no reason at all. Bunny didn't have to die—I wish to God I'd been able to keep him from killing himself.'" With the benefit of more than forty years' perspective, Berigan sidemen like Bushkin, Dixon, Conniff, and Kutch echo these thoughts. They admit to a vague sense of having been cheated, a feeling born of ambivalence. They harbor feelings of personal loss rooted in the dream that, had Bunny lived his personal life differently, they could have been a part of "the greatest" swing band, beyond question. Coupled with that sense of personal loss is the gnawing sense of their own responsibility or culpability: could they have done more to change Bunny's habits? Did they contribute to his death? And these and other musi-

6. Miller, "A Tribute to Bunny Berigan."
7. Irving Kolodin, "Bunny Berigan Died in Irony," New York *Sun,* June 3, 1942.

cians feel deprived of hearing more of Bunny's great music, a feeling shared by the jazz listening world. Critic and entrepreneur John Hammond hinted at this feeling of frustration, of having been cheated:

Bunny Berigan is dead and the music world is shedding tears. Some of that sympathy is belated, and would have done far more good if it had been applied judiciously during his life. . . .

He dissipated his talents in every conceivable way and yet, even at the end, he remained an inspired musician. Nothing that he might do could rob him of that. . . .

He was a funny guy: unhappy when he worked for somebody else, uncomfortable when he was his own boss. I don't know how much moral there is in the story of Bunny Berigan—there must be one—but I see no reason to bring it up now. He was usually a delightful, friendly and human person, acutely self-conscious of his shortcomings. It's a tragedy that he could not adjust himself to the vagaries of the music business.[8]

Two months after Berigan's death, manager Palmer was moved to grant *Down Beat* an exclusive interview about Berigan's financial situation and about some of the negative rumors—and truths—in circulation. Headlined "Manager Nails Berigan Lies," the partial interview follows:

"Take it from me, those stories you hear about Bunny Berigan drinking himself to death are so much hot air. They couldn't be more wrong.

"If ever a guy put his whole heart and soul into making an organization click, that guy was Bunny Berigan. That's why these false rumors bother me and the rest of Bunny's friends so much. It just isn't fair that the thousands of kids all over the country, who thought of him as a great musician and someone to model their music life on, should be disillusioned by lies and gossip spread by squares who never even knew Bunny. . . .

"I'm not going to tell you that Bunny didn't take a drink while I was with him because that wouldn't be true. But he was far from being the irresponsible drunkard that they've made him out. And you don't have to take my word for that, either. Just look up the records. During that last twelve months, there wasn't one complaint sent in to Harry Moss of M.C.A. who handled the band's account. Just the opposite was true. Not only did Bunny break attendance records set up by bands like Gray Gordon, Will Osborne and Russ Morgan, but bookers all over the country sent in enthusiastic accounts to the New York office about the band and his behavior. Even then,

---

8. *Down Beat*, IX (July 1, 1942); John Hammond, "Bunny Was Never Happy," *Music and Rhythm*, July, 1942.

they'd heard the stories about Bunny and were almost surprised to see him reach the band stand sober and on time.

"But to really prove what I'm telling you, here's a story that not many people know and that shows just what a real guy Bunny was. When Harry Moss took the band over on July 28, 1941, Bunny was twenty thousand dollars in debt. At the time of his death, he was less than five thousand dollars in debt. Does that sound as though he hadn't been working hard and plugging to get places? He traveled all over the country and did two hundred one-nighters in a year's time. No screwball drunk could do that.

"Bunny had one big idea and that was to produce the best band in the business. Nothing else mattered. We knew that he was working too hard and told him so. . . .

"I tried to get him to take a lay-off and let the band use his name while he rested, and take enough of a cut to keep him going, but he wouldn't listen to me. We nearly had a fight one night when he was ill and I tried to keep him from working. Another time, Harry Moss flew to Norfolk to get him to quit, but without success. . . .

"I'm glad I can say that Bunny died happily. Vido Musso, who took over the band, Tommy Dorsey and I were at his bed-side. One of his last wishes was that the band should stay together and go places. I don't have to tell you that we're going to do just that. A lot of people have written in to me asking what happened to Bunny's trumpet. I have it and the mouthpiece that he used for his 'I Can't Get Started' number. I intend to hold on to them for the time being, perhaps later they'll be placed in a jazz historical collection.

"I want to say that a lot of credit should be given to Harry Moss for the fine job he did after he took over the band and for the personal interest that he took in Bunny. Tommy Dorsey, too, did everything that he could for Bunny, and gave his family a wonderful lift after his death.

"Maybe this article will do something to clear up the confusion about Bunny's death. The whole musical world should know what a loss they've suffered and that the most wonderful musician who ever lived spent his last days in the best of show tradition, working to do the stuff he loved in the best way that he possibly could."[9]

Some of Palmer's impassioned testimony may simply have been company line. Palmer's own ties to MCA and his genuine loyalty to Berigan may have been in conflict, and his denial of the drinking problem, though typical, tends to lessen his credibility. Donna's statements, and those of too many of the musicians present at the

9. *Down Beat*, IX (September 1, 1942). Partly because of this printed interview, Donna Berigan thought highly of Palmer. It seems clear that Palmer extended himself in caring for Bunny for the same reasons that his sidemen voice almost unanimously: Bunny was a great guy and a great musician to play with. Those associated with the band at this time ascribed ambivalent motivations to some of Palmer's actions, however.

time, cast serious doubt on Palmer's apologist stance regarding Moss's motivation and his actions. The information about the reduction of the debt seems reasonable. Given the punishing schedule the band kept, and the unrelenting pressure maintained by the agency to which Berigan owed a large sum of money, it is not surprising that the debt should have been reduced substantially. Although Palmer's arithmetic on the number of one-nighters played by the band in Bunny's last ten months is not accurate, the thrust is. From July 31, 1941, through June 2, 1942, the band actually played 167 dates, including fairly long strands of three or four weeks each. The projected dates through September were solid, suggesting a return to popularity. Bunny's doggedness in the face of constant adversity and the loyalty of his band members in playing through these difficult times are truly admirable.

With obvious disgust, Donna recounted some of the sad facts of the morning of Bunny's death. "Not only did they steal Bunny's trumpet and his special mouthpiece, some souvenir hunters also took his pen and cuff links and his tie clasps." Donna supported Altpeter's contention that Bunny wanted his friend and former trombonist, Altpeter, to have his trumpet. While it is true that Bunny carried more than one trumpet much of his career, since his promotional contracts probably gave him access to other horns, it is possible that more than one "Bunny Berigan's trumpet" existed at the time of his death. Given his severely reduced financial status, however, it is likely that any extra horns of the type Koss described might have been sold. Moreover, Bunny had always been nonchalant in his treatment of his horns, often leaving them on the stand during off days, as he sometimes did at the Sherman. Even on his last jobs, Bunny was still switching between Kutch's borrowed Conn and his dented Martin, which Kutch had gotten repaired. Kutch got his Conn back when Bunny died. George Quinty at least partially supported Palmer's statement that Palmer had one trumpet and mouthpiece and that he intended to hold onto them "for the time being."[10]

Palmer made no secret of the trumpet he had. In addition to the September, 1942, *Down Beat* article cited above, an item appeared in *Metronome* of the same date, stating that Palmer had been offered

10. Chilton and Sudhalter, *Bunny Berigan*, 26; Quinty interviews with Mickolas and with author.

$4,000 for Bunny's horn but had "nixed the offer." If Donna and Altpeter believed that Palmer commandeered the trumpet that Bunny intended for Altpeter, they most likely could have insisted that Palmer honor Bunny's wishes. At the time, however, Palmer's persuasiveness probably prevailed; he must have convinced Donna that the horn's value would increase and that he would preserve the horn for such an eventuality. It is not unlikely that Palmer would entrust it temporarily to the stable Quinty. Interviewed more than thirty years after Bunny's death, Quinty talked about the horn: "For about two years I had the trumpet that Palmer took from Bunny's apartment for safekeeping. My son used it with a mouthpiece that Bunny had given him. [In about 1944] Don Palmer came over and got them, saying that Donna wanted them. Like a fool, I gave them to him. If Donna got the trumpet, she probably hocked it for some booze." Palmer had also expressed this latter concern at the time of Bunny's death. "As for Bunny's mouthpiece with a shank on it," continued Quinty, "Don Palmer's got it at his house. He had it fitted into a little plastic box with a light. It's got a little glass door in front and has two gold bands and it lights up. Bunny used this cornet mouthpiece with a shank to fit into his trumpet."[11] Kutch confirmed that Palmer reclaimed the trumpet from Quinty for Donna in about 1944, when she was living in Philadelphia. Perhaps the worst fears of Quinty and Palmer were realized. The question remains: where is "Bunny Berigan's trumpet"?

The fate of the Berigan music library is likewise a tangled story. At Bunny's death, many people, realizing the sentimental value attached to this music, appropriated various pieces of the library, from a single part for one tune to the complete arrangements for some numbers. As the band traveled under the leadership of Musso, it became more and more Musso's band, eventually dropping the Berigan name. With the continuing turnover of personnel and the eventual dissolution of the band when Musso broke it up after an engagement at the Arcadia Ballroom in New York on September 30, the music scattered even further. Quinty stored some parts in his Trenton garage. Kutch retains some full arrangements but regrets the one that got away. He had framed the score for "I Can't Get Started." But, like Bunny's trumpet, it too eventually disappeared.

11. Quinty interview with author.

27

I Poured My Heart into a Song

Song from an air check, September 26, 1939
by Bunny Berigan and His Orchestra

Whitney Balliett, the premier jazz writer whose work appears regularly in the *New Yorker,* wrote of Bunny Berigan:

Louis Armstrong was the first sunburst in jazz—the light a thousand young trumpeters reflected. But two other trumpeters, both less imitable than Armstrong, were also closely attended. One was Jabbo Smith . . . the other was Bix Beiderbecke. . . . The two men had an equally evanescent admirer. Bunny Berigan, who has been out of fashion most of the forty years since his death but was once revered as a kind of Beiderbecke replacement, seems to have successfully absorbed both players (along with Armstrong, of course) and then constructed his own over-arching style. . . .

One side of Berigan's style was lyrical, romantic, melodramatic, and garrulous. It had a kind of Irish cast. The other side was blue, emotional, down, funky. He would root around in his lowest register, playing heavy, resonant notes—gravestone notes. He would play blue note after blue note. Both sides of his style would appear in a single solo. He might start two choruses of the blues in his down style. He would stay in his low register (only Ruby Braff has matched the sound he achieved down there), growling and circling like a bear. He would use four or five notes, shaping them into short, insistent reiterated phrases. These would summon up the baying of hounds, the call of train whistles. At the start of his second chorus, he would suddenly jump to a high C or D, go into a flashy descending arpeggio, and wing through a couple of large intervals. His vibrato would become noticeable, and his tone would become generous and sunny. He might dip into his low register at the end of the solo, but he'd finish with a ringing Irish high C. Berigan had a superb technique. His sense of dynamics was unmatched, and his beautiful tone had the same texture and thickness and luxuriousness no matter what register he was in. His execution was almost flawless. He was a daring and advanced improviser, who fooled with offbeat and behind-the-beat rhythms and with all sorts of tonal effects. Yet his melodic lines were invariably long, logical, and graceful. There was an outsize quality to all Berigan's playing. He sounded like a three-man trumpet section pressed into one. He dominated every group he was in: on Benny Goodman's recordings of "Sometimes I'm Happy" and "King Porter Stomp" and on Tommy Dorsey's of "Marie" and "Song of India" his famous solos stand like oaks on a plain. Only Red Allen and Roy Eldridge achieved a similar majesty in their big-band work. (Louis Armstrong's big-band majesty was ready-made; he was often the only soloist.) . . .

Whatever the material, Berigan is everywhere, playing lead trumpet, soloing, filling the air with his serene and muscular lyricism.[1]

This assessment of the Berigan style is frequently matched in spirit, though rarely in presentation, throughout the literature of jazz criticism. With his description, Balliett has come closest to capturing the essence of Berigan's trumpet sound and to evoking the reaction of the sensitive listener upon encountering Berigan's playing. Other writers have evaluated Berigan's playing in their individual ways.

John Chilton described Bunny's style development during his early studio years in this manner:

On many sessions he was an anonymous member of a studio band's brass section, but on others his individualism was unmistakably evident as his solos knifed through many a sedate ensemble. Records from this period show how swiftly he was developing. His powerful attack was growing month by month, and his ideas were increasingly stimulating. He was gaining complete mastery of difficult lip trills, a lip technique that creates rapid alternation between two different notes without the use of the valves, and he was developing extraordinary endurance and range. He could hit a top G with ease and certainty, in a day when a top C, a fifth lower, was generally given in instruction manuals as the trumpet's highest point.[2]

Brian Case and Stan Britt state simply: "A first-class technician, Berigan's playing was noted for its fire and sheer emotionalism. Berigan exhibited a fierce attack, yet never was less than lyrical. His work in the lower register of his instrument was especially memorable, far superior to most other jazz trumpet players. Together with Bix Beiderbecke . . . Bunny Berigan was the greatest white trumpet player to be produced from the 1920s/1930s period—indeed one of

---

1. Whitney Balliett, "Bunny Berigan," *New Yorker*, November 8, 1982, pp. 124, 127.
2. Chilton and Sudhalter, *Bunny Berigan*, 13.

the greatest of all-time—and truly a giant performer on his chosen instrument."[3]

Scott Yanow declared: "Bunny Berigan was one of the most exciting jazz trumpeters of all time. His mastery of the lower register of his horn along with the trumpeter's higher notes allowed him to construct many dynamic spectacular solos. Bunny's trumpet work during his heyday, the thirties, compared favorably with the classic solos of Louis Armstrong and Roy Eldridge."[4]

Berigan's impact on his listening public, his fans, is a special one. For those who have been touched—many of them would say captured—by the Berigan sound, the experience is dramatic. Former Berigan fans do not exist; once captivated by the unique force of Berigan's jazz persuasion, a listener willingly becomes a lifelong believer. The openness, the honesty, the vulnerability, the daring, the capriciousness, the fullness, the sheer beauty of the Berigan sound cut through to the center of his listeners' feelings. Berigan's sound can cause melancholy, joy, pain, exaltation, or simply involuntary foot-tapping, but in my case it always produces empathy. The man communicates! For me, as for his legions of fans, Berigan must be heard with regularity.

Another such Berigan fan is Alfred Gage. In upstate New York in the 1930s Gage was a high-school trumpeter with an ear for jazz and a desire to play it, an ambition he realized on a part-time basis. As many do, he recalls his introduction to Bunny Berigan:

Back in 1937 I used to sneak a "Rube Goldberg" radio under the bed covers so I could listen to the 11:30 P.M. remote broadcasts of bands and not disturb my family. One night I turned the dial and suddenly I hear this terrific trumpet. In two seconds I was absolutely on cloud nine. Right then I swore I'd give an arm or thirty years to be able to play like that for even just one night! And all too soon, the announcer was telling me that the time had come to "say goodnight for Bunny Berigan, his trumpet and his orchestra, coming to you from the beautiful Madhattan Room of the Hotel Pennsylvania in the heart of downtown New York City. This is WEAF, New York." Wow! From then on I haunted the record shops to buy anything I could get my hands on by Bunny Berigan. And then, while visiting in Gloversville, we wandered downtown and I headed for the record shop and asked if they had anything

3. Brian Case and Stan Britt, *The Illustrated Encyclopedia of Jazz* (London, 1978), 24.
4. Scott Yanow, "Bunny Berigan Retrospective," *Record Review*, December, 1980, p. 30.

by Bunny. The clerk said he did just get a new one in and he handed me a big twelve-inch record, and I went into the little listening booth where you could try out a record to see if you wanted it. And I heard "I Can't Get Started" for the first time. They would have had to call the cops to get that record away from me. And for the next three months, as soon as I could get the $1.25, I bought another copy so that, if anything happened to my record, I'd still have other copies. Like a true addict, I didn't want to ever chance being without a good copy of that record. I still have eighteen copies of the tune in all mediums, including two music boxes.

I saw him and his band in the spring [May 10] of 1938 at the Palorama Ballroom in Colonie, New York, just outside Albany. He was terrific! My recollection is of: A band boy placing a gold trumpet on a chair in front of the band that was tuning up. A crowd around the bandstand saying things like, "Let's see what this guy's got." A big, rather rumpled, sheepish man ambling out from the wings and picking up the horn. A distinctive and unusual sideways motion of the right leg as he stomped off the beat. The band playing. Bunny grinning at the crowd. Then casually, almost carelessly, he puts the horn to his mouth and plays. Every trumpet man in the place was as enthralled as I was. The bulk of the crowd was dancing. Bunny played every title requested, one after the other—all the popular recordings he'd made. He never looked at a sheet of music. When he wasn't playing solo in front of the band, he'd step back in line with the two trumpets sitting on a raised tier, and he'd play lead horn. He did this for about an hour and a half without letup. He smiled and stomped off "Spanish Town" immediately when someone yelled it out. Bunny bent over and played at Georgie Auld, and then finally lifted the horn and blew the house down on his chorus. Intermission, and Bunny reached down and braced a hand on the shoulders of friends. The group disappeared through the crowd, to the exit, laughing and talking. It was eleven o'clock and I was seventeen, and my parents were waiting in the car. I didn't see him again that evening—or ever.[5]

In a Mist is the name of the Sunday evening radio record show hosted by Neal Payne on WXDR, the public radio station in Newark, Delaware. Berigan's recording of the Beiderbecke song is the theme for the program. And Berigan is the special delight of the host, a bricklayer and retired Wilmington fireman. Payne began as a volunteer disc jockey on May 20, 1979, with an hour's presentation—since grown to three hours—of vintage jazz and "big band era" music. He knew well that the first show's date, the third Sunday in May, coincided with the sixth Bunny Berigan festival in Fox Lake, Wisconsin.

5. Alfred K. Gage, to author, November 19 and December 6, 1985, in author's possession.

Each Payne program features at least one Berigan record in addition to the theme, most from Payne's private collection; some programs are saturated with Bunny's music. "Yes, I fell in love with that fabulous trumpet in 1948, six years after Berigan died, and time has done nothing to diminish the love affair," admits Payne.

If Bunny had been a guru, and were still alive, I'd be one of the group following him worldwide. That is how he affected me. I well recall that day in 1948 when I first heard "I Can't Get Started." Man, I just knew I couldn't live without that. Almost forty years have passed since then, during which I spent two years in the service as a Seabee in the Korean fiasco, got married to the gal I fell in love with when I fell for Bunny, raised four children, got a good job, retired, and am now playing Bunny on the air. I'll keep the flame burning as long as I'm able to. And one of these days I'm going to skip my anniversary show and make it to Bunny's day up in Fox Lake. [He did, in 1987.] I'd call myself Bunny's number one fan, but I understand there's already a guy near Detroit who claims that honor.[6]

He is recognizable by his vanity license plate, "BUNNY 1." Or by the three-quarter-size trumpet that rests on the rear window deck of his car. Or by his trumpet-shaped belt buckle. Or by his stationery, "Bunny Berigan's No. 1 Fan." Or by his Bunny Berigan T-shirt. Or by the buttons bearing Bunny's image that he wears. If he knows you, he might permit a look through his prized Berigan scrap book, warning, "Don't take anything out of the plastic covers please; someone took some stuff last time I passed it around." If admitted to his inner sanctum, you might admire the beautiful plaque—"Bunny Berigan, One of the Immortals of Jazz; May 16, 1982"—presented to the Berigan family at the ninth Bunny Berigan Day festival, a plaque subsequently given to him by Bunny's brother. Norm Krusinski of New Baltimore, Michigan, proudly claims the title of Bunny Berigan's Number One Fan. His collection of records, tapes, photographs, articles, and general Berigan memorabilia makes the claim difficult to deny. Like many Berigan fans, Krusinski is now retired but vigorous, still haunting used-record bins, flea markets, and auction lists for copies of the good music. Musically unschooled, Krusinski's ear for vintage jazz, Berigan in particular, is well tempered by years of listening, and he is seldom fooled by new discoveries of "Bunny" records:

6. Neal Payne, to author, *ca.* May 1, 1986, in author's possession.

Ever since the first time I heard him I knew there was something special about Bunny's playing. It's just so beautiful, and no one else can sound like him. For a long time it seemed like I was the only one who still appreciated Bunny. Now I've discovered a lot of people who feel the same way, and I think that maybe I wasn't so dumb all these years. Every time I go to Fox Lake for Bunny Day I stop by the cemetery and visit his grave. I always say a prayer and sometimes I leave a decoration or a marker of some kind. I don't suppose that anyone can understand this, but sometimes it makes me cry to be there near him.[7]

As extensive and as affecting as Krusinski's collection of Beriganiana may be, that of a young Trenton, New Jersey, enthusiast surpasses it. Deborah Mickolas is a teacher and an artist and the mother of a young child. But motherhood, while it may have temporarily relegated other pursuits to the back burner, has not dampened Mickolas' passion for the music of Bunny Berigan. Among her possessions is a *complete* collection of 78-rpm records that bear Berigan's name, whether as leader or sideman, with duplicates of most. In addition, she cherishes LPs in an infinite variety of combinations of Berigan music, some from extremely limited editions and rare performances, and including most, perhaps all, of the air checks and acetates that have been unearthed. Photographs, books, sheet music, magazines, tapes, autographs—all are abundantly represented in the Mickolas collection.

The sound of his trumpet, that's what turned me on to Bunny. It was fantastic! I first heard him with Billie Holiday doing "Billie's Blues," and I didn't know who it was. I read George Simon's book on the big bands and he mentioned that Bunny and Billie had recorded together, so I just put two and two together. I started to collect Bunny, and it just mushroomed from there. His sound was just so wonderful. I read Martin Kite's name on the back of one of the LPs, and when I contacted him he was very helpful to me and made tapes of some of the rarer sides. Then I got connected with Bozy White, and we've exchanged things. Now ten years later, here I am surrounded by all this stuff. When I was about four years old my father gave me all of his 78s; my favorite was "Little Brown Jug" by Glenn Miller. But I was listening to Basie and Ellington and Fitzgerald a lot as I grew older. Toward the end of my college days I really got interested in jazz, especially the vocalists like Ella and Billie and Sarah, then I discovered Bunny. I became a member of the IAJRC [International Association of Jazz Record Collectors] and that provided a network of supporting people. Then I met my husband, and he's a

7. Norm Krusinski, interview with author, September 23, 1984, tape in author's possession.

relentless collector of records and memorabilia. He helped me by showing me how to secure what I wanted to add to my collection. It would be almost impossible to start collecting Berigan 78s now; they've become so much in demand and so terribly expensive.[8]

Mickolas has become recognized as a bona fide Berigan expert and has contributed both artwork and information to the production of several Berigan albums on Shoestring. Her experience offers proof that younger listeners will transmit their interest in securing Berigan's well-deserved niche in the jazz pantheon.

And how do professional musicians—especially fellow trumpeters—regard Berigan? Those who heard him or played with him, and even many who were constrained to enjoy and evaluate his playing via his recordings and broadcasts, remain convinced of Berigan's dominance as a jazz performer. His direct and indirect influence on his peers and on later generations of trumpeters—indeed, on all jazz soloists—is significant. Balliett's naming of Armstrong, Beiderbecke, Smith, Berigan, and Eldridge leads us directly to Dizzy Gillespie, the next landmark trumpeter. Whereas, according to Balliett, Berigan "absorbed" his three predecessors, then developed his own unique voice, it is fair to say that those who have come after Berigan (and his contemporary, Eldridge,) reflect his brilliance. All five of the trumpeters Balliett named have a distinctive voice, a unique, identifiable sound, as has their heir, Gillespie.

Berigan established a new plateau for jazz-trumpet playing in several ways. First, he virtually redefined the short trumpet break by viewing even a two- or four-bar solo, not as a throwaway, but as an integral part of the whole performance while still branding it with an identifiable, personal sound. Most soloists of the day, when playing short breaks, either attempted to tell their entire life story in a frantic flurry of notes, or else disdained them. Bunny, though he sometimes entered a short solo with a fusillade, was often content to lay back and relate a relaxed vignette that enhanced the flow of the tune, rather than intruding on it. Bunny imbued each solo, no matter its length, with a form unto itself, shaped so as to tell a story. Invariably, his more extended solos were likewise architectural marvels, structured and logical, but daring. Further, Berigan elevated the accompani-

---

8. Deborah Mickolas, interview with author, June 25, 1985, tape in author's possession.

ment of vocalists to a special kind of art form by complementing vocal performances with accents, harmonies, rhythmic variations, and—where taste indicated—with silences. The sheer power and elegance of his pulsating tone could drive and inspire a vocalist or an instrumental group of whatever size. The imagination and fearlessness of his own solos pushed him to new frontiers of jazz improvisation, often sweeping his peers along with him. The quandary for subsequent trumpeters who may be Berigan pretenders lies in his complete mastery of the instrument, in his unique tone quality, and in his improvisational and compositional skill. Some players have attempted note-for-note Berigan imitations, though lacking either the tone or technique to duplicate Bunny's solos. Some have tried to emulate the richness and thickness of Bunny's tone, only to produce a schmaltzy, ersatz "soulful" sound. Berigan's legacy to succeeding generations of trumpet players may well be that by his attempting and usually achieving the "impossible" on his horn, he opened up the whole concept of jazz trumpeting, challenging those who followed to aspire to his high level of competence both technically and tonally. One result has been that the general level of technical facility and tone production among today's young musicians far surpasses that of the pre-Berigan era. As pianist and arranger Lipman emphasized, "Bunny was that rare combination of studio musician and jazz musician. Very few people have that quality. Later on, in California and New York, some of these people like Doc Severinsen began to blossom, whether on trumpet or other instruments. But don't forget, those very same people were influenced by Berigan." Trumpeter Red Rodney, one of the important links from early bop to today's young players, put it succinctly: "Today the kids have the whole history to listen to . . . and each year the younger players are getting better and better." Closer to Berigan's playing years, Roy Eldridge made this assessment:

I honestly believe there are more really great horn men around today than ever before. That's only natural because every youngster who takes up an instrument is inspired by the work of somebody else, and every once in a while a musician comes along who not only reaches the standard of the man he was using for a model, but also goes a little further. This leaves a higher standard for the next man to shoot at.

So today the average trumpet man has a bigger range than the average man had five years ago; and five years ago the average range was bigger than five years before that. The same thing applies not only to range, but to speed and general technique, and consequently trumpet players are more flexible and have more command of the instrument with which to express a style. Maybe they had the same inspiration in the old days but not the means of expressing it. That's why, today, there are so many men who produce really exciting jazz.[9]

One does not claim for Berigan the sole credit for this obvious improvement: technical advances in radio, television, and recording have made exposure to good playing accessible; colleges, high schools, and even junior high schools have developed courses in jazz studies; jazz teaching methods have improved greatly. These and other factors have made an important contribution to the elevated level of playing by young musicians. Some of these young players may never have heard Berigan, but his influence upon their teachers (or their teachers' teachers) is unmistakable. Even so, technical facility and tone quality in young musicians do not by themselves assure the emergence of great new jazz trumpeters. Creativity and taste, at best, are difficult to teach. Benny Carter, the master composer, arranger, pianist, trumpeter, and altoist, is still a vital player and writer at age eighty. Referring to his workshops at a number of colleges, Carter recently said on National Public Radio, "The kids are fantastically endowed with technique. They do more today than I would have thought possible fifty and sixty years ago. But, they sacrifice a lot of emotional content for technique. There's something to be said for street knowledge, for going around and sitting in at clubs, as I did when I was young, when they let me." And as Eldridge said later in his *Metronome* article, "The best white trumpet player I ever heard was Bunny Berigan. Bunny played with real soul, a fine sense of chord changes and an individual style and tone."[10] Other musicians honor Berigan as well.

Pee Wee Erwin: "I think practically all of the trumpeters of the thirties were, in one way or another, influenced by Bunny. Bunny and I were contemporaries and good friends; you might even say intimate associates. We hung out together in the same saloons. The last time I saw Bunny was at Hurley's bar and grill on 49th Street. I never

9. Red Rodney quoted in Ira Gitler, "Red Rodney: Lighting a Fuse,"*JazzTimes*, August, 1987, p. 17; Roy Eldridge, "Roy Eldridge on Trumpeters," *Metronome*, LIX (October, 1943), 27.
10. Nat Hentoff, "The Gentleman of Jazz," *Wall Street Journal*, April 6, 1987, See. A., p. 27; Eldridge, "Roy Eldridge on Trumpeters."

played with Bunny, but I followed him into several bands and into CBS, and when he couldn't make a commercial record date, I'd make them. I never tried to copy Bunny except on 'Marie,' where I was expected to follow his solo. Tommy Dorsey admired Bunny as everybody else did. When Bunny recorded 'Marie' he was thirty feet from the microphone. When I made 'Who,' which people used to confuse with 'Marie,' I was fifteen feet from the microphone. Bunny had the biggest sound of anybody I ever heard, especially in the low register. Bunny was a very powerful man, and there's an awful lot physical about playing the trumpet, especially the need for a strong air column, and Bunny was a very strong guy. You could never fully appreciate that tone he had, and the power, unless you stood in front of his horn and heard it. He'd hit a note and it would be just like a cannon. I'm not talking about volume. It was sheer body of sound. I think he was probably the greatest white trumpet player I ever heard." [11]

John Best (trumpeter with Glenn Miller, Artie Shaw, Ray Conniff): "I'm a Bunny fan, and so are some good friends of mine like [trumpeter] Billy Butterfield. When I was still back in North Carolina, I would listen to him on CBS with the house band—I think they were called the Music Makers. Then he had that *Saturday Night Swing Club*. I first met Bunny at about that time, and I have always loved his playing. In early 1942 [cornetist, trumpeter, and guitarist] Bobby Hackett and I were with Glenn Miller at the Pennsylvania Hotel, and Bunny had his band up on the Penn Roof playing for a private party. Bobby said, 'Let's go up and hear Bunny during our intermission.' So we did, and Bunny came over and spoke to us. We were amazed. Bunny looked terrible to me; his eyes could hardly focus. Bunny cracked, 'There's a rumor goin' around that I'm no longer alive. Ain't I the damnedest lookin' ghost you ever saw?' That was just a few months before he actually died. I'll never forget that." [12]

Ray Bauduc, drummer: "I was on that first Bunny's Blue Boys session in 1935 kinda by mistake. I went down to the session with Eddie Miller. Davie Tough was supposed to play the drums, but he was sick or something, and Bunny says, 'Where's your drums?' I told him they were out on Long Island and he says, 'Well, get in a cab and go get

11. Erwin interview. Some of this quotation is also from Sudhalter's record jacket notes for RCA 5657-1-RB, *The Complete Bunny Berigan, Vol. II.*

12. John Best, interview with Norm Krusinski, *ca.* 1987, copy of tape in author's possession.

'em and come on down here!' I felt wonderful. I really thought it was great to make records with a guy like Bunny. He was just one of the greatest in the world. There'll never be anybody like Bunny." [13]

Jack Teagarden, trombonist: "I thought Bunny was one of the finest trumpet players in the world. And I'll tell you another wonderful compliment, and it really means a lot because it comes from a guy who does a little bit of braggin'—let's say he's his own best publicity agent—Wingy Manone. He used to say, 'Now me and Louis'—he even put himself before Louis—'me and Louis is the best trumpet players.' About that time Bunny came to town and was playing at one of the hotels with Hal Kemp. I said, 'Wingy, why don't you go down and hear this new fellow, Bunny Berigan, and see what you think?' I saw Wingy on the street the next day and asked him if he'd gone to see the new boy. He said, 'Yup. Now there's three of us: me, and Louis Armstrong, and Bunny Berigan!'" [14]

Joe Bushkin, pianist: "Ain't I a lucky son of a bitch? I've played with and known all these great trumpeters. I played with Armstrong and Berigan, and they were my extra fathers. Bobby Hackett and Billy Butterfield were my brothers. And now Warren Vache, Jr., is my son."

Teddy Wilson, pianist: "Those Parlophone records I made with Bunny for Mildred Bailey were among the best records I ever made. They were the most fun. What a wonderful guy Bunny was." [15]

Don Jacoby, trumpeter: "Bunny was not just a musicians' player, he was a people's player. I would watch people standing around with their mouths hanging open, drinking in every note he played. He could *communicate!* Any trumpet player who sat next to him was truly honored. I feel like I was cheated because I missed out on that great ambition." [16]

Joe Dixon, reedman: "Bunny never held back. In fact, sometimes he'd play better for small crowds than for large ones. He thought every tune could be played to sound good. Bunny was unique. He was a natural blower and had such great lip control that he didn't finger the high stuff the same way every time. His notes had *pulse*, and

13. Ray Bauduc, from John Grams's *Grams on Jazz*, WTMJ, Milwaukee, June 3, 1972.
14. Jack Teagarden, from *Grams on Jazz*, June 3, 1972.
15. Teddy Wilson, from *Grams on Jazz*, June 3, 1972.
16. Don Jacoby, telephone interview with author, March 10, 1988, tape in author's possession.

his sound would get inside you. When he played lead he lifted the whole band. He was the heart and soul of that band. If Bunny's place in history isn't written soon, then soon every white trumpet player will be called an imposter."[17]

Charlie Spivak, trumpeter: "Bunny Berigan was my idol. I worked alongside Bunny, and before, when I free-lanced in radio, he and I did some dates together. I used to marvel at the wonderful things he did on the horn. He was a very gifted trumpet player in that he did so many things that I thought were awfully hard to do. I used to try to mimic him in some of the things I did, but he sure had such an ungodly range for that time. He was just an exceptional talent."[18]

George Shearing: "I had my first contact with jazz in [Claude Bampton's All-Blind] Band. Someone would pick up the new Armstrong or Berigan or Tatum record and say, 'Here's the new sender'— a good musician being known at the time as a solid sender."[19]

Clif Gomon, trumpeter: "Bunny had what we called lower jaw control, which didn't require a lot of pressure. He used his diaphragm to produce his vibrato, and would just finish off a note with a little hand vibrato sometimes. He was just a marvelous player."[20]

In his liner notes for the long-awaited *Complete Bunny Berigan, Volume II*, Sudhalter makes an important point. Taking note of the fact that records and broadcasts simply did not capture the enormity of Berigan's sound and the magic of his creativity, Sudhalter quotes many of the musicians who played with and heard Bunny over a period of time in different settings. All experience frustration in attempting to describe Bunny's playing. Sudhalter relates their common, independently achieved conclusion: YOU HAD TO *HEAR* BUNNY.[21]

---

17. Dixon interview.
18. Margaret M. Duggan, Glenda G. Fedricci, and Cara L. White, eds., *Conversations with Jazz Musicians* (Detroit, 1977), 183, Vol. II of Matthew J. Bruccoli and C. E. Clark, Jr., *Conversations*, 3 vols. to date.
19. Whitney Balliett, "Bob's Your Uncle," *New Yorker*, February 23, 1987, p. 130.
20. Clif Gomon, interview with author, May 20, 1987.
21. Sudhalter, notes for RCA 5657-1-RB.

28

I Can't Get Started

Song recorded August 7, 1937
by Bunny Berigan and His Orchestra

Bunny Berigan's "I Can't Get Started" was heard in the highly acclaimed film *Chinatown*, starring Jack Nicholson, Faye Dunaway, and John Huston.

Bunny Berigan's "I Can't Get Started" was featured in a 1985 advertisement for a swing era record prominently displayed in the news bulletin of the American Association of Retired Persons.

Bunny Berigan's "I Can't Get Started," a special favorite of the featured guest, played in the background as film star Jack Lemmon was interviewed on the top-rated CBS television program *60 Minutes*.

Bunny Berigan's "I Can't Get Started" is a member of the Hall of Fame of the National Academy of Recording Arts and Sciences.

Bunny Berigan's "I Can't Get Started" is the record that Louis Armstrong bought five copies of from his favorite Harlem record store.

Bunny Berigan's "I Can't Get Started" plays a role in a love story in the June, 1987, *Redbook*.

Bunny Berigan's "I Can't Get Started" is still found on jukeboxes in every part of the country, in big cities and small towns.

Bunny Berigan and "I Can't Get Started" are inextricably bound together in the memories of all who have heard the record. If Berigan's name calls forth even the barest spark of recognition, almost inevitably the response follows: "Oh, yes. 'I Can't Get Started.'"

Judy Garland—"Over the Rainbow." Coleman Hawkins—"Body and Soul." Artie Shaw—"Begin the Beguine." Glenn Miller—"In the Mood." Vaughn Monroe—"Racing with the Moon." Stan Kenton—

"Artistry in Rhythm." Al Jolson—"Swanee." Bunny Berigan—"I Can't Get Started." When asked why he did not record the tune, Armstrong replied, "That's Bunny's. You just don't touch that one since he made it."

From the moment artist, advertiser, and songwriter Johnny De-Vries brought the song into the Famous Door, Bunny was smitten by the tune. Whenever possible, Bunny and the merry gang of musicians at the Door featured it. Bunny recorded the song three different times, first on April 3, 1936, with Red McKenzie and His Rhythm Kings, with vocal by Red. Ten days later, as Bunny led his Blue Boys in his third recording session as a leader, he recorded it again, this time taking the vocal himself. On this session, Bushkin insists Eddie Condon set up the chords for Bunny's solo. Some devotees prefer this simpler, more direct treatment to the August 7, 1937, twelve-inch Victor recording with Bunny's full band. Although leader Berigan's two versions were recorded nearly a year and a half apart, and with vastly different instrumentation, both Bunny's vocal chorus and his horn playing are strikingly similar, probably because of the regularity of his performing it and to his bending to the expectations of listeners. Similarities aside, in the fifty years since Bunny ennobled this above-average Vernon Duke–Ira Gershwin song, the version that has attached itself to the hearts of casual listeners, jazz fans, dancers, lovers, trumpet players, and other musicians is the August 7, 1937, recording, which became a hit. There is an irony in the fact that Bunny's only true hit, this four minutes and forty-five seconds of magic, became a kind of trap for him. Having once created this masterpiece, Bunny was expected to re-create it nightly, on demand.

Vladimir Dukelsky and his family arrived in New York, refugees from the Russian Revolution, in 1922. Vladimir was nineteen and had been trained in classical music. In 1930, he began to use the name Vernon Duke and, befriended by George Gershwin, to write popular songs. Among the better-known Duke compositions are "April in Paris," "Autumn in New York," "Cabin in the Sky," "I Like the Likes of You," "Taking a Chance on Love," and "What Is There to Say?" He has also composed three symphonies and a piano concerto. Ira Gershwin's lyric contributions to American music are well known, particularly his collaborations with his brother, George. In 1932, he was the first lyricist to be awarded the Pulitzer Prize, for *Of Thee I Sing*. "I

Can't Get Started" was included in the Broadway presentation of *Ziegfeld Follies of 1936*, starring Bob Hope and Eve Arden. In the show, Hope attempted to impress Arden and to win her over as he sang of his accomplishments, chronicled in the lyrics. When she finally submitted after a long, amorous kiss, the Hope character left her, strutting off triumphantly. "I Can't Get Started" may have more variations of its lyrics than any other song in history. Nearly every performer either requested new lyrics from Gershwin, or else made up new ones, either to fit a given situation or simply to update them. As Gershwin wrote in 1959:

> Vernon played me this tune and told me it had had a lyric called "Face the Music with Me"; that nothing had happened to that version; that the tune was free and I could write it up if I liked it. I liked it and wrote it up. However, there is seemingly no end of lines for "I Can't Get Started." Besides the original version for Hope and Arden, . . . a radio version avoiding proper names was requested by my publisher. After that, I was asked to write a version for a possible recording by Bing Crosby, here again avoiding wherever possible the proper noun. Then there was a request for a female version to be recorded by Nancy Walker. All in all, I have fooled around with many, many lines for this piece. The sheet-music sale never amounted to much (I would say that in more than twenty years it has totaled less than forty thousand copies), but the early recording by Bunny Berrigan [*sic*]—considered by jazz devotees a sort of classic in its field—may have been a challenge (or incentive) for the great number of recordings that have followed. Not a year has gone by, in the past fifteen or so, that up to a dozen or more new recordings haven't been issued.[1]

"I Can't Get Started" is a straightforward, 32-bar ballad, in A-A-B-A form, to which Lipman, the arranger for Bunny's classic, added a commanding introduction. The five sections of the recording may be expressed in the following schematic:

I. Four-part cadenza-like, out-of-tempo introduction by trumpet

II. A—Trumpet statement of melody (eight bars)
A—Reed section (eight bars)

III. A—Berigan vocal (eight bars)
A—Berigan vocal (eight bars)
B—Berigan vocal bridge (eight bars)
A—Berigan vocal (eight bars)

1. Ira Gershwin, *Lyrics on Several Occasions* (New York, 1959), 100.

IV. Turnaround and interlude in cadenza-like form by trumpet (ten bars)

V. A—Trumpet (eight bars)
   A—Trumpet (eight bars)

Berigan took certain small liberties with Gershwin's lyrics in both of his vocal versions. A comparison of the written and sung lyrics follows:

WRITTEN: I've flown around the world in a plane;
SUNG: I've flown around the world in a plane;

WRITTEN: I've settled revolutions in Spain;
SUNG: I've settled revolutions in Spain;

WRITTEN: The North Pole I have charted,
SUNG: And the North Pole I have charted,

WRITTEN: But can't get started with you.
SUNG: Still I can't get started with you.

WRITTEN: Around a golf course, I'm under par.
SUNG: On the golf course, I'm under par.

WRITTEN: And all the movies want me to star;
SUNG: Metro-Goldwyn have asked me to star;

WRITTEN: I've got a house, a showplace, but I get no place with you.
SUNG: I've got a house, a showplace, still I can't get no place with you.

WRITTEN: You're so supreme, lyrics I write of you;
SUNG: 'Cause you're so supreme, lyrics I write of you;

WRITTEN: Scheme, just for the sight of you.
SUNG: I dream, dream day and night of you.

WRITTEN: Dream, both day and night of you,
SUNG: And I scheme, just for the sight of you,

WRITTEN: And what good does it do?
SUNG: Baby, what good does it do?

WRITTEN: When J. P. Morgan bows, I just nod;
SUNG: I've been consulted by Franklin D.

WRITTEN: "Green Pastures" wanted me to play God;
SUNG: Greta Garbo has had me to tea,

WRITTEN: But you've got me downhearted,
SUNG: Still I'm broken-hearted,

WRITTEN: 'Cause I can't get started with you.
SUNG: 'Cause I can't get started with you.[2]

2. Written lyrics, *ibid.*, 99.

On his first vocal version, Berigan sings still other small variations. Of most interest is the fact that in the bridge he orders the "scheme" and "dream" lines as Gershwin wrote them, but intermingles them— "scheme day and night of you; dream for the sight of you"—probably because of simple error. On the classic version, Bunny inverts the order, as shown in the comparison. And Bunny's perhaps inadvertent change in the latter is the stronger order, making for a crescendo of urgency. His other lyric variations have mainly to do with the fact that Bunny sang much as he played the trumpet; he phrased instrumentally. The extra words and substituted words are mainly for accent and rhythmic integrity. The major change lies in Bunny's conversion of Gershwin's very proper, "but I get no place with you" to the colloquial double-negative, "still I can't get no place with you." This folksy version works perfectly in expressing the frustration of the singer, adding to the power of the lyric. And Bunny's two-beat pause as he sings "Still I'm - - broken-hearted" is a natural and musical masterstroke.

Any objective evaluation of Bunny's singing voice would surely conclude that it possesses significant deficits. It is high-pitched and distinctly throaty, so that even Bunny's mother would probably have admitted that his singing never fulfilled the promise she might have sensed in his church debut as a child. Whereas his trumpet tone and vibrato are controlled, deep, and enveloping, his voice is often quavery, shallow, and vapid. Yet, somehow—at least with *this* song—it works. Billie Holiday, Louis Armstrong, Johnny Mercer, Mel Torme: none of their voices, as instruments, could withstand careful scrutiny. But they are musical singers, and they do *communicate!* And so does Bunny, with an open and vulnerable quality that creates an empathy between the forlorn Bunny and his listeners: we instantly identify with him and the problem he voices.

But it is through his trumpet that Bunny truly communicates his artistry as a musician, imparting majesty to this song. From the annunciatory first chord of the introduction and Bunny's entrance on his rich low D, the listener is on notice that something special is about to happen. The four declarations of this cadenza test all but the highest reaches of Bunny's range as he begins what many have called a concerto for trumpet. Stretching and winding, Bunny strikes each note in the center as he sets up his statement of the melody with a penetrating A above the staff. His melody treatment is as simple as that on his earlier record, but this time he commands an assurance, a nobility of phrasing, a richness that are all sublime. Bunny's perfectly controlled diaphragmatic vibrato enriches the melody, coloring and deepening some of the notes. The saxophone ensemble's eight bars are faithful to the melody. When Bunny takes over with his strangely affecting vocal, drummer Wettling's backing with a pattern of brushes on the snare drum—eighth notes on beats one and three, followed by a short roll—seems to lift the performance and help to propel it. On a second take, which was also issued in a limited manner, this drum pattern is not employed, and the vocal seems poorer for it.

The vocal ended, Bunny immediately steps back from the microphone to resume one of the most celebrated moments in recorded jazz. It is all Bunny's trumpet as the band lays down the chords for his cadenza. The first two sets of figures are in the upper-middle register, the next two sets in the lower-middle. The tension and expectation build with each measure. All the notes are rich and fat, the attacks clear, probing. The runs, utilizing frequent triplets and requiring much difficult fingering, are fluid and clean. Then comes the clarion call to the climax: three ringing high C's, the first two enhanced by suicidal lip trills. The next eight measures are taken aloft, exposed to the rarefied air of Bunny's upper register, where he sculpts a melody now become his own, rising to a high F, and punctuated with three piercing E-flats. All this is played without sacrifice of tonal quality or size. The emotional level peaks as well. Immediately then he drops down nearly three octaves to his low G, restating the theme for the last time in his voluptuous low register, before moving to a rich, vibrant, mid-range E-flat in preparing for the finale. This ending is not done in the same throwaway manner as the earlier version. A more experienced Berigan has acquired some showmanship. Using the same buildup, Bunny arrives at the high B-flat, invests it with a rich vibrato, and holds it. Now, instead of moving up, Bunny drops to a G, before soaring to hold the magnificent final E-flat. The dramatic and emotional impact are searing.

YOU HAVE TO *HEAR* IT!

Coda

Fox Lake, Wisconsin
May 15, 1988

Fox Lake's Community Building has changed little since my first visit four years ago. The Fifteenth Annual Bunny Berigan Day marks a return appearance for bandleader and clarinetist Norrie Cox and his Riverboat Ramblers, a sextet in the Dixieland tradition. Again the third Sunday of May in central Wisconsin has provided the faithful with an almost ideal day for festivity. Hot and sunny for the fifteenth year, the weather has once more blessed Bunny's day, and one of the believers ventures an opinion that perhaps Bunny's luck is starting to even out. On this, my sixth trip to Fox Lake, I am more relaxed, feeling as though I'm among friends. During the program, Skip Schweitzer, still the chairman of Bunny Berigan Day, even introduces me to the crowd along with several others who have come from some distance. Almost without exception, those so cited are now numbered among my regular correspondents: Norm Krusinski, Bunny Berigan's "No. 1 Fan"; Neal Payne, the Delaware disc jockey; Bill Hunkins, the jazz lover with a thousand tapes; Loretta Berigan, Bunny's sister-in-law who this year has traveled from Milwaukee with my wife and me, and who will make the scholarship presentation. Although this is just my fifth "BB Day," an extra trip intervened and served two purposes: interviewing local residents for additional information and attending the scholarship fund "booster" held in the fall. During the latter occasion, I sensed the first signals of my acceptance as I was asked to help in a special fund-raising activity.

My apprehension at the time of my first trip was needless. I feel a sense of welcome now, probably brought about by the many kindnesses shown me by the friends and relatives of Bunny Berigan. Through our many letters, phone calls, and personal visits, Loretta has become a friend. She has offered ideas, memorabilia, and, most of all, her insights about Bunny and his family. Artie Beecher and Tom Cullen, who seemed so formidable at first meeting, have continuously provided me with information and encouragement. Artie has helped set up several interviews and has maintained his end of a steady correspondence, ever ready to help. Tom has freely shared his private insights about Bunny. Marion Schultz, who was the Berigans' neighbor, volunteered to share her remembrances and give up a file of valued clippings. Many others have helped in similar ways. A cadre of cheerleaders, Berigan boosters all, are eager to see the story of their hero in print, anxious for me to finish my writing and make that a reality. With this 1988 Fox Lake visit, my endeavor has come nearly full circle, but the information base is not yet finished; a few wedges of updated input may complete that circle.

First I must trace some threads that lead to a few fellow travelers who survived Bunny. Shortly after Bunny's death, Patricia and Joyce were taken in and raised for several years by Darrell McArthur and his wife, Donna's brother and sister-in-law. Donna was unable to shoulder the financial and other responsibilities of raising the children, and shortly after her daughters witnessed her being taken by ambulance to Belleview Hospital for detoxification, their temporary custody was awarded to Darrell and Joyce McArthur. As of this writing, Patricia, now Mrs. Patricia Slavin, is living near Kansas City, Missouri. She works full-time as a counselor to parolees who have a history of substance abuse; in her free time she continues to develop her considerable painting talent. Joyce resides in Woodstock, Illinois, with her second husband, Robert Davis, a musicologist, writer, and potential Berigan biographer. Between them, Bunny's daughters would have made him a grandfather nine times—all boys!

Mary (Mayme) Berigan outlived her son by nearly two years, dying of liver and intestinal cancer on May 26, 1944. At that point, Loretta, soon to be divorced from Don after a long estrangement, left the home at 204 Green Street in Fox Lake and moved to Chicago temporarily, then to Milwaukee to further her career as an interior decorator. Loretta made sure that an appropriate headstone marked the graves of Bunny's and Don's mother and father.

Don Berigan drank his way through two more marriages and divorces before settling down to a long marriage with his fourth wife, Anna. A series of debilitating physical problems forced Don to check into the Veterans' Administration Hospital frequently. The same physical problems apparently persuaded Don to confront his drinking and renounce the use of alcohol. Don died on May 21, 1983, shortly after attending the Tenth Annual Bunny Berigan Day program.

Donna, just beyond her thirtieth birthday at the time of Bunny's 1942 death, married pianist George Zack in 1946. Zack had been the first person to visit Donna in her apartment on the morning of Bunny's death. Many in the music business considered Zack an excellent pianist, an especially strong blues player, but he was, if anything, more addicted to alcohol than Bunny was. Donna's twelve-year marriage to him was lived mostly in Chicago. Whereas, according to Donna, Bunny drank "a little," Zack drank "too much." Donna recalled that Zack made good money but that he would spend it before he got home. More than one visitor to their home spoke of its poor appearance and of the generally trying conditions under which Donna lived. One described Zack as a "mean drunk." In a Zack tribute article by Bert Whyatt, a friend observed that he had never seen Zack sober after noon.[1] During a 1985 interview, Donna offered, "I suppose he's dead now." After divorcing Zack, who indeed died November 7, 1977, Donna married Bernard Burmeister. During my extended interview visit with them in Houston, both Mr. and Mrs. Burmeister were gracious and helpful, apparently adjusted to their reduced financial status and serious physical problems. Donna was bed-bound, suffering from a broken hip that had not received proper attention and from advanced emphysema that required regular, sometimes constant, oxygen inhalation. Her third husband's most obvious physical characteristic was a pair of severely deformed, nonfunctional legs, a legacy of polio. Bernard Burmeister died in Houston in 1985. Donna then went to live with her daughter Pat in Kansas City, Missouri. Later moved to a nursing home, Donna died there on March 15, 1986.

Bunny's grave, financed with the nearly forgotten insurance policy,

1. Bert Whyatt, "The Unforgettable George Zack," *Mississippi Rag*, XV (January, 1988), 8.

lay unmarked from 1942 until October 8, 1950. Artie Beecher chaired a committee that solicited funds from the American Federation of Musicians locals in Fond du Lac, Baraboo, Beaver Dam, and Madison, but mostly from individuals. "I figured it would take me about six months, but was I wrong! It took me over a year and a half," recalled Beecher.

My wife and I contacted almost everyone we knew, and especially musicians. Mostly, it was a buck or two at a time; money was still scarce around here. The Madison local only contributed $10 because that's all their by-laws would allow. The other three put in $25 each. The man at the monument company in Randolph was a bass player; he knocked off $100 from the price of the stone, which brought the price down to $375. The original design was done by Bunny's cousin, Charles Casey. For the dedication day, we sent out a hundred announcement postcards to the people who had contributed. When we got there for the ceremony nearly 350 people were there! We just kinda made up a program on the spot: Merrill Owen, Bunny's first leader, "Doc" DeHaven, the last local musician to play with Bunny, Tom Cullen, who was then working on the biography, and Ray Groose, and myself each said a few words. When it was all over, Casey invited everyone—of course, that included a lot of musicians—down to his tavern, and that's when the jam session began. Two days! That's how long it lasted. The Schlitzberg sisters joined right in; Cull [Cora] was the drummer. She was also an opera singer, and when she sang "Kansas City Kitty" out at the country club later, you could hear her downtown. I've got pictures of that whole thing you wouldn't believe!

From Artie's description, Bunny would have loved it.

One grave site in the Berigan plot still remained unmarked, that of Barbara Ann Berigan, whose birth and death both occurred on Bunny's twenty-fifth birthday. She had been quietly buried at what later became the foot of her father's grave. With Artie Beecher again serving as spearhead, a loose-knit committee was formed with the goal of correcting this oversight. Again pursuing a policy of modest contributions, raised mostly through his personal contacts, Beecher saw the fund begin to take on substance. At the scholarship booster concert in the fall of 1984, this cause was brought to the attention of the audience; some contributed. I became an auctioneer for the first time, seeking a high bidder for a tape of selected Bunny Berigan recordings that had been contributed by his Number One Fan. It was purchased by a local jazz devotee, the daughter-in-law of funeral director Orville Kratz. On November 17, 1985, Artie Beecher saw another project completed with the placing of an appropriate grave marker. Perhaps this is but one more manifestation of the legacy of love and loyalty Bunny generated in his friends and fans.

One touching postscript to the Fourteenth Bunny Berigan Day was the death of Larry Becker, one of the members, with Bunny, of Merrill Owen's Pennsylvanians. Becker, eighty-six, died in Waukesha on June 2, the forty-fifth anniversary of Bunny's death. Owen himself died in Madison, at age 86, on February 8, 1988—the last of the Pennsylvanians. The same month also saw the death of Erle Smith, Bunny's early co-leader in Madison.

Sadly, it must also be reported that Arthur Parks Beecher, Jr., died on May 18, 1990, on the eve of the Seventeenth Annual Bunny Berigan Day. At eighty, Artie had been ill for more than a year. Tom Cullen delivered part of the eulogy.

One more parcel of information will serve to complete my quest for knowledge about Bunny Berigan. Posthumous honors and praises, by nature, are classics of the "too little, too late" syndrome. Although his formally conferred honors have materialized slowly, Bunny would probably have enjoyed being present for the celebrations they occasioned, and for the parties that inevitably followed them. And though he would have tried to dismiss the honors with a modest joke, even Bunny would have been impressed with the seriousness of the intent to salute him and to remember him for the beauty and joy he brought to people through his unique talent. Not the least of these tributes is the Bunny Berigan Day series, initially sponsored by the Fox Lake Chamber of Commerce, that began in Fox Lake on Saturday, May 18, 1974. The inaugural program featured a concert by the "Doc" De-Haven Jazz Combo, trumpeter Kaye Berigan, a proclamation of Bunny Berigan Day from Governor Patrick Lucey, and a "fish boil" dinner. Among those present were Don Berigan, uncle "Big Bob" and cousins "Little Bob" and Chuck Berigan, Cora Schlitzberg, Tom Cullen, and several political dignitaries. Joyce Berigan Bryden, Bunny's daughter, was present with her son; the program's master of ceremonies was Bob Davis, who would later become Joyce's second husband. One of the highlights of the proceedings was the presentation of a ten-foot wooden replica of a trumpet, an icon that still decorates the sign at the town limits welcoming visitors to Fox Lake. This first Bunny Berigan Day began a tradition that endures: friends, family, and fans of Bunny gathering to pay tribute to a musical giant in an atmosphere charged with the emotion and loving conversation of the true believers.

On May 16, 1976, the occasion of the third Bunny Berigan Day in Fox Lake, a Wisconsin State Official Marker honoring Bunny Berigan was dedicated and placed outside the Community Building. The program was begun in 1951, and Bunny's marker—number 226—was the first to be dedicated in honor of a musician. The marker, approximately 4½ feet wide and 6 feet high, bears the heading, BERNARD R. "BUNNY" BERIGAN (1908–1942). The inscription reads:

> This was the hometown of famed jazz trumpeter and band leader, Bunny Berigan. As a child he played in the Fox Lake Juvenile Band directed by his grandfather, John C. Schlitzberg.
>
> In his early teens, he began his professional career with the Merrill Owen dance band at Beaver Dam. A few years later in Madison, he was in demand for campus dances.
>
> Beginning in 1930, he became the featured soloist for such band leaders as Paul Whiteman, Benny Goodman, and the Dorsey Brothers. Singers Bing Crosby and the Boswell Sisters were among those who recorded with him. With his own orchestra in 1937, he recorded his most popular hit and theme song "I Can't Get Started With You."
>
> Jazz great Louis Armstrong predicted Berigan would be the trumpeter most likely to succeed him in the affection of music lovers, but Berigan's life and music came to an untimely end at the age of 33 in New York City. He is buried in St. Mary's Cemetery south of Fox Lake.
>
> Erected May 1976

At the presentation ceremony for this marker, both Berigan daughters, Pat and Joyce, appeared. Those who organized the efforts to procure this honor for Bunny included Fox Lake mayor Wayne Ruenger, Tom Cullen, and Ray Sivesind of the Wisconsin State Historical Society. Cullen was instrumental in rewording the marker to its present form. John Grams, a university professor from Milwaukee and erstwhile host of a popular jazz radio program, served as emcee, and the Riverboat Ramblers provided the jazz.

The latest of Bunny's posthumous honors was proferred on September 20, 1985, in Milwaukee, and it, too, bears a favorite-son flavor. The Wisconsin Performing Artists Hall of Fame, cosponsored by the Milwaukee *Sentinel* newspaper and the Performing Arts Center, pays tribute to those outstanding practitioners of the temporal arts who have Wisconsin roots. In an installation ceremony at the Bradley Pavilion in Milwaukee, Bunny was so honored, along with actress Charlotte Rae. Another inductee was a fellow trumpeter far better known for his popular singing, Vaughn Monroe.

The most prestigious of the honors accorded Bunny since his death is the installation of his August 7, 1937, recording of "I Can't Get Started" into the Hall of Fame of the National Academy of Recording Arts and Sciences. This is the organization that since 1957 has sponsored the annual awarding of Grammys for the outstanding records of each year in a wide range of categories. The hall of fame, a separate category, was founded by the trustees of the academy to honor distinguished recordings made before the first Grammy Awards in 1958. The first five hall of fame selections were honored in 1974; Bunny's certificate and recognition (shared by those who participated in the recording in a major way) came in 1975. Nominations may come from academy members, record companies, music historians, critics, and musicologists. They are then screened by a ninety-member elections committee, chosen by vote of the academy's trustees, that narrows the list to twenty-five finalists. The elections committee then votes again to select the five winners for a given year.

The first ten hall of fame inductees are a formidable group, particularly in view of the fact that the nominees could have come from any recording prior to 1957. Here, with release dates cited, are the recordings so honored:

1974—"Body and Soul"; Coleman Hawkins, 1939
    "The Christmas Song"; Nat "King" Cole, 1946
    "Rhapsody in Blue"; Paul Whiteman and George Gershwin, 1927
    "West End Blues"; Louis Armstrong, 1928
    "White Christmas"; Bing Crosby, 1942
1975—*Beethoven: Complete Piano Sonatas, Volumes I–XII*; Artur Schnabel, 1932–38
    Carnegie Hall Jazz Concert, 1938; Benny Goodman, 1950
    "I Can't Get Started"; Bunny Berigan, 1937
    "Mood Indigo"; Duke Ellington, 1931
    "Vesti La Giubba" from *I Pagliacci*; Enrico Caruso, 1907
Not bad company for a boy from Fox Lake!

*   *   *

I have been asked the question many times, much as I have asked it myself: How would Bunny have played if he had survived in good health to an age of sixty or seventy? Would he have changed his style? Would he, as a creator attuned to new ideas, have accommodated his playing to the bop sounds, in the manner of Roy Eldridge and Coleman Hawkins, two of his outstanding contemporaries? Would he have taken Louis Armstrong's path, denouncing bop as "Chinese music," and clung to familiar, comfortable performances? Would he have lost the creative urge completely, and retreated into a commercially oriented, spiritless musical existence? Intriguing though they may be, and inviting of speculation, these questions simply have no definitive answers. Could Bunny have left us a hint? On the May 28, 1940, air check of a BBC broadcast, from New York to London, the Tommy Dorsey Orchestra plays "East of the Sun." This version is substantially different from the recording made on April 23; for one thing, Bunny's solo is twice as long. In the thirteenth measure, Bunny plays a little phrase— whether planned or to cover a potential fluff—that Dizzy Gillespie would have been proud to have played a few years later. You must hear it if you can. Bunny the bopper?

Through my efforts in bringing this book into being, I have come to know Bunny and his music much better. The Bunny Berigan I know has enriched my life through the beauty and vitality of his music. I am sad that his artistry was cut short, but he owes me no more. Assuming that Bunny left nothing but "I Can't Get Started," perhaps Artie Shaw's view of the artist's potential legacy applies: "Maybe twice in my life I reached what I wanted to. [In 'These Foolish Things'] at the end the band stops and I play a little cadenza. That cadenza—*no one* can do it better. Let's say it's five bars. That's a very good thing to have done in a lifetime. An artist should be judged by his best, just as an athlete is. Pick out my one or two best things and say, 'That's what he did: all the rest was rehearsal.'"[2]

2. *Newsweek*, January 2, 1984, p. 8.

Appendix A

List of Guests on *Saturday Night Swing Club* During Its First Year

The following individuals or groups (in addition to Bunny Berigan, Frank Trumbauer, Lee Wiley, and Red Norvo, all of whom were on the first program) were heard on the *SNSC* from June 13, 1936, to June 5, 1937, and were listed in the program for the First Anniversary Program, June 12 and 13, 1937:

Red Nichols
Artie Shaw
Gogo de Lys
Adrian Rollini
Charlie Teagarden
Casper Reardon
Billie Holiday
Hoagy Carmichael
Miff Mole
Verginia Verill
Carl Kress
Dick McDonough
Dolly Dawn
Johnny Green
Babe Russin
Willard Robison
Dick Stabile
Frank Froeba
Lennie Hayton

Al Duffy
Teddy Wilson
The Modernaires
Claude Thornhill
Tommy Dorsey
The Original Dixieland Jazz Band
The Blue Flames
Earl Hines
The V-8 Octet
Lucky Millinder
Will Hudson
Ray Biondi
Sharkey Bonano
Art Gentry
Willie Smith
Loretta Lee
Margaret McCrae
Mary Lou Williams
Red Allen

Jack Teagarden

Fats Waller

Frank Victor

Harry Volpe

Claude Hopkins

Joe Sodja

Hazel Scott

The Raymond Scott Quintet

Chick Webb

Doris Kerr

Joe Haymes

Ella Fitzgerald

Chauncey Morehouse

John Calli

Tony Gatuso

Ramona

Paul Sterrett

Duke Ellington

Ivie Anderson

Joe Marsala

Red Evans

Billy Kyle

Noble Sissle

Les Lieber

Eddie Condon

Manny Klein

Adele Girard

Wingy Manone

The Onyx Club Trio

Joan Edwards

Joe Bushkin

SOURCE: Soundcraft LP-1013, *The Saturday Night Swing Club—On the Air,* jacket notes.

Appendix B

Schedule of Berigan Band, April 1 to December 31, 1937

DATE	ACTIVITY
April 1	Recording date; four titles at Victor studios, New York City
April 3	Bunny appears on *Saturday Night Swing Club* with Stuff Smith
April 4	Band at Reade's Casino, Asbury Park, N.J.
April 5–10	Probable one-nighters and rehearsals in New York City vicinity
April 10	Bunny appears on *Swing Club* with Joe Marsala
April 14	Probable date of band battle with Artie Shaw at Roseland State Ballroom, Boston
April 16	Dance at State College for Teachers, Albany, New York
April 17	Possible date of first dance at Victor Hall, Camden, N.J.
April 18	First *Fun in Swingtime* broadcast, to continue each Sunday through October 10, WOR, 6:30–7:00 P.M.
April 18–28	Rehearsals at Nola studios, New York City
April 25	*Swingtime* broadcast
April 29	Opening of band in Manhattan Room, Pennsylvania Hotel, New York City

DATE	ACTIVITY
May 1	First Saturday broadcast from Penn Hotel, WABC, 11:00–11:30 P.M.
May 2	*Swingtime* broadcast
May 5	First Wednesday broadcast from Penn Hotel, WABC, 11:05–11:30 P.M.
May 6	First Thursday broadcast from Penn Hotel, WABC, 12:00–12:30 A.M. This pattern of Saturday, Wednesday, Thursday broadcasts continues through July 7, the band's last night at the Penn Roof
May 8	Penn broadcast
May 9	*Swingtime* broadcast
May 12	Penn broadcast
May 13	Recording date; five titles at Victor studios
May 13	Penn broadcast
May 15	Penn broadcast
May 16	*Swingtime* broadcast
May 19	Penn broadcast
May 20	Penn broadcast
May 22	Bunny appears on *Swing Club* with Fats Waller
May 22	Penn broadcast
May 23	*Swingtime* broadcast
May 23–June 18	Probable time period for band's cutting series of radio transcriptions for Norge Refrigerator, Decca studios, New York City
May 26	Penn broadcast
May 27	Penn broadcast
May 29	Penn broadcast
May 30	*Swingtime* broadcast
June 1	Band moves to Penn Roof
June 2	Penn broadcast
June 3	Penn broadcast
June 5	Penn broadcast

DATE	ACTIVITY
June 6	*Swingtime* broadcast
June 9	Penn broadcast
June 10	Penn broadcast
June 12	Penn broadcast. This is the first anniversary of the SNSC. Bunny's band is featured from Penn Roof, along with all-star lineup from around the world.
June 13	Bunny and band guest on *Magic Key* radio program
June 13	*Swingtime* broadcast
June 15	Possible special shortwave broadcast to England
June 16	Penn broadcast
June 17	Penn broadcast
June 18	Recording date; three titles at Victor studios
June 19	Penn broadcast
June 20	*Swingtime* broadcast
June 23	Penn broadcast
June 24	Penn broadcast
June 25	Recording date; four titles at Victor studios
June 26	Penn broadcast
June 27	*Swingtime* broadcast
June 29	Penn broadcast (pattern now Tuesday, Thursday, Saturday)
July 1	Penn broadcast
July 3	Penn broadcast
July 4	*Swingtime* broadcast
July 6	Last Penn broadcast
July 8	Band begins stand at Pavilion Royal, Valley Stream, Long Island
July 10	First of series of Saturday and Tuesday broadcasts from Pavilion Royal, WABC, 11:00–11:30 P.M. on Saturdays

DATE	ACTIVITY
July 11	*Swingtime* broadcast
July 13	First Tuesday broadcast from Pavilion Royal, WABC, 11:05–11:30 P.M.
July 17	Pavilion broadcast
July 18	*Swingtime* broadcast
July 20	Pavilion broadcast
July 24	Pavilion broadcast
July 25	*Swingtime* broadcast
July 31	Pavilion broadcast
August 1	*Swingtime* broadcast
August 3	Pavilion broadcast
August 7	Recording date; four titles at Victor studios including twelve-inch version of "I Can't Get Started"
August 7	Pavilion broadcast
August 8	*Swingtime* broadcast
August 10	Pavilion broadcast
August 14	Bunny guests on *Swing Club*
August 14	Pavilion broadcast
August 15	*Swingtime* broadcast
August 17	Pavilion broadcast
August 18	Recording date; three titles at Victor studios
August 21	Last broadcast from Pavilion Royal
August 22	*Swingtime* broadcast
August 25	Probable closing date for Pavilion Royal stand
August 29	*Swingtime* broadcast
September 3	Recording date; five titles at Victor studios
September 5	*Swingtime* broadcast
September 5	Band at Rotin Point, Conn.
September 7	Probable opening date for stand at the Meadowbrook, Cedar Grove, N.J., lasting through (probably) September 20

DATE	ACTIVITY
September 12	*Swingtime* broadcast
September 19	*Swingtime* broadcast
September 20	Probable closing date for Meadow-brook
September 23	Band at Casino Hall, Scranton, Pa.
September 25	Band at Sunnybrook Ballroom, Potts-town, Pa.
September 26	*Swingtime* broadcast
September 26	Band at Savoy Ballroom, Harlem, N.Y.
October 3	*Swingtime* broadcast
October 7	Recording date; four titles at Victor studios
October 10	Last *Fun in Swingtime* broadcast
October 11	Band at unknown N.Y. ballroom
October 12	Band at Roseland State Ballroom, Boston
October 13	Band at Casino Hall, Carbondale, Pa.
October 14	Band at unknown N.Y. ballroom
October 15–21	Band plays one-week stand at Hippo-drome Theater, Baltimore
October 22	Band at unknown ballroom in Phila-delphia
October 23	Band at Roger Sherman Hotel, New Haven, Conn.
October 24–26	Band in N.Y. at unknown location(s)
October 27	Band in Wheeling, W.Va.
October 28	Band in Akron, Ohio
October 29–November 4	Band plays one-week stand at Stanley Theater, Pittsburgh
November 5–11	Band plays one-week stand at Fox The-ater, Detroit
November 12	Band at unknown hall in Cleveland
November 13	Band at Valley Dale Ballroom, Colum-bus, Ohio
November 14	Band at unknown hall in Fremont, Ohio

DATE	ACTIVITY
November 15	Band at unknown hall, New York City
November 17–December 7	Band plays three-week stand at Paramount Theater, New York City
December 9–15	Band plays one-week stand at Metropolitan Theater, Boston
December 19	Band at Ritz Ballroom, Bridgeport, Conn.
ca. December 16–24	Band plays other one-nighters in New England area; exact places unknown
December 23	Recording date; five titles at Victor studios
ca. December 25	Band Christmas party
ca. December 27	Band opens stand at Earle Theater, Philadelphia

SOURCES: Bozy White Outline, researched by White and Tom Cullen; author's research in miscellaneous other sources.

Appendix C

Schedule of Berigan Band, January 19 to April 23, 1939

DATE	CITY	LOCATION
January 19	Scranton, Pa.	Casino Hall
January 20	Kingston, Ontario	Queens University
January 21	Travel to Detroit	
January 22	Detroit	Graystone Ballroom
January 23	Off—rested in Detroit	
January 24	Lorain, Ohio	Colosseum Ballroom
January 25	Bradford, Pa.	Shea's Theater
January 26	Toronto	Royal York Hotel
January 27	Oneida, N.Y.	National Guard Armory
January 28	York, Pa.	Valencia Ballroom
January 29	New York City	Manhattan Center
January 30	White Plains, N.Y.	Westchester County Center
January 31	Boston	Southland nightclub
February 1–4	Boston	Southland
February 5	Newark, N.J.	Mosque Ballroom
February 6–8	Boston	Southland
February 9	Charlottesville, Va.	Canceled
February 10–11	Blacksburg, Va.	Virginia Polytechnic Institute
February 12	Baltimore	Keith's Roof Ballroom
February 13	New York City	Webster Hall
February 14	Off	

DATE	CITY	LOCATION
February 15	Berwick, Pa.	Canceled—snow, bad roads
February 16	Allentown, Pa.	Mealy's Auditorium
February 17	Andover, Mass.	Andover Prep School
February 18	Exeter, Mass.	Exeter Academy
February 19	Waterbury, Conn.	Hamilton Park Pavilion
February 20	Worcester, Mass.	Municipal Auditorium
February 21	Kingston, R.I.	Rhode Island State College
February 22	Hartford, Conn.	Capital Park Casino
February 23	Travel	
February 24–25	Lexington, Va.	Virginia Military Institute
February 26	Travel	
February 27–28	Tuscaloosa, Ala.	University of Alabama
March 1	Macon, Ga.	Capitol Theater
March 2	Jacksonville, Fla.	County Armory
March 3–4	Gainesville, Fla.	University of Florida
March 5	Travel	
March 6	Daytona Beach, Fla.	Pier Casino
March 7	Columbus, Ga.	Royal Theater— canceled
March 8	Birmingham, Ala.	City Auditorium
March 9	Atlanta	Shrine Mosque
March 10–11	Durham, N.C.	Duke University
March 12	Travel	
March 13	Off	
March 14	New York City	Rehearsal—Gray Studios
March 15	New York City	Recording session
March 16	Off	
March 17	Rochester, N.Y.	Convention Hall
March 18	Providence, R.I.	Arcadia Ballroom
March 19	New York City	New Yorker Hotel
March 20	Off	
March 21–22	New York City	Rehearsal—Gray Studios

DATE	CITY	LOCATION
March 24–25	Brooklyn, N.Y.	Riviera Theater
March 26	Brooklyn and Harlem, N.Y.	Riviera Theater and Savoy Ballroom
March 27	Brooklyn, N.Y.	Riviera Theater
March 28–April 4	Week off before Easter	
April 5–7	Cleveland, Ohio	Rehearsals
April 8	Cleveland, Ohio	Hotel Cleveland
April 9	Cleveland, Ohio	Trianon Ballroom
April 10	Charleston, W.Va.	WCHS Auditorium
April 11	Cleveland, Ohio	Trianon Ballroom
April 12	Canton, Ohio	Meyer's Lake Park Pavilion
April 13	Cleveland, Ohio	Trianon Ballroom
April 14	Detroit	Masonic Auditorium
April 15	Cleveland, Ohio	Trianon Ballroom
April 16	Vermilion, Ohio	Crystal Beach Park
April 17	Toronto	Palais Royale Ballroom
April 18	Cleveland, Ohio	Trianon Ballroom
April 19	Beaver Falls, Pa.	Broadhead Hotel
April 20	Cleveland, Ohio	Trianon Ballroom
April 21	Cleveland, Ohio	Hotel Cleveland
April 22	Cleveland, Ohio	Trianon Ballroom
April 23	Columbus, Ohio	Valley Dale Ballroom

SOURCE: Eddie Jenkins Diary, in White Materials, White and Cullen Research Materials, and in Jerry Kline, ed., "Touring with Bunny," *Mississippi Rag*, X (February, 1983).

Appendix D

Schedule of Berigan Band, July 31, 1941, to June 2, 1942

DATE	CITY	LOCATION
July 31	Luna Pier, Mich.	Ballroom
August 1	Dayton, Ohio	Lakeside Park
August 2–September 1 (inclusive)	Buckeye Lake, Ohio	Crystal Danceteria
September 4	Pulaski, Va.	Monticello Club (Louis Armstrong visits)
September 6–October 2 (inclusive)	Jacksonville, Fla.	Hotel Roosevelt patio
October 3	Charleston, S.C.	County Hall
October 8	Berwick, Pa.	Westside Park
October 10–11	Richmond, Va.	University of Virginia
October 17	Bethlehem, Pa.	Lehigh University
October 18	Boston	Raymor Ballroom
October 19	Fitchburg, Mass.	Lyric Theater (three shows)
October 24–25	Boston	Raymor Ballroom
October 31	Baltimore	Keith's Roof Ballroom (broadcast)
November 1	New York City	Manhattan Center
November 4	New York City	Recording, "Pepsi-Cola"

DATE	CITY	LOCATION
November 6–7	Raleigh, N.C.	University of North Carolina (two broadcasts)
November 11	Bunny's father dies	
November 14	Camden, N.J.	Convention Hall (Policemen's Ball)
November 15	Williamstown, Mass.	Williams College
November 19	East Park, N.Y.	East Park High School
November 21	Chester, Pa.	El Rancho Club
November 24	New York City	Imperial Record Co.; cut four Elite sides
November 28	Chester, Pa.	Saint Robert's High School
November 29	Newark, N.J.	Krueger Auditorium
December 5	New York City	Hotel Pennsylvania
December 6	Hempstead, Long Island	Elks Club
December 7	Boston	Tic Toc Club
December 12	Lancaster, Pa.	Moose Hall
December 13	Hartford, Conn.	Foot Guard Hall
December 19	Sanford, N.C.	Sanford Armory
December 20	Knoxville, Tenn.	Cherokee Country Club
December 25	Erie, Pa.	Waldamer Park (broadcast)
December 26	Wilmington, Del.	Hotel Dupont
December 27	New York City	Hotel Pennsylvania
December 29	Coatsville, Pa.	Scott High School
December 30	Milford, Del.	Milford Armory
December 31	Altoona, Pa.	Jaffa Mosque Masonic Temple

ca. January 1, 1942   Bunny leaves for California to take part in the film *Syncopation*. He returns at the end of January. During Bunny's absence, the band played only six dates:

January 10–11	Chester, Pa.	El Rancho Club
January 17–18	Chester, Pa.	El Rancho Club
January 25–26	Chester, Pa.	El Rancho Club

DATE	CITY	LOCATION
February 7	Cincinnati	Cincinnati University
February 8	Cleveland	Aragon Ballroom
February 10	Pittsburgh	Aragon Ballroom
February 11	Olean, N.Y.	Palace Theater (three shows)
February 12	Youngstown, Ohio	Nu-Elms Ballroom (broadcast)
February 13	Galt, Ontario	The Highlands
February 14	Cleveland	Aragon Ballroom
February 17	Fremont, Ohio	Rainbow Gardens
February 21	Baltimore	Lord Baltimore Hotel
February 23–28	Auburndale, Mass.	Totem Pole (broadcasts February 25, 26)
March 1	New Britain, Conn.	Hotel Stanley arena
March 6	Nashua, N.H.	N.R.C. Ballroom
March 7	Portland, Maine	Ricker Gardens
March 8	Waterbury, Conn.	Hamilton Park Pavilion
March 11	New York City	Last four records for Elite (old NBC studios at 711 5th Avenue)
March 13	Wilmington, Del.	Black Cat Casino
March 14	Philadelphia	Brookline Country Club (broadcast)
March 15	Holyoke, Mass.	Holyoke Theater (five shows; local broadcast)
March 16	New Rochelle, N.Y.	Fort Slocum (unpaid job)
March 19	Pittsburgh	William Penn Hotel
March 20	Pittsburgh	Military Ball, William Penn Hotel (four bands: Ted Weems, Sammy Watkins, Rusty Williams, BB)
March 21	Bowling Green, Ohio	Bowling Green University
March 22	Hornell, N.Y.	Majestic Theater
March 24	Pittsburgh, Pa.	Aragon Ballroom
March 27	Ann Arbor, Mich.	University of Michigan

DATE	CITY	LOCATION
March 28	Flint, Mich.	IMA Auditorium
March 29	Toledo, Ohio	Trianon Ballroom
April 1	Toronto, Ontario	Palais Royale Ballroom
April 4	Cincinnati	Castle Farms
April 5	Vermilion, Ohio	Crystal Beach Park
April 6	Detroit	Graystone Ballroom ("black Easter" dance)
April 8	Cumberland, Md.	Maryland Theater
April 10	Wooster, Ohio	Wooster College
April 11	Saginaw, Mich.	Saginaw Auditorium
April 12	Youngstown, Ohio	Nu-Elms Ballroom
April 13	Norwalk, Ohio	Cole Auditorium
April 14	Youngstown, Ohio	Nu-Elms Ballroom
April 16	Youngstown, Ohio	Nu-Elms Ballroom
April 17	Granville, Ohio	Granville College
April 18	Grove City, Pa.	Grove City College
April 19	Youngstown, Ohio	Nu-Elms Ballroom
April 20	Bunny hospitalized in Allegheny, Pa.; rejoins band on May 8 in Baltimore. Band carries on as follows:	
April 21	Pittsburgh	Aragon Ballroom
April 22	Allentown, Pa.	Empire Ballroom
April 23–May 13	Baltimore	Summit Inn
May 14	Aberdeen, Md.	USO benefit, U.S. Army camp
May 16	New York City	Manhattan Center
May 17–23	Boston	Tic Toc Club
May 25–27	Norfolk, Va.	Palomar Ballroom
May 28	Milford, Conn.	[Milford College?]
May 29	Scranton, Pa.	Scranton University
May 30	Pottstown, Pa.	Sunnybrook Farms (missed job)
May 31	New York City	Manhattan Center (Bunny ill)
June 2	Alexandria, Va.	Saint Mary's Academy (Bunny died, 3:30 A.M.)

SOURCE: Gene Kutch Diary, copy in author's possession.

Appendix E

Partial Berigan Genealogy

William Berigan was born in County Kilkenny, Ireland, about 1784. His parents are unknown. He died in Fox Lake, Dodge County, Wisconsin, on May 8, 1878. While still in Ireland, William married Ellen Stapleton, who was born there *ca.* 1803 and died in Fox Lake in 1878. William, Ellen, and their seven children came to Dodge County, Wisconsin, in 1848. Their fourth child, Nicholas, who was born in Ireland, *ca.* 1840, married on January 28, 1875, Margaret McMahon, who was born *ca.* 1857, daughter of Bridget Finerty and Michael McMahon. Their first child was William, born in Fox Lake on December 22, 1875. He married Mary "Mayme" Schlitzberg, who was born in Packwaukee, Marquette County, Wisconsin, on October 5, 1904, daughter of John Schlitzberg and Julia Philipson.

William and Mary had two sons. Donald was born in Madison, Wisconsin, on September 3, 1905, and died May 21, 1983. He married first Loretta Reichenberger on July 3, 1938. Roland Bernard "Bunny" Berigan was born in Hilbert, Calumet County, Wisconsin, on November 2, 1908, and died in New York City on June 2, 1942.[1] In Syracuse, New York, on May 25, 1931, he married Donna McArthur, born in Berlin, New Hampshire, April 19, 1912. Her father was John J. McArthur.

Donna and Bunny's two daughters were born in New York City. Patricia was born July 23, 1932; Joyce was born April 22, 1936. A middle

---

1. Bunny's birth certificate reads Rowland Bernart, which was a German-influenced interpolation by the hospital clerk of his parents' intended name, Roland Bernard.

BERIGAN GENEALOGY CHART

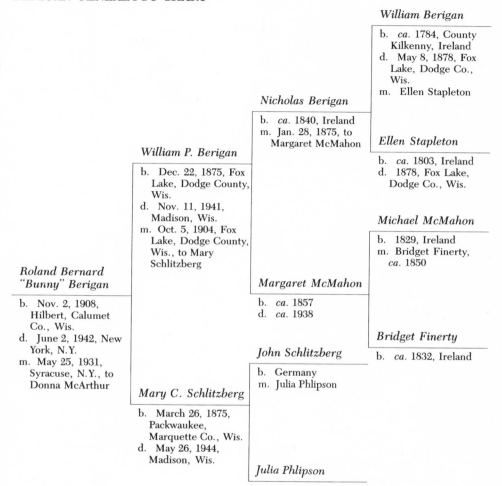

William Berigan

b. *ca.* 1784, County Kilkenny, Ireland
d. May 8, 1878, Fox Lake, Dodge Co., Wis.
m. Ellen Stapleton

Nicholas Berigan

b. *ca.* 1840, Ireland
m. Jan. 28, 1875, to Margaret McMahon

Ellen Stapleton

b. *ca.* 1803, Ireland
d. 1878, Fox Lake, Dodge Co., Wis.

William P. Berigan

b. Dec. 22, 1875, Fox Lake, Dodge County, Wis.
d. Nov. 11, 1941, Madison, Wis.
m. Oct. 5, 1904, Fox Lake, Dodge County, Wis., to Mary Schlitzberg

Michael McMahon

b. 1829, Ireland
m. Bridget Finerty, *ca.* 1850

Margaret McMahon

b. *ca.* 1857
d. *ca.* 1938

Roland Bernard "Bunny" Berigan

b. Nov. 2, 1908, Hilbert, Calumet Co., Wis.
d. June 2, 1942, New York, N.Y.
m. May 25, 1931, Syracuse, N.Y., to Donna McArthur

Bridget Finerty

b. *ca.* 1832, Ireland

John Schlitzberg

b. Germany
m. Julia Phlipson

Mary C. Schlitzberg

b. March 26, 1875, Packwaukee, Marquette Co., Wis.
d. May 26, 1944, Madison, Wis.

Julia Phlipson

SOURCES: Birth Certificate for Roland Bernard Berigan, Register of Deeds, Vol. V, p. 409, in Bureau of Vital Statistics, Hilbert, Calumet County, Wis.; Certificate of Death for Roland Bernard Berigan, No. 11660, Department of Health, City of New York, Borough of Manhattan, N.Y.; Certificate of Death for William P. Berigan, Local Registrar's No. 2005, and Certificate of Death for Mary Schlitzberg Berigan, Local Registrar's No. 5, both in Bureau of Vital Statistics, Madison, Dane County, Wis.; Certificate of Death for William Berigan, No. 01809, Fox Lake, Dodge County, Wis.; information on births of William Berigan, Ellen Stapleton, and Nicholas Berigan from *Ninth Census of the United States, 1870*, Dodge County, Wis., Township of Fox Lake, 197; information on births of William P. and Mary Schlitzberg Berigan from family documents, courtesy of Lorraine Berigan (copies in author's possession).

child, Barbara Ann, was born prematurely on November 2, 1933, and lived only a few hours.

Patricia and Thomas Colburn had five sons: Thomas, born March 23, 1951; Stephen, born February 16, 1952; Wayne, born November 16, 1954; Gary, born September 30, 1956; William, born January 15, 1958. Joyce and Robert Bryden had four sons: Robert, born June 20, 1957; Joseph, born February 4, 1959; James, born October 17, 1960; Peter, born November 4, 1963.

Appendix J

Berigan's Recorded Legacy

Berigan's recorded legacy might be divided into three major categories, which fall roughly in chronological order: as a member of countless studio orchestras that cranked out commercially oriented backgrounds for singers of "popular" songs; as a major member of various smaller jazz groups, sometimes backing jazz-oriented vocalists; and as a lead and solo trumpeter with big swing bands, principally his own. What follows is a listing of several selections from each category, most of which are still available in one form or another. Even given the technical limitations of his surviving recordings, some of which have been made from poor reproductions of original radio broadcasts, or remastered from original records of questionable quality, most of the selections mentioned throughout this book, and especially those listed here, are recommended for careful listening.

The first selected listing includes mainly those recordings with studio orchestras and vocalists pitched toward the popular market. In these, Bunny usually provides the only jazz sound and often freshens the entire session. Most of these come from the period from 1931 to 1933, but two Bob Howard selections were recorded in 1936. Bunny can usually be heard playing strong lead horn, clean and sometimes almost too sweet, as the job demanded. But when his solos surface, not only do they provide a breath of invigorating air, they remake the whole *feel* of the performance. The rhythmic pulse is changed, not the tempo, and the tunes only seem quicker. Often the listener is transported in time: so fresh and new is his sound, so free of the clichés of the day, the recordings seem to leap ten years—from 1931 to 1941, or beyond. To illustrate this effect, the following list is offered:

"I Raised My Hat" (Adrian Rollini and His Orchestra)
"I've Got a Sweet Somebody to Love" (Hal Kemp Orchestra)
"Love Is Like That" (probably Fred Rich Orchestra)
"Much Too Much" (Bob Howard and His Orchestra)
"Nevertheless" (Sam Lanin and His Orchestra)
"Now You're in My Arms" (Probably Fred Rich Orchestra)
"Parkin' in the Moonlight" (Dorsey Brothers Orchestra)
"She Reminds Me of You" (Paul Hamilton and His Orchestra)
"Smile, Darn You, Smile" (Carolina Club Orchestra)
"Whose Big Baby Are You?" (Bob Howard and His Orchestra)

In the second category, the jazz content is far richer, and even the following partial listing of the "must hear" selections Bunny recorded with jazz-oriented groups is a long one. Among them are several made with groups Bunny led, which I have designated as follows: Bunny Berigan and His Blue Boys, (BB); Bunny Berigan and His Boys, (HB); Bunny Berigan and His Studio Orchestra, (SO). For the other titles the nominal leader of the group is indicated in parentheses following the name of the selection. Much of Berigan's finest recorded work is in this setting:

"A Fine Romance" (Billie Holiday)
"Basin Street Blues" (Bill Dodge)
"Billie's Blues" (Billie Holiday)
"Blues" (BB)
"Blues" (Jam Session at Victor)
"Bughouse" (Red Norvo)
"By the Sycamore Tree" (Dorsey Brothers Orchestra)
"Chicken and Waffles" (BB)
"Dardanella" (SO)
"Davenport Blues" (HM)
"Did I Remember?" (Billie Holiday)
"Dinah" (Bill Dodge)
"Doggone, I've Done It Again" (Boswell Sisters with Dorsey Brothers Orchestra)

"Downhearted Blues" (Mildred Bailey)
"Easy to Find, Hard to Lose" (Rhythm Makers)
"Empty Saddles" (SO)
"Everybody Loves My Baby" (Boswell Sisters with Dorsey Brothers
    Orchestra)
"Going, Going, Gone" (Chick Bullock with His Levee Loungers)
"Honeysuckle Rose" (Bill Dodge)
"I Can't Get Mississippi Off My Mind" (Dorsey Brothers Orchestra)
"I Can't Get Started" (April 13, 1936, version)
"I Can't Give You Anything but Love, Baby" (Bill Dodge)
"If I Had My Way About My Sweetie" (Studio Orchestra; Owen
    Fallon and His Californians)
"I Just Couldn't Take It, Baby" (Bill Dodge)
"I'm an Old Cowhand" (SO)
"I'm Coming, Virginia" (BB)
"I'm Gonna Sit Right Down and Write Myself a Letter" (Chick
    Bullock)
"Is That Religion?" (Mildred Bailey with Dorsey Brothers Orchestra)
"It's Been So Long" (HB)
"Junk Man" (Bill Dodge)
"Keep Smilin' at Trouble" (Bud Freeman and His Windy City Five)
"Let Yourself Go" (HB)
"Mama Don't Allow It" (Mound City Blue Blowers)
"Me Minus You" (Connee Boswell)
"Nobody's Sweetheart Now" (Bill Dodge)
"No Regrets" (Billie Holiday)
"Nothin' but the Blues" (Gene Gifford and His Orchestra)
"Organ Grinder's Swing" (Frank Froeba)
"Savage Serenade" (Adrian Rollini and His Orchestra)
"Squareface" (Gene Gifford)
"Summertime" (Billie Holiday)
"Sweet Sue" (Bill Dodge)
"'Tain't So, Honey, 'Tain't So" (Rhythm Makers)
"There's Something About an Old Love" (Rhythm Makers)
"Tillie's Downtown Now" (take two; Bud Freeman)
"Troubled" (Frank Trumbauer and His Orchestra)
"When Love Has Gone" (Red McKenzie and His Rhythm Kings)

"Why Did It Have to Be Me?" (Dorsey Brothers Orchestra)
"Willow Tree" (Mildred Bailey)
"You Took Advantage of Me" (BB)
"You've Got Me Crying Again" (Lee Wiley and Dorsey Brothers
   Orchestra)

Finally, with the big band format, certainly the classics with Benny Goodman—"King Porter Stomp" and "Sometimes I'm Happy" (the air check from the Palomar Ballroom has a better solo on the latter)—and with Tommy Dorsey—"Marie," "Song of India," "East of the Sun," and "Liebestraum," among others—should be heard, and are readily available in a variety of reissues that display Berigan to advantage. Two sides he made with the first Glenn Miller orchestra—"In a Little Spanish Town" and "Moonlight on the Ganges"—spotlight Berigan in great solos and demonstrate why Miller chose him for these sides. With his own band, many of Bunny's best-known sides are easy to obtain in a variety of formats. Among several that should be listened to:

"Black Bottom"
"Caravan"
"Frankie and Johnnie"
"Jelly Roll Blues"
"Mahogany Hall Stomp"
"The Prisoner's Song"
"Russian Lullaby"
"Shanghai Shuffle"
"Sobbin' Blues"
"Trees"
(and the Beiderbecke tunes with the reduced band:)
"Candlelights"
"Davenport Blues"
"Flashes"
"In a Mist"
"In the Dark"

Many lesser-known titles in the full-band context reveal Berigan's power and inventiveness as well:

"All God's Chillun Got Rhythm"
"And So Forth"
"Blue Lou"
"Carelessly"
"Devil's Holiday"
"Ebb Tide"
"The First Time I Saw You"
"Gee, but It's Great to Meet a Friend (From Your Hometown)"
"Heigh Ho" (air check from Paradise Restaurant preferred)
"I'm Confessin'" (air check from Detroit's Westwood Gardens)
"I Poured My Heart into a Song" (air check from WNEW)
"Kiss Me Again" (air check from Paradise Restaurant)
"Me and My Melinda"
"Melancholy Baby" (air check from Westwood Gardens)
"Mother Goose"
"Never Felt Better, Never Had Less"
"Panama" (air check)
"The Pied Piper"
"Roses in December"
"A Serenade to the Stars"
"Somebody Else Is Taking My Place"
"Stardust" (A Demonstration in Swing)
"Swanee River"
"Sweet Varsity Sue"
"That Foolish Feeling"
"Turn on That Red Hot Heat"
"The Wearin' of the Green"
"You Can't Run Away from Love Tonight"

Some explanation is in order regarding the large number of "Bill Dodge" selections in the second category. Both historically and musically, these samplings represent a significant meeting of talents as they present Bunny and Benny Goodman in particularly fine early form. These titles come from a 24-tune collection recorded on three 16-inch World electrical transcriptions, designed for exclusive play on radio. These ETs were vertically cut, inside out, at *33 and* ⅓ rpm, probably in two sessions during February and March, 1934. The discovery of these ETs, and their subsequent reissue in three different formats, has generated great interest and some speculation through the years. Bill Dodge is almost certainly a pseudonym for Goodman. The latest reissue, *Swinging '34: Bill Dodge and His All-Star Orchestra* (1966 on Melodeon MLP 7328, 7329), appears with liner notes by Howard J. Waters that provide some perspective about these rare recordings:

The musicians featured on these recordings were drawn from the select group of free-lance men in New York at the time. Perhaps never before or since the recording dates did this exact group exist as an orchestra. Yet such were their talents that the music has a strong unity of concept, and a poise and a polish as well, that many fine bands never achieved. . . .

Benny Goodman, featured on all selections, was just 25 years old. Even by 1931, Benny's style had matured and taken on a polish which was envied by every clarinet player with two ears. And by 1934, with rounded experience in radio, films, pit bands and free-lance recording, BG had a well-earned reputation among leaders as well as his peers. He was then only one year away from the public launching of his career as the King of Swing.

Bunny Berigan, not yet 25 years old [*sic*] when these sides were made, is also featured throughout both on lead trumpet and hot solos. He was not far from his own debut as a band leader, and already had a growing reputation in music circles. Beginning his free-lance career in radio early in 1931, Bunny's reputation grew during his tenure with the Paul Whiteman Orchestra and he returned to the free-lance field in New York in 1934. Here, in these recordings, he is perhaps at the alltime peak of his ability.

Dick McDonough and Arthur Schutt, free-lance specialists from the late '20's, appear here in some of their last recordings as featured jazz soloists. McDonough continued to record until his death in 1937 but rarely in anything resembling a jazz setting. Schutt became a successful musical director for the Hollywood film studios and except for some obscure solo transcriptions, this was virtually the last jazz recording session on which he can be heard.

Art Rollini, younger brother of the famed jazzman and orchestra leader Adrian Rollini, is heard here in what is probably the earliest known example on record of his hot style. He plays with terrific swing, good tone, and fine ideas. It's no surprise that he was Goodman's first choice for the jazz tenor chair when Goodman organized his first swing band.

While the brass section was completely dominated by Berigan, the trombonist and second trumpet do get occasional solo opportunities and acquit themselves well in the ensembles. The identity of the trombonist has long been a mystery to researchers. . . . Jenney gets our vote. . . . The second trumpet, though occasionally playing lead parts on some selections, was by the great Mannie Klein. . . .

In the rhythm section we find a blend of talent well-matched to the powerful front line. Artie Bernstein's playing on this set of recordings easily demonstrates his mastery of the instrument and what a great asset he was to the rhythm section. Gene Krupa had recently left the Mal Hallett band in Boston and was due to spend a brief period with Buddy Rogers' band in Chicago before joining BG's Victor band in early 1935. There's no feature for Gene in this set, as there were to be so many with Goodman later on, but nevertheless his presence is felt at important moments during the first session. If he weren't there you'd know something was missing. Stan King, we believe, handles the drum department on the second session.

D. Russell Connor is the author of a monumental compilation of Goodman's history of recordings, *Benny Goodman: Listen to His Legacy* (Metuchen, N.J., 1988). His considerable research on the "Bill Dodge" sides has led him to conclude that Shirley Clay was the second trumpet for the twelve sides on the first session, Klein on the second; that Joe Harris was the trombonist on the first session, Jenney on the second; that an unknown tenorist appeared on the first session, Rollini on the second; and that "Krupa's opinion, upon listening to all the sides, was that he cut them all" (42–43). Waters' assertion that these particular sides represen. "the alltime peak of [Bunny's] ability" will certainly raise some eyebrows among Berigan aficionados. Nevertheless, these 1934 efforts do showcase some of Bunny's transcendent ability in a series of performances, fortuitously preserved.

More detailed information about some of the above recordings, and others, appears in the Selected Discography. This annotated discography includes possible sources for purchasing these records. It is through these records and others that the Berigan musical legacy endures.

Selected Discography

This section contains a discography of many of the recordings, transcriptions, and air checks that make up the main body of Berigan's recorded legacy. Selections are listed in chronological order and, in a rough sense, divide Berigan's work into the three categories, as discussed in Appendix F. Many of these discographical entries also contain annotations, mostly related to Berigan's solo work, with some comments directed to the work of his playing partners or the setting of the music.

According to the authoritative research of Bozy White, Berigan made his first known recordings with Hal Kemp on May 14, 1930. These are featured on White's SS-110. Berigan's last recordings were made on Elite, March 11, 1942. Gunther Schuller and others have claimed that Bunny's first recordings were made with the Wisconsin University Skyrockets in 1928. In *The Swing Era: The Development of Jazz, 1930–1945* (New York, 1989), Schuller goes to some length to analyze Berigan's early style on these records (see p. 465). There are some problems: The research of White and others clearly places Berigan in Philadelphia when these records were made. In addition, Tom Cullen interviewed several of the men who were in the band for these recordings; none of them remembers Berigan on the scene.

Exact dates have been given wherever possible. The matrix number of the recording (Mx—usually etched inward from the last used grooves, toward the hole) and its original issue number follow the personnel listings. All of these, except for the transcriptions, the Bill Dodge All-Stars records, and the air checks, were 78 rpm recordings.

These 78s, if they could be found, would probably be very expensive. Several LP reissues of various kinds have come on the market and are available in varying degree. Some compact discs (CDs) have begun to appear on the market. Reissues on CD will no doubt continue, making Berigan's sound available more widely. For example, J-CD-627 contains all of the transcription tunes recorded on July 20, 1936, and five from the June 27, 1938, session. A planned companion CD will complete the two 1938 Thesaurus dates. Following the issue number of most titles is another number, indicating on which LPs or CD this title might be more readily found. Absence of an availability number simply indicates the author's lack of knowledge regarding the accessibility of other reissues. Berigan researcher Bozy White is compiling, and will soon have published, the definitive Berigan discography, including reissue availability.

Many of these listings are available through collectors' channels only. Shoestring records may be purchased from Shoestring, P.O. Box 10208, Oakland, Calif., 94610-0208. Only SS-115 is currently available; 110 and 112 are temporarily out of print. The Bill Dodge records may be purchased from Circle Records, 1206 Decatur Street, New Orleans, LA, 70116. J-CD-627 may be purchased from Jass Records, 611 Broadway, #411B, New York, NY, 10012. The other CD is generally available. The key for availability of records listed here is as follows:

1. *Time-Life Giants of Jazz series (Bunny Berigan)*, P3-15957
2. *Time-Life Giants of Jazz series (Billie Holiday)*, P3-14787
3. *The Complete Bunny Berigan, Vol. I*, RCA AXM2-5584
4. *The Complete Bunny Berigan, Vol. II*, RCA 5657-1-RB
5. *The Indispensable Bunny Berigan*, PM 43689 (French-issued RCA Jazz Tribute)
6. *IAJRC 5* (International Association of Jazz Record Collectors)
7. *Hal Kemp and His Orchestra, Featuring Bunny Berigan, Vol. I*, Shoestring SS-110
8. *Hal Kemp and His Orchestra, Featuring Bunny Berigan, Vol. II*, Shoestring SS-112
9. *Bunny Berigan, 1931*, Shoestring SS-115
10. *Mildred Bailey: Her Greatest Performances*, Columbia/CBS JC3L 22

11. *Tommy Dorsey and His Orchestra, Featuring Bunny Berigan,* Fanfare Records 4-104·
12. *Swinging '34: Bill Dodge and His All-Star Orchestra, Vols. I and II,* Melodeon MLP-7328 and MLP-7329
13. *Lee Wiley and Bunny Berigan: The Complete Session of April 10, 1940,* Blu-Disc T-1013
14. *Bunny and Red: Bunny Berigan—Red McKenzie and the Mound City Blue Blowers (1935–1936),* Jazz Archives Recordings
15. *Portrait of Bunny Berigan,* CD AJA 5060 (Academy Sound and Vision, Ltd., 1989)
16. *Bunny Berigan and the Rhythm Makers, Vol. I: 1936 & 1938,* J-CD-627 (Jass Records)

February 18, 1931. "Smile, Darn You, Smile"

Carolina Club Orchestra: Hal Kemp, director, clarinet, alto sax; Bunny Berigan, Harry Preble, trumpets; Gus Mayhew, trombone; Kemp, Ben Williams, unknown, Saxie Dowell, reeds; John Scott Trotter, piano; Claude Thornhill, xylophone; Pinky Kintzle, banjo, guitar; Paul Weston, tuba, string bass; Skinnay Ennis, drums; Ennis, Kemp, Dowell, unknown, vocal. Mx E-35870; Melotone M-12110. Availability 8.

Bunny, noodling nicely, is heard muted behind a vocal group in an arrangement sounding very dated. When he follows the vocal with sixteen bars of muted solo, the whole mood changes from cutesy to swingy. The rhythm section grooves in behind him.

April 16, 1931. "Now You're in My Arms"

Probably Fred Rich Orchestra: A large orchestra, using such soloists as Bunny Berigan, trumpet; Tommy Dorsey, trombone; Jimmy Dorsey, reeds; Joe Venuti, violin; Eddie Lang, guitar; and others. Scrappy Lambert, vocal. Availability 9.

An early eight-bar muted trumpet solo is definitely not Bunny. As he comes in muted for the bridge, however, the voice is unmistakable. Bunny uses no tricks, remaining in the middle register. The pulse and the feel change as he gently punches and pushes, the music no longer just a perfunctory exercise.

July 30, 1931. "I Can't Get Mississippi off My Mind"

Dorsey Brothers Orchestra: Bunny Berigan and unknown, trumpets; Tommy Dorsey, trombone; Jimmy Dorsey, clarinet, alto sax; unknown, alto sax; Elmer Feldkamp, tenor sax, vocal; unknown, piano, guitar; probably Artie Bernstein, string bass; possibly Stan King, drums. Mx E-36946; Melotone M-12230. Availability 9.

After a brief intro, Bunny plays all of the first chorus, except the bridge, with mute. Sticking closely to the melody before the bridge, he displays a few characteristics that are essential to his style: half-valve slurs, rhythmic variations, and his rich tone. The eight bars after the bridge move away from the tune, revealing his debt to Louis. Tommy and Jimmy are heard to advantage; Elmer Feldkamp is vocalist and tenor saxist.

June 17, 1932. "Doggone, I've Done It Again"

The Boswell Sisters, accompanied by Bunny Berigan, trumpet; Tommy Dorsey, trombone; Jimmy Dorsey, clarinet; Joe Venuti, violin; Martha Boswell, piano; Dick McDonough, guitar; Artie Bernstein, string bass; Stan King, drums. Mx B11948-A; Brunswick 6335.

Joe Venuti takes a tasty violin solo after the snappy, close-harmony first vocal by the sisters, whose rhythmic variations remain a delight. Bunny takes over from Venuti and almost bursts through his mute as he punches through sixteen bars that provide a perfect bridge between Venuti and the sisters' vocal wrap-up. This is a typical, fun-filled Boswell-Dorsey collaboration, with Bunny supplying more than his share of improvised backing.

September 27, 1932. "Me Minus You"

Connee Boswell, vocal, accompanied by: Bunny Berigan, trumpet; Tommy Dorsey, trombone; Jimmy Dorsey, clarinet, alto sax; Larry Binyon, tenor sax; Martha Boswell, piano; Dick McDonough, guitar; Artie Bernstein, string bass; Stan King, drums. Recorded for ARC; Mx-B-12379-A; Brunswick 6405. Availability 1, 15.

March 7, 1933. "You've Got Me Crying Again"

Lee Wiley with the Dorsey Brothers Orchestra: Bunny Berigan, trumpet; Tommy Dorsey, trombone; Jimmy Dorsey, clarinet; Joe Venuti, two unknown, violins; Fulton McGrath, piano; Dick McDonough, guitar; Artie Bernstein, string bass; Stan King, drums. Mx B-13122; Epic SN 6095 (LP).

This was the first record date Wiley did under her own name, and it was probably her first meeting with Berigan. Bunny, Tommy, and Jimmy all show up well here on solo work, but the highlight is Bunny's smoky, muted backing of Wiley's vocal. His often double-time feel behind her straight melodic rendition provides a perfect fill, and when he pushes them buoyantly toward the ending, the artistry fuses as though they were meant to make music together.

April 8, 1933. "Is That Religion?"

Mildred Bailey, vocal, with Dorsey Brothers Orchestra: Bunny Berigan, trumpet; Tommy Dorsey, trombone; Jimmy Dorsey, clarinet; Larry Binyon, tenor sax; Fulton McGrath, piano; Dick McDonough, guitar; Artie Bernstein, string bass; Stan King, drums. Recorded for ARC; Mx B-13208-A; Brunswick 6558. Availability 1, 10.

November 24, 1933. "I Raised My Hat"

Adrian Rollini and His Orchestra, issued as Gene Kardos and His Orchestra: Adrian Rollini, director, bass sax, vibraphone; Bunny Berigan, trumpet; Al Philburn, Arthur Rollini, Pee Wee Russell, reeds; Fulton McGrath, piano; Dick McDonough, guitar; Art Miller, string bass; Herb Weil, drums, vocal; others unknown. ARC 14381-2; Banner 32912.

The vocal is by Herb Weil, and despite the appearance of Rollini and a number of certifiable jazz players, this record is just another of the endless sales-oriented, heavily arranged numbers cranked out by the hundreds. But when Bunny enters for the last bridge—open, low, and dirty—you know something else is happening. Over a shuffle rhythm he twists his way upward, again through effecting a double-time feeling, and constructs an eight-bar gem. He also stands out on lead.

ca. February–March, 1934. "Dinah"

The Bill Dodge All-Stars: Bunny Berigan, Mannie Klein or Shirley Clay, trumpet; Jack Jenney or Joe Harris, trombone; Benny Goodman, clarinet; Arthur Rollini, tenor sax; Arthur Schutt, piano; Dick McDonough, guitar; Artie Bernstein, string bass; Gene Krupa or Stan King, drums; Red McKenzie, vocal. World Transcription; Mx BB 6451; 300-50. Availability 12.

This opens with a sparkling chorus by Goodman (including a rare reed squeak), followed by Red McKenzie's vocal chorus and a well-played chorus by Harris (or Jenney). Then Bunny bursts in for sixteen sunlit bars played open and strong, using most of the horn's range. He pauses for the bridge, then returns to lead the group out in a happy gallop. This is swing!

ca. February–March, 1934. "Nobody's Sweetheart Now"
World Transcription; Mx BB 6453; 200-57. Personnel and Availability same as for "Dinah" above.
Again without introduction, Bunny charges into a muted first chorus that is just straight-ahead swing, pushed along by half-time triplet figures accented by his sharp attack. Rollini (or unknown) shines on a chorus, and Goodman crackles on his. Bunny comes in again to lead the last ensemble chorus with open horn, and the swinging is relentless.

ca. February–March, 1934. "Sweet Sue—Just You"
World Transcription; Mx BB 6460; 200-65. Personnel and Availability same as for "Dinah" above.
Another opportunity appears for a comparison between a muted melody chorus by Klein and Berigan's robust open horn, as Bunny solos only on the bridge of the third chorus. Jenney and Goodman are heard prominently. Bunny sounds like a rogue, abetted by Krupa, on his short burst between Jenney's muted, placid trombone and Klein's firm, polite trumpet.

ca. February–March, 1934. "I Can't Give You Anything but Love, Baby"
World Transcription; Mx BB 6461; 200-72. Personnel and Availability same as for "Dinah," above.
Bunny's opening chorus, begun without intro, seems to say "I love you, Louis!" He doesn't mess around, just begins with a bold statement hovering near the melody, using some lip trills and the double-time feel once more. After the bridge, he hints at the melody again, then leaps an octave up to an E-flat to restate the figure before returning mainly to the mid-range to finish out the chorus. It all flows so well and sounds so easy. Bunny leads an ensemble chorus after Art Rollini's tasty tenor chorus, firing it near the end with a figure whose difficulty is almost unnoticed because he pulls it off. Klein's (or Clay's) muted half-chorus out is pallid by comparison.

March 14, 1934. "She Reminds Me of You"

Paul Hamilton and His Orchestra: Bunny Berigan, trumpet; Tommy Dorsey, trumpet, trombone; Lloyd Turner, trombone; Jimmy Dorsey, clarinet, alto sax; Lyle Bowen, alto sax; Larry Binyon, tenor sax; Fulton McGrath, piano; Dick McDonough, guitar; Artie Bernstein, string bass; Stan King, drums; George Beuchler, vocal. Mx 14927-1; Vocalion 2662. Availability 1, 15.

What starts out as a Hal Kemp–like, ricky-tick treatment of this pop tune is suddenly transformed into something different when Bunny comes in after a brief modulation. He ruminates around his lower register, then leaps an octave to a pulsating high C, carrying the whole rhythm section with him in a way that probably surprised even them. Jimmy Dorsey is heard on both clarinet and alto to good advantage. A series of high Cs by Bunny brings on the vocal by George Beuchler. After the vocal, the ensemble takes over, sparked all the way by Bunny's insistent horn. The climax is reached when Bunny holds a high D for two brisk measures, then accents that by reaching up to a high G. And this was supposed to be just another pickup job to play another dog tune!

November 20, 1934. "Troubled"

Frankie Trumbauer and His Orchestra: Trumbauer, leader, c-melody sax; Nat Natoli, Bunny Berigan, trumpet; Glenn Miller, trombone; Artie Shaw, clarinet, alto sax; Jack Shore, alto sax; Larry Binyon, tenor sax; Roy Bargy, piano; Lionel Hall, guitar; Artie Bernstein, string bass; Jack Williams, drums. Recorded for Victor; Mx 86222-1; Victor 24834. Availability 1, 15.

April 25, 1935. "In a Little Spanish Town"

Glenn Miller and His Orchestra: Miller, leader, trombone, arranger; Charlie Spivak, Bunny Berigan, trumpet; Jack Jenney, trombone; Johnny Mince, clarinet, alto sax; Eddie Miller, tenor sax; Harry Bluestone, Wladimir Selinsky, violin; Harry Waller, viola; Bill Schumann, cello; Claude Thornhill, piano; Larry Hall, guitar; Delmar Kaplan, string bass; Ray Bauduc, drums. Recorded for ARC; Mx CO-17381-1; Columbia 3058-D. Availability 1, 15.

May 13, 1935. "Nothin' but the Blues"

Gene Gifford and His Orchestra: Gifford, director-arranger; Bunny Berigan, trumpet; Morey Samel, trombone; Matty Matlock, clarinet;

Bud Freeman, tenor sax; Claude Thornhill, piano; Dick McDonough, guitar; Pete Peterson, string bass; Ray Bauduc, drums. Mx 89794-1; Victor 25041. Availability 1, 15.

This tune represents part of the only session in which Bunny and Wingy Manone appeared together, with Manone only on the vocal of "Squareface." Claude Thornhill, Dick McDonough, bassist Pete Peterson, drummer Ray Bauduc, and tenorman Bud Freeman completed the group that responded so well to Gifford's effective arrangements of "Squareface" and this tune. Sudhalter describes this classic Berigan solo:

Berigan opens the number with an eight-bar announcement of mood and tone, the sound of his horn glowing rich and silvery-bright. . . . A full-band chord, with Berigan holding a D on top, begins a trumpet chorus whose resounding beauty has been admired by many through the years but seldom equaled—at least on records. It has passion, sweep, dignity, pathos. It reaches for the heights and plumbs the depths. His first two bars are built around that sustained D. He drops to a C, then B, then B flat, returning each time to the D in a rhythm pattern whose irregularity and intensity had been found in few trumpet players, except for Louis Armstrong, up to that time. Berigan leaps then to his clarion upper register for a proclamation that moves him ahead over shifting chords to a long phrase full of felicities: well-chosen notes, a variety of rhythms, sensitive dynamics—all portraying emotions on a grand scale. Notice the eloquent Armstrong touch of the major seventh in bar five and the hush at the end of bar six that tugs at the heart like a catch in the voice of the singer. All passion spent for the moment, Berigan ends on a cheery, upbeat phrase. [After the vocal] Berigan returns with a more contemplative but no less emotionally charged chorus, over the same sort of marching background given to Matlock earlier. . . . His long, annunciatory, top-of-the-staff G leads the ensemble into one final ad-lib chorus nearly as intense as the trumpet solos. With Freeman's tenor wailing and Bauduc bashing cymbal backbeats, Berigan stamps out a high E to unleash a passionate double-time run, then winds up with a broad, rhapsodic outburst of *bel canto* Armstrong to carry him into a reprise of the introduction. Even after all this strenuous playing, his control, broad tone and faultless execution are as they were at the outset. His only variation is a single playful octave leap, G to G, to show that he is not ready to quit even as the band winds down to a single final Bauduc cymbal crash. (John Chilton and Richard M. Sudhalter, *Giants of Jazz: Bunny Berigan* [Alexandria, Va., 1982], 32)

Such an elegant, analytical description of one of his records would probably have surprised Bunny. Ever the natural player, Bunny once told an interviewer, "I just sort of follow the chords; they tell you where to go." In jest he would often tell inquirers after his style, "You push the first valve down, and the music. . . ."

May 13, 1935. "Squareface"
Gene Gifford and His Orchestra: Personnel same as for "Nothin' but the Blues," above, plus Wingy Manone, vocal. Mx 89796-1; Victor 25065. Availability 1, 15.

Matty Matlock opens with a lovely, appropriately bluesy clarinet solo, followed by Wingy's vocal about the evil temptation of gin. Morey Samel's muted trombone first backs the vocal, then makes a full solo statement, followed by Berigan. The trumpet enters in a relaxed, low mood, toys with two or three notes, works its way up into mid-range, then explodes up an octave and a fourth to a high D, repeating the phrase mid-range again before it yields to a reprise of the vocal. Bunny's closing cadenza ends in another emphatic high D.

July 1, 1935. "Sometimes I'm Happy"
Benny Goodman and His Orchestra: Goodman, leader, clarinet; Bunny Berigan, Nate Kazebier, Ralph Muzzillo, trumpet; Red Ballard, Jack Lacey, trombone; Toots Mondello, Hymie Shertzer, alto sax; Arthur Rollini, Dick Clark, tenor sax; Frank Froeba, piano; George Van Eps, guitar; Harry Goodman, string bass; Gene Krupa, drums; Fletcher Henderson, arranger. Recorded for Victor; Mx 92546-1; Victor 25090. Availability 1.

December 4, 1935. "Tillie's Downtown Now"
Bud Freeman and His Windy City Five: Bunny Berigan, trumpet; Bud Freeman, tenor sax, clarinet; Claude Thornhill, piano; Eddie Condon, guitar; Grachan Moncur, string bass; Cozy Cole, drums. Recorded for EMI; Mx 60192-B; Parlophone R-2210. Availability 1, 15.

December 4, 1935. "Keep Smilin' at Trouble"
Bud Freeman and His Windy City Five: Personnel the same as "Tillie's Downtown Now," above, except Freeman plays only tenor sax. Recorded for EMI; Mx 60193-A; Parlophone R-2285. Availability 1.

A fine rhythm section with Claude Thornhill, piano, Eddie Condon, guitar, Grachan Moncur, bass, and Cozy Cole, drums, moves the four tunes on this session along nicely. The opening chorus here finds the leader and Bunny curling and pirouetting around one another as they carry the brisk tempo along. Freeman sounds as though he's using a slightly better grade of cardboard than usual for his reed on this day. The tenorman, despite his ability to swing, has consistently produced the worst *sound* of any of the major jazzmen. When Bunny takes over for his chorus, he begins a fluid, low-register series of phrases, soon emerging into the higher and middle range. The bridge is the highlight, as he repeats a D followed by three descending accents three times before moving into the final eight bars. Bunny leads the ensemble on the out-chorus, blazing out with a high C, sustained over two-and-a-half measures, that propels them into a fine, final frenzy.

December 6, 1935. "Willow Tree"
Mildred Bailey and Her Alley Cats: Bunny Berigan, trumpet; Johnny Hodges, alto sax; Teddy Wilson, piano; Grachan Moncur, string bass; Bailey, vocal. Recorded for EMI; Mx 60201-A; Parlophone R2201. Availability 1, 10.

This is one of the records Teddy Wilson thought of as among the finest he ever made, and the most fun. Wilson, Moncur on bass, Johnny Hodges on alto, and Bunny accompany Mildred. If schools attempt to teach jazz horn players how to complement vocalists, this record should be part of the curriculum. There's no flash here, just solid musical empathy and taste, with Bunny restraining his massive sound while playing open horn all the way and demonstrating his sense of dynamics as well as form.

December 13, 1935. "I'm Coming, Virginia"
Bunny Berigan and His Blue Boys: Berigan, trumpet; Edgar Sampson, alto sax; Eddie Miller, tenor sax; Cliff Jackson, piano; Grachan Moncur, string bass; Ray Bauduc, drums. Recorded for EMI; Mx 60231-A; Parlophone 2316. Availability 1, 15.

In 1927, Bix recorded this tune with the Frankie Trumbauer Orchestra, and his solo on it remained one of his most searing and emotional efforts. Bunny, though employing a much brighter tempo, would have us understand that he was well aware of Bix's treatment, without in any way copying his predecessor's solo. Staying in his rich middle register, Bunny makes generous use of lip trills and rhythmic accents, as well as a "popping" feel on the arpeggios. There are no bravura sounds here, just pure, emotional jazz playing.

January 8–9, 1936. "I'm Gonna Sit Right Down and Write Myself a Letter"

Mound City Blue Blowers: Bunny Berigan, trumpet; Forrest Crawford, clarinet, tenor sax; Eddie Condon, Carmen Mastren, guitar; Sid Weiss, string bass; Stan King, drums; Red McKenzie, comb; Spooky Dickenson, vocal. Mx 60311-A; Champion 40082. Availability 14.

Recorded shortly after Bunny left Goodman, and at about the time he was beginning his reign on 52nd Street, this tune finds the trumpeter in great form. Bunny's big, open horn leads the way as Forrest Crawford takes a fine tenor chorus and Red McKenzie provides one of his patented comb solos. Bunny series of stabbing, driving high Cs creates the torrid ending. Bunny recorded another, quite different, version of the same tune with Chick Bullock just ten days later. His solo there is remarkable for its virtuosity.

February 24, 1936. "Let Yourself Go"

Bunny Berigan and His Boys: Berigan, leader, trumpet; Bud Freeman, tenor sax, clarinet; Forrest Crawford, tenor sax; Joe Bushkin, piano; Dave Barbour, guitar; Mort Stuhlmaker, string bass; Dave Tough, drums; Chick Bullock, vocal. Recorded for ARC; Mx 18720-1; Vocalion 3178. Availability 1.

April 13, 1936. "I Can't Get Started"

Bunny Berigan and His Boys: Berigan, leader, trumpet, vocal; Artie Shaw, clarinet; Forrest Crawford, tenor sax; Joe Bushkin, piano; Mort Stuhlmaker, string bass; Cozy Cole, drums. Recorded for ARC; Mx 19013-1; Vocalion 3225. Availability 1. See comments in Chapter 28.

July 10, 1936. "No Regrets"

Billie Holiday and Her Orchestra: Holiday, leader, vocal; Bunny Berigan, trumpet; Artie Shaw, clarinet; Joe Bushkin, piano; Dick McDonough, guitar; Pete Peterson, string bass; Cozy Cole, drums. Recorded for Vocalion; Mx 19536-1; Vocalion 3276. Availability 2.

July 10, 1936. "Summertime"

Billie Holiday and Her Orchestra: Personnel same as for "No Regrets," above. Recorded for Vocalion; Mx 19537-1; Vocalion 3288. Availability 2.

July 20, 1936. "Empty Saddles"

Bunny Berigan and His Studio Orchestra: Berigan, leader, trumpet; two unknown, trumpet; Artie Drelinger and two unknown, reeds; possibly Frank Froeba, piano; unknown, string bass; unknown, drums. Recorded for Thesaurus Transcriptions; Mx 102943-1; 273, also 1172. Availability 16.

One of twenty tunes recorded on this date for Thesaurus Transcriptions with a largely unknown personnel makeup, this mundane song and arrangement are cited only because of the life Berigan breathes into them. He does it all here—lead, open horn solo, muted solo—and in so doing provides the side with its only virtue. Somehow Bunny manages to invest even this song with an often bluesy and swinging feel.

September 29, 1936. "A Fine Romance"

Billie Holiday and Her Orchestra: Bunny Berigan, trumpet; Irving Fazola, clarinet; Clyde Hart, piano; Dick McDonough, guitar; Artie Bernstein, string bass; Cozy Cole, drums; Holiday, vocal. Recorded for Vocalion; Mx 19971-1; Vocalion 3333. Availability 2.

This is Holiday's second session as leader, with some personnel changes from July 10. Bunny's open eight-bar intro here is piercing and pure, setting the pace as Billie romps into the first chorus. Bunny noodles behind her, then lays out for the beautiful low-register Irving Fazola clarinet on the second chorus until taking over with a dazzling high E-flat. Bunny nearly misses this note, then amazes by turning it into a lip trill. Next, just to prove the point, he stabs the E-flat on the nose again before working his way down and yielding to Billie for the last chorus.

January 29, 1937. "Song of India"

Tommy Dorsey and His Orchestra: Dorsey, leader, trombone; Bunny Berigan, Jimmy Welch, Joe Bauer, Bob Cusumano, trumpet; Les Jenkins, E. W. "Red" Bone, trombone; Joe Dixon, clarinet, alto sax; Fred Stulce, alto sax; Bud Freeman, Clyde Rounds, tenor sax; Dick Jones, piano; Carmen Mastren, guitar; Gene Traxler, string bass; Dave Tough, drums. Recorded for Victor; Mx 04533-2; Victor 25523. Availability 1 and many others. See comments in Chapter 14.

January 29, 1937. "Marie"

Tommy Dorsey and His Orchestra: Personnel same as for "Song of India," above. Recorded for Victor; Mx 04534-1; Victor 25523. Availability 1, 15, and many others. See comments in Chapter 14.

February 18, 1937. "Liebestraum"

Tommy Dorsey and His Orchestra: Personnel the same as for "Song of India," above, except Andy Ferretti replaces Cusumano on trumpet; Slats Long replaces Dixon on clarinet, alto sax. Recorded for Victor; Mx 04933-1; Victor 25539.

March 31, 1937. "Blues"

Jam session at Victor: Bunny Berigan, trumpet; Tommy Dorsey, trombone; Fats Waller, piano; Dick McDonough, guitar; George Wettling, drums. Recorded for Victor; Mx 06582-1; Victor 25559. Availability 5.

April 1, 1937. "Carelessly"

Bunny Berigan and His Orchestra: Berigan, leader, trumpet; Nat Natoli, Steve Lipkins, trumpets; Ford Leary, Frank D'Annolfo, trombone; Frank Langone, Henry Freeman, clarinet, alto sax; Clyde Rounds, George Auld, tenor sax; Joe Lipman, piano; Tom Morgan, guitar; Arnold Fishkind, string bass; George Wettling, drums; Carol McKay, vocal. Recorded for Victor; Mx 06592-1; Camden CAL-550. Availability 3.

This ballad of the day was included in Bunny's first Victor session. It is cited here only as a typical example of the leader's style, including a missed note in the opening muted solo, and the never-hold-back communication found in Bunny's playing. His massive sound again threatens to disintegrate his mute, and the expressiveness and emotive values are all here, complete with full high E in the muted solo, finished off with a shimmering high F.

June 18, 1937. "All God's Chillun Got Rhythm"

Bunny Berigan and His Orchestra: Berigan, leader, trumpet; Steve Lipkins, Irving Goodman, trumpets; Sonny Lee, Morey Samel, trombones; Joe Dixon, clarinet, alto sax; Sid Perlmutter, alto sax; Clyde Rounds, George Auld, tenor sax; Joe Lipman, piano; Tom Morgan, guitar; Arnold Fishkind, string bass; George Wettling, drums; Ruth

Bradley, vocal. Recorded for Victor; Mx 010597-1; Victor 25609. Availability 3, 5.

This tune from the third Victor session features a bright arrangement and a well-modulated vocal by Ruth Bradley. Bunny's powerful muted eight-bar statement leads into the vocal, which he follows with an audacious open solo that climbs quickly to a resounding high F. The effect created is of jumping up two steps, then falling back one, repeated until the peak is reached. Another eight bars of cooling off is followed by a tasty Joe Dixon clarinet solo, this time without the band shouting behind him, as was so often the case.

June 25, 1937. "Mahogany Hall Stomp"

Bunny Berigan and His Orchestra: Personnel the same as for "All God's Chillun Got Rhythm"; no vocal. Recorded for Victor; Mx 011122-1; Victor 25622. Availability 1, 3, 5.

For this comment, I again draw upon the expertise of Richard Sudhalter:

Ten introductory bars at a relaxed, unhurried tempo, with the brass prominently featured, bring on Berigan, playing with a straight mute and opening with Armstrong's famous break before setting out the melody of the number's principal strain. He is not playing Armstrong note for note here, yet it is doubtful whether he or anyone else ever came closer to Armstrong's inflections and unique sense of phrase placement. . . . Then at last [after solos by Sonny Lee and George Auld] it is Berigan's turn, and he kicks things off with three barked-out notes that establish both majesty and rhythmic momentum. Armstrong's influence saturates this solo. The second four bars are typical: For all practical purposes, the notes are the notes of Louis, but Berigan, by slurring them in a long legato phrase where Armstrong would have tongued them short, makes them Berigan notes. He winds up the solo with a declarative phrase that leaves the listener waiting, hoping for another solo chorus. Instead, the brass, with Berigan leading, pilots the band into the key of D flat for a strutting, joyous final chorus. Berigan solos briefly in the middle, then dives back into the ensemble to lead "Mahogany Hall Stomp" to a spirited conclusion. (Chilton and Sudhalter, *Bunny Berigan,* 42–43)

August 7, 1937. "Turn On that Red Hot Heat"

Bunny Berigan and His Orchestra: Personnel the same as for "All God's Chillun Got Rhythm," except Al George replaces Samel, trombone; Mike Doty, alto sax, replaces Perlmutter; Hank Wayland replaces Fishkind, string bass; Gail Reese, vocal. Recorded for Victor; Mx 011674-1; Victor 25646; Availability 3, 5.

Recorded on the same date as Bunny's theme, this tune reveals the leader in quite another mood. He opens festivities with a growling, plunger solo of sixteen bars, strong and dirty. Joe Dixon is again featured, opening his solo with a woody low register, then moving to an earthy middle register before singing out high. Bunny follows Reese's vocal with a lowdown open-horn sixteen bars that travels nearly the full range of the horn, twisting, turning, and stabbing.

August 7, 1937. "I Can't Get Started"
Bunny Berigan and His Orchestra: Personnel the same as for "Turn On that Red Hot Heat," above; Berigan, vocal, replaces Reese. Recorded for Victor; Mx 011675-1; Victor 36208. Availability 1, 3, 5 (alternate take), 15, and many other reissue LPs. Comments in Chapter 28.

September 3, 1937. "Gee, but It's Great to Meet a Friend (From Your Home Town)"
Bunny Berigan and His Orchestra: Personnel the same as for "Turn On that Red Hot Heat," above; chorus on vocal (in addition to Reese). Recorded for Victor; Mx 013330-1; Victor 25664. Availability 3.

December 23, 1937. "Black Bottom"
Bunny Berigan and His Orchestra: Personnel the same as for "Turn On that Red Hot Heat," above; no vocal. Recorded for Victor; Mx 017766-1; Victor 26138. Availability 1, 4, 5, 15.

December 23, 1937. "Trees"
Bunny Berigan and His Orchestra: Personnel the same as for "Turn On that Red Hot Heat," above; no vocal. Recorded for Victor; Mx 017767-1; Victor 26138. Availability 4.

December 23, 1937. "Russian Lullaby"
Bunny Berigan and His Orchestra: Personnel the same as for "Turn On that Red Hot Heat," above; no vocal. Recorded for Victor; Mx 017768-1; Victor 26001. Availability 4, 5.
Berlin's plaintive melody gets a compelling, upbeat treatment here, with bouncy solos from Auld and Dixon. Yet, both on his open horn solo and on the later growling plunger bit, Bunny evokes a mournful, pleading feel. His repeated high E-flats, followed each of the five times by an octave skip down, then to a D and back up again to the E-flat, are enough to make any brass player cry with envy.

January 26, 1938. "A Serenade to the Stars"

Bunny Berigan and His Orchestra: Personnel the same as for "Turn On that Red Hot Heat," above, except Fulton McGrath replaces Lipman, piano; Dave Tough replaces Wettling, drums. Recorded for Victor; Mx 018415-2; Victor 25781. Availability 4.

This is a seemingly unremarkable performance on a better-than-average ballad. But listen closely: first to Bunny's lead on the first half-chorus; then to the gorgeous, shimmering, low-register treatment of the last half of that chorus; and especially to the reflective, pleading, open solo after the vocal. In the latter, Bunny's great sound is intact as he hits several high Es so naturally and fully that they can easily be overlooked.

May 26, 1938. "The Wearin' of the Green"

Bunny Berigan and His Orchestra: Berigan, leader, trumpet; Irving Goodman, Steve Lipkins, trumpet; Ray Conniff, Nat Lobovsky, trombone; Mike Doty, Joe Dixon, clarinet, alto sax; Clyde Rounds, George Auld, tenor sax; Joe Bushkin, piano; Dick Wharton, guitar; Hank Wayland, string bass; Johnny Blowers, drums; Joe Lipman, arranger. Recorded for Victor; Mx 023291-1; Victor 25872. Availability 1, 4, 5.

June 27, 1938. "Frankie and Johnny"

Bunny Berigan and His Orchestra (as The Rhythm Makers): Berigan, leader, trumpet; Steve Lipkins, Irving Goodman, trumpet; Ray Conniff, Nat Lobovsky, trombone; Joe Dixon, clarinet, alto sax; Mike Doty, alto sax; George Auld, Clyde Rounds, tenor sax; Joe Bushkin, piano; Dick Wharton, guitar; Hank Wayland, string bass; Johnny Blowers, drums. Recorded for Thesaurus Transcriptions; Mx 023740-1; 544. Availability 6.

June 27, 1938. "Shanghai Shuffle"

Bunny Berigan and His Orchestra: Personnel the same as for "Frankie and Johnny," above. Recorded for Thesaurus Transcriptions; Mx 023741-1; 563. Availability 6.

This is a crackling Fletcher Henderson arrangement recorded as one of twenty tunes for the day. Bunny's band sounds especially tight here as they play an arrangement that they had had time to get comfortable with before recording. The ensemble work in the reeds is especially pleasing. Sectional dynamics are admirable. Auld, Dixon, and Doty all take fine solos of the kind that would have extended to several choruses when playing dances. Bunny's solo here begins with a series of nine high Es before wending its way down to the middle and lower registers. Two radio checks of the same tune taken from the famous Paradise Restaurant run in April, 1938, reveal how the concept of the chart changed. The April 10 rendition is at a medium tempo; by April 24, the tempo was much slower; the Thesaurus version is at a breakneck tempo. Bunny's solos are as different as the tempi. On the April 24 version, he enters about two-and-a-half octaves lower than on this transcription, at the very bottom of his trombonelike range. Arrangers often took advantage of this ability by writing third trombone parts for Bunny, thus broadening and deepening the sound of the trombone section.

November 22, 1938. "I Cried for You"

Bunny Berigan and His Orchestra: Berigan, leader, trumpet; Irving Goodman, Johnny Napton, trumpet; Ray Conniff, Bob Jenney, trombone; Murray Williams, Gus Bivona, clarinet, alto sax; George Auld, Clyde Rounds, tenor sax; Joe Bushkin, piano; Dick Wharton, guitar; Hank Wayland, string bass; Buddy Rich, drums; Kathleen Lane, vocal. Recorded for Victor; Mx 030301-1; Victor 26116. Availability 1.

Recorded about a month after the hurricane experience in Boston, this great ballad treatment features Kathleen Lane in a pleasant-toned vocal and demonstrates how a master can turn a fluff into a highlight. Listen to the relaxed, lustrous playing as Bunny begins his gorgeous open solo, and feel the development of intensity. The fluff-into-highlight comes when Bunny misses one of three high Cs but then repeats it, turning it into a difficult, spontaneous lip trill. Who but Bunny, the consummate gambler, would test and expose himself so consistently by constructing mistake-prone passages, then leave them in his recordings for all the world to hear?

November 22, 1938. "Jelly Roll Blues"

Bunny Berigan and His Orchestra: Personnel same as for "I Cried for You," above; no vocal. Recorded for Victor; Mx 030302-1; Victor 26113. Availability 1.

From Bunny's opening four-bar, muted mood-setting solo to the final accent, this treatment of Jelly Roll Morton's classic blues melody is itself a classic. The colors of the ensemble playing are exquisite. Bunny's own open solo is basic in its emotional appeal, not going for the spectacular, but drawing us in with its warmth and with a sense of loneliness that the blues can evoke.

November 30, 1938. "In a Mist"
Bunny Berigan and His Men: Berigan, leader, trumpet; Irving Goodman, trumpet; Ray Conniff, trombone; Murray Williams, Gus Bivona, clarinet, alto sax; George Auld, tenor sax; Joe Lipman, piano, arranger; Hank Wayland, string bass; Buddy Rich, drums. Recorded for Victor; Mx 030168-1; Victor 26123. Availability 1, 5.
See comments in Chapter 10.

November 30, 1938. "Davenport Blues"
Bunny Berigan and His Men: Personnel same as for "In a Mist," above. Recorded for Victor; Mx 030170-1; Victor 26121. Availability 5.

January 12, 1939. "Blue Lou"
Metronome All-Star Band: Charlie Spivak, Bunny Berigan, Sonny Dunham, trumpet; Jack Teagarden, Tommy Dorsey, trombone; Benny Goodman, clarinet, alto sax; Hymie Shertzer, alto sax; Eddie Miller, Arthur Rollini, tenor sax; Bob Zurke, piano; Carmen Mastren, guitar; Bob Haggart, string bass; Ray Bauduc, drums. Recorded for Victor; Mx 031445-2; Victor 26144. Availability 1, 5.

April 10, 1940. "Let's Do It"
Lee Wiley, vocal, accompanied by Bunny Berigan's Music: Berigan, trumpet; Joe Bushkin, piano; Sid Weiss, string bass; George Wettling, drums. P-27151-1; LMS (Liberty Music Shops) L-297. Availability 13.

April 10, 1940. "Hot House Rose"
Lee Wiley, vocal, accompanied by Bunny Berigan's Music: Personnel the same as for "Let's Do It," above. P-27152-1; LMS L-297. Availability 13.

May 28, 1940. "East of the Sun"
Tommy Dorsey and His Orchestra (probable personnel): Bunny Berigan, Ray Linn, Jimmy Blake, John Dillard, trumpet; Dorsey,

leader, trombone; Les Jenkins, George Arus, Lowell Martin, trombone; Johnny Mince, clarinet, alto sax; Fred Stulce, Hymie Shertzer, alto sax; Don Lodice, Paul Mason, tenor sax; Joe Bushkin, piano; Clark Yocum, guitar; Sid Weiss, string bass; Buddy Rich, drums; Frank Sinatra, vocal; Berigan, Dorsey, Mince, Stulce, Bushkin, Yocum, Weiss, Rich, chorus. Victor recording Mx 048939-1 made April 23, 1940; issued as Bluebird BB B-10726. Availability 11.

This is an air check broadcast over BBC, London, and differs in many ways from the recorded version. Note the boplike figure played by Berigan in the thirteenth measure of his solo. See further comments in Coda.

June 22, 1940. "I'm Nobody's Baby"

Tommy Dorsey and His Orchestra: Personnel the same as "East of the Sun," above, except Leon Debrow or Clyde Hurley replaces Dillard on trumpet. Air check from the Astor Hotel Roof, New York City. Availability 11.

November 24, 1941. "'Tis Autumn"

Bunny Berigan and His Orchestra: Berigan, leader, trumpet; (all probable) Arthur Mellor, Bobby Mansell, Freddy Norton, trumpet; Charles Stewart, Max Smith, trombone; Walt Mellor, George Quinty, alto sax; Wilbur Joustra, Red Lang, tenor sax; Gene Kutch, piano; Tony Estren, string bass; Jack Sperling, drums; Lynn Richards, vocal. Recorded for Elite; Mx W-111-2; Elite 5005.

Recorded less than two weeks after the death of Bunny's father, this tune is included for comparison's sake. Bunny's trumpet is heard mainly in a statement of the melody on the first chorus, sans bridge. Bunny's nephew Kaye is an accomplished trumpet player very definitely of the modern school. On hearing this and other Bunny Berigan numbers during an interview on *Grams on Jazz* (WTMJ, Milwaukee, May, 1976), Kaye Berigan commented:

Even though it's not a style I like, *Bunny was different.* I really didn't know him, so I listen to him as I would to anyone else. And it's difficult because of the poor technical quality of the recordings, and because I wasn't brought up on that style of music. But Bunny's tone quality stands out; it has a fatter, wider, brighter sound to it. He had a quality of playing low and high, and of soloing as well as reading, which was a rare quality at that time. He could do it all, and he definitely was and still is admired by other trumpet players and musicians.

And even with his diminished powers at the time of this recording, Bunny's distinctive sound stands out.

Bibliography

Books and Monographs

Berton, Ralph. *Remembering Bix: A Memoir of the Jazz Age.* New York, 1974.

Case, Brian, and Stan Britt. *The Illustrated Encyclopedia of Jazz.* London, 1978.

Chilton, John. *Who's Who of Jazz: Storyville to Swing Street.* Alexandria, Va., 1978.

Chilton, John, and Richard M. Sudhalter. *Giants of Jazz: Bunny Berigan.* Time-Life. Alexandria, Va., 1982.

Condon, Eddie. *We Called it Music: A Generation of Jazz.* New York, 1947.

Connor, D. Russell. *Benny Goodman: Listen to His Legacy.* Metuchen, N.J., 1988.

Danca, Vince. *Bunny: A Bio-discography of Jazz Trumpeter Bunny Berigan.* Rockford, Ill., 1978.

Dance, Stanley. *The World of Earl Hines.* New York, 1977.

Duggan, Margaret M., Glenda G. Fedricci, and Cara L. White, eds. *Conversations with Jazz Musicians.* Detroit, 1977. Vol. II of Matthew J. Bruccoli and C. E. Clark, Jr., eds., *Conversations.* 3 vols. to date.

Esquire Jazz Book, 1947. New York, 1947.

Feather, Leonard. *The New Edition of the Encyclopedia of Jazz.* Rev. ed. New York, 1960.

Frazier, George. *The One with the Mustache Is Costello.* New York, 1947.

Gershwin, Ira. *Lyrics on Several Occasions.* New York, 1959.

Goodman, Benny, and Irving Kolodin. *The Kingdom of Swing.* New York, 1939.

Green, Benny. *The Reluctant Art: The Growth of Jazz.* New York, 1962.

Johnson, Vernon E. *I'll Quit Tomorrow.* Rev. ed. San Francisco, 1980.

Keepnews, Orrin, and Bill Grauer, Jr. *A Pictorial History of Jazz.* New York, 1955.

Maddocks, Melvin. *Giants of Jazz: Billie Holiday.* Time-Life. Alexandria, Va., 1979.

McCarthy, Albert. *Big Band Jazz.* New York, 1974.

Panassié, Hugues. *Hot Jazz: The Guide to Swing Music.* Translated by Lyle Dowling and Eleanor Dowling. Rev. ed. New York, 1936.

Rust, Brian. *Jazz Records, 1897–1942.* 5th ed. 2 vols. Chigwell, Eng., 1982.

Schuller, Gunther. *Early Jazz: Its Roots and Musical Development.* New York, 1968.

———. *The Swing Era: The Development of Jazz, 1930–1945.* New York, 1989.

Shaw, Arnold. *The Street That Never Slept.* New York, 1971.

Simon, George T. *The Big Bands.* New York, 1967.

Sudhalter, Richard M., and Philip R. Evans. *Bix: Man & Legend.* New York, 1974.

Periodicals, Newspapers, and Articles

Balliett, Whitney. "Bob's Your Uncle." *New Yorker,* February 23, 1987, p. 130.

———. "Bunny Berigan." *New Yorker,* November 8, 1982, pp. 124, 127.

Billboard, 1928–42.

Crosbie, Ian. "Bunny Berigan." *Jazz Journal,* XXVII (September, 1974), 8–14.

Down Beat, 1934–42.

Eldridge, Roy. "Roy Eldridge on Trumpeters." *Metronome,* LIX (October, 1943), 27.

Feather, Leonard G. "Bunny Berigan: Master of the Blues." *Melody Maker,* November 28, 1936, p. 2.

Gitler, Ira. "Red Rodney: Lighting a Fuse." *JazzTimes,* August, 1987, pp. 16–17.

Goodman, Benny, with Richard Gehman. "That Old Gang of Mine." *Collier's,* January 20, 1956, pp. 27–31.

Hammond, John. "Bunny Was Never Happy." *Music and Rhythm,* July, 1942.

Hentoff, Nat. "The Gentleman of Jazz." *Wall Street Journal,* April 6, 1987, Sec. A, p. 27.

Kline, Jerry, ed. "Touring with Bunny." *Mississippi Rag,* X (February, 1983), 1–3.

Kolodin, Irving. "Bunny Berigan Died in Irony." New York *Sun,* June 3, 1942.

Leerhsen, Charles, with Tessa Namuth. "Alcohol and the Family." *Newsweek,* January 18, 1988, pp. 62–68.

Melody Maker, ca. May, 1931.

Metronome, 1935–43.

Miller, Paul Eduard. "A Tribute to Bunny Berigan." *Down Beat*, IX (July 1, 1942), p. 14.
Newsweek, January 2, 1984, January 18, 1988.
New York *Times*, October 10, 1929, May 29, June 3, 1942.
New York Times Biographical Service, VI (December, 1975), 1630.
Fox Lake (Wis.) *Representative*, 1928–40.
Swing, September, 1940.
Variety, 1929–38.
Whyatt, Bert. "The Unforgettable George Zack." *Mississippi Rag*, XV (January, 1988), 8.
Yanow, Scott. "Bunny Berigan Retrospective." *Record Review* (December, 1980), 30–33.

Typescript

Wilson, Bob. "Beauty, Drive, and Freedom." Typescript in possession of author.

Record Jacket Notes

Melodeon MLP 7328, 7329. *Swinging '34: Bill Dodge and His All-Star Orchestra*. Notes by Howard J. Waters.
RCA AXM2-5584. *The Complete Bunny Berigan, Vol. I*. Notes by Mort Goode.
RCA 5657-1-RB. *The Complete Bunny Berigan, Vol. II*. Notes by Richard M. Sudhalter.
Shoestring SS-100. *Bunny Berigan—Vol. I (1938–39)*. Notes by Bozy White.
Shoestring SS-115. *Bunny Berigan, 1931*. Notes by John McDonough.
Soundcraft LP-1013. *The Saturday Night Swing Club—On The Air.*

Radio and Television Programs

"Alcohol & Cocaine: The Secret of Addiction." *Closeup*. ABC-TV. May 29, 1987.
Grams, John. *Grams on Jazz*. WTMJ, Milwaukee. June 3, 1972.

Interviews

Most of the quotations in the text come from interviews tape recorded during face-to-face conversations. The subjects knew they were being interviewed for the purpose of contributing to the writing of a biography of Bunny Berigan.

Interviews by the Author
Beecher, Art. May 19, 1986.
Benson, Clifford. By telephone, April 15, 1984, October 5, 1989.
Berigan, Joyce. May 14, 1988.
Berigan, Loretta. May 21, 1985, and by telephone, April 1, 1986.
Bivona, Gus. August 14, 1987.
Blowers, Johnny. June 26, 1985, and by telephone, May 20, 1985.
Burmeister, Donna Berigan. September 6–8, 1984.
Bushkin, Joe. June 26, 1985.
Cullen, Tom. May 21, 1985.
Dixon, Joe. By telephone, July 14, October 23, December 1, 1986.
Eisenbarth, Erlyne Keefer. May 19, 1985.
Gomon, Clif. August 30, 1985, May 20, 1987.
Jacoby, Don. By telephone, March 10, 1988.
Koss, Edwin "Buddy." By telephone, March 13, 1988.
Kratz, Orville. May 19, 1986.
Krusinski, Norm. September 23, 1984.
Kutch, Gene. June 25, 1985.
Lake, Bonnie. June 28, 1985.
Lipman, Joe. By telephone, January 20, 1985.
Litscher, Emerson "Diver." May 19, 1985.
Mickolas, Deborah. June 25, 1985.
Morgan(elli), Tom. By telephone, February 9, April 10, 1988.
Owen, Merrill. May 20, 1984.
Quinty, George. By telephone, February 9, 1988.
Richards, Danny. By telephone, November 9, 1985.
Sheskey, Joe. May 18, 1986.
Slavin, Patricia Berigan. August 10, 1988, and by telephone, June 14, 1988.
Smith, Bobby. August 13, 1987, and by telephone, February 23, 1988.
Smith, Jack. May 19, 1985.
Sperling, Jack. By telephone, February 10, 1988.
Stacy, Jess. August 13, 1987, and by telephone, August 15, 1987.
Streich, Howard. May 19, 1986.
Thrasher, Mary. August, 1985.

Interviews by Persons Other Than the Author
Auld, George, with Tom Cullen. N.d.
Bernstein, Artie, with Bozy White. February, 1961.
Best, John, with Norm Krusinski. *Ca.* 1987.
Dorsey, Jimmy, with Tom Cullen. *Ca.* June, 1952.
Erwin, Pee Wee, with Deborah Mickolas. October 30, 1977.
Forbes, Graham, with Tom Cullen. *Ca.* September, 1960.
Koss, Edwin "Buddy," with Deborah Mickolas. July 28, 1978.
Langone, Frank, with Deborah Mickolas, from questions by Bozy White.
    September 5, 1981.

Lee, Sonny, with Tom Cullen. February, 1961.
Mayhew, Gus, with Bozy White. May, 1959.
Mitchell, Sue, with Deborah Mickolas, from questions by Bozy White. September 10, 1975.
Napton, Johnny, with Bozy White, *Ca.* 1952.
Quinty, George, with Deborah Mickolas, from questions by Bozy White. September 6, 1976.
Roberts, Keith "Curly," with Tom Cullen. June, 1959.
Rounds, Clyde, with Tom Cullen. May, September, 1960.
Shertzer, Hymie, with Bozy White. *Ca.* 1961.
Teagarden, Jack, with Bozy White. August, 1959.
Towers, Julie, with Bozy White. February, 1953.
Walsh, Larry, with Tom Cullen. June, 1960.

White and Cullen Research Materials

This is a large body of information about Bunny Berigan, including interviews, periodical entries, book references, letters, and discographical information, as well as Berigan memorabilia, collected by Bozy White and Tom Cullen. White and Cullen collaborated for twelve to thirteen years on research for a Berigan biography-discography. Later, Martin L. Kite also contributed some research. This material covers the period from approximately 1908 to 1942. It is in the possession of White and Norm Krusinski, with copies of applicable sections also in possession of the author. It is used with the permission of Bozy White and Tom Cullen.

Other Unpublished Materials

Letters to the author from:
Berigan, Joyce. March 21, May 24, 1988, February 7, August 14, 1989, September 5, 1990.
Berigan, Loretta. June 11, August 20, September 14, 1985, March 4, June 21, August 11, September 11, September 27, October 22, 1986, January 14, 1987, November 6, 1988, October 10, 1989.
Blowers, Johnny. March 3, August 19, 1989, April 6, 1990.
Butterfield, Billy. May 7, 1987.
Campbell, Fran. June 23, 1985.
Dixon, Joe. March 25, July 1, 1987, January 5, February 28, August 15, 1989.
Gage, Alfred K. November 19, December 6, 1985, March 20, 1987.
Jacoby, Don. March 4, March 21, 1988.
Koss, Edwin "Buddy." March 1, March 24, 1988, January 20, February 25, 1989.
Kutch, Gene. January 22, 1987, February 5, 1988, February 27, 1989.
Morganelli, Tom. March 12, 1988, February 2, March 9, 1989.

Payne, Neal. *Ca.* May 1, 1986, April 13, April 26, August 23, 1987.
Smith, Erle. June 5, 1985.
Troisi, Madeline "Madie." October, 1987.
Weston, Paul. August 25, September 18, 1985, June 3, 1986, February 27, 1989.
White, Bozy. June 17, August 14, 1986, January 12, January 13, 1987, February 27, March 15, March 16, May 28, June 7, June 14, 1988.

Diaries
Eddie Jenkins Diary. In White Materials, White and Cullen Research Materials.
Gene Kutch Diary. Copy in author's possession.

Index